The New
Concise British Flora

'O all ye green things upon the earth, bless ye the Lord,
Praise him and magnify him for ever.'

The New Concise British Flora

W. Keble Martin

MA, DSc, FLS

With nomenclature edited and revised by
Douglas H. Kent

and Foreword by
H.R.H. The Duke of Edinburgh
KG, PC, KT, GMBE, FRS

Mermaid Books

First published in this Mermaid Books edition
by Michael Joseph Limited,
44 Bedford Square, London WC1
and Ebury Press, National Magazine House,
72 Broadwick Street, London W1
1986

This book was designed and produced by
The Rainbird Publishing Group Limited
40 Park Street, London W1
and first published in Great Britain by
Michael Joseph Limited
and Ebury Press
1982

The Concise British Flora
First published May 1965
Second Impression (with revisions) June 1965
Third Impression September 1965
Fourth Impression November 1965
Fifth Impression April 1967
Second (revised) Edition 1969
Second Impression December 1969
Third Impression June 1971
Fourth Impression October 1972
Fifth Impression 1974
Sixth Impression 1976
Seventh Impression 1978
Third Edition 1982
(as *The New Concise British Flora*)

British Library Cataloguing in Publication Data
Martin, W. Keble
The new concise British flora—3rd ed.
1. Wild flowers—Great Britain—Identification
I. Title   II. Kent, Douglas H.
582.13′0941   QK306
ISBN 0–7181–2700–5

The publishers would like to express their gratitude to
Douglas Kent for his invaluable assistance in updating
the text for the 1982 edition. They would also like to thank
the following for their help with this book:
Margaret Kapff, Bridget Gibbs, Nicholas Gibbs,
David Spink and George Rainbird

Printed and bound by Jarrold and Sons Limited, Norwich

Foreword

The Reverend W. Keble Martin's classic work *The Concise British Flora* was first published in 1965, but only after many difficulties in finding a publisher prepared to overcome the printing problems. In the end The Rainbird Publishing Group took on the task and eventually printed a total of 558,000 copies.

The success of this book reflects the growing interest in natural history and the mounting concern for our natural environment. The conservation of nature, and that includes every plant illustrated in this book, depends on public awareness of the facts and of the problems.

On these pages is recorded the full extent of Britain's heritage of wild flowers, and thanks to the advances in printing technology, this new edition reproduces Keble Martin's original work much more faithfully than the first. As the text has also been brought up to date, I am sure that it will prove to be even more popular.

Contents

Preface to the Original Edition

In recent years many illustrated works on the British flora have issued from the press. It may appear at first sight to be superfluous to publish another. But there seem to be good reasons for this. The present work is on a somewhat different scale, comprising as it does some 1480 figures mostly in colour, drawn with all the care of which the draughtsman was capable, over a period of about sixty years. It is an attempt to attain scientific accuracy without losing the attractive appearance of the flowers. Although this work has been such a long while in preparation, an effort has always been made to keep it in touch with changing ideas through contact with leading botanists of each period. The drawings however are in a form in which their sequence could not be altered. With small exceptions this follows that of the National Herbarium at the British Museum, and *The London Catalogue of British Plants*, XIth Edition.

A further reason for desiring publication is that a number of experts have helped by selecting and identifying specimens for these drawings, thus ensuring suitable and accurate material for the purpose. In addition some three hundred of the specimens drawn were sent by a wide circle of botanists. Valuable help, as acknowledged below, has been given in the preparation of the short text, especially in bringing the nomenclature into accord with the Rules of the International Botanical Congress. The production of this work has therefore been very much a combined effort, and it is only fair to all these botanists that the result should be published.

Every figure of these plates was drawn direct from nature. The drawings were first made in the form of pen outlines on small separate sheets. On each sheet the name of the species was recorded, with the date, the place from which the specimen came, and the name of the sender, if any, or of the referee who named it.

In building up the plates the draughtsman's aim has been to show an average fragment, with its essential features, and to give each a place in the sun without crowding. He has tried where possible to show white or pale coloured flowers against green foliage, as in the hedgerow, though this was not always possible. These aims involved much patience in rearranging and redrawing. During the years there have always been gaps on the plates, because the necessary specimens could not be obtained. Some of these gaps have waited for twenty or even twenty-five years before being filled. The author's own visits to distant botanical spots have of necessity been rather few and brief. Owing to the pressure of the author's parochial work the specimens received by post sometimes perished. Some species difficult to obtain had to be sent in two or more seasons, but, owing to great kindness and much forbearance shown by correspondents, the gaps were all filled at last.

It was the desire to know the food plants of Lepidoptera that first promoted the effort to identify the plants required. Then the author was studying for his degree in the Botany School at Oxford, under Professor S. H. Vines and Mr A. W. Church. It was Mr Church who specially urged his students to draw whatever they saw under the microscope and started them in the habit of drawing. The desire to help others in recognizing the plants around them led to the idea of this present work. In this the text is short, mentioning for the most part features that cannot be shown effectively in the figures.

It is an amateur work, which was from the beginning treated as a secondary interest and a recreation. For after further training at a Theological College the author was plunged at his own request in the Church work of large industrial parishes, which was happy work, but it left little time indeed for botany. Progress with these drawings was therefore extremely slow and mostly confined to an annual holiday; and yet before 1918 work on the present lines was well under way.

For a few years, from 1921 to 1926, the author was in a small parish, and his work for a neighbouring housing estate had not yet begun. He had more time for this work, and several plates were redrawn. From 1949 he no longer held a benefice. And it happened that in five successive years as a Public Preacher he was in charge of some parish for more than six months in the winter, but had more interrupted engagements in the summer, and several other plates were redrawn.

We should like to make two suggestions about gathering flowers: first that it should be done sparingly, and secondly that collectors should be fully courteous to the owner of enclosed land.

We have tried to take care of the flowers, and only to gather rare species very sparingly or not at all. Often we have hidden them with foliage from less scrupulous fingers. And when leading walks or expeditions of field clubs, we have tried to persuade others to do the same. Unfortunately there was sometimes one in the party, who thought it his special privilege to pick the only specimen seen or even to come back afterwards and do so! It really is important that we should preserve rare and interesting flowers for future generations.

Real botanists understand this. Gathering the flower prevents the casting of seed. Even for drawing these figures we have sometimes been content with two florets from a good spike with an upper and a lower leaf. We have walked miles in mountain mist and rain to restore a small rare plant to its own niche.

We commend botanizing as a means of healthy recreation for young and old. It is an interest that takes us out to the beautiful places of the earth. And if we really know the wild flowers around us at home, the plants almost speak to us of their struggles to grow. This interest stays with us to the end of our pilgrimage. It is not exactly an armchair study. To fulfil it properly we need good boots, a compass and a companion, and must face the thorns and steep places, the dense clouds and sharp mountain thunderstorms or the tides and island crossings. But we take no undue risks. It is good fun and healthy.

We said that valuable help had been given in editing the short text. Mr Douglas Kent, formerly Editor of the *Proceedings of the Botanical Society of the British Isles*, has kindly helped much with it, making many adjustments, especially to the nomenclature, and adding a list of authorities for the names. The brief descriptions are indebted to the earlier Floras. The first pages were written before the publication of the Flora by Messrs Clapham, Tutin and Warburg; but the whole is now doubtless indebted in greater or less degree to this latter work. We gratefully acknowledge the debt, and commend that work to all who wish to make a more serious study of the British Flora. We have followed Mr H. W. Pugsley's *Prodromus of the British Hieracia* and his *Revision of Euphrasiae*, both of them published in the *Journal of the Linnean Society*, and also Dr C. E. Hubbard's *Grasses*.

We are much indebted to the Keeper of Botany and his staff at the British Museum (Natural History) and also to the Director and the Herbarium staff at the Royal Botanic Gardens at Kew. In both we have had valuable advice accompanied by the selection of suitable material from the National Herbaria for drawing. This has been especially the case in the choice of Sedges and Grasses, but in other groups also.

In drawing the figures we have had helpful advice or determination of specimens from those who have specialized in several groups. This was often coupled with the posting of fresh specimens as follows: *Fumaria*, H. W. Pugsley, who also personally conducted us around Cornwall in search of these; *Cruciferae* and many other groups, Dr G. C. Druce; *Rubus*, Wm

Watson, who himself wrote the notes for the text on those figured; the Rose plate was redrawn after kind criticism of N. Y. Sandwith; *Sorbus*, A. J. Wilmott; *Mentha*, R. Graham; *Salix*, R. D. Meikle; *Potamogeton*, Dr G. Taylor; *Cyperaceae*, E. Nelmes and A. W. Stelfox; *Gramineae*, Dr C. E. Hubbard. All these gave valuable help and we are much indebted to them. For other drawings we acknowledge with gratitude that many botanists past and present kindly helped by sending fresh specimens, carefully determined and posted for this work. They are too numerous to name here. Their names are on the separate drawings referred to above.

We wish further to acknowledge our debt to Dr W. S. Bristowe (of Spider fame, President of the Ray Society) for earlier research into the possibility of publication. We are extremely grateful to His Royal Highness the Duke of Edinburgh for his active interest and to Squadron-Leader David Checketts for introducing the project to Mr George Rainbird and his colleagues.

After these acknowledgements we hope that the plates may have a chance of speaking for themselves. The author is very conscious of their limitations.

W. Keble Martin

Preface to the New Edition

Since the publication of the last edition of *The Concise British Flora* many changes have taken place, a few species may have become extinct, while others have become rare, new native taxa have been found and some introduced foreign species have become established.

In preparing the text for *The New Concise British Flora* these factors have been taken into account, and descriptions have been added of eighteen species which may be native as well as details of more than eighty introduced species, many of which are now spreading rapidly in various parts of Britain and Ireland. A number of hybrids which appear to be widespread, based on the work of Stace (1975), are also noticed. English names have been completely revised and standardized in accordance with the list published by The Botanical Society of the British Isles (Dony, *et al.*, 1980), and the distributional and habitat data has been revised and enlarged.

As a result of the revision *The New Concise British Flora* may justly claim to provide the most up-to-date account of the rapidly changing flora of these islands.

D. H. Kent

Glossary

achene A small dry indehiscent fruit, strictly of one free carpel.
acicle A very slender prickle or stoutish bristle.
acuminate With a long fine point.
acute Narrowed into a sharp point.
alternate Arranged successively on opposite sides of a stem.
amplexicaul Clasping the stem.
angle(d) (s) The meeting of two planes to form an edge.
annual A plant completing its life cycle from germination to death within one year.
anther The terminal portion of a stamen containing the pollen grains.
antrorse Directed upwards or forward.
apex The growing point of a stem; the tip of an organ.
apiculate Furnished with a small broad point at the apex.
appressed Lying flat along the whole length of an organ.
arcuate Bent like a bow.
aril The exterior covering of the seed in certain plants, e.g. *Taxus baccata*, developed from the stalk or base of the ovule.
aristate Awned.
ascending Sloping or curving upwards.
attenuate Gradually tapering.
auricles Small ear-like appendages at the base of a leaf.
awn A bristle-like part.
axil The upper angle formed by the union of the stem and the leaf.
axillary Growing in an axil.
axis The central part of a plant, around which the organs are developed.

beak A pointed projection.
beard Awn.
biconvex Convex on two sides.
biennial A plant requiring two years to complete its life cycle, growing in the first year, and flowering and fruiting in the second.
bifid Divided halfway down into two parts.
bipinnate When the divisions of a pinnate leaf are themselves pinnate.
biserrate Doubly serrate.
blunt Ending in a rounded form, neither tapering to a point, nor truncate.
bract(s) Modified leaves intermediate between the calyx and the normal leaves.
bracteate Having bracts.
bracteoles Minute bracts.
bulb An underground organ which is really a modified plant bud with fleshy scales, yielding stem and roots.
bulbils Small bulbs or tubers usually arising in the axils of the leaves or amongst the florets of an inflorescence, but sometimes found on the root.

calyx The outermost of the floral envelopes.
campanulate Bell-shaped.
capillary Hair-like.
capitate Growing in heads; pin-headed.
capitulum A close cluster of sessile flowers.
capsule A dry, dehiscent fruit.
carpel A modified leaf of one, or several, of which the pistil is formed.
carpophore The continuation of the stalk between the carpels.

cauline Borne on the stem, not radical.
cernuous Nodding.
ciliate Fringed with hairs.
cladode A leaf-like branch, as in *Ruscus aculeatus*.
clasping Grasping.
claw The narrow base of a petal in certain genera, e.g. *Dianthus*.
cleft Deeply cut, but not to the midrib.
commissure The faces by which two carpels adhere, particularly in the *Umbelliferae*.
confluent United at some part.
connate Similar organs distinct in origin but eventually becoming united.
connivent Making contact or converging.
contiguous Adjacent to each other; making contact at the edges.
convex Having a more-or-less rounded surface.
cordate Heart-shaped.
corm Bulb-like fleshy underground stem, as in *Anemone*, etc.
corolla The petals as a whole.
corona The circumference or margin of a radiated compound flower, particularly in the *Compositae*.
cotyledon(s) The first leaf or leaves of the embryo.
crenate With rounded marginal teeth.
crenulate Minutely crenate.
cruciform Cross-shaped.
cryptogam A flowerless plant.
cuneate Wedge-shaped.
cuspidate Spear-shaped at the tip.
cyme A flower-cluster of a broad and flattened type, as in *Sambucus nigra*.

deciduous Dropping off; shedding its leaves in the autumn.
decumbent Lying on the ground but tending to rise at the end.
decurrent Extending downwards, as when leaves are extended beyond their insertion and run down by a wing on the stem as in *Carduus* and *Cirsium*.
deflexed Bent sharply downwards.
dehiscent Opening to shed its seeds.
deltoid Shaped like an equilateral triangle.
dentate Toothed; notched.
denticulate Minutely toothed.
depressed When flattened vertically or at top.
dichotomous Forked, parted by pairs from top to bottom.
diffuse Widely or loosely spreading.
digitate A compound leaf divided into five leaflets, as in *Aesculus hippocastanum*.
dioecious Having the sexes on different plants.
disk The central part of a capitulum in the *Compositae* as opposed to the ray florets; the expanded base of a style in the *Umbelliferae*.
distant When similar parts are not close to each other.

elliptic(al) Oval but acute at each end.
elongate Drawn out.
emarginate Slightly notched at the edges.
entire Not toothed or cut at the edges.
epicalyx An involucre resembling an accessory calyx, as in *Malva*.
epichile The terminal part of the labellum of an orchid when it is distinct from the basal portion.

excurrent Where the stem remains central, the other parts being regularly placed around it.
exserted Protruding.

family A group of related genera.
fascicle(d) A close cluster or bundle.
fastigate Tapering to a point like a pyramid.
filament The stalk of an anther.
filiform Thread-like.
fimbriate With a fringed margin.
flexuose Wavy.
floret A small flower, one of a cluster.
follicle A dry dehiscent fruit formed of one carpel opening by a ventral suture to which the seeds are attached.
fringe(d) With hair-like appendages on the margins.
fruit The ripe seeds and their surrounding structure.

gamopetalous Having the petals united at the edges in the form of a tube.
genus The smallest natural group containing related but distinct species.
gibbous Swollen on one side.
glabrous Without hairs.
gland A wart-like structure on the surface, embedded or protruding, from any part of a plant.
glandular Having glands.
glaucous Bluish-grey.
globose Spherical.
glume A small bract with a flower in the axil as in grasses.

hastate Spear-shaped.
herb Any non-woody vascular plant.
herbaceous Having the texture of leaves.
hirsute Hairy, with long, usually soft, hairs.
hispid Clothed with stiff hairs or bristles.
hooded Formed into a hood at the end.
hyaline Very thin and translucent.
hybrid A plant produced by the fertilization of one species by another.
hypochile The basal portion of the labellum in an orchid.

incumbent Overlapping.
inferior Below the ovary.
inflorescence The arrangement of the flowers on a stem or branch.
intercalary Inserted between or amongst others.
internode The space between two adjacent nodes.
involucre The whorl of bracts enclosing a number of flowers as in the *Compositae* and *Umbelliferae*.
involute Having the margins rolled upwards.

keel(ed) The lower petal or petals when shaped like the keel of a boat as in *Astragalus*, *Lathyrus*, *Vicia*, etc.

labellum The lower petal of certain flowers, particularly orchids.
laciniate Jagged; deeply and irregularly divided into segments.
lanate Covered with soft, flexuous, densely matted hairs.

lanceolate Narrow, tapering at each end.
lateral Fixed on, or near, the side of an organ.
leaflet A subdivision of a compound leaf.
lemma The flowering glume of a grass.
lenticel Corky spots having the shape of a double-convex lens on young bark.
ligulate Strap-shaped.
ligule A small thin projection from the top of the leaf-sheath in grasses; a strap-shaped petal, e.g. in the *Compositae*.
limb The border or exposed part of a calyx or corolla, as distinct from the tube or throat.
linear Slender.
linear-lanceolate Slender but tapering to a point at the tip.
lobed Said of leaves which are divided, but not into separate leaflets.
lunate Shaped like the new moon.

membranous Thin, dry and semi-transparent.
mucronate Abruptly tipped with a short, straight point.
muricate With sharp points or prickles.

nectary The honey gland of a flower.
nerve A vein or slender rib.
node A point in a stem where a leaf is borne.
notch An indentation.

ob- As a prefix means inversely or oppositely.
oblong Longer than broad.
obtuse Blunt.
ochrea Provided with a tubular membranous stipule.

opposite Growing in pairs at the same level on opposite sides of a stem.
orbicular Nearly round and flat.
oval Broadly elliptic.
ovary The vessel in which the seeds are formed.
ovate Egg-shaped.
ovate-oblong Egg-shaped, but much longer than broad.
ovoid Of a solid object which is egg-shaped in outline.

palea The inner bract or glume of a grass; the chaffy scales on the receptacle in many species of the *Compositae*.
palmate Lobed or divided in the manner of an outspread hand.
panicle A raceme with branching pedicels.
papillae Small elongated protuberances.
papillose Warty; having papillae.
pappus The tufts of hairs on achenes or fruits, particularly in the *Compositae*.
pectinate Resembling the teeth of a comb.
pedicel The stalk of a single flower.
peduncle The stalk supporting either a flower or a flower-cluster.
pellucid Transparent.
peltate Shield-shaped with the stalk in the centre.
perennial A plant that lives for more than two years and usually flowers annually.
perfoliate With the leaf united round the stem, as in *Montia perfoliata*.
perianth The floral envelopes, calyx or corolla, or both.

pericarp A seed vessel, including the adhering calyx if present.
petal A flower leaf, often brightly coloured, forming part of a corolla.
petaloid Resembling a petal.
petiole A leaf-stalk.
petiolate Having a petiole.
pilose Hairy, usually with long soft hairs.
pinnate With leaflets arranged on opposite sides of a common stalk or rachis.
pinnatifid Deeply cut into segments nearly to the midrib.
pinnatisect Pinnately divided almost to the midrib but not into separate leaflets.
pistil The female organ of a flower, consisting when complete of ovary, style and stigma.
pollinia A pollen mass composed of large numbers of cohering pollen grains.
polypetalous Having many separate petals.
pore A small aperture.
procumbent Trailing; lying loosely on the ground. .
proliferous Bearing progeny as off-shoots.
prostrate Lying closely on the surface of the ground.
pruinose Covered with a whitish bloom.
pubescent Covered with fine short hairs.
pyriform Pear-shaped.

raceme An unbranched inflorescence with flowers borne on equal pedicels.
rachis The axis of an inflorescence, compound leaf or branch.
radical Growing from the root.

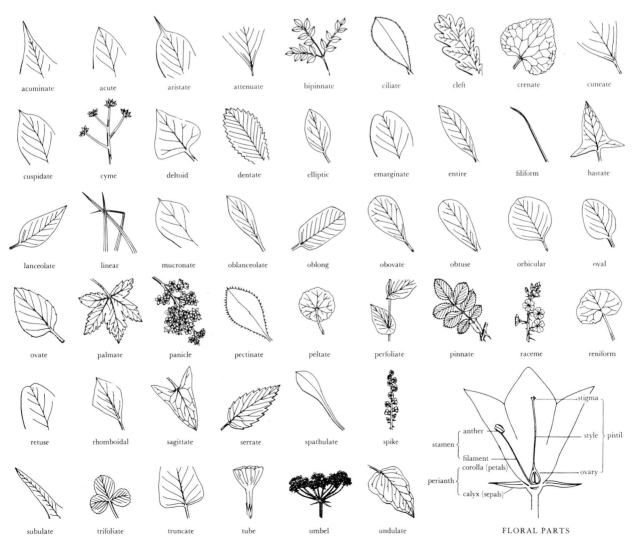

acuminate   acute   aristate   attenuate   bipinnate   ciliate   cleft   crenate   cuneate

cuspidate   cyme   deltoid   dentate   elliptic   emarginate   entire   filiform   hastate

lanceolate   linear   mucronate   oblanceolate   oblong   obovate   obtuse   orbicular   oval

ovate   palmate   panicle   pectinate   peltate   perfoliate   pinnate   raceme   reniform

retuse   rhomboidal   sagittate   serrate   spathulate   spike

subulate   trifoliate   truncate   tube   umbel   undulate

FLORAL PARTS

stigma · style · pistil · anther · stamen · filament · corolla (petals) · ovary · perianth · calyx (sepals)

ray The outer part of a compound radiate flower.

receptacle The uppermost part of the stem nearing the flowers.

recurved Bent moderately backwards in a curve.

reflexed Bent abruptly backwards.

reniform Kidney-shaped.

reticulate Marked with a network of veins.

retrorse Pointing backwards.

retuse Terminating in a rounded end, the centre of which is slightly indented.

revolute Rolled or curved downwards.

rhizomatous Having the character of a rhizome.

rhizome An underground, creeping stem, producing roots and leafy shoots.

rhomboid(al) Similar in shape to a diamond in a pack of playing cards.

rib(bed) A primary vein; furnished with ribs.

rosette A cluster of leaves in circular form, as in *Plantago major*.

rotate (of a corolla) Wheel-shaped, circular and flat with a short tube.

rugose Wrinkled.

saccate Pouched.

sagittate Shaped like an arrow-head.

saprophyte A plant that lives on decaying vegetable matter.

scabrid Rough.

scale A thin scarious structure, often a degenerate leaf.

scape A leafless flower-stalk rising from the root.

scarious Very thin, dry and semi-transparent.

secund All turned to one side.

segment A division into which a plant organ, e.g. a leaf, may be cleft.

sepal A leaf of the calyx, the outer whorl of the perianth

septate Divided into partitions.

serrate Toothed like a saw.

sessile Without a stalk.

setae Bristles.

silicula(e) A pod (in *Cruciferae*) less than three times as long as broad.

siliqua(e) A pod (in *Cruciferae*) more than three times as long as broad.

sinuate Having a deep wavy outline.

sinuous Undulating.

sinus A depression between two teeth.

spadix A succulent spike with a fleshy axis, as in *Arum maculatum*.

spathe A large bract enclosing a flower cluster, usually a spadix.

spathulate Paddle-shaped.

spike An inflorescence in which the flowers are sessile round an axis.

spikelet A small spike; the inflorescence of grasses.

spine A thorn.

spur A slender projection from the base of a perianth segment, or of a corolla, as in *Aquilegia vulgaris*.

stamen One of the male reproductive organs of a plant.

staminodes Infertile, often reduced, stamens.

standard The large, often erect, posterior petal of a corolla in the *Leguminosae*.

stellate Star-shaped.

stigma The part of the pistil or style which receives the pollen.

stipule A leaf-like appendage usually at the base of the petiole.

stipulate Having stipules on it.

stolon A creeping stem which roots at intervals.

stoloniferous Having stolons.

striate(ions) Marked with slender streaks or furrows.

strict Narrow, upright and very straight.

style The space between the ovary and the stigma.

sub- Under or below.

subulate Awl-shaped.

succulent Juicy.

teeth Small marginal lobes.

tepals (*Rumex*) Inner and outer perianth segments.

terete Long and round, without ridges or grooves.

terminal Borne at the top of the stem.

testa The outer coat of the seed.

tomentose Densely pubescent, with woolly entangled hairs.

trifid Three-cleft but not to the base.

trifoliate Having three leaflets.

trigonous Three-sided.

triquetrous Triangular and acutely angled.

truncate As though abruptly cut off at the end.

tube The united parts of a corolla or calyx.

tuber A thickened part of an underground stem or root of one year's duration.

tubercle A small spherical or ovoid swelling.

umbel A type of inflorescence in which equal pedicels proceed from a common centre.

umbellate With partial or secondary umbels.

unarmed Without spines or prickles.

undulate Wavy.

unisexual Of one sex only.

valvate When parts of a flower bud meet but do not overlap.

valve (*Rumex*) The inner tepals when they have reached maximum development following fertilization.

vascular Furnished with vessels.

vernal Appearing in spring.

villous Covered with shaggy hairs.

viscid Clammy or sticky.

vitta(e) The aromatic oil tubes of the pericarp in many species of the *Umbelliferae*.

viviparous Producing young plants instead of flowers.

whorl(ed) A ring of leaves or flowers around a stem at the same level as each other.

wing(ed) The lateral petals in the flowers of the *Papaveraceae* and *Leguminosae*; the flat membranous appendages of some seeds.

Abbreviations

Abbreviations of Authors' Names for the Plant Species

No dates are given for living authors

Adams–M. F. Adams, 1780–1833
Adema–F. Adema
Aellen–P. Aellen, 1896–1973
Airy Shaw–H. K. Airy Shaw
Ait.–W. Aiton, 1731–1793
Ait.f.–W. T. Aiton, 1766–1849
Albert–A. Albert, 1836–1909
All.–C. Allioni, 1728–1804
D. E. Allen–D. E. Allen
Allman–G. J. Allman, 1812–1898
Anderss.–N. J. Andersson, 1821–1880
Andreas–C. H. Andreas
Andrz.–A. L. Andrzejowski, 1784–1868
Arcangeli–G. Arcangeli, 1840–1921
Ard.–P. Arduino, 1728–1805
Arn.–G. A. W. Arnott, 1799–1868
Arrondeau–E. T. Arrondeau, d. 1882
Aschers.–P. F. A. Ascherson, 1834–1913
Ashe–W. W. Ashe, 1872–1932
auct.–auctor, auctores; author(s)
Auquier–P. Auquier, 1939–1980

Bab.–C. C. Babington, 1808–1895
Backh.–J. Backhouse, 1825–1890
C. Bailey–C. Bailey, 1838–1924
Bak.–E. G. Baker, 1864–1949
H. G. Bak.–H. G. Baker
J. G. Bak.–J. G. Baker, 1834–1920
Balb.–G. B. Balbis, 1765–1831
J. Ball–J. Ball, 1818–1889
P. W. Ball–P. W. Ball
Bartal.–B. Bartalini, 1746–1822
Bast.–T. Bastard, 1784–1846
Batt.–J. A. Battandier, 1848–1922
Baumg.–J. C. G. Baumgarten, 1765–1843
Beauv.–A. M. F. J. Palisot de Beauvois, 1752–1820
Bechst.–J. M. Bechstein, 1757–1822
Beck–G. Ritter Beck von Mannagetta und
    Larchenau, 1856–1931
W. Becker–W. Becker, 1874–1928
Beeby–W. H. Beeby, 1849–1910
Béguinot–A. Béguinot, 1875–1940
Bellardi–C. A. L. Bellardi, 1741–1826
A. Benn.–A. Bennett, 1843–1929
Benth.–G. Bentham, 1800–1884
Bernh.–J. J. Bernhardi, 1774–1850
Bertol.–A. Bertoloni, 1775–1869
Bess.–W. S. J. G. von Besser, 1784–1842
Betcke–E. F. Betcke, 1815–1865
Bicknell–C. Bicknell, 1842–1918
Bieb.–F. A. Marschall von Bieberstein, 1768–1826
Bigel.–J. Bigelow, 1787–1879
Billot–P. C. Billot, 1796–1863
Biv.–A. de Bivona-Bernardi, 1774–1837
Blanche–E. Blanche, 1824–1908
Bluff–M. Bluff, 1805–1837
Böcher–T. Böcher
Boenn.–C. M. F. von Boenninghausen, 1785–1864
Boiss.–P. E. Boissier, 1810–1885
Bonnier–G. E. M. Bonnier, 1853–1922
Boott–F. Boott, 1792–1863
Bor.–A. Boreau, 1803–1875
Borbás–V. von Borbás, 1844–1905
Borkh.–M. B. Borkhausen, 1760–1806
Börner–C. Börner, 1880–1953

Borrer–W. Borrer, 1781–1862
Boucher–J. A. G. Boucher de Crèvecoeur, 1757–1844
R. Br.–R. Brown, 1773–1858
M. E. Bradshaw–M. E. Bradshaw
A. Braun–A. C. H. Braun, 1805–1877
F. Braun–F. Braun
Bréb.–L. A. de Brébisson, 1798–1872
Britton–N. L. Britton, 1859–1934
Brodesson–E. Brodesson, fl. 1906–1912
Bromf.–W. A. Bromfield, 1801–1851
Brot.–F. da Avellar Brotero, 1744–1828
Brügg.–C. G. Brügger, 1833–1899
Brummitt–R. K. Brummitt
Bub.–P. Bubani, 1806–1888
Buchen.–F. G. P. Buchenau, 1831–1906
Bunge–A. A. von Bunge, 1803–1890
Burbidge–F. W. T. Burbidge, 1847–1905
Burgsd.–F. A. L. von Burgsdorf, 1747–1802
Burm.f.–N. L. Burman, 1734–1793
Burnat–E. Burnat, 1828–1920
Buser–R. Buser, 1857–1931
Butcher–R. W. Butcher, 1897–1971

Caruel–T. Caruel, 1830–1898
Casp.–J. X. R. Caspary, 1818–1887
Cass.–A. H. G. de Cassini, 1781–1832
Cav.–A. J. Cavanilles, 1745–1804
Cavara–F. Cavara, 1857–1929
Čelak.–L. J. Čelakovsky, 1834–1902
Chaix–D. Chaix, 1730–1799
Cham.–A. L. von Chamisso, 1781–1838
Chatel.–J. J. Chatelain, 1736–1822
Chater–A. O. Chater
Chaub.–L. A. Chaubard, 1785–1854
Chazelles–M. de Chazelles, fl. 1790
Chevall.–F. F. Chevallier, 1796–1840
Chiov.–E. Chiovenda, 1871–1940
Chouard–P. Chouard, fl. 1921–1970
Clairv.–J. P. de Clairville, 1742–1830
Clapham–A. R. Clapham
Clarion–J. Clarion, 1780–1856
Clavaud–A. Clavaud, 1828–1890
Cockayne–L. Cockayne, 1855–1934
Colem.–W. H. Coleman, 1816–1863
Colgan–N. Colgan, 1851–1919
Compton–R. H. Compton, 1886–1979
C. D. K. Cook–C. D. K. Cook
D. E. Coombe–D. E. Coombe
Corb.–L. Corbière, 1850–1941
Cosson–E. S. C. Cosson, 1819–1889
Coult.–J. M. Coulter, 1851–1928
Court.–R. J. Courtois, 1806–1835
Coutinho–A. X. P. Coutinho, 1851–1939
Coville–F. V. Coville, 1867–1937
Crantz–H. J. N. von Crantz, 1722–1799
Crép.–F. Crépin, 1830–1903
Cronq.–A. Cronquist
Cunn.–A. Cunningham, 1791–1839
Curt.–W. Curtis, 1746–1799
Custer–J. L. Custer, 1755–1828
Cyr.–D. Cyrillo, 1739–1799
Czern.–V. M. Czernjew, 1796–1871

Dahl–O. C. Dahl, 1862–1940
Dahlst.–H. G. A. Dahlstedt, 1856–1934

Dandy–J. E. Dandy, 1903–1976
Danser–B. H. Danser, 1891–1943
Davey–F. H. Davey, 1868–1915
E. W. Davies–E. W. Davies
Davies–H. Davies, 1739–1821
DC.–A. P. de Candolle, 1778–1841
Del.–A. R. Delile, 1778–1850
Delarb.–A. Delarbre, 1724–1814
Déségl.–P. A. Déséglise, 1823–1883
Desf.–R. L. Desfontaines, 1750–1833
Desv.–A. N. Desvaux, 1784–1856
Dickson–J. Dickson, 1738–1822
Dippel–L, Dippel, 1827–1914
Don–D. Don, 1799–1841
G. Don–G. Don, 1798–1856
Donn–J. Donn, 1758–1813
Dostál–J. Dostál
Dougl.–D. Douglas, 1798–1834
Drej.–S. T. N. Drejer, 1813–1842
Druce–G. C. Druce, 1850–1932
Dryander–J. C. Dryander, 1748–1810
Duby–J. E. Duby, 1798–1885
Duchesne–A. N. Duchesne, 1747–1827
Düll–R. Düll
Dumort.–B. C. J. Dumortier, 1797–1878
Durieu–M. C. Durieu de Maisonneuve, 1796–1878
Duroi–J. P. Duroi, 1741–1785
D'Urv.–J. C. S. D. D'Urville, 1790–1842
Duvigneaud–J. Duvigneaud
Dyer–W. T. Thiselton Dyer, 1843–1928

Edmondst.–T. Edmondston, 1825–1846
Ehrh.–J. F. Ehrhart, 1742–1795
Ehrend.–F. Ehrendorfer
Ell.–S. Elliot, 1771–1830
Engelhorn–T. Engelhorn

A. Félix–A. Félix, fl. 1912
Fenzl–E. Fenzl, 1808–1879
Fernald–M. L. Fernald, 1873–1950
R. Fernandes–R. Fernandes
Fieb.–F. X. Fieber, 1807–1872
Fiori–A. Fiori, 1865–1950
Fisch.–F. E. L. von Fischer, 1782–1854
Flügge–J. Flügge, 1775–1816
Foggitt–W. Foggitt, 1835–1917
Forsk.–P. Forskål, 1732–1763
E. Forst.–E. Forster, 1765–1849
G. Forst.–J. G. A. Forster, 1754–1794
J. R. Forst.–J. R. Forster, 1729–1798
T. F. Forst.–T. F. Forster, 1761–1825
Fouc.–J. Foucaud, 1847–1904
P. Fourn.–P. Fournier, 1877–1964
Fourr.–P. J. Fourreau, 1844–1871
Fr.–E. M. Fries, 1794–1878
Franch.–A. R. Franchet, 1834–1900
Fritsch–K. Fritsch, 1864–1934
Fuss–M. Fuss, 1814–1883

Gaertn.–J. Gaertner, 1732–1791
Garcke–F. A. Garcke, 1819–1904
Gaudich.–C. Gaudichaud-Beaupré, 1789–1854
Gaudin–J. F. A. T. G. P. Gaudin, 1766–1833
Gay–J. E. Gay, 1786–1864
Gilib.–J. E. Gilibert, 1741–1814

Gilmour–J. S. L. Gilmour
Girard–F. de Girard, fl. 1842
Gled.–J. G. Gleditsch, 1714–1786
C. C. Gmel.–C. C. Gmelin, 1762–1837
S. G. Gmel.–S. G. Gmelin, 1744–1774
Godfery–M. J. Godfery, d. 1945
Godr.–D. A. Godron, 1807–1880
Good.–S. Goodenough, 1743–1827
Gouan–A. Gouan, 1733–1821
Goupil–C. J. Goupil, 1784–1858
Graebner–K. O. R. P. P. Graebner, 1871–1933
R. A. Graham–R. A. Graham, 1915–1958
A. Gray–A. Gray, 1810–1888
S. F. Gray–S. F. Gray, 1766–1836
Gregory–Mrs. E. S. Gregory, 1840–1932
Gremli–A. Gremli, 1833–1899
Gren.–J. C. M. Grenier, 1808–1875
Greuter–W. R. Greuter
Grimm–J. F. K. Grimm, 1737–1821
Griseb.–A. H. R. Grisebach, 1814–1879
H. Groves–H. Groves, 1855–1912
J. Groves–J. Groves, 1858–1933
Guinochet–M. Guinochet
Gunn.–J. F. Gunnerus, 1718–1773
Guss.–G. Gussone, 1787–1866

Hack.–E. Hackel, 1850–1926
Hagerup–O. Hagerup, 1889–1961
Haller f.–A. von Haller, 1758–1823
Halliday–G. Halliday
F. J. Hanb.–F. J. Hanbury, 1851–1938
Hardouin–L. Hardouin, 1800–1858
Hartig–H. J. A. R. Hartig, 1839–1901
Hartm.–K. J. Hartman, 1790–1849
Harz–K. O. Harz, 1842–1906
Hassk.–J. C. Hasskarl, 1811–1894
Hausskn.–H. K. Haussknecht, 1838–1903
Hayek–A. E. von Hayek, 1871–1928
Hayne–F. G. Hayne, 1763–1832
Hedlund–T. Hedlund, 1861–1953
Heg.–J. J. Hegetschweiler, 1789–1839
Hegi–G. Hegi, 1876–1932
Henrard–J. T. Henrard
Henry–L. Henry, 1853–1913
Henslow–J. S. Henslow, 1796–1861
Hepper–F. N. Hepper
Herbert–W. Herbert, 1778–1847
F. Hermann–F. Hermann, 1873–?
Herter–W. G. Herter, 1884–1958
Heuffel–J. Heuffel, 1800–1857
Heynh.–G. Heynhold, fl. 1838–1850
Heywood–V. H. Heywood
Hiern–W. P. Hiern, 1839–1925
Hiit.–H. I. A. Hiitonen
Hill–J. Hill, 1716–1775
Hochst.–C. F. Hochstetter, 1787–1860
Hoffm.–G. F. Hoffmann, 1760–1826
Hoffmanns.–J. C. Hoffmannsegg, 1766–1849
Holmberg–O. R. Holmberg, 1874–1930
Holub–J. Holub
Honck.–G. A. Honckeny, 1724–1805
Hook.–W. J. Hooker, 1785–1865
Hook.f.–J. D. Hooker, 1817–1911
Hoppe–D. H. Hoppe, 1760–1846
Hork.–J. Horkel, 1769–1846
Hornem.–J. W. Hornemann, 1770–1841
Hose–J. Hose, d. 1800
Host–N. T. Host, 1761–1834
House–H. D. House, 1878–1949
Houtt.–M. Houttuyn, 1720–1798
Howard–H. W. Howard
Howell–T. J. Howell, 1842–1912
C. E. Hubbard–C. E. Hubbard, 1900–1980
Huds.–W. Hudson, 1730–1793
W. E. Hughes–W. E. Hughes
Hull–J. Hull, 1761–1843
Hülphers–K. A. Hülphers, 1882–1948
Hultén–E. O. G. Hultén, 1894–1981
P. F. Hunt–P. F. Hunt
Hyland.–N. Hylander, 1904–1970

Iljin–M. M. Iljin, 1889–1967
Ilse–H. Ilse, 1835–1900
Ives–E. Ives, 1779–1861

Jacq.–N. J. von Jacquin, 1727–1817
Jacq.f.–J. F. von Jacquin, 1766–1839
Jalas–J. Jalas
Jansen–P. Jansen, 1882–1955
Johans.–K. K. Johansson, 1856–1928
Jord.–A. Jordan, 1814–1897
Juss.–A. L. de Jussieu, 1748–1836
Juz.–S. V. Juzepczuk, 1893–1959

Kar.–G. S. Karelin, 1801–1872
Karst.–G. K. W. H. Karsten, 1817–1908
Kenyon–W. Kenyon, fl. 1847
Ker-Gawl.–J. Gawler (né J. B. Ker), 1764–1842
Kerguélen–M. F.-J. Kerguélen
Kerner–A. J. Kerner von Marilaun, 1831–1898
Kir.–I. P. Kirilow, 1821–1842
Kirschleger–F. R. Kirschleger, 1804–1869
Kit.–P. Kitaibel, 1757–1817
Kittel–M. B. Kittel, 1796–1875
Kneucker–J. A. Kneucker, 1862–1946
Knuth–R. G. P. Knuth, 1874–1957
Koch–W. D. J. Koch, 1771–1849
K. Koch–K. (C.) H. E. Koch, 1809–1879
Walo Koch–Walo Koch, 1896–1956
Koel.–G. L. Koeler, 1765–1807
Koerte–F. Koerte, 1782–1845
E. H. L. Krause–E. H. L. Krause, 1859–1942
Krecz.–V. I. Kreczetowicz, 1901–1942
Kunth–K. S. Kunth, 1788–1850
Kuntz.–K. (C.) E. O. Kuntze, 1843–1907
Kütz.–F. T. Kützing, 1807–1892

L.–C. von Linné (C. Linnaeus), 1707–1778
L.f.–C. von Linné, 1741–1783
Laest.–L. L. Laestadius, 1800–1861
Lag.–M. La Gasca y Segura, 1776–1839
Lagr.-Foss.–A. R. A. Lagrèze-Fossat, 1814–1874
Laichard.–J. N. von Laicharding, 1754–1797
Lam.–J. B. A. P. Monnet de la Marck, 1744–1829
Lamotte–M. Lamotte, 1820–1883
Láng–A. F. Láng, 1795–1863
Lange–J. M. C. Lange, 1818–1898
Lapierre–J. M. Lapierre, 1754–1834
Latourr.–M. A. L. C. de Latourette, 1729–1793
Latterade–J. F. Latterade, 1784–1858
Lawalrée–A. Lawalrée
Lebel–J. E. Lebel, 1801–1878
Lecoq–H. Lecoq, 1802–1871
Ledeb.–C. F. von Ledebour, 1785–1851
Leers–J. D. Leers, 1727–1774
Le Gall–N. J. M. Le Gall, 1787–1860
Lehm.–J. G. C. Lehmann, 1792–1860
Leight.–W. A. Leighton, 1805–1889
Lejeune–A. L. S. Lejeune, 1779–1858
Le Jolis–A. F. Le Jolis, 1823–1904
Leresche–L. F. J. R. Leresche, 1808–1885
Less.–C. F. Lessing, 1809–1862
Léveillé–A. A. H. Léveillé, 1863–1918
Levier–E. Levier, 1838–1911
Ley–A. Ley, 1842–1911
Leyss.–F. W. von Leysser, 1731–1815
L.-Garland–L. V. L. Garland, (né Lester), 1860–1944
L'Hérit.–C. L. L'Héritier de Brutelle, 1746–1800
Liebl.–F. K. Lieblein, 1744–1810
Lightf.–J. Lightfoot, 1735–1788
Liljeb.–S. Liljeblad, 1761–1815
Lindblad–M. A. Lindblad, 1821–1899
Lindl.–J. Lindley, 1799–1865
Lindm.–C. A. M. Lindman, 1856–1928
Link–J. H. F. Link, 1767–1851
E. F. Linton–E. F. Linton, 1848–1928
Lois.–J. L. A. Loiseleur-Deslongchamps, 1774–1849
Lönnr.–Lönnroh, 1802–1884
Loret–H. Loret, 1810–1888
Lousley–J. E. Lousley, 1907–1976
Á. Löve–Á. Löve
D. Löve–D. Löve
Lyons–L. J. C. Lyons, 1792–1874

Mabille–P. Mabille, fl. 1864–1872
Mackenzie–K. K. Mackenzie, 1877–1934
Macreight–D. C. Macreight, 1799–1868
Manton–I. Manton

Marsh.–H. Marshall, 1722–1801
E. S. Marshall–E. S. Marshall, 1858–1919
Martyn–T. Martyn, 1735–1825
Mattuschka–H. G. von Mattuschka, 1734–1779
Mauri–E. Mauri, 1791–1836
Maxim.–K. J. Maximowicz, 1827–1891
McNeill–J. McNeill
Medic.–F. K. Medicus, 1736–1808
Meerb.–N. Meerburgh, 1734–1814
Meikle–R. D. Meikle
Meissn.–C. F. Meissner, 1800–1874
Melderis–A. Melderis
Melville–R. Melville
Merát–F. V. Merát, 1780–1851
Mert.–F. K. Mertens, 1764–1831
Mey.–C. A. Meyer, 1795–1855
E. Mey.–E. H. F. Meyer, 1791–1858
Michx.–A. Michaux, 1746–1802
Michx.f.–F. A. Michaux, 1770–1855
Mikan f.–J. C. Mikan, 1769–1844
Mill.–P. Miller, 1691–1771
Moench–C. Moench, 1744–1805
D. Moresby Moore–D. Moresby Moore
Moq.–C. H. B. A. Moquin-Tandon, 1804–1863
More–A. G. More, 1830–1895
Moss–C. E. Moss, 1872–1931
Muhl.–G. H. I. Muhlenberg, 1753–1815
Murb.–S. S. Murbeck, 1859–1946
Murr.–J. A. Murray, 1740–1791
A. Murr.–A. Murray, 1812–1878
J. Murr–J. Murr, 1864–1932

Naeg.–O. Naegeli, 1871–1938
Nakai–T. Nakai, 1882–1952
Neck.–N. J. von Necker, 1729–1793
Nees–C. G. D. Nees von Esenbeck, 1776–1858
Th. Nendtvich–Th. Nendtvich
Neves–J. de Barros Neves
Nevski–S. A. Nevski, 1908–1938
Newbould–W. W. Newbould, 1819–1886
Neygenf.–F. W. Neygenfind, fl. 1821
Nicholson–G. Nicholson, 1847–1908
Nied.–F. J. Niedenzu, 1857–1937
Nolte–E. F. Nolte, 1791–1875
Nordb.–G. Nordborg
Nordh.–R. Nordhagen, 1894–1979
Nutt.–T. Nuttall, 1786–1859
Nyman–C. F. Nyman, 1820–1893

Oborny–A. Oborny, 1840–1925
Ockendon–D. J. Ockendon
Oeder–G. C. von Oeder, 1728–1791
Oefelein–H. Oefelein, 1905–1970
Opiz–P. M. Opiz, 1787–1858
Ostenf.–C. E. H. Ostenfeld, 1873–1931

Pall.–P. S. Pallas, 1741–1811
Palla–E. Palla, 1864–1922
Panz.–G. W. F. Panzer, 1755–1829
Paol.–G. Paoletti, 1865–1941
Parl.–F. Parlatore, 1816–1877
Parnell–R. Parnell, 1810–1882
Pedersen–A. Pedersen
Pennell–F. W. Pennell, 1886–1952
Perring–F. H. Perring
Pers.–C. H. Persoon, 1762–1836
Peter–G. A. Peter, 1853–1937
Petermann–W. L. Petermann, 1806–1855
Petrak–F. Petrak, 1886–1973
Pilg.–R. K. F. Pilger, 1876–1953
Piré–L. A. H. J. Piré, 1827–1887
Planch.–J. E. Planchon, 1823–1888
Podp.–J. Podpěra, 1878–1954
Poggenb.–J. F. Poggenburg, 1840–1893
Pohl–R. W. Pohl
Poir.–J. L. M. Poiret, 1755–1834
Polatschek–A. Polatschek
Poll.–J. A. Pollich, 1740–1780
Porter–T. C. Porter, 1822–1901
Pourr.–P. A. Pourret de Figeac, 1754–1818
Prantl–K. A. E. Prantl, 1849–1893
C. Presl–C. (K.) B. Presl, 1794–1852
J. Presl–J. S. Presl, 1791–1849
Prime–C. T. Prime, 1909–1979
Pritchard–N. M. Pritchard

M. C. F. Proctor–M. C. F. Proctor
Pugsley–H. W. Pugsley, 1868–1947
Pursh–F. T. Pursh, 1774–1820
Rabenh.–G. L. Rabenhorst, 1806–1881
Raf.–C. S. Rafinesque-Schmaltz, 1783–1840
Rafn–C. G. Rafn, 1769–1808
Raunk.–C. Raunkiaer, 1860–1938
Räusch.–E. A. Räuschel, fl. 1772–1797
Raven–P. H. Raven
Rech.f.–K. H. Rechinger
Regel–E. A. von Regel, 1815–1892
Rehd.–A. Rehder, 1863–1949
Rehm.–A. Rehman, 1840–1917
Reichard–J. J. Reichard, 1743–1782
Reichb.–H. G. L. Reichenbach, 1793–1879
Reichb.f.–H. G. Reichenbach, 1823–1889
Renner–O. Renner, 1883–1960
Req.–E. Requien, 1788–1851
Retz.–A. J. Retzius, 1742–1821
Reut.–G. F. Reuter, 1805–1872
Rich.f.–L. C. M. Richard, 1754–1821
A. J. Richards–A. J. Richards
Riddelsd.–H. J. Riddelsdell, 1866–1941
Ridley–H. N. Ridley, 1855–1956
Robson–E. Robson, 1763–1813
Rochel–A. Rochel, 1770–1847
Roem.–J. J. Roemer, 1763–1819
Roffey–J. Roffey, 1860–1927
Ronn.–K. Ronniger, 1871–1954
Rosser–E. M. Rosser
Rostański–K. Rostański
Rostk.–F. W. G. Rostkovius, 1770–1848
Rostrup–F. G. E. Rostrup, 1831–1907
Roth–A. W. Roth, 1757–1834
Rothm.–W. Rothmaler, 1908–1962
Rouy–G. C. C. Rouy, 1851–1924
Royle–J. F. Royle, 1779–1858
Runemark–H. Runemark
Rupr.–F. J. Ruprecht, 1814–1870
Ruthe–J. F. Ruthe, 1788–1859
Ryd.–P. A. Rydberg, 1860–1931

St Amans–J. F. B. St Amans, 1748–1831
St John–H. St John
Salisb.–R. A. Salisbury, (né Markham), 1761–1829
Salmon–C. E. Salmon, 1872–1930
Samp.–G. A. da Silva Ferreira Sampaio, 1865–1937
Sándor–I. Sándor, 1853–?
Sauter–A. E. Sauter, 1800–1881
Savi–G. Savi, 1769–1844
Savigny M. J. C. L. de Savigny, 1777–1851
Savouré–H. S. Savouré, 1861–1921
Schau.–J. C. Schauer, 1813–1848
Scheele–G. H. A. Scheele, 1808–1864
Scherb.–J. Scherbius, 1769–1813
Schiffn.–V. F. Schiffner, 1862–1944
Schimp.–C. C. F. Schimper, 1803–1867
Schinz–H. Schinz, 1858–1941
Schischk.–B. K. Schischkin, 1886–1963
Schkuhr–C. Schkuhr, 1741–1811
Schlecht.–D. F. L. von Schlechtendal, 1794–1866
Schleich.–J. C. Schleicher, 1768–1834
Schleid.–M. J. Schleider, 1804–1881
Schmidt–F. W. Schmidt, 1764–1796
F. Schmidt–F. Schmidt, 1832–1908
C. K. Schneid.–C. K. Schneider, 1876–1951
Schönh.–F. C. G. Schönheit, 1789–1870
Schönl.–S. Schönland, 1860–1940
Schott–H. W. Schott, 1794–1865
Schousb.–P. K. A. Schousboe, 1766–1832

Schrad.–H. A. Schrader, 1767–1836
Schrank–F. von Paula von Schrank, 1747–1835
Schreb.–J. C. D. von Schreber, 1739–1810
F. Schroeder–F. Schroeder
Schult.–J. A. Schultes, 1773–1831
C. H. Schultz–C. H. Schultz, 1805–1867
F. W. Schultz–F. W. Schultz, 1804–1876
K. F. Schultz–K. F. Schultz, 1765–1837
O. E. Schulz–O. E. Schulz, 1874–1936
R. Schulz–R. Schulz, 1873–1926
Schumach.–H. C. F. Schumacher, 1757–1830
Schur–P. J. F. Schur, 1799–1878
Schwarz–O. Schwarz
Schweigg.–A. F. Schweigger, 1783–1821
Schwein.–G. A. Schweinfurth, 1836–1925
Scop.–G. A. Scopoli, 1723–1788
A. J. Scott–A. J. Scott
Seb.–A. Sebastiani, 1782–1821
P. D. Sell–P. D. Sell
Senn.–Frère Sennen (E. M. Grenier-Blanc), 1861–1937
Sibth.–J. Sibthorp, 1758–1796
Sieb.–P. F. von Siebold, 1796–1866
Silva–A. R. Pinto da Silva
Simmons–H. G. Simmons, 1866–1943
Simonkai–L. von Simonkai, 1851–1910
Simonet–M. Simonet, 1899–1965
Sims–J. Sims, 1749–1831
Sm.–J. E. Smith, 1759–1828
G. E. Sm.–G. E. Smith, 1804–1881
H. Sm.–H. Smith
P. M. Sm.–P. M. Smith
Small–J. K. Small, 1869–1938
Sobol.–G. F. Sobolevski, 1741–1807
Sobrinho–L. G. Sobrinho
Soland.–D. C. Solander, 1736–1782
Soó–R. de Soó, 1903–1980
Soy.-Wil.–H. F. Soyer-Willemet, 1791–1867
Spach–E. Spach, 1801–1879
Spreng.–C. (K.) P. J. Sprengel, 1766–1833
Stace–C. A. Stace
Stapf–O. Stapf, 1857–1933
Stearn–W. T. Stearn
Stefánsson–S. Stefánsson, 1863–1921
Steph.–F. Stephani, 1842–1927
T. Stephenson–T. Stephenson, 1855–1948
T. A. Stephenson–T. A. Stephenson, 1898–1961
Sterneck–J. von Sterneck, fl. 1864–1901
Sterner–K. R. Sterner, 1891–1956
Sterns–E. E. Sterns, 1846–1926
Stev.–C. von Steven, 1781–1863
Stokes–J. Stokes, 1755–1831
Suckow–G. G. A. Suckow, d. 1867
Suksd.–W. N. Suksdorf, 1850–1932
Summerhayes–V. S. Summerhayes, 1897–1974
Sutton–C. Sutton, 1756–1846
Sw.–O. Swartz, 1760–1818
Sweet–R. Sweet, 1783–1835
Syme–J. T. I. B. Syme, (né Boswell), 1822–1888

Tausch–I. F. Tausch, 1793–1848
Ten.–M. Tenore, 1780–1861
Thell.–A. Thellung, 1881–1928
C. Thomas–C. Thomas, fl. 1938–1973
Thuill.–J. L. Thuillier, 1757–1822
Timm–J. C. Timm, 1734–1805
Tod.–A. Todaro, 1818–1892
Torr.–J. Torrey, 1796–1873
Tourlet–E. H. Tourlet, 1843–1907
Towns.–F. Townsend, 1822–1905

Tratt.–L. Trattinick, 1764–1849
Trimen, H. Trimen, 1843–1896
Trin.–K. B. von Trinius, 1778–1844
Turcz.–N. Turczaninow, 1796–1864
D. Turner–D. Turner, 1775–1858
Turra–A. Turra, 1730–1796
Turrill–W. B. Turrill, 1890–1961
Tutin–T. G. Tutin
Tzvelev–N. N. Tzvelev

Ucria–B. Ucria, 1739–1796
Ulbr.–E. Ulbrich, 1879–1952

Vaarama–A. Vaarama
Vahl–M. H. Vahl, 1749–1804
Valentine–D. H. Valentine
Van Hall–H. C. Van Hall, 1801–1874
Velloso–J. M. Conceição Velloso, 1742–1811
Vermeul.–P. Vermeulen
Vest–L. C. von Vest, 1776–1840
Vierh.–F. Vierhapper, 1876–1932
Vig.–A. L. G. Viguier, 1790–1867
Vill.–D. Villar(s), 1745–1814
Viv.–D. Viviani, 1772–1840

Wachter–W. H. Wachter, 1882–1946
Wahlb.–P. F. Wahlberg, 1800–1877
Wahlenb.–G. G. Wahlenberg, 1780–1851
Waldst.–F. A. Graf von Waldstein-Wartemberg, 1759–1823
E. Walker–E. Walker
Wall.–N. Wallich, 1786–1854
Wallr.–K. F. W. Wallroth, 1792–1857
Walp.–W. G. Walpers, 1816–1853
Walters–S. M. Walters
E. F. Warb.–E. F. Warburg, 1908–1966
H. C. Wats.–H. C. Watson, 1804–1881
W. C. R. Wats.–W. C. R. Watson, 1885–1954
Weatherby–C. A. Weatherby, 1875–1949
Webb–P. B. Webb, 1793–1854
D. A. Webb–D. A. Webb
Weber–F. Weber, 1781–1823
Weig.–C. E. von Weigel, 1748–1831
Weihe–K. E. A. Weihe, 1779–1834
K. Wein–K. Wein, 1883–1968
Wessely–I. Wessely, 1814–1898
C. West–C. West
Weston–R. Weston, 1773–1806
Wettst.–R. Ritter von Wettstein, 1863–1931
W. Wettst.–W. von Wettstein
L. C. Wheeler–L. C. Wheeler
F. B. White–F. B. W. White, 1842–1894
Wibel–A. W. E. C. Wibel, 1775–1814
Wieg.–K. M. Wiegand, 1873–1942
Willd.–C. (K.) L. Willdenow, 1765–1812
Willk.–H. M. Willkomm, 1821–1895
Wilmott–A. J. Wilmott, 1888–1950
Wimm.–C. F. H. Wimmer, 1803–1868
Wirtg.–P. Wirtgen, 1806–1870
With.–W. Withering, 1741–1799
Wolf–J. Wolf, 1765–1824
Wolfg.–J. F. Wolfgang, 1776–1859
Wulf.–F. X. von Wulfen, 1728–1805

D. P. Young–D. P. Young, 1917–1972

Zahn–K. H. Zahn, 1865–1940
Zimmeter–A. Zimmeter, 1849–1897
Ziz–J. B. Ziz, 1779–1829
Zucc.–J. G. Zuccarini, 1797–1848

Abbreviations Used in the Text

*indicates plant is not illustrated

agg.	aggregate	fr.	fruit(s)	o.	absent
c.	approximately	inflo.	inflorescence	ssp.	subspecies
flo.	flower(s)	introd.	introduced	var.	variety

Plate 1

DICOTYLEDONES

Ranunculaceae

Clematis vitalba L. Traveller's-joy. Stems rope-like, climbing by twisted leaf stalks; flo. *c.* 2 cm, greenish; fr. feathery. Hedges, thickets, etc., on calcareous and alluvial soils, S. England, Midlands and Wales, local in N. England, introd. in Scotland and Ireland. Flo. July–Aug.

Thalictrum alpinum L. Alpine meadow-rue. Small, wiry, 7.5–15 cm; flo. purplish, drooping; stamens pendulous. Wet mountain turf and rocks, N. Wales and Yorkshire northwards. Flo. July.

Thalictrum minus L. agg. Closely related forms; leaflets variable, their length not much exceeding breadth; stamens drooping. Flo. June–Aug.
Ssp. **minus**. Lesser meadow-rue. *T. montanum* Wallr. *T. collinum* auct. Shortly creeping or not; branching above the middle; leaflets medium. Limestone sea cliffs, mountain rocks and chalk, local.
Ssp. **arenarium** (Butcher) Clapham. Sand meadow-rue. *T. dunense* auct. Stolons widely creeping; stem short, branched and leafy to base. Coastal sand dunes, from S. Wales and Norfolk northwards.
Ssp. **majus** (Crantz) Rouy & Fouc. Greater meadow-rue. *T. kochii* Fr. Stem 60–120 cm branching from about the middle; leaflets large. Shady rocks and riversides, Wales, N. England and Scotland.

Thalictrum flavum L. Common meadow-rue. Stems 60–100 cm, stout, subsimple; leaflets oblong; flo. crowded; stamens erect. Damp meadows, ditches and stream sides, mostly England and Wales, local and decreasing. Flo. June–July.

Pulsatilla vulgaris Mill. Pasqueflower. *Anemone pulsatilla* L. Stem 10–30 cm; leaves finely divided, hairy; flo. violet, silky outside; fr. feathery. Calcareous and limestone slopes, S. and E. England, rare and decreasing. Flo. April–May.

Anemone nemorosa L. Wood anemone. Rootstock horizontal; stem up to 25 cm; sepals petaloid, white, rarely lilac, var. *purpurea* DC., or pale blue, var. *caerulea* DC. Woods, except on acid soils, common. Flo. March–April.

Anemone ranunculoides L. Yellow anemone. Similar in habit to *A. nemorosa*; leaves deeply divided, very shortly stalked; sepals petaloid, golden-yellow, solitary, or in pairs. Garden escape. Naturalized in woods and plantations, rare. Flo. April–May.*

Anemone apennina L. Blue anemone. Similar in habit to *A. nemorosa* but with a tuberous, blackish, elongated rhizome; stem leaves in whorls of 3, glabrous above pubescent below; flo. solitary, with 8–15 narrow, bright blue, rarely white, perianth segments. Garden escape. Naturalized in woods and plantations, rare. Flo. April–May.*

Adonis annua L. Pheasant's-eye. Annual, stem 10–35 cm; leaves finely divided; flo. scarlet; achenes with straight beak. Cornfields, S. and E. England, very rare and decreasing. Flo. May–Sept.

Myosurus minimus L. Mousetail. Annual, 5–12 cm; leaves basal, linear; flo. greenish; sepals with spur; carpels many, spiked. Damp arable fields, England, rare, and decreasing. Flo. April–June.

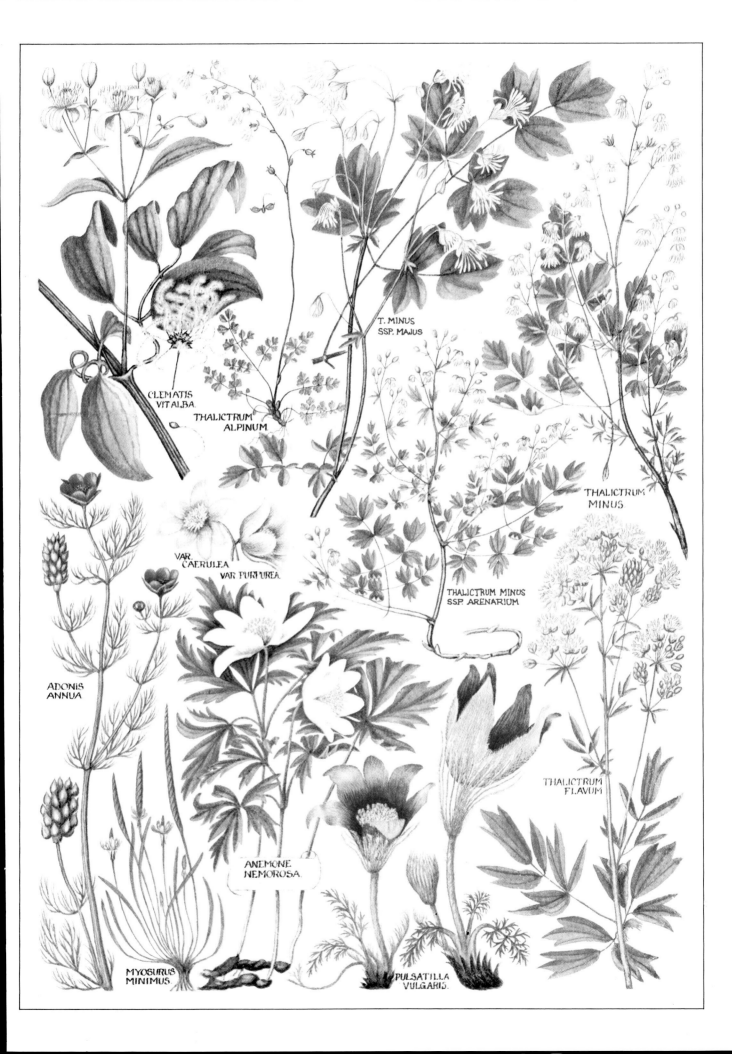

T. MINUS
SSP. MAJUS

CLEMATIS
VITALBA.

THALICTRUM
ALPINUM

THALICTRUM
MINUS.

VAR.
CAERULEA.
VAR PURPUREA.

THALICTRUM MINUS
SSP. ARENARIUM

ADONIS
ANNUA

THALICTRUM
FLAVUM

ANEMONE
NEMOROSA.

MYOSURUS
MINIMUS.

PULSATILLA
VULGARIS.

Plate 2

Ranunculaceae *(continued)*

The *Batrachian* species of *Ranunculus* were revised by Cook (1966) and the data given below is based on his treatment.

Ranunculus fluitans Lam. River water-crowfoot. Stems long and stout; submerged leaves 7.5–25 cm; flo. large, petals 5–8; stamens shorter than achenes. In rather rapid streams, widespread. Flo. June–Aug.

Ranunculus peltatus Schrank. Pond water-crowfoot. Floating leaves with rounded segments; submerged leaves rather stiff; peduncles long and tapering; flo. large. Ponds and slow streams, common. Flo. May–Aug.
Var. **floribundus** (Bab.) Druce. Petals not contiguous; peduncles short and slender. Now regarded as a mere habitat form and unworthy of varietal status.

Ranunculus fluitans × peltatus. Intermediate, occurs with the parents in the Midlands.*

Ranunculus fluitans × trichophyllus. Similar in appearance to *R. penicillatus* but very robust and highly sterile, spreading vegetatively. Known from several river systems in Britain.*

Ranunculus trichophyllus Chaix. Thread-leaved water-crowfoot. *R. drouetii* F. W. Schultz ex Godr. Leaves all submerged, segments short, dark, rigid; petals narrow; achenes hairy, crowded. Ponds and slow streams, England, S. Scotland and Ireland. Flo. June.

Ranunculus aquatilis L. Water-crowfoot. *R. heterophyllus* Weber. Floating leaf segments, wedge-shaped or variously cut. Submerged leaves not rigid; peduncles short; stamens exceeding achenes. Ponds, etc., widespread. Flo. May–June.

Ranunculus × lambertii A. Félix. *R. aquatilis × baudotii*. Intermediate, found with the parents in W. Cornwall.*

Ranunculus aquatilis × trichophyllus. Intermediate, though developing leaves intermediate between capillary and entire. Known from a number of areas in S. England and the Midlands.*

Ranunculus aquatilis × tripartitus. Intermediate, found with the parents in W. Cornwall.*

Ranunculus penicillatus (Dumort.) Bab.
Var. **penicillatus**. Stream water-crowfoot. *R. pseudofluitans* (Syme) Newbould ex J. G. Bak. & Foggitt. *R. peltatus* Schrank ssp. *pseudo-fluitans* (Syme) C. D. K. Cook. Floating leaves alternate; submerged leaves long, tassel-like, much branched; flo. large. Fast-flowing streams, E. and S. England, the Midlands, Wales and Ireland. Flo. May–June.*
Var. **calcareus** (Butcher) C. D. K. Cook. *R. calcareus* Butcher. Similar to var. *penicillatus* but floating leaves absent; submerged leaves shorter and very much branched with up to 150 ultimate segments. Calcareous streams, mostly S.E. England and the Midlands. Flo. May–June.
Var. **vertumnus** C. D. K. Cook. *R. sphaerospermus* auct. angl., non Boiss & Blanche. Entire leaves absent; divided leaves globose to reniform in outline; shorter than mature internodes; segments rigid, much branched. Canals, ditches and slow streams, S. England and the Midlands. Flo. May–June.

Ranunculus circinatus Sibth. Fan-leaved water-crowfoot. Leaves all submerged, segments short, in one plane, wheel-like. Canals, ponds and slow streams, mainly lowland. Flo. June–Aug.

Ranunculus baudotii Godr. Brackish water-crowfoot. Floating leaves cut into 3 subequal segments; submerged leaves rigid; stamens shorter than head of many achenes. Brackish water near sea, widespread. Flo. May–Sept.
Var. **confusus** (Godr.) Syme. More slender with longer stamens. Now regarded as a mere habitat form and unworthy of varietal status.

Ranunculus tripartitus DC. Three-lobed water-crowfoot. Stems very slender; floating leaves small, with obovate or lobed segments; submerged leaves very fine or absent (f. *lutarius*); flo. minute, petals 3 mm; achenes few, 3–5. Shallow pools, S. and W. England and Wales. Flo. May.

Ranunculus omiophyllus Ten. Round-leaved crowfoot. *R. lenormandii* F. W. Schultz. With floating leaves only, divided half-way into 3 rounded, crenate segments; petals 5–6 mm. Moorland pools, mostly W. and N. Britain. Flo. May–Sept.

Ranunculus omiophyllus × tripartitus. Similar to *R. tripartitus* but petals longer (up to 6 mm); entire leaves often 5-lobed with shallow sinuses; pedicels often remaining erect at maturity. *R. tripartitus* f. *lutarius* may be referable to this hybrid. Known from the New Forest where it sometimes replaces the parents.*

Ranunculus hederaceus L. Ivy-leaved crowfoot. Leaves notched, with shallow lobes, broadest at their base; petals often hardly longer than the sepals. Creeping on mud and in shallow water, widespread but rather local. Flo. June–Sept.

RANUNCULUS

PENICILLATUS VAR. VERTUMNUS.

RANUNCULUS AQUATILIS

R. TRIPARTITUS.

RANUNCULUS TRICHOPHYLLUS.

× 4

BAUDOTII.

RANUNCULUS CIRCINATUS.

R. TRIPARTITUS f. LUTARIUS.

VAR. CONFUSUS.

× 5

R. FLUITANS.

R. HEDERACEUS.

× 4

RANUNCULUS PENICILLATUS VAR. CALCAREUS

RANUNCULUS PELTATUS.

RANUNCULUS OMIOPHYLLUS.

R. PELTATUS.

VAR. FLORIBUNDUS.

Plate 3

Ranunculaceae *(continued)*

Ranunculus sceleratus L. Celery-leaved buttercup. Annual, 20–60 cm; petals small, yellow; receptacle elongated; achenes many. Muddy ditches and sides of ponds, common. Flo. May–Sept.

Ranunculus ophioglossifolius Vill. Annual, 10–40 cm; flo. small 6–8 mm, pale yellow, achenes covered with tubercles. Marshes, Gloucestershire, formerly in Jersey and Dorset, very rare. Flo. June–July.

Ranunculus flammula L. Lesser spearwort.
Ssp. **flammula**. Suberect, 10–45 cm; basal leaves oval. Wet places, common. Flo. May–Sept.*
Var. **tenuifolius** Wallr. Fairly stout, arching, rooting at some nodes.
Ssp. **scoticus** (E. S. Marshall) Clapham. Lower leaves often without a blade. Gravelly lake margins, N. England, Scotland and Ireland.

Ranunculus reptans L. Creeping spearwort. Stem creeping, slender, rooting at every node; leaves linear-lancolate; achenes with slender, curved beak. Sandy lake margins, N. England and Scotland, very rare. Material previously referred to this species is now regarded as the hybrid *R. flammula × reptans*. Flo. July.

Ranunculus lingua L. Greater spearwort. Stem 60–100 cm, hollow; leaves very large, ovate-oblong, clasping stem; flo. 3–5 cm wide. Marshes, fens and ditches, local. Flo. July–Sept.

Ranunculus auricomus L. Goldilocks. Stem 10–30 cm; petals often imperfect; achenes on tubercles of receptacle, downy with hooked beak. Woods and thickets, common. Flo. April–July.

Ranunculus acris L. Meadow buttercup. Stem 20–90 cm, without stolons; leaves with middle lobe subsessile; sepals not reflexed. Meadows, etc., very common. Flo. April–Sept.

Ranunculus parviflorus L. Small-flowered buttercup. Stem 10–30 cm, prostrate, spreading; flo. very small; achenes few, bordered with short, hooked tubercles. Arable land and short grass, common in S.W. England, rare elsewhere. Flo. May–June.

Ranunculus repens L. Creeping buttercup. Stems 20–50 cm, with leafy stolons rooting at nodes; mid lobe of leaves stalked; sepals not reflexed. Cultivated land and pastures, very common. Flo. May–Aug.

Ranunculus bulbosus L. Bulbous buttercup. Stem 15–45 cm, base bulbous; mid lobe of leaves stalked; sepals reflexed. Dry pastures, common. Flo. April–July.

Ranunculus mucronatus L. Prickly fruited buttercup. Stem 10–40 cm; much branched; sepals glabrous, reflexed; achenes large, tapering abruptly into a curved beak, the face covered with short spines. Introd. Mediterranean region. Established in bulb fields, Isles of Scilly and W. Cornwall. Flo. March–May.*

Ranunculus sardous Crantz. Hairy buttercup. Annual, 15–45 cm; sepals hairy, reflexed; achenes bordered and tuberculate. Damp arable, waste and grassland on heavy soils near the sea, local. Flo. June–Sept.

Ranunculus marginatus D'Urv. ssp. **trachycarpus** (Fisch. & Mey.) Hayek. St Martin's buttercup. Similar to *R. sardous* but less hairy; flo. small, petals scarcely exceeding spreading sepals; achenes small with a short beak, entire face covered with wrinkled tubercles. Introd. Near East. Established in arable fields, Isles of Scilly. Flo. May.*

Ranunculus arvensis L. Corn buttercup. Annual, 15–60 cm; fr. bordered with long, curved spines. Formerly common in cornfields, particularly on calcareous soils, S. England, now rare. Flo. May–July.

Ranunculus paludosus Poir. Jersey buttercup. Plant with tubers and stolons; 18–30 cm, silky; leaf segments narrow; flo. large, bright yellow. Dry places, Jersey. Flo. May.*

Ranunculus ficaria L. Lesser celandine. Tuberous; leaves cordate; flo. glossy yellow. Shady places, common. Flo. March–May.
Ssp. **ficaria**. Flo. 20–30 mm diam., petals broad and overlapping, fertile seed produced.*
Ssp. **bulbifer** (Albert) Lawalrée. Flo. up to 20 mm, petals usually narrow and not overlapping, infertile; small bulbils produced in axils of leaves; reproduce the plant vegetatively.

RANUNCULUS
SCELERATUS.

VAR.
TENUIFOLIUS.

RANUNCULUS
FLAMMULA.

RANUNCULUS
LINGUA.

SSP.
SCOTICUS

RANUNCULUS
REPTANS.

RANUNCULUS
AURICOMUS

RANUNCULUS
ACRIS.

RANUNCULUS BULBOSUS.

RANUNCULUS
REPENS.

RANUNCULUS
ARVENSIS.

RANUNCULUS
OPHIOGLOSSIFOLIUS.

RANUNCULUS
SARDOUS.

RANUNCULUS PARVIFLORUS.

RANUNCULUS
FICARIA

Plate 4

Ranunculaceae *(continued)*

Caltha palustris L. Marsh-marigold.
Ssp. **palustris**. Stems suberect, flo. 3 cm wide, bright yellow. Marshes etc., common. Flo. March–April.
Ssp. **minor** (Mill.) Clapham. Stems decumbent or rooting; leaves often triangular; flo. few and smaller. Mountains, N. England and Scotland. Flo. April–June.*

Trollius europaeus L. Globeflower. Stems 20–60 cm; flo. 2.5 cm, globular; perianth segments orbicular, pale yellow, inner (petals) with nectaries. Subalpine meadows, Wales and Derbyshire northwards, and N.W. Ireland. Flo. June–July.

Helleborus viridis L.
Ssp. **occidentalis** (Reut.) Schiffn. Green hellebore. Stems 20–40 cm; leaves glabrous beneath; flo. 2.5–4.5 cm, green. Woods, mostly on calcareous and limestone soils, England and Wales, introd. in Scotland. Flo. March–April.

Helleborus foetidus L. Stinking hellebore. Stems 20–80 cm, flo. many, drooping, green with purple edges. Bushy places on calcareous soils, S. England and Wales, introd. elsewhere. Flo. Feb.–March.

Eranthis hyemalis (L.). Salisb. Winter aconite. Stems 5–15 cm; sessile leaflets forming an involucre; flo. bright yellow. Garden escape. Naturalized in plantations, local. Flo. Jan.–March.

Aquilegia vulgaris L. Columbine. Perennial, 30–90 cm; spur much curved inwards; fr. 1.5–2.5 cm. Native on shady slopes and in woods, on calcareous and limestone soils, elsewhere as a garden escape, local. Flo. May–July.

Aquilegia pyrenaica DC. *Aquilegia alpina* auct. angl., non L. Has spur less curved; fr. 12 mm. Planted and naturalized in Caenlochan Glen, Clova Mountains, Angus. Flo. June–July.*

Consolida ambigua (L.) P. W. Ball & Heywood. Larkspur. *Delphinium ambiguum* L. *D. ajacis* auct. Annual, 30–60 cm; fr. of 1 pubescent follicle, tapering to beak. Introd. Mediterranean region. More or less established in cultivated ground, uncommon. Flo. June–July.

Aconitum napellus L. Monks-hood. *A. anglicum* Stapf. Perennial, 60–120 cm, leaves light green. Native in shady places by streams, S.W. England and Wales, elsewhere as a garden escape, rare. Flo. May–June.

Actaea spicata L. Baneberry. Rhizome stout; stem 30–60 cm, herbaceous; flo. white; fr. globose black, poisonous. Woods on limestone soils, Yorkshire, Lancashire and Westmorland. Flo. May.

Paeoniaceae

Paeonia mascula (L.) Mill. Peony. Stem 50 cm; flo. red; fr. large and downy. In rock clefts, Steepholme, Bristol Channel. Perhaps brought by monks in Middle Ages. Flo. May–June.

Berberidaceae

Berberis vulgaris L. Barberry. Spinous shrub, 1.2–2 m; fl. yellow with irritable stamens. Garden escape. Naturalized in hedges and copses, widespread but local. Flo. May–June.

Berberis darwinii Hook. Evergreen spinous shrub, 2–3.5 m; leaves obovate, dark green, shining, 3-spined at apex; flo. bright yellow, tinged red, in pendulous racemes; fr. 6–8 mm long, ovoid, dark purple. Garden escape. Naturalized in thickets and hedges particularly near the coast, S.W. England, Wales, Scotland and W. Ireland, rare. Flo. April–May.*

Mahonia aquifolium (Pursh) Nutt. Oregon-grape. *Berberis aquifolium* Pursh. Shrub with dark green, ovate, spinose, dentate, evergreen leaflets; flo. bright yellow in clustered, suberect, racemes; fr. globose, bluish-black, pruinose. Introd. N. America. Flo. April–May.*

Epimedium alpinum L. Barrenwort. Rhizomatous; stem 6–30 cm; perianth segments red and pale yellow. Garden escape. Subalpine woods, mostly N. England and Scotland. Flo. May.

CALTHA
PALUSTRIS

HELLEBORUS
VIRIDIS
S.S.P.
OCCIDENTALIS.

TROLLIUS
EUROPAEUS

HELLEBORUS
FOETIDUS.

ACONITUM
NAPELLUS.

BERBERIS
VULGARIS.

AQUILEGIA
VULGARIS.

CONSOLIDA
AMBIGUA

ERANTHIS
HYEMALIS.

ACTAEA SPICATA

PAEONIA
MASCULA.

EPIMEDIUM
ALPINUM.

Plate 5

Nymphaeaceae

Nuphar lutea (L.) Sm. Yellow water-lily. Leaves floating; flo. 4–6 cm diam.; stigma 10–20-rayed, margin entire. Canals, ponds and slow streams, common. Flo. June–Sept.

Nuphar pumila (Timm.) DC. Least water-lily. Flo. 1.5–3.5 cm diam.; stigma with 8–10 rays projecting as teeth on the margin. Lakes, mostly Scotland, rare elsewhere. Flo. June–Aug.

Nuphar × spennerana Gaud. *N. lutea × pumila. N. intermedia* Ledeb. Intermediate. Stigma 9–14 rayed. Northern Britain.*

Nymphaea alba L. White water-lily.
Ssp. **alba** Flo. very large; stigma 15–20-rayed. Ponds, canals and slow streams. Frequently planted for ornamental purposes. Flo. July–Aug.
Ssp. **occidentalis** Ostenf. Smaller in all parts. Scotland and W. Ireland.*

Papaveraceae

Papaver rhoeas L. Common poppy. Filaments of stamens not dilated; capsule round, glabrous; stigma rays 8–12. Cornfields, waste ground, etc., common. Flo. June–Sept.

Papaver dubium L. Long-headed poppy. Filaments not dilated above; capsule long, glabrous; stigma rays 6–12, lobes spreading. Cornfields and waste places, common. Flo. June–July.

Papaver lecoqii Lamotte. Yellow-juiced poppy. Very near *P. dubium*, but sap always yellow; leaves more cut and acute; stigma lobes depressed. Sandy or calcareous fields, mostly England and Wales. Flo. June–July.*

Papaver argemone L. Prickly poppy. Filaments dilated above; capsule long and bristly; stigma rays 4–6. Cornfields and dry places, widespread but local. Flo. June–July.

Papaver hybridum L. Rough poppy. Filaments dilated above; capsule round and bristly; stigma rays 4–8. Sandy fields, mostly S. and E. England, rare and decreasing. Flo. June–July.

Papaver somniferum L. Opium poppy. Variable; leaves lobed, glaucous; flo. large, lilac, white or pink. Introd. S. Europe, etc. A weed of cultivation especially in fens, also introd. with bird-seed, common. Flo. June–Aug.

Papaver atlanticum (Ball) Cosson. *P. lateritium* C. Koch. Perennial, petals orange- to brick-red-coloured; capsule long, up to 2.5 cm, tapering. Garden escape. Established on old walls, mostly S. and E. England, rare but increasing. Flo. June–July.*

Meconopsis cambrica (L.) Vig. Welsh poppy. Perennial, 20–50 cm, with yellow sap. Damp, shady rocks, S.W. England, Wales and Ireland, introd. elsewhere. Flo. June–July.

Glaucium flavum Crantz. Yellow horned-poppy. Perennial, 30–90 cm; flo. yellow; pod up to 30 cm. Shingly beaches, etc., widespread. Flo. June–Oct.

Roemeria hybrida (L.) DC. Violet horned-poppy. Annual, 20–40 cm; flo. violet; capsule 5–7 cm. Introd. S. Europe, etc. Ephemeral.

Chelidonium majus L. Greater celandine. Perennial, 30–90 cm; flo. yellow. Banks and hedgerows near houses, common. Possibly introd. by herbalists. Flo. May–Sept.

PAPAVER HYBRIDUM.

PAPAVER
ARGEMONE.

CHELIDONIUM
MAJUS

PAPAVER
SOMNIFERUM.

MECONOPSIS
CAMBRICA.

PAPAVER
RHOEAS.

PAPAVER DUBIUM.

ROEMERIA
HYBRIDA.

GLAUCIUM
FLAVUM.

NYMPHAEA
ALBA.

NUPHAR
LUTEA.

NUPHAR
PUMILA.

Plate 6

Papaveraceae *(continued)*

Corydalis lutea (L.) DC. Yellow corydalis, yellow fumitory. Perennial, 15–30 cm; branched from root. Garden escape. Old walls. Flo. May–Sept.

Corydalis bulbosa (L. emend. Mill.) DC. Purple corydalis. *C. solida* (L.) Sw. Perennial, 10–20 cm; tuber solid; flo. purplish-rose; bracts digitate. Garden escape. Naturalized in a few places, rare. Flo. April–May.*

Corydalis cava (L.) Schweigg & Koerte. *C. bulbosa* auct. *C. tuberosa* DC. Resembling *C. bulbosa* but tuber hollow; small floral leaves entire; flo. white to purple, larger than those of *C. bulbosa*; bracts ovate, entire. Garden escape. Naturalized in a few places, rare. Flo. April–May.*

Corydalis claviculata (L.) DC. Climbing corydalis. Annual, stems 30–120 cm. Heathy woods and shady slopes, especially on peaty soil, widespread. Flo. June–Sept.

In the genus *Fumaria* Mr H. W. Pugsley gave liberal help both in finding and determining specimens for this work.

Fumaria occidentalis Pugsley. Flo. very large, 12–15 mm; lower petal with broad margin; fr. 3 × 3 mm, keeled and rugose. Field borders in Cornwall and the Isles of Scilly, endemic. Flo. June.

Fumaria capreolata L.
Ssp. ***babingtonii*** (Pugsley). P. D. Sell. White ramping-fumitory. *F. pallidiflora* Jord. Peduncle long; flo. large 10–13 mm; lower petal with narrow margin; upper petal narrow; wings not exceeding keel; fr. 2 × 2 mm, not keeled, pedicel recurved. Hedges and fields, widespread but uncommon. Flo. June.*
Var. ***devoniensis*** Pugsley. Flo. more suffused with pink; fr. 2.5 × 2.5 mm.*

Fumaria purpurea Pugsley. Purple ramping-fumitory. Peduncle long; flo. large, 10–13 mm, reddish-purple; upper petal rather broad; wings exceeding keel; pedicel less recurved. Hedges and field borders, mostly W. and N. Britain, local, endemic. Flo. June.

Fumaria martinii Clavaud. *F. paradoxa* Pugsley. Peduncle much shorter than the long lax raceme; pedicel recurved in flo., straight in fr.; flo. 10–13 mm, light rose. Formerly in field borders in S. and W. England, but possibly extinct. Flo. June–Sept.

Fumaria bastardii Bor. Tall ramping-fumitory. Peduncle shorter than lax raceme; flo. 9–12 mm; upper petal narrow, without dark tip. Field borders, local. Flo. June–Sept.

Fumaria muralis Sond. ex Koch.
Ssp. ***muralis***. Peduncle equalling lax few-flowered raceme; flo. 9–11 mm, upper petal apiculate, not broad. Field borders, rare.*
Ssp. ***boraei*** (Jord.) Pugsley. Common ramping-fumitory. *F. boraei* Jord. Leaf segments broad and flat; raceme lax, few-flowered; upper petal broad. Cultivated ground, local. Flo. May–Aug.
Ssp. ***neglecta*** Pugsley. Raceme lax, many-flowered; upper petal obtuse, not broad. Cultivated land, W. Cornwall, rare.*

Fumaria densiflora DC. Dense-flowered fumitory. *F. micrantha* Lag. Leaf segments linear, channelled; peduncle much shorter than the long raceme; sepals large and rounded; flo. small, 6–7 mm. Arable fields, S. and E. England, local, or rare elsewhere. Flo. June–Sept.

Fumaria officinalis L. Common fumitory.
Ssp. ***officinalis***. Peduncle shorter than the many-flowered raceme; usually more than 20-flowered; sepals narrower than corolla; fr. truncate or retuse. Arable ground, on light soils, widespread. Flo. May–Sept.
Ssp. ***wirtgenii*** (Koch) Arcangeli. Similar to ssp. *officinalis*, but raceme 10–20-flowered and sepals narrower. Arable ground, chiefly on calcareous soils, E. and S.E. England.*

Fumaria vaillantii Lois. Few-flowered fumitory. Leaves linear, flat, often glaucous; peduncle shorter than raceme; flo. small, 5–6 mm; sepals minute. Arable land on calcareous soil, mostly S.E. England, rare. Flo. June–Sept.

Fumaria parviflora Lam. Fine-leaved fumitory. Leaf segments small, linear, channelled, very glaucous; raceme subsessile; flo. small, white, 5–6 mm; sepals minute. Arable land on calcareous soil, mostly S. and E. England, rare. Flo. June–Sept.

Cruciferae

Matthiola sinuata (L.) R. Br. Sea stock. Herbaceous, diffuse; lower leaves sinuate, dentate. Shores and cliffs of coasts of Channel Islands, S.W. England and S. Wales, local. Flo. May–Aug.

Matthiola incana (L.) R. Br. Hoary stock. Shrubby and erect; lower leaves entire. Sea cliffs, mostly S. and S.W. England and Wales. Flo. May–July.*

Cheiranthus cheiri L. Wallflower. Stem 20–60 cm, woody; leaves lanceolate, entire; flo. large, yellow, orange or brownish, fragrant; pod *c.* 4 cm. Garden escape. Established on old walls, castles and rock cuttings, local. Flo. April–May.*

CORYDALIS
LUTEA

CORYDALIS
CLAVICULATA

FUMARIA
CAPREOLATA

×2

FUMARIA
OCCIDENTALIS.

×2

FUMARIA
PURPUREA

×2

F. MURALIS
S.S.P. BORAEI

FUMARIA
MARTINII.

FUMARIA DENSIFLORA.

FUMARIA
BASTARDI.

×2

×2

FUMARIA
OFFICINALIS.

FUMARIA PARVIFLORA.

×2

FUMARIA VAILLANTII.

MATTHIOLA
SINUATA.

Plate 7

Cruciferae *(continued)*

Nasturtium officinale R. Br. Water-cress. *Rorippa nasturtium-aquaticum* (L) Hayek. Perennial, stem 10–70 cm, rooting; seeds in two rows; siliquae *c.* 2 × 16 mm. Streams etc., common. Flo. May–Oct.

Nasturtium microphyllum (Boenn). Reichb. Narrow-fruited water-cress. *N. uniseriatum* Howard & Manton. *Rorippa microphyllum* (Boenn) Hyland. Similar to above but seeds in one row; siliquae slender, 1 × 20 mm; leaves often smaller. Flo. May–Oct.*

Nasturtium × sterile (Airy Shaw) Oefelein. *Nasturtium microphyllum × officinale. Rorippa × sterilis* Airy Shaw. Intermediate. Common.*

Rorippa sylvestris (L.) Bess. Creeping yellow-cress. *Nasturtium sylvestre* (L.) R. Br. Rootstock creeping; stem 20–45 cm; leaves pinnate; siliquae linear. River banks and wet places, widespread. Flo. June–Sept.

Rorippa islandica (Oeder ex Murray) Borbás. *Nasturtium palustre* (L.) DC. var *pusillum* (Willd.) DC. Plant prostrate; leaves with narrow and numerous lateral segments, together with a very small terminal lobe; petioles with inconspicuous wings and no auricles; sepals shorter than 1.6 mm; flo. small, yellow; fruit 2–3 times as long as pedicels. Sea coasts, W. Ireland, I. of Man, Orkneys, W. mainland of Scotland, very local. Flo. June–Sept.*

Rorippa palustris (L.) Bess. Marsh yellow-cress. *Nasturtium palustre* (L.) DC., non Crantz. *Rorippa islandica* auct., non (Oeder ex Murray) Borbás. Root fibrous; stem 10–50 cm; leaves pinnatifid with irregularly toothed lateral segments, together with a very prominent ovate terminal lobe; petioles auricled; fruit not more than *c.* 2 times as long as pedicels; sepals longer than 1.6 mm. Streamsides, marshes, damp waste ground, etc. S. Scotland southwards, common; local in Ireland. Flo. June–Sept.

Rorippa amphibia (L.) Bess. Great yellow-cress. *Nasturtium amphibium* (L.) R. Br. Rootstock stoloniferous; stem 40–120 cm; leaves serrate or pinnate; fruit ovoid. Watery places from York southwards, very local in Wales and Ireland. Flo. June–Sept.

Rorippa amphibia × palustris. Intermediate between the parents, with cauline leaves 2–3 times as long as broad and usually acutely serrate. A rare sterile hybrid, which occasionally occurs where the parents grow together, e.g. R. Thames between Hammersmith and Richmond.*

Rorippa amphibia × sylvestris. Intermediate between the parents, with ripe pods up to 1.5 mm broad and petals shorter than 3 mm. A fertile hybrid which often occurs where the parents grow together. Recorded from the R. Arun, Sussex; R. Thames, Oxford; frequent by the R. Severn in Shropshire, Worcestershire and Gloucestershire, etc.*

Rorippa austriaca (Crantz) Bess. Austrian yellow-cress. Rootstock stoloniferous; stem 30–90 cm; leaves elliptical, irregularly toothed; flo. 3–4 mm, yellow; fr. 3–6 mm, ovoid with prominent style. Introd. Europe. Naturalized on waste ground, etc. S. England, Midlands and Wales, rare. Flo. June–Aug.*

Rorippa × armoracioides (Tausch) Fuss. *R. austriaca × sylvestris.* Intermediate between the parents, occurs in Essex and Middlesex.*

Barbarea vulgaris R. Br. Winter-cress, common yellow rocket. Uppermost leaves undivided, toothed; flo. *c.* 8 mm wide; buds glabrous; siliquae 20–25 mm; style 3 mm. Hedge banks, waste ground etc., common. Flo. May–Aug.

Barbarea stricta Andrz. Small-flowered winter-cress. Uppermost leaves undivided, toothed; flo. 5–6 mm wide; buds downy at top; appressed, siliquae 20–25 mm; style *c.* 1 mm. Riversides, damp grassy places, very local and rare. Flo. May–Aug.

Barbarea intermedia Bor. Medium-flowered winter-cress. Leaves all pinnatifid, terminal lobe oval; flo. 5–6 mm wide; buds glabrous; siliquae 10–25 mm. Introd. Europe. Cultivated fields and waysides, local. Flo. May–Aug.*

Barbarea verna (Mill.) Aschers. American winter-cress. *B. praecox* (Sm.) R. Br. Upper leaves with linear-oblong lobes; flo. *c.* 9 mm wide; siliquae *c.* 5 cm long, rather spreading. Introd. Mediterranean region. Naturalized in waste places. Flo. May–July.

Cardaminopsis petraea (L.) Hiit. Northern rock-cress. *Arabis petraea* (L.) Lam. Stem 7.5–25 cm; leaves stalked, spathulate, lower toothed; flo. 10–12 mm wide, white or tinted purple. High mountains, N. Wales, Scotland and S. Ireland. Flo. July.

Arabis alpina L. Alpine rock-cress. Stem leaves clasping with rounded basal lobes, 3–6 teeth each side and clothed with stellate hairs; flo. white, 2 sepals saccate. Mountains, Skye, at 820 m. Flo. July–Aug.

Arabis caucasica Willd. Garden arabis. *A. albida* Stev. ex Jacq. f. *A. alpina* auct., non L. Stem leaves with *c.* 2 teeth each side, and basal lobes pointed; flo. rather larger than those of *A. alpina.* Garden escape. Garden walls, rocks, etc., uncommon. Flo. March–May.*

Arabis scabra All. Bristol rock-cress. *A. stricta* Huds. Perennial; stems erect, purple, 10–25 cm; leaves forming dense rosette, toothed, hispid; siliquae *c.* 5 cm long. Cliffs above R. Avon, Bristol. Flo. March–May.

Arabis hirsuta (L.) Scop. Hairy rock-cress. Stem erect, leafy; rosette leaves stalked, hispid, subentire; stem leaves slightly clasping stem; siliquae 1.5–6 cm; seeds winged. Limestone rocks, walls, etc., local. Flo. June–Aug.

Arabis brownii Jord. Fringed rock-cress. *A. ciliata* auct. Similar to *A. hirsuta* but with stem leaves subglabrous or ciliate, with rounded base not clasping stem; seeds not winged. Perhaps best treated as a ssp. of *A. hirsuta.* Sand dunes, W. Ireland. Flo. July–Aug.*

Arabis turrita L. Tower-cress. Rosette leaves elliptical, stalked; stem leaves narrow, base cordate clasping stem, stellate hairy; flo. yellowish; siliquae 8–12 cm, recurved. Introd. C. Europe, etc. Walls at Cambridge, formerly at Oxford, Kinross and elsewhere, now very rare. Flo. May–Aug.*

Arabis glabra (L.) Bernh. Tower mustard. *A. perfoliata* Lam. *Turritis glabra* L. Stem leaves glabrous, clasping stem; flo. yellowish; siliquae 3–6 cm, erect; seeds not winged. Dry banks, mostly E. and S. England, rare and decreasing. Flo. May–July.

Cardamine amara L. Large bitter-cress. Stoloniferous, 10–60 cm, leaflets tapering below; flo. white; siliquae 2–4 cm; anthers purple. Moist meadows and riversides, local. Flo. April–June.

Cardamine pratensis L. Cuckoo flower, lady's smock. Perennial, 15–60 cm, subglabrous; flo. lilac, rarely white; siliquae 2.5–4 cm; anthers yellow. Moist meadows, etc., common. Flo. April–June.

Cardamine hirsuta L. Hairy bitter-cress. Annual, 6–30 cm; basal leaves many, sparsely hairy; stamens 4; fr. pedicels erect. Dry bare ground, etc., common. Flo. March–Sept.

Cardamine flexuosa With. Wavy bitter-cress. *C. sylvatica* Link. Biennial, 10–50 cm; basal leaves few; stamens 6; fr. pedicels spreading. Moist shady places, common. Flo. April–Sept.

Cardamine raphanifolia Pourr. *C. latifolia* Vahl, non Lej. Similar to *C. pratensis* but with robust, glabrous stem, large thick bright green lyrate-pinnate leaves, each with large orbicular terminal leaflet; flo. deep lilac, petals 8–12 mm long; siliquae 15–30 mm long. Garden escape. Naturalized in moist shady places, mostly S.W. and N. England and Scotland. Flo. May.*

Cardamine trifolia L. Basal leaves with 3 roundish leaflets; flo. white or pale pink, petals 9–11 mm; siliquae 20–25 mm. Garden escape. Naturalized in shady places, very rare. Flo. April–June.*

RORIPPA
AMPHIBIA.

NASTURTIUM OFFICINALE

BARBAREA
VERNA

BARBAREA
VULGARIS.

RORIPPA SYLVESTRIS.

RORIPPA
PALUSTRIS

BARBAREA
STRICTA.

ARABIS
SCABRA

CARDAMINE
AMARA.

CARDAMINOPSIS
PETRAEA.

CARDAMINE
FLEXUOSA.

ARABIS
ALPINA.

CARDAMINE
PRATENSIS.

ARABIS GLABRA.

ARABIS HIRSUTA.

CARDAMINE HIRSUTA.

Plate 8

Cruciferae *(continued)*

Cardamine impatiens L. Narrow-leaved bitter-cress. Stem leaves with basal auricles like stipules; leaflets toothed; flo. small; siliquae spreading. Shady limestone rocks and woods, local. Flo. May–Aug.

Cardamine bulbifera (L.) Crantz. Coralroot, coral-wort. *Dentaria bulbifera* L. Root white and scaly; stem 30–70 cm with purple bulbils in axils of branches; petals pink or lilac, siliquae 20–35 mm. Woods mostly on calcareous soils, mostly S.E. England and Chilterns, very local. Flo. April–May.

Alyssum alyssoides (L.) L. Small Alison. *A. calycinum* L. Stem 8–25 cm, hoary with stellate hairs; flo. yellow; calyx not persistent; siliculae rounded. Introd. Europe. Naturalized on arable land and sandy tracks, S. and E. England rare. Flo. May–June.*

Lobularia maritima (L.) Desv. Sweet Alison. *Alyssum maritimum* (L.) Lam. Stem 15–30 cm, grey, with forked hairs; calyx not persistent; petals white, entire. Garden escape. Waste ground, etc., common. Flo. June–Sept.

Berteroa incana (L.) DC. Hoary Alison. *Alyssum incanum* L. Stem 20–60 cm, grey, with stellate hairs; petals white, deeply bifid; stamen filaments toothed or winged at base. Introd. Europe. Casual on arable land, rare. Flo. June–Sept.*

Draba muralis L. Wall Whitlow grass. Stem 8–30 cm, stem leaves broadly ovate, sessile, dentate; flo. small; petals narrow, white. Limestone rocks and walls, rare. Flo. April–May.

Draba incana L. Hoary Whitlow grass. Stem 5–50 cm, leafy; leaves lanceolate, toothed, with stellate hairs; flo. white; siliquae twisted. Mountain rocks to 900 m, Derbyshire northwards and W. Ireland. Flo. June–July.

Draba norvegica Gunn. Rock Whitlow grass. *D. rupestris* R. Br. Stem 2–5 cm, usually leafless; leaves mostly entire; flo. white; siliquae not twisted. Mountains above 900 m, Scotland, rare. Flo. June–July.

Draba aizoides L. Yellow Whitlow grass. Stem 5–15 cm, leafless; leaves acute, margins ciliate; flo. larger, 8 mm, bright yellow. Rocks and walls, Gower Peninsula, S. Wales, doubtful native. Flo. March–May.

Erophila verna (L.) Chevall.
Ssp. **verna.** Common Whitlow grass. Stem 2–20 cm; leaves with forked hairs; siliculae boat-shaped. Walls and dry places, mostly on calcareous soil. Flo. March–May.*
Ssp. **spathulata** (Láng) Walters. *Erophila spathulata* Láng. *E. boerhaavii* (Van Hall) Dumort. Round-podded Whitlow grass. Stem with short, forked hairs; siliculae obovoid, rounded at top; flo. smaller. Local.
Var. **brachycarpa** (Jord.). Petals 1.5 mm; siliculae orbicular.
Ssp. **praecox** (Stev.) Walters. *Erophila praecox* (Stev.) DC. Leaves with long, simple hairs; siliculae obovate. Local.*

Arabidopsis thaliana (L.) Heynh. Thale cress. *Sisymbrium thalianum* (L.) Gay. Annual; stem 5–30 cm, slender; flo. white; siliquae slender, spreading. Banks, wall tops and fields, common. Flo. April–May.

Cochlearia officinalis L. Common scurvygrass *C. scotica* Druce. Stem 5–50 cm, lower leaves fleshy, cordate, long stalked; siliculae subglobose. Sea cliffs and shores, widespread. Flo. April–Aug.

Cochlearia danica L. Danish scurvygrass. Lower leaves cordate; stem leaves stalked and lobed; flo. white or pinkish. Seaside cliffs and shores, common, also inland on railway ballast. Flo. Feb.–June.

Cochlearia micacea E. S. Marshall. Leaves small; siliculae 2–3 times as long as broad, tapering at apex. Mountains, N. Scotland, very rare. Flo. July–Aug.

Cochlearia pyrenaica DC. Alpine scurvygrass. *C. alpina* (Bab.) H. C. Wats. *C. officinalis* L. ssp. *alpina* (Bab.) Hook. Lower leaves not fleshy, cordate; stem leaves triangular or ovate, lobed; siliculae obovate. Mountains, mostly N. England; N. Wales and Scotland. Flo. June–Sept.*

Cochlearia anglica L. English scurvygrass. Lower leaves ovate; upper leaves clasping stem; siliculae large, obovoid. Muddy shores and estuaries, common. Flo. April–July.

Cochlearia × hollandica Henrard. *C. anglica × officinalis.* Intermediate. Common where the parents grow together.*

Bunias orientalis L. Warty cabbage. Perennial. Stem 25–120 cm, glabrous; leaves pinnatifid; flo. pale yellow, petals 8 mm; siliculae 5–10 mm, ovoid, warty, on long stalks. Introd. E. Europe. Established on waste ground, rare in N. England and Scotland. Flo. May–July.*

Lunaria annua L. Honesty. *L. biennis* Moench. Annual or biennial. Stem 30–100 cm, stiffly hairy; leaves cordate-acuminate, coarsely toothed; flo. reddish-purple or white. Pods large, circular and flattened. Garden escape. Hedge-banks, etc. Flo. April–May.*

Armoracia rusticana Gaertn., Mey. & Scherb. Horse-radish. *A. lapathifolia* Gilib. Stem up to 120 cm; leaves 30–50 cm, oblong; root thick and used for flavouring; inflo. a panicle; flo. white on slender pedicels. Garden escape. Naturalized by streams, on waste ground, etc., common. Flo. June–Sept.*

Hesperis matronalis L. Dames-violet. Stem 40–90 cm; leaves broadly lanceolate, toothed, rough, hairy; flo. 16 mm, white or lilac. Garden escape. Naturalized on banks, etc. Flo. May–July.

Sisymbrium officinale (L.) Scop. Hedge mustard. Stem 30–90 cm, stiff and erect; flo. yellow; siliquae hairy, rarely glabrous (var. *leiocarpum* DC.), appressed. Hedge banks, waste land, etc., common. Flo. June–Aug.

Sisymbrium altissimum L. Tall rocket. *S. pannonicum* Jacq. Lower leaves with many triangular lobes, upper sessile with pairs of linear lobes; siliquae ridged, long thin, spreading; pedicel 6–9 mm. Introd. E. Europe. Naturalized in waste places, common. Flo. May–Oct.*

Sisymbrium orientale L. Eastern rocket. *S. columnae* Jacq. Stem hispid; leaves petiolate, lobes few, 2–3 pairs; upper leaves hastate with oblong terminal lobe; siliquae ridged, long and thick; pedicel 3–4 mm. Waste places, etc., common. Flo. May–Oct.*

Sisymbrium irio L. London rocket. Stem 10–60 cm, glabrous; lower leaves many, with oblong lobes; upper leaves with hastate terminal lobe; flo. pale yellow; siliquae short, beaded. Introd. Mediterranean region. Waste places, rare. Called London rocket since it appeared in quantity after the fire of 1666. Flo. May–Oct.

Sisymbrium loeselii L. False London rocket. Similar to *S. irio* but stem with long stiff hairs; flo. large, petals bright yellow, twice as long as sepals and siliquae beaded, not overtopping the open flo. Introd. S.E. Europe. Waste places, etc., mostly S. England. Flo. June–Oct.*

Descurainia sophia (L.) Webb ex Prantl. Flixweed. *Sisymbrium sophia* L. Stem 30–90 cm, slightly downy, branched above; leaves finely divided; flo. small, pale yellow. Waste places, rare. Flo. June–Aug.

Alliaria petiolata (Bieb.) Cavara & Grande. Garlic mustard. *Sisymbrium alliaria* (L.) Scop. Stem 25–120 cm; leaves broad, cordate or reniform, garlic-scented when crushed; flo. white. Hedge banks, shady places, etc., widespread and common. Flo. April–June.

COCHLEARIA
DANICA.

COCHLEARIA
OFFICINALIS.

E. VERNA SSP.
SPATHULATA

COCHLEARIA
OFFICINALIS

DRABA
AIZOIDES.

COCHLEARIA
ANGLICA.

COCHLEARIA
MICACEA

CARDAMINE
IMPATIENS.

CARDAMINE
BULBIFERA.

DRABA
NORVEGICA

DRABA
INCANA

LOBULARIA
MARITIMA.

ALLIARIA
PETIOLATA

SISYMBRIUM
IRIO.

ARABIDOPSIS
THALIANA.

SISYMBRIUM
OFFICINALE.

DESCURAINIA SOPHIA.

DRABA MURALIS.

HESPERIS
MATRONALIS.

Plate 9

Cruciferae *(continued)*

Erysimum cheiranthoides L. Treacle mustard. Stem 20–60 cm, with a few forked hairs; leaves lanceolate; flo. yellow, often in a neat ring. Cultivated lowland fields, local. Flo. June–Sept.

Camelina sativa (L.) Crantz. Gold-of-pleasure. Stem 60–90 cm; leaves oblong-lanceolate, with pointed auricles; flo. small, yellow; siliquae obovate, 6–9 mm. Introd. E. Europe. Arable fields, on rubbish tips, etc., rare. Flo. June–Sept.*

Subularia aquatica L. Awlwort. Root of many white fibres; stem 2–8 cm; leaves all radical, subulate; siliquae 3 mm, oblong. Margins of alpine lakes, N. Wales, N. England and Scotland. Flo. June–Aug.

Brassica oleracea L. Wild cabbage. Biennial, 30–60 cm; leaves very broad, glaucous; flo. large, in long spike. Sea cliffs, England and Wales, local. Flo. May–Aug.

Brassica napus L. Rape, swede. *B. oleracea × rapa*. Root spindle-shaped; leaves glaucous; flo. yellow; Rape, grown for fodder. Root more tuberous; leaves glaucous; flo. pale orange. Swede, introd. Flo. May–Aug.*

Brassica rapa L. Wild turnip. *B. campestris* L. Root tuberous; leaves bright green; flo. overtopping the buds, bright yellow. Arable fields and river banks, common. Flo. May–Aug.

Brassica nigra (L.) Koch. Black mustard. *Sinapis nigra.* L. Siliquae 10–20 mm, 4-angled, glabrous, appressed; beak short, narrow, seedless, valve 1-nerved. Riversides, cliffs, banks, waste ground, etc. Locally common. Flo. June–Aug.

Brassica juncea (L.) Czern. & Coss. *B. nigra × rapa.* Annual, stems to 1 m, glabrous, branched; leaves lyrate-pinnatifid with large ovate terminal segment; flo. pale yellow; siliquae 30–60 mm, constricted, beak 5–10 mm, seedless. Introd. Asia. Rubbish tips, waste ground, etc. Flo. June–Sept.*

Erucastrum gallicum (Willd.) O. E. Schulz. Hairy rocket. *Brassica gallica* (Willd.) Druce. Stem erect, 20–60 cm, densely clothed with short greyish-white hairs; basal leaves lyrate, upper leaves deeply pinnatifid; sepals erect; flo. pale yellow; siliquae 2–4 cm, curved, beak slender,

seedless. Introd. C. Europe. Naturalized on waste ground, mostly S. England, rare. Flo. June–Sept.*

Rhynchosinapis monensis (L.) Dandy. Isle of Man cabbage. *Brassicella monensis* (L.) O. E. Schulz. Mostly decumbent, glabrous; leaves radical, pinnatifid; siliquae 4–7 cm, spreading, beak 1–3 seeded; valves 3-nerved. Sea shores, N.W. England and Wales. Flo. May–June.

Rhynchosinapis cheiranthos (Vill.) Dandy. Wallflower cabbage. *Brassicella erucastrum* auct. Stem erect, branched, leafy, hispid below; leaves lobed, hispid beneath. Introd. S. Europe. Naturalized on waste ground, S. and E. England and Wales. Flo. June–Aug.

Rhynchosinapis wrightii (O. E. Schulz) Dandy. Lundy cabbage. *Brassicella wrightii* O. E. Schulz. Like *R. cheiranthos* but more robust; erect 45–90 cm, stem clothed with deflexed hairs; leaves very hairy; siliquae thicker, hairy with *c.* 40 seeds; flo. larger, 2.5 cm across. Lundy Island, N. Devon only, and endemic there. Flo. June–July.*

Conringia orientalis (L.) Dumort. *Erysimum orientale* (L.) R. Br. Stem 30–70 cm; leaves glaucous, oval, cordate, clasping the stem; flo. yellowish-white. Introd. Europe. Cultivated land, very rare. Flo. May–July.*

Sinapis arvensis L. Charlock. *Brassica arvensis* (L.) Rabenh., non L. *B. kaber* (DC.) L. C. Wheeler. Hispid; siliquae 25–40 mm, spreading and longer than the conical beak; valves usually 3-nerved; seeds dark. Cultivated and waste ground, common. Flo. May–July.

Sinapis alba L. White mustard. *Brassica hirta* Moench. *B. alba* (L.) Rabenh. Hispid with reflexed hairs; siliquae short, *c.* 3-seeded, equalling the wide sword-like beak; seeds pale. Arable land, local. Flo. June–Aug.

Hirschfeldia incana (L.) Lagr.-Foss. Hoary mustard *Brassica adpressa* Boiss. Plant hoary; uppermost leaves narrow, entire, often subglabrous siliquae very short, appressed with short 1-seeded beak. Introd. Mediterranean region. Naturalized on waste ground, mostly S. and E. England and Wales, rare but increasing. Flo. June–Sept.*

Diplotaxis tenuifolia (L.) DC. Perennial wall-rocket. Stem leafy, branched; leaves glaucous, segments long; flo. long-pedicelled. Walls, waste places, etc., widespread, but absent from Ireland. Flo. July–Sept.

ERYSIMUM
CHEIRANTHOIDES.

BRASSICA OLERACEA.

BRASSICA RAPA

RHYNCHOSINAPIS.
CHEIRANTHOS.

RHYNCHOSINAPIS
MONENSIS.

SINAPIS
ALBA

SINAPIS
ARVENSIS.

SUBULARIA AQUATICA.

BRASSICA
NIGRA.

DIPLOTAXIS TENUIFOLIA.

Plate 10

Cruciferae *(continued)*

Diplotaxis muralis (L.) DC. Annual wall-rocket, sand rocket, stinkweed. Stem 15–60 cm, simple or branched at base; leaves often mostly basal, lobed; flo. short-stalked. Waste land and railway ballast, common. Flo. Aug.–Sept.

Capsella bursa-pastoris (L.) Medic. Shepherd's-purse. Basal leaves forming rosette; stem leaves amplexicaul; siliculae triangular or obcordate. A very common weed, but variable. Flo. March–Nov.

Capsella × gracilis Gren. *C. bursa-pastoris × rubella.* Intermediate, but siliculae usually abortive, apical notch very shallow, style prominent. Sometimes occurs with the parents, very rare.*

Capsella rubella Reut. Similar to *C. bursa-pastoris* but with smaller flo., the petals scarcely exceeding the sepals; flo. buds red; apical notch of siliculae shallow. Introd. Mediterranean region. Waste ground, S. England, rare.*

Coronopus squamatus (Forsk.) Aschers. Swine-cress, wart-cress. *C. procumbens* Gilib. *C. ruellii* All. *Senebiera coronopus* (L.) Poir. Prostrate; petals small; fr. not notched, longer than stalk. Bare waste ground, common. Flo. June–Sept.

Coronopus didymus (L.) Sm. Lesser swine-cress. *Senebiera didyma* (L.) Pers. Prostrate, foetid; petals minute or o; fr. notched, shorter than stalk. Introd. S. America. Bare waste ground, mostly S. and S.W. England. Flo. June–Sept.

Lepidium latifolium L. Dittander. Stem 50–130 cm, branched; leaves large, basal lobed, upper oblong; flo. many; siliculae elliptical. Salt marshes, mostly E. England, adventive on canal and river banks, in gravel pits, etc., in the London area. Flo. July–Aug.

Lepidium ruderale L. Narrow-leaved pepperwort. Stem 10–30 cm; leaves mostly pinnate; petals usually o; siliculae oval or nearly round, deeply notched. Waste land, rubbish tips, etc., common. Flo. May–June.

Lepidium neglectum Thell. Least pepperwort. Similar to *L. ruderale*, but stem with spreading hairs, stem leaves entire and siliculae orbicular. Introd. N. America. Rubbish tips, etc. Flo. May–June.*

Lepidium bonariense L. Similar to *L. ruderale*, but stem unbranched, hairy; leaves pinnate, hairy; siliculae orbicular with shallow notch. Introd. S. America. Established on waste ground, S. England, rare. Flo. May–June.*

Lepidium sativum L. Garden cress. Stem 30 cm; lower leaves pinnatifid, upper entire, linear, not clasping the stem; siliculae deeply notched; narrowly winged above. Introd. W. Asia. Rubbish tips etc., common. Flo. June–Sept.*

Lepidium campestre (L.) R. Br. Field pepperwort. Stem 20–60 cm, branched at top; upper leaves clasping stem, soft and hairy; anthers yellow; siliculae papillose; style short. Dry banks, local. Flo. May–Aug.

Lepidium heterophyllum Benth. var. **canescens** Godr. Smith's pepperwort. *L. smithii* Hook. Perennial; stems many, branched mostly from below or from base; anthers violet; siliculae nearly smooth; style longer than notch. Dry banks, roadsides, etc., on light soils, widespread but local. Flo. May–Aug.
Var. **alatostylum** (Towns.) Thell. Siliculae without a notch, wing continued to style.

Cardaria draba. (L.) Desv. Hoary cress. *Lepidium draba* L. Stoloniferous; stem 30–90 cm, branched above; leaves oblong, sagittate, clasping the stem; fr. cordate, tapering above. Introd. Europe. Cultivated and waste ground, railway banks etc., widespread and common, mostly S. England and Wales to S. Scotland, rare in Ireland. Flo. May–June.

Cardaria chalepensis L. Similar to *C. draba* but with fruit tapering at base as well as above. Introd. S.W. Asia. Cultivated and waste ground, N. England, rare. Flo. May–June.*

Thlaspi arvense L. Field penny-cress. Glabrous annual, leaves clasping; siliculae very large, 10–15 mm, nearly round, broadly winged and notched. Cultivated land, common. Flo. May–Aug.

Thlaspi perfoliatum L. Perfoliate penny-cress. Annual, stem 7.5–25 cm; stem leaves deeply cordate; siliculae smaller; style short. Fields, on limestone soil, Worcestershire, Gloucestershire, Oxfordshire, Wiltshire, adventive on railway tracks, elsewhere rare. Flo. April–May.

Thlaspi alpestre L. Alpine penny-cress. Stem 15–40 cm, erect; stem leaves narrow, cordate; flo. white or pink; anthers often purple; style longer. Rocks, mountains. Somerset and N. Wales to Forfar. Flo. May–Aug.

Thlaspi alliaceum L. Garlic penny-cress. Annual, stem 15–60 cm, hairy below; stem leaves with auricles; flo. white; fr. winged with apical notch; whole plant smelling strongly of garlic. Introd. C. Europe. Cultivated land, mostly S. and E. England, rare. Flo. April–June.*

Iberis amara L. Wild candytuft. Stem 16–30 cm, erect; leaves lanceolate, mostly lobed; flo. pink or white with outer petals larger; siliculae winged and notched. Fields, on calcareous soil, mostly S. and E. England, local. Flo. July–Aug.

Teesdalia nudicaulis (L.) R. Br. Shepherd's cress. Stem 8–40 cm; leaves mainly radical with broad terminal lobe; flo. white, 2 outer petals longer than inner; stamens 6 with minute white basal scale. Bare places on sandy, gravelly, and acid soils, widespread but local. Flo. April–June.

Hornungia petraea (L.) Reichb. *Hutchinsia petraea* (L.) R. Br. Hutchinsia. Stem 5–15 cm, branched; leaves pinnate, lobes small; petals small, equal; siliculae elliptical. Limestone rocks and dunes, England and Wales, local. Flo. March–May.

Isatis tinctoria L. Woad. Stem 50–120 cm, branched; radical leaves oblong, crenate., stem leaves with basal lobes; flo. yellow; fr. pendulous. A prehistoric introduction. Formerly naturalized on chalk and clay cliffs in a number of localities, now known only in Gloucestershire and Surrey. Flo. June–Sept.

CAPSELLA
BURSA-PASTORIS.

CORONOPUS
DIDYMUS.

CARDARIA
DRABA.

LEPIDIUM
RUDERALE.

DIPLOTAXIS
MURALIS.

CORONOPUS
SQUAMATUS.

LEPIDIUM
LATIFOLIUM.

THLASPI PERFOLIATUM

X2

LEPIDIUM
HETEROPHYLLUM

THLASPI
ALPESTRE.

THLASPI
ARVENSE

LEPIDIUM
CAMPESTRE.

IBERIS
AMARA.

ISATIS TINCTORIA.

TEESDALIA
NUDICAULIS

HORNUNGIA PETRAEA

Plate 11

Cruciferae *(continued)*

Crambe maritima L. Sea-kale. Stem 30–60 cm; leaves glabrous, glaucous, broad and fleshy; flo. white; fr. spherical or oval. Shingle and sea cliffs. Widespread, mostly England, but local. This was first cultivated and introd. to Covent Garden by Mr Curtis in 1795 from the S. Devonshire coast, where it was plentiful, but it is now very rare. Flo. June–Aug.

Rapistrum rugosum (L.) All. Bastard cabbage. Annual, stem 15–60 cm, hispid; lower leaves pinnate with large terminal lobe; flo. pale yellow with dark veins, petals 10 mm; siliculae in two sections, the upper large, ovoid, wrinkled, abruptly contracted into a beak, the lower narrow and appressed to stem. Introd. Mediterranean region. Naturalized on waste ground, etc., especially in R. Thames estuary. Flo. June–Sept.*

Cakile maritima Scop. Sea rocket. Branches 15–45 cm; leaves mostly with oblong lobes; flo. lilac or white; fr. of 1 or 2 unequal cells. Sea sand and shingle, local. Flo. June–Aug.

Raphanus raphanistrum L.
Ssp. **raphanistrum.** Wild radish. Annual, 20–60 cm; leaf segments few; flo. pale yellow, golden, white, lilac, or rarely, violet; fr. slightly constricted; seeds 4–8. Arable land, common. Flo. May–Sept.
Ssp. **maritimus** (Sm.) Thell. Sea radish. *Raphanistrum maritimus* Sm. Biennial, very hispid; leaf segments many, often overlapping; flo. yellow; fr. deeply constricted; seeds 2–3. Sandy seashores and cliffs, local. Flo. June–Aug.

Raphanus sativus L. Garden radish. Root tuberous; stem often tall; pod inflated, scarcely constricted. An escape from cultivation, origin unknown. Flo. June–Sept.

Resedaceae

Reseda alba L. White mignonette. Stems erect, glabrous; leaves pinnate; petals 5–6, all trifid, white; stigmas usually 4. Introd. Mediterranean region. Waste places, etc., rare. Flo. June–Aug.*

Reseda lutea L. Wild mignonette. Stem bushy, 30–50 cm; leaves pinnate; petals 6, the lower entire, the lateral 2-cleft; stigmas 3. Disturbed calcareous ground, mostly England, but frequently adventive by railways. Flo. June–Aug.

Reseda luteola L. Weld. Stem erect, 40–120 cm; leaves oblong, entire; petals 5, 2 lower entire, lateral 3-cleft. Waste places, etc., on stony and calcareous soils, common. Flo. June–Aug.

Cistaceae

Tuberaria guttata (L.) Fourr. Spotted rock-rose. *Helianthemum guttatum* (L.) Mill. *H. breweri* Planch. Erect herbaceous annual, stellate hairy; upper leaves oblong with stipules, much narrower than the lower; bracts absent; petals yellow with red spot. Dry cliffs and rocky places near the sea, Channel Islands, N. Wales and W. Ireland, local. Flo. June–Sept.

Helianthemum canum (L.) Baumg. Hoary rock-rose.
Ssp. **canum.** Shrubby, dwarf; leaves hairy; green or greyish above and hoary beneath, without stipules; flo. usually 2–5, yellow, 12 mm wide. Limestone rocks, S. Wales to Westmorland, and isolated colonies in W. Ireland, rare. Flo. May–July.
Ssp. **levigatum** M. C. F. Proctor. Similar to ssp. *canum* but very prostrate; leaves small, dark green, glabrous or subglabrous above; flo. usually 1–3, yellow, with short inflo. Upper Teesdale, very local.

Helianthemum nummularium (L.) Mill. Common rock-rose. *H. chamaecistus* Mill. Shrubby, diffuse; leaves with stipules, white beneath; 2 outer sepals small; flo. yellow, 20 mm wide. Banks and dry places, mostly on calcareous soil, common, but very rare in Ireland. Flo. June–Sept.

Helianthemum apenninum (L.) Mill. White rock-rose. *H. polifolium* Mill. Shrubby, hoary; leaves grey above and beneath, with stipules, margin revolute; flo. white. Sea cliffs, Somerset and S. Devonshire, local. Flo. May–July.

H. × sulphureum Willd. *H. apenninum × nummularium.* Intermediate, with sulphur-yellow flo. Sometimes occurs where the parents grow together.*

Polygalaceae

Polygala vulgaris L. Common milkwort. Leaves lanceolate, lower small; flo. blue, white or pink, in racemes of 10–30; calyx wing as broad as fr., its lateral veins looping up with central vein. Rough pastures and banks, especially on calcareous soils, locally common. Flo. May–Sept.

Polygala oxyptera Reichb. Stems prostrate; leaves narrow lanceolate; flo. pink or white; calyx wing narrower than fr. Sandy shores and stony hills, local. This is now regarded as a form of *P. vulgaris.* Flo. May–Aug.

Polygala serpyllifolia Hose. Heath milkwort. *P. serpyllacea* Weihe. Flower stem branched above; leaves all small elliptical; flo. deep blue-purple, in racemes of 6–10; calyx wing as wide as fr., its veins looping up. Heaths and peaty moors, widespread and common. Flo. May–Aug.

Polygala calcarea F. W. Schulz. Chalk milkwort. Lower leaves large, obovate; flo. purer blue, in racemes of 10–30; calyx wing longer than fr., veins slightly rejoining or not. Downs and grassy places on calcareous soils, S. and E. England. Flo. May–July.

Polygala amarella Crantz. Dwarf milkwort. *P. austriaca* Crantz. *P. amara* auct. angl., non L. Similar to *P. calcarea* but much smaller; flo. tiny, bluish-lilac, white or pink (never bright blue); calyx wings ½ width of fr. Calcareous downs, Kent and limestone grassland in N. England, and formerly in Surrey, very rare. Flo. June–Aug.

CAKILE
MARITIMA

RAPHANUS
RAPHANISTRUM

R. RAPHANISTRUM
SSP. MARITIMUS

X 2

FRUIT OF
RAPHANUS
SATIVUS.

CRAMBE
MARITIMA.

POLYGALA OXYPTERA.

TUBERARIA
GUTTATA

RESEDA
LUTEOLA.

POLYGALA
SERPYLLIFOLIA

X 2

POLYGALA
VULGARIS

POLYGALA
CALCAREA.

RESEDA
LUTEA.

HELIANTHEMUM
APENNINUM

POLYGALA
AMARELLA

HELIANTHEMUM
NUMMULARIUM

HELIANTHEMUM
CANUM.

POLYGALA AMARELLA

Plate 12

Violaceae

(a) Leaves enlarging after flowering.

Viola palustris L. Marsh violet.
Ssp. **palustris.** Stems white and creeping; leaves orbicular-reniform; flo. lilac, rarely white, with dark veins; spur short. Wet boggy places, especially on peat, widespread. Flo. April–July.
Ssp. **juressii** (Link ex K. Wein) Coutinho. *Viola epipsila* auct. angl. *V. juressi* Link ex K. Wein. Leaves often with hairy petioles and more toothed than ssp. *palustris*; flo. larger; spur longer. In similar habitats to ssp. *palustris*. Mostly S. England and Wales. Flo. April–July.

Viola odorata L. Sweet violet. Plant with stolons; leaves cordate; petioles and peduncles with deflexed hairs; stipules glandular; flo. fragrant, blue-purple. Flo. April–May. 'a'
Var. **dumetorum** (Jord.) Rouy & Fouc. Flo. white with violet spur; lateral petals bearded. Common in S.W. England. 'c'
Var. **praecox** Gregory. Summer leaves pointed; flo. small, blackish-purple. Flo. early, Jan.–March. 'b'
Var. **subcarnea** (Jord.) Parl. Flo. all pink. 'd'
Var. **imberbis** (Leight.) Henslow. Flo. white with violet spur; lateral petals beardless.*

Viola hirta L. Hairy violet. Plant without stolons; leaves triangular-cordate, hairy; flo. from rosette.
Ssp. **hirta.** Leaves large, elongate; flo. large; spur hooked. Fields and banks, mostly on calcareous soil. Flo. April–May.
Ssp. **calcarea** (Bab.) E. F. Warb. Leaves shorter; flo. smaller, petals narrow; spur short and straight. Growing with ssp. *hirta* and intermediates.

Viola × scabra F. Braun. *V. hirta × odorata*. *V. × permixta* Jord. Variable. 'x'

(b) Leaves not enlarging after flowering.

Viola rupestris F. W. Schmidt. Teesdale violet. Small pubescent plant; leaves roundly cordate; flo. on short branches; spur short; capsule downy. Limestone rocks and turf above Teesdale. Flo. May–June.

Viola reichenbachiana Jord. ex. Bor. Early dog-violet. *V. sylvestris* auct. Branched from the base; flo. lilac; spur long, red-purple; appendages of calyx small. Woodland glades, banks etc., local. Flo. March–May.

Viola × bavarica Schrank. *V. reichenbachiana × riviniana*. *V. intermedia* Reichb., non Krock. Intermediate between the parents.*

Viola riviniana Reichb. Common dog-violet.
Ssp. **riviniana.** Branched freely from base; leaves cordate-ovate; flo. blue-purple; spur board, furrowed and pale. Woodland borders, hedge banks etc., common. Flo. April–June.
Var. **diversa** Gregory. Plant dwarf and floriferous; petals and spurs variable in colour. Upland pastures.*
Ssp. **minor** (Murb. ex Gregory) Valentine. Dwarf plant; leaves very small and often purple beneath; spur yellow. Upland or moorland grassland.

Viola × burnatii Gremli. *V. riviniana × rupestris*. Intermediate between the parents. Known from upper Teesdale.*

Viola canina L. Heath dog-violet.
Ssp. **canina.** Branched from base; leaves cordate, prolonged; flo. almost pure blue; spur yellow. Heaths and dunes. Flo. April–June.
Ssp. **montana** (L.) Hartm. Bushy plants with underground stems; leaves thin, triangular; flo. pale blue; spur slender, green. Fens, Cambridgeshire and Huntingdonshire. Flo. April–June.

Viola × militaris Savouré *V. canina × lactea*. Intermediate between the parents, sometimes occurs where they grow together.*

Viola canina × riviniana. Variable, but usually intermediate between the parents, sometimes occurs where they grow together.*

Viola × ritschliana W. Becker *V. canina × persicifolia*. Occurs rarely where the parents grow together.*

Viola lactea Sm. Pale dog-violet. Upper leaves tapering at both ends; stipules larger with green teeth; petals pale, subacute. Heaths, mostly S. and W. England, very rare in Ireland. Flo. May–June.

Viola lactea × riviniana. Intermediate between the parents, sometimes occurs where they grow together.*

Viola persicifolia Schreb. Fen violet. *V. stagnina* Kit. Plant with underground stolons; leaves triangular; petals very pale, round; spur yellowish, bent downwards. Fens and calcareous marshes, E. England and Ireland, rare and decreasing. Flo. May–June.

Melanium Section. Pansies.
The British Pansies have sometimes been treated as belonging to several micro-species but Mr R. D. Meikle of Kew Herbarium has kindly advised us to reduce them to the following arrangement.

Viola arvensis Murr. Field pansy (including many named forms).
Annual plants with petals shorter than sepals. Very variable, with leaves lanceolate and hairy or finely pubescent or broadly oval and glabrous. The mid lobe of stipules may be rather broad and foliaceous or narrow and lanceolate. Arable land, especially cornfields, mostly S. Britain, widespread. Flo. April–Oct. The form with oval, glabrous leaves was figured as var. *obtusifolia*.

Viola arvensis × tricolor (including *V. variata* Jord.) 'A very common, variable and widespread hybrid.' R.D.M.*

Viola tricolor L. Wild pansy (including many named forms).
Ssp. **tricolor.** Annual plants (except forma *lepida*); petals longer than sepals, often highly coloured; variable, with leaves ovate or oblong lanceolate; the mid lobe of stipules may be broad and crenate or narrow entire. Cornfields and other cultivated land, mostly coastal areas of N. Britain and Ireland, local. Flo. April–Sept.
Forma **lepida** Jord. With shoots rising from twiggy underground stems. 'A form with perennial habit induced by environment.' R.D.M.
Ssp. **curtisii** (E. Forst.) Syme. Seaside pansy. *V. curtisii* E. Forst. Perennial; underground stems rising 15 cm or more with slender branches at surface; flo. yellow; spur slender, exceeding small calyx appendages. Dunes on the W. coast and elsewhere. 'The hybrid *V. arvensis × tricolor* ssp. *curtisii* arises freely and has purple flowers.' R.D.M.

Viola lutea Huds. Mountain pansy. Perennial; stems slender, rising singly a few centimetres from underground rhizomes; leaf stipules with linear-lanceolate mid lobe; flo. large, 2.5–3 cm, yellow or purple; spur long and slender. Mountain pastures, often on limestone, local. Flo. June–Aug.

Viola lutea × tricolor. Intermediate between the parents, sometimes occurs where they grow together, mostly N. England.*

Viola kitaibeliana Schult. Dwarf pansy. *V. nana* (DC.) Godr. Plant small in all its parts; flo. very small, pale, with short entire calyx appendages. On sand in Channel Islands and Isles of Scilly. Flo. April–July.

VIOLA
ODORATA

V. ODORATA.

c.

d

b

.x

a

VIOLA
REICHENBACHIANA

VIOLA PALUSTRIS.

V. ODORATA
X 3

VIOLA
HIRTA

VIOLA
LACTEA

V. HIRTA
SSP.
CALCAREA

V. RIVINIANA
SSP. MINOR

VIOLA
RIVINIANA

VIOLA
PERSICIFOLIA

SSP.
MONTANA

VIOLA
CANINA

VIOLA
CANINA

VIOLA
ARVENSIS

VIOLA RUPESTRIS

SSP.
CURTISII.

VIOLA
TRICOLOR.

V. TRICOLOR
F. LEPIDA

VIOLA
LUTEA.

VAR.
OBTUSIFOLIA

V. KITAIBELIANA

Plate 13

Frankeniaceae

Frankenia laevis L. Sea-heath. Stems prostrate, wiry; leaves small, oblong, heath-like, margins strongly revolute; flo. pink. On sand and gravel, S. and E. coasts, of Britain, local. Flo. July–Aug.

Caryophyllaceae

Dianthus armeria L. Deptford pink. Stem 30–60 cm, erect; leaves green, tapering; flo. clustered, crimson; calyx bracts acuminate, as long as calyx. Sandy soils, mostly S. and E. England, local and rare. Flo. July–Aug.

Dianthus deltoides L. Maiden pink. Perennial, barren shoots green; flo. stems erect, slender; leaves lanceolate; calyx bracts ovate, nearly $\frac{1}{2}$ length of calyx; petals pink with dark spot. Dry banks and hilly pastures, widespread but local. Flo. June–Sept.

Dianthus gallicus Pers. Jersey pink, western pink. Perennial, stems minutely downy; leaves short, stiff, blunt; flo. pink, petals cut to $\frac{1}{3}$ of length. Dunes, Jersey. Flo. June–Aug.*

Dianthus gratianopolitanus Vill. Cheddar pink. *D. caesius* Sm. Leaves of barren shoots linear-lanceolate, glaucous, rather blunt, edges rough; calyx bracts roundly ovate, $\frac{1}{4}$ length of calyx; flo. pink, petals with shallow teeth. Limestone cliffs, Cheddar Gorge. Flo. June–July.

Dianthus plumarius L. Pink. Leaves of barren shoots linear, glaucous, very acute, with rough edges; calyx bracts $\frac{1}{4}$ length of calyx; petals cut nearly to the middle, fragrant. Garden escape. Old walls. The origin of the garden pink. Flo. June–Aug.

Dianthus caryophyllus L. Clove pink. Leaves long, linear, glaucous with smooth edges; calyx bracts $\frac{1}{4}$ length of calyx; petal teeth shallow; very fragrant. Garden escape. Old walls, rare. The origin of the garden carnation. Flo. July–Aug.

Dianthus barbatus L. Sweet-William. Stem 30–70 cm, erect; basal leaves in a rosette; stem leaves broadly lanceolate; flo. short-stalked in dense cymes; petals bearded, dark purple to pink, streaked with white. Garden escape, sometimes established in chalky railway cuttings etc., mostly S. England. Flo. July–Aug.*

Vaccaria pyramidata Medic. *Saponaria vaccaria* L. Cowherb. Annual, stems 30–60 cm; leaves oblong; calyx inflated, 5-angled. Introd. Europe. Waste ground, etc., uncommon. Flo. June–July.

Saponaria officinalis L. Soapwort. Perennial, stoloniferous; stems 30–90 cm; leaves ovate; calyx cylindrical, not angular. Banks of streams and rivers, S.W. England and Wales, introd. elsewhere. Flo. Aug–Oct.

Petrorhagia nanteulii (Burnat) P. W. Ball & Heywood. *Kohlrauschia prolifera* auct. *Dianthus prolifer* auct. Childling pink. Annual, erect, 10–50 cm; flo. clustered within inflated oval bracts; leaves linear; petals small, rose coloured, notched. On sand and gravel, near sea, S. England, very rare. Flo. June–Oct.

Petrorhagia saxifraga (L.) Link. *Tunica saxifraga* (L.) Scop. Perennial, stems up to 45 cm, erect, glabrous; leaves linear; flo. white or pink, petals notched, in loose heads on long stalks, calyx-teeth obtuse. Introd. C.

Europe. Established on walls, in sandy places, etc., England and Wales, rare. Flo. June–Sept.*

Cucubalus baccifer L. Berry catchfly. Plant long, climbing over bushes; leaves oval; calyx teeth broad and open; petals long, narrow, bifid, greenish-white; fr. obovate, black. Copses and bushy sea cliffs, widespread but very rare, perhaps introd. by migratory birds. Flo. July–Sept.*

Silene vulgaris. (Moench). Garcke. Bladder campion. *S. cucubalus* Wibel. Ssp. **vulgaris**. Perennial, erect, 20–80 cm; branched above, bracts small, scarious; calyx inflated; flo. many; petals white, rarely with a corona. Cultivated and waste ground, common. Flo. May–Aug.
Ssp. **maritima** (With.) Á & D Löve. Sea campion. *Silene maritima* With. Plant decumbent; bracts leaf-like; flo. mostly solitary; petals broad, with a corona. Cliffs and shingle, common; rare by alpine streams. Flo. June–Aug.
Ssp. **macrocarpa** Turrill. Plant slightly smaller than ssp. *vulgaris*, with long stolons; leaves longer and narrower; petals pink or greenish. Introd. Mediterranean region. Long naturalized on Plymouth Hoe, S. Devonshire. Flo. June–Aug.*

Silene conica L. Sand catchfly. Annual, erect, 10–35 cm, glandular; leaves narrowly lanceolate; calyx many-veined, conical in fr.; flo. pink. Sandy fields, mostly near E. and S. coasts of England. Flo. May–June.

Silene conoidea L. Similar to *S. conica* but leaves broadly lanceolate, glabrous. Introd. Mediterranean region. Waste ground, etc., mostly S. England, rare. Flo. May–June.*

Silene gallica L. Small-flowered catchfly. *S. anglica* L. Annual, erect, 15–45 cm; leaves hairy; calyx viscid; flo. dull white or pink; petals slightly cloven. Fields, etc., on sandy and gravelly soils, rare. Flo. June–Oct.
Var. **quinquevulnera** (L.) Mert. & Koch. *S. quinquevulnera* L. Petals white with dark blotch. Channel Islands, casual in S. England.

Silene dichotoma Ehrh. Forked catchfly. Annual, erect, 20–60 cm, branched; leaves lanceolate; inflo. forked; flo. white, 15 mm wide; petals deeply cleft. Introd. E. Europe. Waste ground, etc., mostly S. England, rare. Flo. June–Aug.*

Silene acaulis (L.) Jacq. Moss campion. Stems densely matted; leaves small, linear; flo. stalks short, solitary. High mountain rocks, N. Wales northwards, local. Flo. July–Aug.

Silene otites (L.) Wibel. Spanish catchfly. Stems erect, 20–90 cm, viscid below; leaves mostly radical; flo. small, yellowish, whorled. Sandy fields, Norfolk, Suffolk and Cambridgeshire, rare. Flo. June–July.

Silene nutans L. Nottingham catchfly. Stem 25–80 cm, viscid above; flo. drooping. Flo. May–July.
Var. **salmoniana** Hepper. Slender with narrow leaves; flo. yellowish; capsule 11–14 mm on stalk (carpophore) 3–4.5 mm. Dry places, mostly on calcareous soil, S.E. England, local.*
Var. **smithiana** Moss. Stronger plant; leaves broader; petals white; capsule 8–10 mm, carpophore 2–2.5 mm. Cliffs, E. Devonshire, E. Kent, Nottinghamshire, N. Wales, E. Scotland, local.

Silene italica (L.) Pers. Italian catchfly. Stem 25–70 cm, hairy and viscid; flo. on opposite branches, suberect, yellowish-white above; carpophore as long as capsule. Plant resembling *S. nutans*. In quarries, Kent, etc., rare. Introd. S. Europe. Flo. June–July.*

FRANKENIA
LAEVIS.

PETRORHAGIA
NANTEULII

DIANTHUS
DELTOIDES

*DIANTHUS
PLUMARIUS.

*DIANTHUS
CARYOPHYLLUS.

SAPONARIA
OFFICINALIS.

*VACCARIA PYRAMIDATA.

DIANTHUS
GRATIANOPOLITANUS

DIANTHUS
ARMERIA.

VAR. QUINQUE-
-VULNERA.

SILENE
NUTANS

SILENE
OTITES

SILENE CONICA.

SILENE
VULGARIS.

SILENE GALLICA.

SILENE ACAULIS.

S. VULGARIS SSP. MARITIMA

— *Plate 14* —

Caryophyllaceae *(continued)*

Silene noctiflora L. Night-flowering catchfly. *Melandrium noctiflorum* (L.) Fr. Stem 15–60 cm, hairy and viscid; calyx 10-veined; flo. pale pink above, fragrant at night; styles 3. Cultivated land, mostly S. and E. England, rare. Flo. July–Aug.

Silene pratensis (Rafn) Godr. & Gren. White campion. *Lychnis alba* Mill. *L. vespertina* Sibth. *Silene alba* (Mill.) E. H. L. Krause. *Melandrium album* (Mill.) Garcke. Flo. dioecious, white; fertile calyx 18–25 mm, teeth linear-lanceolate; styles 5; capsule teeth erect. Cultivated and waste ground, widespread and common. Flo. May–Sept.

Silene dioica (L.) Clairv. Red campion. *Lychnis dioica* L. *L. diurna* Sibth. *Melandrium dioicum* (L.) Coss. & Germ.
Ssp. **dioica**. Flo. dioecious, deep pink, rarely white; fertile calyx 15 mm, teeth triangular; styles 5; capsule teeth revolute. Woods, etc., widespread and common. Flo. mostly May–June.
Ssp. **zetlandica** (Compton) Clapham. Similar to ssp. *dioica* but stem much stouter and densely hairy; basal leaves slender stalked; stem leaves narrower and pubescent on both surfaces; flo. larger. Orkney and Shetland.*
Hybrids between *S. dioica* and *S. pratensis* are intermediate and fairly common.

Lychnis flos-cuculi L. Ragged-robin. Upper leaves narrow, glabrous; petals with 4 spreading segments, rose; coronal scales narrow. Marshes, wet meadows and fens, widespread and common. Flo. May–June.

Lychnis viscaria L. Sticky catchfly. *Viscaria vulgaris* Bernh. Stem 30–60 cm, very sticky at nodes; petals broad, slightly notched and with coronal scales. Rocks, N. Wales and Scotland, very local. Flo. June–July.

Lychnis alpina L. Alpine catchfly. *Viscaria alpina* (L.) G. Don. Rootstock branches ending in rosettes or flo. stems 5–20 cm; flo. clustered, dull rose, petals bifid. Alpine moors to 900 in, Lake District and Clova Mountains. Flo. June–July.

Agrostemma githago L. Corncockle. *Lychnis githago* (L.) Scop. Stem 30–100 cm; leaves linear; flo. large, solitary, purple, without corona; calyx leafy. Cornfields, formerly frequent but now very rare. Flo. June–Aug.

Holosteum umbellatum L. Umbellate chickweed. Stem 3–20 cm, viscid above; flo. umbellate, white or pale pink; sepals with broad scarious tips. Old walls, E. England, perhaps extinct. Flo. April–May.

Cerastium diffusum Pers. Sea mouse-ear. *C. atrovirens* Bab. *C. tetrandrum* Curt. Branched from base, 8–30 cm; bracts, leafy; sepals 4 (or 5) scarious, margin narrow; petals notched, veins branched. Sandy fields, mostly near the sea. Flo. April–Oct.

Cerastium pumilum Curt. Dwarf mouse-ear. Stem 2–12 cm; lower leaves obovate, stalked; sepals and small upper bracts with scarious margins; petals slightly notched, veins branched; fr. drooping, later erect. Downs and banks on calcareous soils, mostly S. England. Flo. April–May.

Cerastium semidecandrum L. Little mouse-ear. Stem 1–20 cm, upper half of bracts and tips of sepals broadly scarious; petals very slightly notched, veins simple. Dry turf, common. Flo. April–May.

Cerastium glomeratum Thuill. Sticky mouse-ear. *C. visosum* auct. Stem glandular; bracts green, very hairy; flo. clusters dense; tips of sepals acute and hairy. Fields, etc., very common. Flo. April–Sept.

Cerastium brachypetalum Pers. Grey mouse-ear.
Ssp. **brachypetalum**. Annual. Stems 5–40 cm, with spreading ascending eglandular hairs; bracts herbaceous; petals ciliate; inflo. lax. Grassy places, Bedfordshire and Northants. First found 1947. Flo. May.*
Ssp. **tenoreanum** (Ser.) Soó. Similar to ssp. *brachypetalum*, but smaller stems 5–18 cm, with ascending-appressed eglandular hairs. Known only from Kent. Flo. May.*

Cerastium fontanum Baumg.
Ssp. **glabrescens** (G. F. W. Meyer) Salman, *et al.* Common mouse-ear. *C. holosteoides* Fr. *C. vulgatum* auct. Stems and lanceolate leaves hairy; flo. larger, not clustered; tips of sepals glabrous. Fields, etc., larger flowered on mountains, common. Flo. April–Sept.
Ssp. **scoticum** Jalas & Sell. Similar to ssp. *glabrescens* but with longer petals, larger seeds bearing large tubercles and basal part of sepals prominently keeled. Scottish mountains, chiefly Clova region.*

Cerastium alpinum L. Alpine mouse-ear.
Ssp. **alpinum**. Plant greyish-green, with soft long hairs and sometimes almost glandular hairs; leaves broadly ovate; bracts with scarious margins; seeds small with acute tubercles. Mountains, N. Wales, N. England and Scotland. Flo. June–Aug.
Ssp. **lanatum** (Lam.) Ascher. & Graebner. Similar to ssp. *alpinum*, but whole plant lanate; glandular hairs absent. Mountains, Scotland.*

Cerastium alpinum × arcticum. Intermediate, but sterile. Frequent where the parents occur in the Scottish and Welsh mountains.*

Cerastium × symei Druce. *C. alpinum × fontanum.* Intermediate. Occurs with parents in the Scottish Highlands.*

Cerastium arcticum Lange. Arctic mouse-ear.
Ssp. **arcticum**. *Cerastium edmonstonii* auct., non (H. C. Wats.) Murb. & Ostenf. Leaves elliptic, yellowish-green, margins sparsely ciliate, otherwise glabrous to slightly pubescent; bracts without scarious margins; seeds large, tubercles obtuse. Mountains, N. Wales and Scotland. Flo. June–Aug.
Ssp. **edmondstonii** (H. C. Wats.) À & D Löve. *C. nigrescens* Edmondst. ex H. C. Wats. Plant dwarf, compact, densely tufted, purplish and glandular; leaves shorter, roundish and darker green. Serpentine rocks, Shetland.*

Cerastium arvense L. Field mouse-ear. Perennial, stems prostrate; leaves narrow, downy; petals twice as long as sepals. Roadsides, banks, etc., on calcareous and sandy soils, local. Flo. April–Aug.

Cerastium tomentosum L. Snow-in-summer. Perennial, stems up to 45 cm; similar to *C. arvense* but whole plant covered with dense silvery-white hairs; petals white, twice as long as sepals; capsule teeth marginless. Garden escape. Naturalized in fields, on banks, etc. Flo. May–Sept.*

Cerastium biebersteinii DC. Similar to *C. tomentosum* but smaller (10–30 cm); leaves smaller; capsule teeth with flat margins. Garden escape, naturalized on banks, waste ground, etc. Much confused with *C. tomentosum*. Flo. May–Sept.*

Cerastium cerastoides (L.) Britton. *Stellaria cerastoides* L. Starwort mouse-ear. Stems prostrate, rooting, with alternate hairy line; pedicels slender, terminal. By high mountain rills, Scotland. Flo. July–Aug.

Moenchia erecta (L.) Gaertn. Mey. & Scherb. Upright chickweed. *Cerastium quaternellum* Fenzl. Glaucous, 3–10 cm; sepals with broad white margins; petals 4, entire. Bare sandy and gravelly places, England and Wales, local. Flo. April–June.

SILENE
PRATENSIS

SILENE
DIOICA.

LYCHNIS
FLOS-CUCULI.

LYCHNIS
VISCARIA

LYCHNIS ALPINA.

SILENE
NOCTIFLORA.

C. FONTANUM
SSP. GLABRESCENS
a   b

AGROSTEMMA
GITHAGO

CERASTIUM
CERASTOIDES.

CERASTIUM
ARVENSE.

C. ALPINUM.

C. PUMILUM.

CERASTIUM
GLOMERATUM.

CERASTIUM
DIFFUSUM.

CERASTIUM
SEMIDECANDRUM.

CERASTIUM
ARCTICUM.

HOLOSTEUM
UMBELLATUM

MOENCHIA
ERECTA.

— *Plate 15* —

Caryophyllaceae *(continued)*

Myosoton aquaticum (L.) Moench. Water chickweed. *Stellaria aquatica* (L.) Scop. Stems long, soft and trailing; leaves subsessile; styles 5; capsule with 4 bifid valves. Wet places and streamsides, England and Wales. Flo. June–Aug.

Stellaria nemorum L. Wood stitchwort.
Ssp. **nemorum**. Leaves mostly long-stalked; bracts decreasing gradually in size at each branching of inflo; styles 3; capsule with 6 valves; margins of seeds with row of rounded tubercles. Wet shady places, N. Devonshire and Midlands to Scotland, rare. Flo. May–Aug.
Ssp. **glochidisperma** Murb. Similar to ssp. *nemorum* but bracts decreasing abruptly in size after first branching of inflo; margins of seeds with long cylindrical papillae. Wet shady places, Wales, rare. Flo. May–Aug.*

Stellaria media (L.) Vill. Common chickweed. Stems annual with single line of hairs; sepals hairy; stamens 5; petals 5, rarely 0; anthers red. Cultivated land, very common. Flo. Feb.–Nov.

Stellaria pallida (Dumort.) Lesser chickweed Piré. *S. apetala* auct. Lesser chickweed. Stems procumbent, slender; leaves small, yellowish-green; sepals small, 3 mm; petals 0 or minute; stamens 3; anthers grey; seeds small and pale. Dunes, sandy places, etc., local. Flo. March–May.*

Stellaria neglecta Weihe. Greater chickweed. Stems 25–90 cm, with single hairy line; leaves broadly ovate, acuminate; pedicels and sepals usually hairy; stamens 10. Hedge banks, etc., local. Flo. April–Aug.*
Var. **elizabethae** (F. W. Schulz) Béguinot, *S. umbrosa* Opiz. Pedicels and sepals glabrous; pedicels straight in fr., deflexed at base, later erect; fr. more sharply tubercled. Hedge banks, etc., local.

Stellaria holostea L. Greater stitchwort. Perennial, angles of stems and leaf margins rough, scabrid; leaves widest below the middle; veins of sepals hardly visible, scarious margin narrow. Hedges, wood borders, etc., common. Flo. April–June.

Stellaria palustris Retz. Marsh stitchwort. *S. glauca* With. Angles of stem and leaf margins smooth; leaves glaucous, tapering from base; sepals 3-nerved, scarious margin wide; stamens red. Marshes and fens, local. Flo. May–July.

Stellaria graminea L. Lesser stitchwort. Stems 25–90 cm, diffuse; leaves bright green, margins smooth, ciliate below; bracts scarious, ciliate; sepals 3-nerved. Heaths, etc., common. Flo. May–Oct.

Stellaria alsine Grimm. Bog stitchwort. *S. uliginosa* Murr. Stems 10–40 cm, glaucous, diffuse; flo. branches short; lobes of adjacent petals near together. Boggy places, local. Flo. May–July.

Minuartia recurva (All.) Schinz & Thell. *Arenaria recurva* All. Small perennial, densely caespitose; stems woody; leaves recurved, awl shaped; sepals 5–7-veined; flo. stems few-flowered; petals white, twice as long as sepals; seeds smooth. Discovered on mountains in Cork and Kerry, Ireland in 1964. Flo. May–July.*

Minuartia verna (L.) Hiern. Spring sandwort. *Arenaria verna* L. Leafy shoots tufted; leaves linear, acute; sepals 3-veined; flo. stems few-flowered; petals longer than sepals; seeds papillose. Calcareous and limestone rocks and moors in W. and N. England and Wales, rare in Scotland and Ireland. Flo. June–Sept.
Var. **gerardii** (Willd.) Hiern. Dwarf plant, leaves blunt, appressed. Kynance Cove, Cornwall.

Minuartia rubella (Wahlenb.) Hiern. Mountain sandwort. *Arenaria rubella* (Wahlenb.) Sm. Stems tufted, 2–8 cm; flo. branches mostly 1-flowered; leaves linear, blunt, 3-veined. High Scottish mountains, very rare. Flo. July–Aug.

Minuartia stricta (Sw.) Hiern. *Arenaria uliginosa* Schleich. ex DC. Teesdale sandwort. Small perennial tufts; leaves filiform, veinless; flo. stalks. 5–10 cm, erect. Calcareous flushes, Teesdale. Flo. June–July.*

Minuartia hybrida (Vill.) Schischk. Fine-leaved sandwort. *Arenaria tenuifolia* L. Stem annual, 5–20 cm, much forked, glabrous, or glandular above; stamens 10. On sandy and calcareous soils, walls and railway tracks, England and Ireland, rare in Wales. Flo. May–June.

Moehringia trinervia (L.) Clairv. Three-veined sandwort. *Arenaria trinervia* L. Stems diffuse, 10–40 cm; leaves broadly ovate, acute, 3–5-veined; seeds with an appendage. Shady places, common. Flo. May–July.

Arenaria serpyllifolia L. Thyme-leaved sandwort. Erect, rigid, pubescent; leaves and sepals ovate, acute; capsule 2.5 mm wide. Dry places, cliffs and walls, common. Flo. June–Aug.

Arenaria leptoclados (Reichb.) Guss. Slender sandwort. Erect, very slender; leaves narrower; inflo. longer; sepals lanceolate; capsule 1.5 mm wide. Now regarded by some botanists as a ssp. of *A. serpyllifolia*, in which case the name used should be *A. serpyllifolia* L. ssp. *leptoclados* (Reichb.) Nyman. Dry soils and walls, common. Flo. June–Aug.

Arenaria ciliata L.
Ssp. **hibernica** Ostenf. & Dahl. Fringed sandwort. Small and prostrate; branches ascending to 5 cm; leaves obovate, blunt, ciliate; petals exceeding 3-ribbed sepals. Ben Bulben, Co. Sligo. Flo. May–Aug.

Arenaria norvegica Gunn.
Ssp. **norvegica**. Arctic sandwort. Stems short, leaves obovate, blunt, glabrous; sepals faintly 3-ribbed; capsule not constricted at top, teeth suberect. Stony places, Argyll, Sutherland, Hebrides, Shetlands and Co. Clare. Flo. July–Aug.
Ssp. **anglica** Halliday. English sandwort. Leaves lanceolate, acute; capsule constricted at top, teeth revolute. High limestone rocks, W. Yorkshire. Flo. May–Sept.

Arenaria balearica L. Mossy sandwort. Slender perennial with many prostrate hairy mat-forming branches; leaves small, ovate or orbicular; pedicels up to 10 times as long as sepals; flo. solitary; petals white, twice as long as sepals. Garden escape. Naturalized in stony places, established on walls, widespread and increasing. Flo. June–Aug.*

STELLARIA
NEGLECTA

MYOSOTON
AQUATICUM.

STELLARIA MEDIA.

STELLARIA
NEGLECTA
VAR ELIZABETHAE.

STELLARIA
HOLOSTEA

STELLARIA
PALUSTRIS.

STELLARIA
NEMORUM.

×6

STELLARIA
GRAMINEA.

STELLARIA
ALSINE

MINUARTIA
RUBELLA

ARENARIA CILIATA

MOEHRINGIA
TRINERVIA

VAR GERARDI

ARENARIA
NORVEGICA
SSP. ANGLICA

MINUARTIA
HYBRIDA

MINUARTIA VERNA

ARENARIA NORVEGICA

ARENARIA
SERPYLLIFOLIA.

ARENARIA
LEPTOCLADOS

Plate 16

Caryophyllaceae *(continued)*

Honkenya peploides (L.) Ehrh. Sea sandwort. *Arenaria peploides* L. Stolons creeping; leaves fleshy, margins membranous; flo. often dioecious; capsule globose. Sandy and pebbly seashores, common. Flo. May–Sept.

Minuartia sedoides (L.) Hiern. Cyphel. *Arenaria sedoides* (L.) F. J. Hanb., *Cherleria sedoides* L. Stems in dense cushions; leaves linear; flo. solitary; petals o, or minute. Scottish mountains, local. Flo. June–Aug.

Sagina maritima Don. Sea pearlwort. Prostrate or erect; leaves blunt or apiculate; sepals suberect in fr.; petals 4, minute. Seaside cliffs and rocks, widespread. Flo. May–Sept.

Sagina apetala Ard.
Ssp. **apetala**. Ciliate pearlwort. *S. ciliata* Fr. Very slender stems, all flowering; outer sepals pointed, all appressed in fr., tips patent; petals minute or o. Dry places, etc., locally common. Flo. May–Sept. The plants are apt to be glandular on dry heaths (*S. filicaulis* Jord.).
Ssp. **erecta** (Hornem.) F. Hermann. Annual pearlwort. *S. apetala* auct. Stems suberect, all flowering; leaves tapering, mucronate; sepals spreading in fr.; petals very minute. Bare places, etc., locally common. Flo. May–Aug.

Sagina procumbens L. Procumbent pearlwort. Branches spreading, prostrate, from a central rosette; sepals blunt, spreading in fr.; pedicel top recurved in unripe fr. Stony places, wall bases, etc., very common. Flo. May–Oct.

Sagina × normaniana Lagerh. Scottish pearlwort. *S. procumbens × saginoides*. *S. scotica* (Druce) Druce. Similar to *S. procumbens* but with fr. smaller, 2.5 × 2 mm, about equal to sepals; stems more slender; rosette leaves longer. Wet turf on mountains, Scotland. Flo. July–Sept.

Sagina saginoides (L.) Karst. Alpine pearlwort. *S. linnei* C. Presl. Branches spreading from central rosette; petals 5, rounded, nearly equal to sepals; fr. large, 3.5–4 × 2.5 mm, exceeding appressed sepals. Mountains, Scotland. Flo. June–Aug.

Sagina nivalis (Lindblad) Fr. Snow pearlwort. *S. intermedia* Fenzl ex Ledeb. *S. nivalis* auct. *S. caespitosa* auct. Small, densely tufted; petals 5; fruiting sepals suberect; pedicels short and straight. Mountain tops, Scotland, very rare. Flo. June–Aug.

Sagina subulata (Sw.) C. Presl. Heath pearlwort. Stems tufted, glandular; leaves tapering, ciliate and hair pointed; petals 5; pedicels long and glandular. Dry heaths, local. Flo. June–Aug.

Sagina nodosa (L.) Fenzl. Knotted pearlwort. Leafy to top of stem, with many bundles of leaf buds in axils; petals large; fr. pedicels straight. Wet sandy places, widespread but local. Flo. July–Sept.

Spergula arvensis L. Corn spurrey. *S. vulgaris* Boenn. Plant scarcely viscid; seeds covered with club-shaped papillae. Sandy cornfields, etc., common. Flo. June–Aug.
Var. **sativa** (Boenn.) Mert. & Koch. Plant very viscid; seeds nearly smooth, with a narrow wing; leaves often grey-green.*

Spergula morisonii Bor. *S. vernalis* auct. *S. pentandra* auct., non L. Stems stiffly erect; leaves not furrowed beneath; seeds with a broad wing. Introd. C. Europe. Sandy cultivated ground, Sussex. Flo. April–May.*

Spergularia rubra (L.) J. & C. Presl. Sand spurrey. Leaves flat; stipules silvery, torn; seeds tubercled, the margin thick, not winged. Bare places on gravelly and sandy soils, common. Flo. May–Oct.

Spergularia bocconii (Scheele) Aschers. & Graebn. *S. campestris* auct., non Aschers. Plant covered with minute glands; branches dichotomous, bearing many small, short-stalked flo.; petals shorter than sepals; stipules broad. Dry sandy and rocky places, coast of Cornwall, rare. Flo. May–Sept.

Spergularia marina (L.) Griseb. Lesser sea-spurrey. *S. salina* J. & C. Presl. Branches spreading or prostrate; leaves flat above, rounded beneath; bracts often leafy; calyx longer than petals, shorter than pedicels, a few of the seeds winged. Salt marshes, widespread. Flo. June–Aug.

Spergularia maritima (All.) Chiov. Greater sea-spurrey. *S. media* (L.) C. Presl. *S. marginata* Kittel. Plant larger, subglabrous; upper bracts small; petals often exceeding calyx, pale pink; capsule almost twice length of calyx; seeds all winged. Muddy salt marshes, widespread. Flo. June–Sept.

Spergularia rupicola Lebel ex Le Jolis. Rock sea-spurrey. Plant glandular; leaves short and fascicled; stipules acute; capsule not much exceeding calyx; seeds pear-shaped, not winged. Sea cliffs and rocks, mostly S.W. England, Wales and Ireland. Flo. June–Sept.

Polycarpon tetraphyllum (L.) L. Four-leaved allseed. Leaves obovate, some opposite, some in whorls of 4; sepals hooded; petals minute, white. Sea cliffs, Isles of Scilly, Cornwall, and Devonshire, and common in Channel Isles, introd. elsewhere. Flo. June–July.

Portulacaceae

Montia sibirica (L.) Howell. *Claytonia sibirica* L. *C. alsinoides* Sims. Pink purslane. Succulent, 15–30 cm; stem leaves opposite but separate; flo. pink. Garden escape. Spreading along streams, in damp woods, etc., local. Flo. May–July.

Montia perfoliata (Willd.) Howell. Springbeauty. *Claytonia perfoliata* Donn ex Willd. 10–30 cm; stem leaves opposite and united; flo. smaller, white. Introd. N. America. Naturalized in cultivated ground on light soils, widespread. Flo. May–July.

The segregates of *Montia fontana* were revised by Walters (1953) and his treatment is followed here.

Montia fontana L. Blinks. All forms grow in trickles of water or in very wet places on acid soil, and of smaller size on pastures. Flo. May–Oct.
Ssp. **fontana**. Seeds smooth and shining. Wales, N. England, Scotland and Ireland.*
Ssp. **chondrosperma** (Fenzl.) Walters. Seeds dull, with rather coarse tubercles. Widespread.*
Ssp. **amporitana** Senn. Ssp. *intermedia* (Beeby) Walters. Seeds smaller, less than 1 mm, finely tuberculate with prominent tubercles. Widespread.
Ssp. **variabilis** Walters. *M. rivularis* auct. Seeds more or less smooth, but less shining than in ssp. *fontana*.*

Portulaca oleracea L. Annual. Stems 10–30 cm, succulent; leaves ovate-oblong, fleshy, shining; flo. yellowish, petals 4–6, opening only in sun; capsule 3–7 mm. Introd. cosmopolitan weed. Cultivated ground, mostly S. England. Flo. June–Aug.*

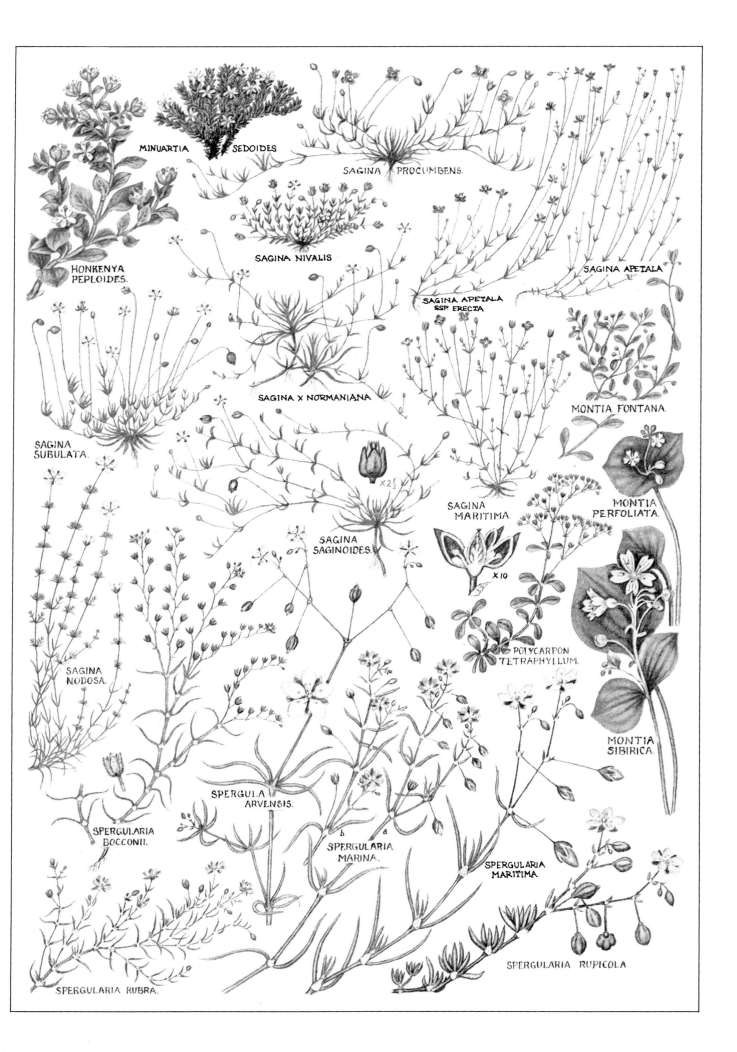

MINUARTIA SEDOIDES

SAGINA PROCUMBENS.

SAGINA NIVALIS

HONKENYA
PEPLOIDES.

SAGINA APETALA

SAGINA APETALA
SSP. ERECTA

SAGINA
SUBULATA.

SAGINA X NORMANIANA

MONTIA FONTANA.

SAGINA
MARITIMA.

MONTIA
PERFOLIATA.

X2½

SAGINA
SAGINOIDES.

X 10

POLYCARPON
TETRAPHYLLUM.

SAGINA
NODOSA.

MONTIA
SIBIRICA.

SPERGULA
ARVENSIS.

SPERGULARIA
BOCCONII.

b. a

SPERGULARIA
MARINA.

SPERGULARIA
MARITIMA

SPERGULARIA RUPICOLA

SPERGULARIA RUBRA.

Plate 17

Tamaricaceae

Tamarix gallica L. Tamarisk. *T. anglica* Webb. Shrub 1–3 m; branches slender; leaves minute, glaucous; flo. buds globose; stamens inserted in depressions of the disk. Introd. Mediterranean region. Sandy shores, S. England and elsewhere, planted. Flo. July–Sept.

Elatinaceae

Elatine hexandra (Lapierre) DC. Six-stamened waterwort. Plants matted, submerged; leaves sessile; flo. stalked; petals 3; stamens 6; seeds nearly straight. Verges of lakes and reservoirs, widespread but uncommon. Flo. July–Sept.

Elatine hydropiper L. Eight-stamened waterwort. Similar to *E. hexandra*, but leaves stalked; flo. sessile; petals 4; stamens 8; seeds curved. Verges of pools, widespread but rare and decreasing. Flo. July–Aug.

Guttiferae

Hypericum androsaemum L. Tutsan. Small shrub, 30–70 cm, slightly aromatic; flo. *c.* 2 cm; leaves ovate, obtuse; stamens in 5 bundles; styles shorter than stamens; fr. red, globose, becoming bluish-black when ripe, indehiscent. Damp woods and hedgerows, local. Flo. June–Aug.

Hypericum × inodorum Mill. Tall tutsan. *H. androsaemum × hircinum*. *H. elatum* Ait. Similar to *H. androsaemum*, but taller, 50–150 cm; leaves slightly smaller, strongly aromatic when bruised; flo. *c.* 1.5 cm; styles longer than stamens; fr. dehiscent. Garden escape. Naturalized in hedgerows and thickets.*

Hypericum hircinum L. Stinking tutsan. Similar to *H. androsaemum* and *H. × inodorum*; stem quadrangular; leaves emitting a strong goat-like odour when bruised; flo, *c.* 3 cm; styles longer than stamens; fr. dehiscent. Garden escape. Naturalized in woods and thickets, rare. Flo. May–Sept.*

Hypericum calycinum L. Rose-of-Sharon. Stems many, creeping, ascending, 40–60 cm; flo. 8 cm. Garden escape. Extensively naturalized in woods, etc. Flo. July–Sept.

Hypericum perforatum L. Perforate St John's-wort. Stem 2-ribbed; leaves elliptic, with many pellucid dots; sepals lanceolate, acute. Field-borders, waste ground, etc., widespread and common, especially on calcareous soils. Flo. June–Sept.

Hypericum maculatum Crantz. *H. quadrangulum* auct. *H. dubium* Leers. Imperforate St John's-wort.
Ssp. **maculatum**. Plant slender with few branches, usually at an angle of 30° from 4-ribbed stem; leaves oval, pellucid dots few or absent, densely reticulate; sepals ovate, obtuse; petals entire with glands on surface in form of dots. Moist places, mostly Scotland. Flo. July–Sept.*

Ssp. **obtusiusculum** (Tourlet) Hayek. Plant stouter with many branches, usually at an angle of 50° from 4-ribbed stem; leaves oval, with pellucid dots, sparsely reticulate; petals sometimes crenate with glands on surface in form of streaks or lines. Damp woods, hedge banks, etc., widespread but local. Flo. July–Sept.

Hypericum × desetangsii Lamotte. *H. maculatum* ssp. *obtusiusculum × perforatum*. Stem upright with 2 very prominent and 2 faint raised lines; leaves ovate-oblong, with or without large pellucid glandular dots. Sometimes occurs where the parents grow together.*

Hypericum undulatum Schousb. ex Willd. Wavy St John's-wort. Stem 2-ribbed; leaves ovate with wavy edges and pellucid dots and veins; sepals ovate, acute; petals partly red outside. Bogs, Devonshire, Cornwall, and Wales, rare. Flo. July–Aug.

Hypericum tetrapterum Fr. Square-stalked St John's-wort. *H. quadrangulum* L., *H. quadratum* Stokes. Stem 4-winged; leaves oval with pellucid veins and small dots; flo. 1 cm; sepals lanceolate, acute. Bogs and streamsides, common. Flo. July–Aug.

Hypericum canadense L. Irish St John's-wort. Stem slender, erect, 10–20 cm, 4-ribbed, reddish; leaves narrow, oblong; flo. *c.* 5 mm; capsule dark red. Bogs and damp fields, W. Ireland. Flo. Aug.–Sept.*

Hypericum humifusum Trailing St John's-wort. Stem slender, prostrate, 2-ribbed; flo. few, 1 cm; sepals unequal. Gravelly banks and heaths, common. Flo. June–Sept.

Hypericum linarifolium Vahl. Toadflax-leaved St John's-wort. Stem erect, nearly round; leaves narrow, obtuse, margin revolute; sepals acute with black glandular teeth. Dry rocky slopes on acid soil, Cornwall, S. Devon and Channel Islands, and formerly in N. Wales, very rare. Flo. June–July.

Hypericum pulchrum L. Slender St John's-wort. Stem erect, round; leaves short, cordate, obtuse, with pellucid dots; bud red; blunt sepals and petals edged with black glands. Dry banks, woods, etc., common. Flo. June–Aug.

Hypericum hirsutum L. Hairy St John's-wort. Stem 40–80 cm, round, pubescent; leaves ovate, striate, with pellucid glands; flo. pale; sepals with black glands. Woodland borders, grassland, etc., mostly on heavy soils, widespread, but rare in S.W. England, Wales and N. Scotland. Flo. July–Aug.

Hypericum montanum L. Pale St John's-wort. Stem round; leaves, bracts and sepals with marginal black glands; inflo. dense; petals pale yellow. Woods, hedgerows, etc., on calcareous soil, England and Wales, local. Flo. July–Aug.

Hypericum elodes L. Marsh St John's-wort. Plant softly tomentose; stems creeping or floating; leaves suborbicular; flo. few; petals erect. Spongy bogs, local and decreasing. Flo. July–Aug.

HYPERICUM
CALYCINUM

H. ANDROSAEMUM.

HYPERICUM
MONTANUM.

TAMARIX
GALLICA

HYPERICUM
TETRAPTERUM

H. MONTANUM

HYPERICUM PULCHRUM

HYPERICUM
UNDULATUM

HYPERICUM
PERFORATUM

ELATINE
HEXANDRA

E. HYDROPIPER

HYPERICUM
LINARIFOLIUM.

HYPERICUM
HIRSUTUM

HYPERICUM HUMIFUSUM

HYPERICUM
MACULATUM

HYPERICUM
ELODES

Plate 18

Malvaceae

Althaea officinalis L. Marsh-mallow. Stout, erect, 60–120 cm, velvety pubescent throughout; flo. clustered; epicalyx bracts 6–9, narrow; sepals ovate, acuminate. Marshes near sea, local. Flo. Aug–Sept.

Althaea hirsuta L. Rough marsh-mallow. Slender, hispid, spreading, 8–60 cm; flo. solitary; epicalyx narrow; sepals long, setaceous. Rough grassy places, Kent, and formerly Somerset, introd. elsewhere, very rare. Flo. July–Aug.

Lavatera arborea L. Tree-mallow. Stem 60–280 cm, stout, woody, pubescent; epicalyx bracts 3, connate, larger than calyx; fr. wrinkled. Sea cliffs and rocks, S.W. England, Wales and W. Ireland, local, introd. elsewhere. Flo. July–Sept.

Lavatera cretica L. Smaller tree-mallow. *L. sylvestris* Brot. Smaller plant, herbaceous, with stellate hairs; epicalyx shorter than calyx; fr. smooth. Plant like *Malva sylvestris*. Sea cliffs, etc., W. Cornwall, Isles of Scilly, Channel Isles, introd. elsewhere. Flo. June.

Malva moschata L. Musk mallow. Erect, 60 cm; stem leaves cut to narrow segments; flo. pink; fr. stalks erect; calyx enlarged; carpels hispid. Dry banks and fields, widespread. Flo. July–Aug.
Var. **heterophylla** Lej. & Court. Lower leaves entire, upper cut into about 3 broad segments. Flo. often more autumnal.

Malva sylvestris L. Common mallow. Leaves 5–8 cm wide, lobes folded, triangular; flo. rose-purple; fr. spreading; carpels reticulate, usually glabrous. Waste ground, etc., widespread and common. Flo. June–Sept.

Malva neglecta Wallr. Dwarf mallow. *M. rotundifolia* auct., non L. Prostrate, pubescent; leaves 4–7 cm wide; flo. 2–2.5 cm, pale; epicalyx shorter than calyx; carpels pubescent, smooth. Roadsides, waste ground, etc., mostly S. England. Flo. June–Sept.

Malva pusilla Sm. Small mallow. *M. rotundifolia* L. *nom, ambig.* Epicalyx equalling deltoid calyx lobes; flo. 5 mm wide; carpels netted, rugose, margined, meeting with a toothed edge. Introd. Europe. Waste ground, rare. Flo. June–Sept.

Malva parviflora L. Least mallow. Flo. 5 mm wide; petal claws glabrous; calyx lobes broadly ovate, enlarged in fr.; carpels pubescent, edges winged and wavy. Introd. Mediterranean region. Waste ground, rare. Flo. June–Sept.*

Malva verticillata L. Chinese mallow. Plant erect, 60–90 cm; flo. 25 mm wide; carpels smooth, angles square; sepals enlarged in fr. Introd. E. Asia. Waste ground, rare. Flo. July–Sept.*

Tiliaceae

Tilia platyphyllos Scop. Large-leaved lime. Twigs and undersides of leaves downy; flo. few, pendulous; fr. with prominent ribs. Woods by R.s Wye, Teme and Severn, planted elsewhere. Flo. June.

Tilia cordata Mill. Small-leaved lime. Twigs glabrous; leaves small, glaucous beneath with hairs at axils of veins; flo. erect; fr. thin-walled, slightly angular. Woods and cliffs, especially on limestone soil, local. Flo. July.

Tilia × vulgaris Hayne. Lime. *T. cordata × platyphyllos. T. europaea* auct. Leaves green and glabrous beneath except for hairs at axils of veins; flo. pendulous; fr. downy, slightly ribbed. Planted, woods, copses, etc. Flo. July.*

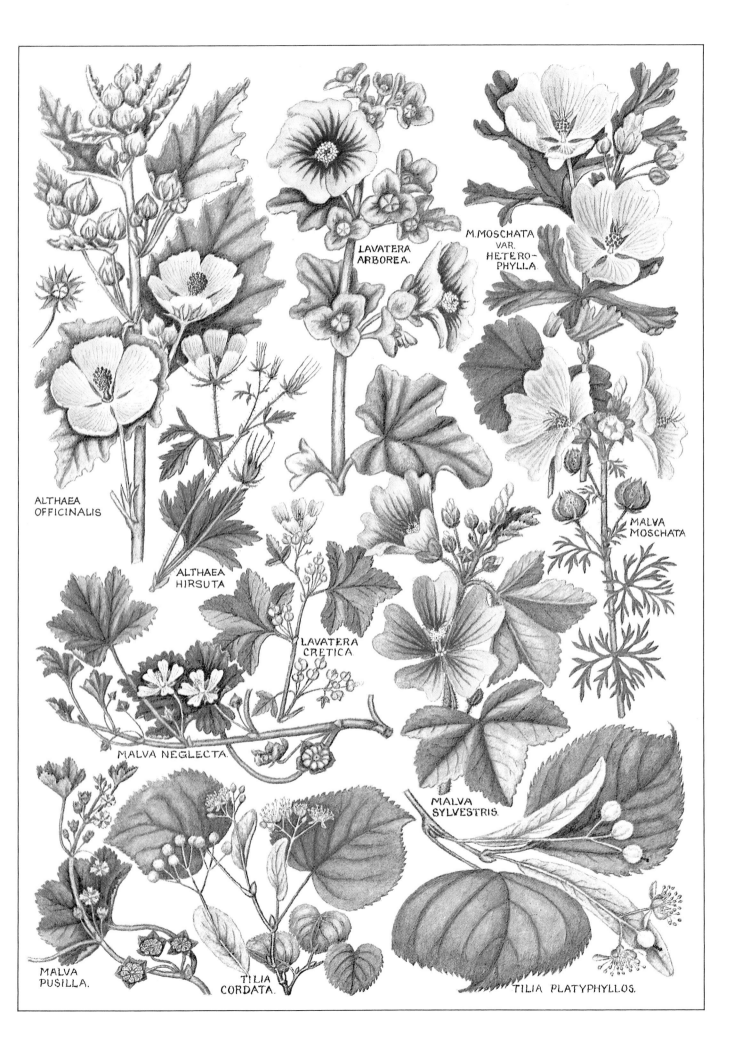

ALTHAEA
OFFICINALIS

LAVATERA
ARBOREA.

M.MOSCHATA
VAR.
HETERO-
PHYLLA.

ALTHAEA
HIRSUTA

MALVA
MOSCHATA

LAVATERA
CRETICA

MALVA NEGLECTA.

MALVA
SYLVESTRIS.

MALVA
PUSILLA.

TILIA
CORDATA.

TILIA PLATYPHYLLOS.

Plate 19

Linaceae

Radiola linoides Roth. Allseed. *R. millegrana* Sm. Very small annual, 1.5–8 cm; repeatedly forked; flo. minute; sepals 3-cleft. Bare sandy places, sometimes with *Anagallis minima*, widespread but local. Flo. July–Aug.

Linum catharticum L. Fairy flax. Annual, stem slender, 5–25 cm; leaves opposite, elliptic; petals white, suberect. Dry banks and basic soils, common. Flo. June–Aug.
Var. **dunense** Druce. Very small, *c.* 2.5 cm long, prostrate. Dunes.

Linum perenne Mill. Perennial flax.
Ssp. **anglicum** (Mill.) Ockendon *L. anglicum* Mill. Perennial, 30–60 cm; leaves alternate, linear; flo. blue; sepals obovate, glabrous, less than ½ length of fr. Chalk and limestone, grassland, local. Flo. June.

Linum bienne Mill. Pale flax. *L. augustifolium* Huds. Perennial, 30–60 cm; leaves linear; flo. very pale mauve; sepals ovate, ciliate, more than ½ length of fr.; fr. 4–6 mm. Dry banks, S. and S. W. England and S. Ireland. Flo. May–Sept.

Linum usitatissimum L. Flax. Annual. Similar to *L. bienne*, but more robust and stems usually single; fr. 6–9 mm. Introd., origin unknown. Rubbish tips, waste ground, etc., common. Flo. May–Oct.*

Geraniaceae

Geranium sanguineum L. Bloody cranes-bill. Stems diffuse, 10–60 cm; flo. solitary, 3 cm wide, crimson; peduncle long. Dry rocks and sea cliffs, etc., widespread and local, but often a garden escape. Flo. July–Aug.
Var. **lancastriense** (With.) Druce. Stems procumbent; flo. pale pink. N. Lancashire coast.

Geranium macrorrhizum L. Plant aromatic; stems erect, hairy, 10–30 cm; leaves smooth, 5-lobed; peduncle 2 r 1 flowered; petals pink or red. Garden escape. Naturalized on walls and banks, mostly S.W. England. Flo. May–Aug.*

Geranium versicolor L. Pencilled cranes-bill. *G. striatum* L. Stems 30–60 cm, erect, hairy; peduncle 2-flowered; petals emarginate, pale with purple veins. Garden escape. Shady places, widespread, but rare in Scotland. Flo. May–Sept.

Geranium endressii Gay. French cranes-bill. Similar to *G. versicolor*, but petals more rounded, deep pink without darker veins. Garden escape. Naturalized on banks, in fields, etc., local. Flo. May–June.*

Geranium endressii × versicolor. Similar to above but petals with dark veins. Garden escape. Naturalized in fields, on banks, etc. Sometimes more frequent than either of the parents. Flo. May–June.*

Geranium nodosum L. Knotted cranes-bill. Erect, glabrous, 20–50 cm; stem leaves with large ovate, acute lobes; flo. pale rose-purple. Garden escape. Grassy places, mostly S. England, rare. Sometimes confused with *G. endressii*. Flo. May–Sept.*

Geranium × magnificum Hyland. *G. ibericum × platypetalum*. *G. ibericum* auct., non L. *G. platypetalum* auct., non L. Stems 3–6 cm, erect; leaves roundish, heart-shaped, long-stalked, deeply 5–7-lobed, woolly; flo. 2.5–4 cm in pairs, or more, in open panicles; petals bluish-violet to purple; calyx rough. Garden escape. Established on waste ground, in fields, etc., uncommon. Flo. May–Aug.*

Geranium × monacense Harz. *G. phaeum × reflexum*. Similar to *G. phaeum* but flo. dull purple, petals narrow-oblong, strongly reflexed. Garden escape. Naturalized in grassy places in Surrey and Sussex and doubtless elsewhere. Flo. May–Aug.*

Geranium sylvaticum L. Wood cranes-bill. Stems 30–80 cm; erect; stem leaves sessile; flo. 25 mm, reddish-purple, filaments filiform; fr. erect. Meadows, banks, etc., N. England and Scotland, introd. elsewhere. Flo. June–July.

Geranium pratense L. Meadow cranes-bill. Stems 30–80 cm, erect; leaves nearly all petiolate; flo. 3 cm, blue-purple; fr. reflexed; filaments wide at base. Meadows, banks, etc., England and Wales, introd. in Scotland and Ireland. Flo. June–Aug.

Geranium phaeum L. Dusky cranes-bill. Stems erect, 30–60 cm; flo. blackish-purple, in pairs; petals ovate-orbicular, wavy; sepals awned. Garden escape. Plantations and waste places, uncommon. Flo. May–Aug.

Geranium pyrenaicum Burm. f. Hedgerow cranes-bill. *G. perenne* Huds. Stems 25–60 cm, diffuse, downy; flo. 12 mm, red-purple; petals deeply notched; carpels smooth. Roadsides and fields, S. and E. England. Flo. June–Aug.

Geranium molle L. Dove's-foot cranes-bill. Prostrate, softly pubescent; flo. 8 mm, pink; petals deeply notched; carpels wrinkled. Cultivated and waste land, very common. Flo. April–Sept.

Geranium pusillum L. Small-flowered cranes-bill. Flo. 6–8 mm, lilac; petals notched; carpels smooth, keeled, hairs appressed. Cultivated fields on light soils, widespread, common in England, local in Wales and Ireland and rare in Scotland. Flo. June–Sept.

Geranium rotundifolium L. Round-leaved cranes-bill. Leaves round, lobes shallow; petals entire, flesh-pink; carpels keeled with spreading hairs. Cliffs, walls and banks, widespread, mostly England, rare or introd. elsewhere. Flo. June–July.

Geranium dissectum L. Cut-leaved cranes-bill. Leaves deeply cut; peduncles short; petals bifid, red-purple; carpels smooth, hairs erect. Hedge banks and arable land, common. Flo. May–Aug.

Geranium columbinum L. Long-stalked cranes-bill. Stems long, spreading; leaf segments narrow; sepals awned; petals rounded, pale rose. On dry, calcareous soils, widespread, rare in Scotland. Flo. June–July.

Geranium lucidum L. Shining cranes-bill. Stems red; leaves round and glossy, lobes shallow; petals rounded, pink. Shady banks, walls, etc., common on calcareous soils. Flo. May–Aug.

Geranium robertianum L. Herb-Robert.
Ssp. **robertianum**. Stems erect, rather hairy; petals spreading, anthers reddish; carpels wrinkled, downy. Banks, etc., common. Flo. April–Oct.
Ssp. **maritimum** (Bab) H. G. Bak. Stem prostrate, succulent, red; leaves and flo. smaller; carpels glabrous. Shingle beaches, England and Scotland.*
Ssp. **celticum** Ostenf. Stems reddish on nodes and petiole bases; leaves light green; flo. pale pink; fr. hairy, large. Limestone rocks, S. Wales and W. Ireland.*

Geranium purpureum Vill. Little-Robin.
Ssp. **purpureum**. Plant upright; leaf segments narrow; stamens yellow; carpels much wrinkled, glabrous; fr. hairy or glabrous with closely set ridges. Sea cliffs, rocky places, etc., sometimes inland, Channel Islands, S. England and Ireland. Flo. May–Sept.
Ssp. **forsteri** (Wilmott) H. G. Bak. Plant prostrate; petioles of rosette leaves very short; fr. hairy or glabrous, often occurring together; ridges less apparent. Stabilized shingle beaches, Hampshire, and formerly in Guernsey and Sussex, very rare.

LINUM BIENNE.

LINUM
SSP.

PERENNE
ANGLICUM

RADIOLA
LINOIDES.

GERANIUM
SYLVATICUM

GERANIUM
PRATENSE.

GERANIUM
VERSICOLOR

GERANIUM
SANGUINEUM

LINUM CATH-
ARTICUM.

GERANIUM
PHÆUM.

GERANIUM MOLLE.

GERANIUM MOLLE
X 5.

GERANIUM
ROTUNDIFOLIUM

GERANIUM
PUSILLUM.

GERANIUM
PURPUREUM

GERANIUM
LUCIDUM.

GERANIUM ROBERTIANUM

GERANIUM COLUMBINUM.

GERANIUM
DISSECTUM.

GERANIUM
PYRENAICUM.

— Plate 20 —

Geraniaceae

Erodium cicutarium (L.) L'Hérit. Common stork's-bill.
Ssp. **cicutarium**. Leaves pinnate, leaflets cut to narrow segments; peduncles 6–9-flowered; petals rose, usually unspotted; filaments gradually enlarged at base. Dry grassy places on sandy soils, dunes, etc., widespread. Flo. June–Sept.*
Var. **pimpinellifolium** Cav. Two upper petals with dark spot.
Ssp. **dunense** Andreas. Dune stork's-bill. *E. lebeli* Jord. Stem short, stout, prostrate, very glandular, sticky; leaflet segments broader; peduncles 3–5-flowered; petals pale; filaments gradually enlarged at base; pit on carpel conspicuous. Coastal dunes, mostly England and Wales.
Ssp. **bipinnatum** (Willd.) Tourlet. *E. glutinosum* Dumort. Sticky stork's-bill. Plant very glandular, sticky; branches more slender, prostrate; peduncles 2–4-flowered; petals pale; filaments suddenly enlarged or dentate below; carpels with small pit at top. Coastal dunes, mostly England and Wales, scarce.*

Erodium moschatum (L.) L'Hérit. Musk stork's-bill. Leaves large, pinnate, leaflets ovate, coarsely toothed, smelling of musk; base of filament toothed. Coastal areas, W. England, Ireland. Flo. June–Aug.

Erodium maritimum (L.) L'Hérit. Sea stork's-bill. Branches prostrate; leaves small, oval, toothed or lobed, not pinnate; petals pale, often absent. Sea cliffs and exposed places inland, widespread but very rare in Scotland. Flo. May–Sept.

Oxalidaceae

The species of *Oxalis* found in the British Isles were revised by Young (1958), and the following account is based on his treatment.

Oxalis rosea Jacq. Stem glabrous; flo. rose-pink with white centre, erect in flo., drooping in bud and fr.; petal *c.* 5 mm. Introd. S. America. Cultivated ground, Isles of Scilly, W. Cornwall and Channel Islands. Flo. May–Sept.*

Oxalis corniculata L. Yellow sorrel. Stem prostrate or procumbent, pubescent; leaves with small stipules; inflo. 1–8; pedicels reflexed in fr.; capsule 12–20 mm, oblong, hairy, erect. Introd. cosmopolitan weed. Persistent garden weed, mostly S. England. Flo. June–Sept.
Var. **atropurpurea** Planch. var. *purpurea* Parl. Leaves and stems purple.*

Oxalis exilis A. Cunn. *A. corniculata* var. *microphylla* Hook. f. Similar to *O. corniculata* but much smaller, stems filiform, creeping, mat-forming; leaves green, tiny, leaflets emarginate; inflo. 1; capsule 5–8 mm. Garden escape. Gravel paths, short turf, etc., widespread, but mostly S. England. Flo. June–Sept.*

Oxalis fontana Bunge. Upright yellow sorrel. *O. europaea* Jord. *O. stricta* mult. auct., non L. Similar to *O. corniculata* but stem erect, glabrous or hirsute with septate hairs, and underground stolons or surface stolons which do not root; stipules o; inflo. 2–5; peduncles not reflexed in fr.; capsule oblong, shorter. Introd. N. America. Widespread garden weed. Flo. June–Sept.*

Oxalis stricta L. *O. dillenii* Jacq. Similar to *O. fontana* but lacking stolons; stipules narrow-oblong; inflo. 2–3; peduncles reflexed in fr.; capsule cylindrical. Introd. N. America. Cultivated ground, Sussex, Channel Islands and Cumbria, very rare. Flo. June–Sept.*

Oxalis acetosella L. Wood sorrel. Leaves radical from creeping rhizome; inflo. 1; petals white, rarely pink; capsule ovoid, 5-angled. Woods, shady places, etc., common. The only native species. Flo. April–May.

Oxalis articulata Savigny. Pink oxalis. *O. floribunda* Lehm. Root tuberous, rhizome thick, horizontal; leaves and flo. borne at end of rhizome to form compact bunches; leaves spotted below with orange blobs; flo. pink, many in an umbel; capsule 10 mm, cylindrical-ovate. Garden escape. Persistent garden weed, mostly S. England. The most common pink *Oxalis* species. Flo. May–Oct.*

Oxalis corymbosa DC. Similar to *O. articulata* but smaller, with clusters of bulbils at stem base; leaves spotted below on margins with small reddish blobs; flo. purplish-pink; capsule smaller. Garden escape. Persistent garden weed, particularly London area. Flo. July–Sept.*

Oxalis debilis Kunth. Similar to *O. corymbosa*, but with smaller bulbils and salmon-pink to brick-red flo. Garden escape. Persistent weed, Royal Botanic Gardens, Kew, also in Berkshire and Lancashire, uncommon. Flo. July–Sept.*

Oxalis latifolia Kunth. Similar to *O. corymbosa* but bulbils borne on horizontal underground stolons up to 2 cm from stem base; leaves broadly triangular, not spotted below; flo. pink; capsule not known in British Isles. Introd. S. America. Pernicious weed of market gardens, old gardens, etc., mostly S. England but especially Devon and Cornwall. Flo. May–Sept.*

Oxalis tetraphylla Cav. Similar to *O. latifolia* but bulb up to 4 cm diam., leaves 4-foliate (all others 3-foliate); flo. bright rose-red. Introd. Mexico. Established in cultivated ground, Isles of Scilly and Channel Islands. Flo. May–Sept.*

Oxalis pes-caprae L. Bermuda buttercup. *O. cernua* Thunb. Bulb 2–4 × 1 cm, ovoid, deeply buried (up to 25 cm) below ground surface; leaves many, up to 20 cm; peduncles 10–30 cm bearing flo. in umbels; flo. bright yellow, large. Introd. S. Africa. Frequent weed of bulbfields, Isles of Scilly and Channel Islands, also on cultivated ground, S.W. England and W. Wales. Flo. March–June.*

Oxalis incarnata L. Similar to *O. acetosella* but bulb up to 2 cm long; stem, annual, slender, erect, bulbil-bearing; flo. white. Garden escape. Established on walls, banks, etc., mostly S. England. Flo. May–July.*

Balsaminaceae

Impatiens noli-tangere L. Touch-me-not balsam. Plant succulent, 20–60 cm; nodes swollen; flo. yellow, 1–3 together; spur tapering, point recurved. By streams, Lake District and N. Wales, introd. elsewhere. Flo. July–Sept.

Impatiens capensis Meerb. Orange balsam. *I. fulva* Nutt. *I. biflora* Walt. Leaves ovate with shallow teeth; flo. orange; spur tapering, reflexed at tip. Garden escape. Naturalized on river banks, etc., mostly S. and E. England and Midlands. Flo. June–Aug.

Impatiens parviflora DC. Small balsam. Stem 30–100 cm; leaves ovate with many acute teeth; flo. 3–10 on peduncle, pale yellow; spur nearly straight. Introd. Siberia. Naturalized in woods, waste ground, etc., widespread. Flo. July–Sept.*

Impatiens glandulifera Royle. Indian balsam. *I. roylei* Walp. Stem stout, 1–2 m; leaves opposite, teeth many, acute; flo. large, rose, pink or white; spur inflated, with short reflexed point. Garden escape. River and stream banks, etc., widespread and increasing, rarely on waste ground. Flo. July–Sept.

Aquifoliaceae

Ilex aquifolium L. Holly. Small tree 3–15 m; flo. white, dioecious; fr. red, poisonous. Woods and hedges, common. Flo. April–May.

Celastraceae

Euonymus europaeus L. Spindle. Shrub or small tree, 2–6 m; flo. small, greenish; fr. beautiful, lobed and pink, with seeds enclosed in an orange aril (an aftergrowth from seed stalk). Copses and hedges, common in S. England, extending to S. Scotland and Ireland. Flo. May–June.

Rhamnaceae

Rhamnus catharticus L. Buckthorn. Shrub or small tree, 4–6 m; branches opposite, ending in thorns; flo. 4-partite, dioecious. Hedges, wood borders, etc., on calcareous soils, widespread, but introd. in Scotland. Flo. May–July.

Frangula alnus Mill. Alder buckthorn. *Rhamnus frangula* L. Branches alternate, without thorns; flo. white, 5-partite, perfect; fr. black when ripe. Peaty heaths and woods and damp hedgerows, widespread but local or rare in Wales, Scotland and Ireland. Flo. May–June.

Aceraceae

Acer pseudoplatanus L. Sycamore. Tree up to 30 m; flo. dense, pendulous; stamens twice as long as petals; juice not milky. An ancient introd., very common. Flo. April–June.

Acer platanoides L. Norway maple. Tree up to 30 m; leaves shining on both surfaces; juice milky; flo. in erect corymbs. Introd. N. Europe. Planted but readily regenerating. Flo. April–May.*

Acer campestre L. Field maple. Small tree 9–20 m; flo. erect; stamens equalling petals; wings of fr. nearly in one line. Hedgerows from Yorkshire southward, introd. elsewhere. Flo. May–June.

ERODIUM
CICUTARIUM
SSP. DUNENSE

ERODIUM
MARITIMUM

ERODIUM
MOSCHATUM

ERODIUM
CICUTARIUM

× 2

VAR.
PIMPINELLIFOLIUM

OXALIS
CORNICULATA.

OXALIS
ACETOSELLA.

ILEX AQUIFOLIUM

IMPATIENS
NOLI-TANGERE.

IMPATIENS
GLANDULIFERA.

IMPATIENS
CAPENSIS

RHAMNUS
CATHARTICUS.

EUONYMUS
EUROPAEUS.

ACER
PSEUDOPLATANUS

ACER CAMPESTRE.

FRANGULA
ALNUS

Plate 21

Leguminosae

Lupinus nootkatensis Donn ex Sims. Nootka lupin. Stem 30–60 cm, stout, herbaceous, subsimple; leaf petioles long; flo. blue. Garden escape. River shingle, frequent in mid Scotland and Orkneys. Flo. July–Aug.*

Lupinus arboreus Sims. Tree lupin. Woody shrub with many spreading branches; petioles short; flo. yellow. Garden escape. Naturalized on dunes, etc., local. Flo. June–Sept.*

Lupinus polyphyllus Lindl. Garden lupin. Stems stout, unbranched; racemes dense; flo. blue, purple, pink or white. Garden escape. Established on railway banks, etc., widespread. Flo. June–July.*

Genista anglica L. Petty whin. Stem 30–60 cm, woody, diffuse, spinous; leaves ovate, glabrous; flo. yellow. Damp heaths, etc., up to 950 m, widespread. Flo. May–June.

Genista pilosa L. Hairy greenweed. Stem 10–40 cm, woody, without spines; leaves ovate, silky beneath; flo. pubescent, yellow; pod downy. Dry heathy places, W. Cornwall, Wales and Sussex, rare. Flo. May–Sept.

Genista tinctoria L. Dyer's greenweed.
Ssp. ***tinctoria***. Stem 30–70 cm suberect, striate; leaves oblong-lanceolate; flo. and pods glabrous. Rough grassy places, S. England to S. Scotland. Flo. July–Sept.
Ssp. ***littoralis*** (Corb.) Rothm. Ssp. *prostrata* (Bab.) Perring & Sell. Stem up to 25 cm, procumbent; leaves ovate or oblong; pods hairy on back of valve. Sea coasts, Cornwall and N. Devon.*

Ulex europaeus L. Gorse, furze. Stem 60–200 cm; spines furrowed and straight; flo. bracts ovate, about 4×2 mm; calyx hairs spreading; flo. yellow. Heaths, etc., common. Flo. March–May.

Ulex europaeus × gallii. Very variable, but usually intermediate between the parents, and probably common where they grow together.

Ulex gallii Planch. Western gorse. Stems 10–90 cm; spines strong, slightly furrowed, often curved; bracts minute; calyx hairs appressed; flo. golden. Heaths and moors, common in W. England, Wales and S. Ireland, rare elsewhere. Flo. July–Oct.

Ulex minor Roth. Dwarf gorse. *U. nanus* T. F. Forst. Stems 5–100 cm; spines weak and slender; bracts minute; flo. pale yellow and small. Heaths, Dorset to Sussex, Norfolk and Cumbria. Flo. July–Oct.

Laburnum anagyroides Medic. Laburnum. *L. vulgare* J. Presl. Shrub or small tree to 7 m; twigs appressed, pubescent, greyish-green; leaves 3-foliate; flo. golden-yellow in lax racemes; seeds black. Garden escape. Established on waste ground in hedgerows, etc., widespread. Flo. May.*

Laburnum alpinum (Mill.) Berchtold & J. Presl. Scottish laburnum. Similar to *L. anagyroides* but smaller (up to 5 m), twigs glabrous, green, racemes denser, flo. paler, seeds brown. Garden escape. Established in hedgerows, etc., S. Scotland. Flo. May.*

Cytisus scoparius (L.) Link. Broom. *Sarothamnus scoparius* (L.) Wimm. ex Koch.

Ssp. ***scoparius***. Erect shrub, 60–200 cm; branches angular, green; leaflets 1–3, silky; flo. large, bright yellow, sometimes blotched with red. Heaths, widespread. Flo. May–June.*
Ssp. ***maritimus*** (Rouy) Heywood. *Sarothamnus scoparius* ssp. *maritimus* (Rouy) Ulbr. Ssp. *prostratus* (C. Bailey) Tutin. Stems prostrate; twigs and leaves densely silky. Sea cliffs, W. Cornwall, Channel Islands and W. Cork.*

Cytisus striatus (Hill) Rothm. Similar to *C. scoparius* but with pale grey, strigate stems, larger and paler flo. and short, inflated, densely grey, pubescent pods. Introd. Spain. Extensively planted on banks of motorways and arterial roads and regenerating. Flo. May–June.*

Cytisus monspessulanus L. Montpelier broom. Similar to *C. scoparius* but upper lip of calyx deeply bifid, lower with 3 distinct teeth and hairy pods. Introd. Mediterranean region. Extensively planted on banks of motorways and arterial roads and regenerating. Flo. April–June.*

Cytisus multiflorus (Ait.) Sweet. White Spanish broom. Shrub to 3 m; branches slender, erect; leaves 3-foliate below, simple above; leaflets oblong-obovate to linear-oblong; flo. 1 cm long, white, numerous; pods appressed, pubescent. Introd. Mediterranean region. Planted on banks of motorways and arterial roads, mostly S. England. Flo. May–June.*

Spartium junceum L. Spanish broom. Similar to *Sarothamnus scoparius* but with terete stems and linear-lanceolate leaves. Introd. S. Europe. Planted but regenerating on railways banks, etc., in S. England. Flo. July–Sept.*

Ononis repens L. Common restharrow. *O. arvensis* auct. Stem rhizomatous, procumbent, hairy all round, usually without spines; pod shorter than calyx. Grassy places, etc., particularly on calcareous soils, widespread. Flo. June–Sept.
Var. ***horrida*** Lange. Plant spinous.

Ononis spinosa L. Spiny restharrow. *O. campestris* Koch & Ziz. Stem erect with two lines of hairs, usually spinous; pod decidedly longer than calyx. Rough pastures, England, except S.W., very rare in Scotland. Flo. June–Sept.

Ononis reclinata L. Small restharrow. Annual, stem 4–8 cm; viscid; fr. pedicels reflexed. In turf on sea cliffs, S. Devon, S. Wales and Channel Islands, rare. Flo. June–July.

Medicago sativa L. Lucerne. Erect, 30–90 cm bushy; leaflets 3 cm; flo. purple; pod 8 mm wide, with 2–3 turns. Introd. S.E. Europe, cultivated, established on field borders, road verges, etc., common. Flo. April–Aug.

Medicago × varia Martyn — *M. falcata × sativa*. *M. silvestris* Fr. Variable; pod forming 1 ring; flo. yellow to green.

Medicago falcata L. Sickle medick. Usually procumbent; flo. 8–10 mm, yellow; pod sickle-shaped, downy. Dry sandy and gravelly places, E. England, introd. elsewhere. Flo. June–July.

Medicago lupulina L. Black medick. Procumbent; flo. 2–3 mm, yellow, in small oval spikes; pods very small, netted circular, becoming black. Fields, etc., very common. Flo. May–Aug.

GENISTA
PILOSA.

GENISTA
ANGLICA

ULEX
GALLII

ULEX EUROPAEUS
X 4

GENISTA
TINCTORIA

ONONIS RECLINATA

CYTISUS
SCOPARIUS

ONONIS
SPINOSA.

VAR HORRIDA

ULEX
EUROPAEUS

ULEX
MINOR

MEDICAGO SATIVA

ONONIS REPENS

MEDICAGO LUPULINA

TRIFOLIUM
ORNITHOPODIOIDES

MEDICAGO
FALCATA

MEDICAGO
X VARIA

Plate 22

Leguminosae *(continued)*

Medicago nigra (L.) Krock. Toothed medick. *M. polymorpha* L. *M. denticulata* Willd. *M. hispida* Gaertn. Stem prostrate; stipules laciniate; flo. yellow, 1–5 on peduncle; pods netted, coiled with spines usually long. Sandy and gravelly places, mostly S. and E. coasts of England, introd. inland. Flo. May–Aug.

Medicago arabica (L.) Huds. Spotted medick. *M. maculata* Sibth. Leaflets usually with dark spot; stipules toothed; pods with 3–5 coils and curved spines. Fields, etc., mostly E. and S. England. Flo. May–Aug.

Medicago minima (L.) Bartal. Bur medick. Prostrate, downy; leaves small; stipules subentire; peduncles very short; pods coiled and spinous. Sandy places, S.E. and E. England, introd. elsewhere, rare. Flo. May–July.

Melilotus altissima Thuill. Tall melilot. *M. officinalis* (Lam.) Hayne. Stems erect, 60–100 cm; leaflets oblong, 15–20 mm; petals all equal; pods 5–6 mm, black, acute, hairy. Fields and roadsides. Flo. June–Aug.

Melilotus officinalis (L.) Pall. Ribbed melilot. *M. arvensis* Wallr. Similar to *M. altissima*, but wing petals and standard longer than keel, pale, yellowish; pods 3–5 mm, brown, mucronate, glabrous, ribbed. Introd. Europe. Cultivated and waste ground, common. Flo. July–Sept.

Melilotus alba Medic. White melilot. More slender, 60–120 cm, flo. white; standard petal longer than keel or wing; pod netted. Introd. Europe. Cultivated and waste ground, common. Flo. June–Aug.

Melilotus indica (L.) All. Small melilot. *M. parviflora* Desf. Plant smaller; flo. small, pale yellow; standard longer than other petals; pods globular, netted. Introd. Mediterranean. Waste ground, etc., rare. Flo. July–Sept.*

Trifolium ornithopodioides L. Fenugreek. *Trigonella ornithopodioides* (L.) DC. Prostrate, glabrous; leaves trifoliate; flo. pink and white, 1–3 on peduncle; pod twice length of calyx. Sandy heaths mostly near the sea, local. Flo. June–Aug. Illus. on pl. 21.

Trifolium subterraneum L. Subterranean clover. Stems prostrate, hairy; leaflets obcordate; flo. few, pale; sterile calyces adapted as anchors to bury pods. Dry pastures, mostly S. England. Flo. May–June.

Trifolium pratense L. Red clover. Leaves often white-blotched; heads subsessile between leaves with broad stipules; flo. pale rose. Pastures, etc., very common. Flo. May–Sept.

Trifolium medium L. Zigzag clover. Leaflets longer; stipules linear, green, tapering; heads peduncled from opposite leaves; flo. deeper colour. Pastures, especially on clay soils, local. Flo. June–Sept.

Trifolium ochroleucon Huds. Sulphur clover. Pubescent; leaflets obovate; stipule tips subulate; flo. cream-coloured; calyx tube ribbed, teeth subulate, lowest longest. Grassy places on gravel and clay soils, mostly E. England, local. Flo. June–Aug.

Trifolium hybridum L. Alsike clover. Plant large, spreading, up to 60 cm; leaflets toothed; heads peduncled, 25 mm wide; flo. pink and white, drooping over fr. A survival from cultivation. Naturalized on roadsides, etc., common. Flo. June–Aug.

Trifolium squamosum L. Sea clover. *T. maritimum* Huds. Leaf stipules long, tapering; heads shortly peduncled, pink; calyx teeth small in flo. becoming enlarged, foliaceous, spinescent, lowest longest, 3-veined. Rough grassy places near the sea, S. and E. England and S. Wales. Flo. June–Aug.

Trifolium molinerii Balb. ex Hornem. Long-headed clover. Stem with appressed hairs; leaflets obcordate; flo. pinkish-white; calyx spreading in fr. In short grass, Lizard Head, Cornwall, and in Jersey. Flo. June–July.

Trifolium stellatum L. Starry clover. Stems short; leaves and ovate stipules softly hairy; heads globose, stalked; flo. small, cream; calyx enlarged in fr., spreading, star-like. Introd. Europe. Shingle beaches, Shoreham, Sussex, very rare.*

Trifolium arvense L. Hare's-foot clover. Stems ascending, hairy; leaflets narrow; heads oblong, stalked; flo. small, white, immersed in long, pink hairs of calyx. Grassy places on sandy soils, widespread. Flo. July–Sept.

Trifolium bocconei Savi. Twin-headed clover. Erect, 5–10 cm; heads ovate, terminal, often in pairs; stipules and calyx teeth subulate; flo. small, whitish. Short turf, Lizard Head, Cornwall, and in Jersey. Flo. July.

Trifolium striatum L. Knotted clover. Leaflets silky with straight veins; stipules broad, striate; heads sessile; calyx ventricose, ribbed; flo. rose-pink. Sandy fields, often by sea, widespread. Flo. June.

Trifolium scabrum L. Rough clover. Procumbent; leaflets pubescent, veins curved; heads sessile; flo. white; calyx tube cylindrical, teeth spreading in fr. Dry sandy places, mostly near the sea, England and Wales, uncommon, very rare in Ireland. Flo. May–July.

Trifolium glomeratum L. Clustered clover. Leaves glabrous; heads axillary, semi-globose; flo. rose-pink; calyx teeth very acute, reflexed. Sandy and gravelly places, mostly S. and E. coasts of England and S.E. Ireland, local and rare, introd. elsewhere. Flo. June.

Trifolium suffocatum L. Suffocated clover. Stems short, nearly buried in sand; leaf petioles long; flo. heads sessile, often confluent; calyx teeth recurved. Grassy places on light soils, mostly S. and E. coasts of England, local and rare. Flo. July–Aug.

Trifolium strictum L. Upright clover. Erect, 3–20 cm; leaflets narrow, toothed; stipules broad; heads globose, peduncled; flo. pink; calyx ribbed. Grassy places, Lizard Head, Cornwall, and in Jersey. Flo. June.

Trifolium incarnatum L. Crimson clover. Stem with spreading hairs; leaflets obovate; calyx very hairy; flo. deep crimson. Introd. Mediterranean region. A fodder crop, persisting on roadsides, rare. Flo. June–Aug.

Trifolium repens L. White or Dutch clover. Closely creeping and rooting; leaf petioles long; heads long-stalked; flo. white or rose, persistent, drooping over the fr. Grassy places, etc., very common. Flo. May–Oct.

Trifolium occidentale D. E. Coombe. Western clover. Similar to *T. repens* from which it differs in its shorter stems; dark green, smaller leaflets without blotchy markings, fewer lateral veins; fewer-flowered heads and creamy-white (never pinkish) flo. Dry warm rocks, pastures and sand dunes near the sea, W. Cornwall, Channel Islands, Isles of Scilly and Ireland. Flo. March–June.*

MEDICAGO ARABICA

MEDICAGO NIGRA

MEDICAGO NIGRA

MEDICAGO MINIMA.

TRIFOLIUM SUBTERRANIUM.

X2

TRIFOLIUM PRATENSE.

TRIFOLIUM HYBRIDUM.

TRIFOLIUM MEDIUM.

MELILOTUS ALTISSIMA

MELILOTUS OFFICINALIS

MELILOTUS ALBA.

T. PRATENSE X 8

TRIFOLIUM REPENS.

T. ARVENSE.

TRIFOLIUM SUFFOCATUM.

TRIFOLIUM SQUAMOSUM

TRIFOLIUM GLOMERATUM.

TRIFOLIUM OCHROLEUCON.

T. INCARNATUM

TRIFOLIUM STRICTUM.

TRIFOLIUM BOCCONEI.

TRIFOLIUM STRIATUM.

TRIFOLIUM SCABRUM

TRIFOLIUM MOLINERII.

Plate 23

Leguminosae *(continued)*

Trifolium fragiferum L. Strawberry clover. Creeping and rooting; leaves and heads long-stalked; flo. pink; calyx of 2 lips, upper lip enlarging and covering fr. Grassy places on heavy soils, mostly S. and E. England, and Ireland, local in Wales, rare in Scotland. Flo. July–Aug.

Trifolium resupinatum L. Reversed clover. Slender, 10–25 cm; leaflets narrow, obovate; flo. small, pink, upside down; calyx inflated, woolly. Introd. Europe. Waste places and docksides, rare. Flo. July.*

Trifolium aureum Poll. Large hop trefoil. *T. agrarium* auct. Mid leaflet sessile; flo. up to 50 in head, bright yellow; style as long as pod. Introd. Europe. Naturalized in fields and by roadsides, rare. Flo. July–Aug.

Trifolium campestre Schreb. Hop trefoil. *T. procumbens* auct. Mid leaflet stalked; flo. yellow, 20–40 in head, standard deflexed; style shorter than pod. Pastures, etc., common. Flo. June–Aug.

Trifolium dubium Sibth. Lesser trefoil. *T. minus* Sm. Mid leaflet stalked; flo. yellow, 10–20 in head; standard folded over pod; style shorter than pod. Pastures, banks, etc., common. Flo. June–Aug.

Trifolium micranthum Viv. Slender trefoil. *T. filiforme* L. Very slender; mid leaflet sessile; flo. yellow, 2–6 in head; standard narrow and deeply notched; peduncle filiform. Dry grassy places on light soils, mostly S. England and Wales, very rare in Ireland. Flo. June–July.

Anthyllis vulneraria L. Kidney vetch. Stem and pinnate leaves silky; flo. usually yellow; heads in pairs; calyx woolly; pod small, 1-seeded. Dry grassy places on calcareous and sandy soils, on sea cliffs, etc., widespread and very variable. Flo. June–Aug.
Var. **coccinea** L. Small, with dark red flowers. Sea coasts.

Lotus corniculatus L. Common bird's-foot trefoil. Decumbent; stipules ovate like leaflets; flo. bright yellow, 5–8 in head; calyx teeth erect, appressed in bud. Grassy places, very common. Flo. June–Aug.

Lotus tenuis Waldst. & Kit. ex Willd. Narrow-leaved bird's-foot trefoil. Stems ascending, long and slender; leaflets and stipules linear; flo. 3–4 in head; calyx teeth erect. Grassy places on heavy soils, local, but rare in Wales and N. England, introd. in Ireland. Flo. June–Sept.

Lotus uliginosus Schkuhr. Greater bird's-foot trefoil. *L. majus* auct. *L. pedunculatus* auct., non Cav. Stoloniferous and tall; leaflets and stipules larger, ovate; flo. dark yellow, 6–10 in head; calyx teeth spreading in bud. Wet meadows, bogs, etc., common. Flo. July–Sept.

Lotus subbiflorus Lag. Hairy bird's-foot trefoil. *L. hispidus* Desf. *nom. nud.* Plant small, hairy throughout; flo. 2–4 in head; standard petal narrow; pod short and broad. Sea cliffs, Cornwall to Hampshire, Pembrokeshire and S. Ireland. Flo. July–Aug.

Lotus angustissimus L. Slender bird's-foot trefoil. Prostrate; peduncles short; flo. yellow, 1–2 in head; standard wide; pod narrow, 20–30 mm long. Near the sea, Cornwall to Kent and Channel Islands, introd. inland. Flo. July–Aug.

Tetragonolobus maritimus (L.) Roth. Dragon's-teeth. *Lotus siliquosus* L. Leaflets 3; peduncles exceeding leaves; flo. *c.* 3 cm long, orange; pod winged. Introd. Europe. Naturalized in grassy places, mostly S. England. Flo. June–Aug.*

Galega officinalis L. Goat's rue. Perennial. Stems 60–150 cm, glabrous erect; leaves pinnate with terminal leaflet; flo. lilac or white, 12–15 in spikes. Garden escape. Established on waste ground, widespread. Flo. June–Aug.*

Oxytropis halleri Bunge ex Koch. Purple oxytropis. *O. uralensis* auct. Leaves 6–10 cm, pinnate, leaflets acute; flo. pale mauve; pod abruptly pointed. Rocks, 900 m, Scotland, local. Flo. June–July.

Oxytropis campestris (L.) DC. Yellow oxytropis. Leaves up to 15 cm, leaflets blunt; flo. yellow, tinged mauve; pod tapering. Rocks, 900 m, Perthshire, Angus and Kintyre, very rare. Flo. June–July.

Colutea arborescens L. Bladder senna. Shrub up to 4 m; stems hairy; leaves pinnate, leaflets silky beneath; flo. deep yellow with red blotches, 2–8 in stalked spikes; pods large, papery, much inflated. Introd. Mediterranean region. Established on waste ground. Flo. May–July.*

TRIFOLIUM
DUBIUM

TRIFOLIUM
MICRANTHUM.

TRIFOLIUM
CAMPESTRE.

TRIFOLIUM
AUREUM.

ANTHYLLIS
VULNERARIA

VAR. COCCINEA

LOTUS
ULIGINOSUS

TRIFOLIUM
FRAGIFERUM

LOTUS
CORNICULATUS.

L. SUBBIFLORUS × 10

LOTUS ANGUSTISSIMUS.

OXYTROPIS
CAMPESTRIS

LOTUS TENUIS.

LOTUS
SUBBIFLORUS

OXYTROPIS HALLERI

— *Plate 24* —

Leguminosae *(continued)*

Astragalus danicus Retz. Purple milk-vetch. *A. hypoglottis* auct., non L. Erect, pubescent; leaves pinnate; stipules connate; flo. erect, purple; pods erect. Dunes, roadsides, etc., on calcareous soil, Gloucestershire, Wiltshire and Chilterns to E. Scotland, uncommon, absent from Wales, and very rare in Ireland. Flo. June–Aug.

Astragalus alpinus L. Alpine milk-vetch. Prostrate, slender, elongate; leaf stipules free; flo. horizontal, whitish, purple-tipped; pods pendulous. Rocks, 780 m, Highlands of Scotland, rare. Flo. July.

Astragalus glycyphyllos L. Wild liquorice. Stems 60–100 cm, stout, spreading; leaflets large; flo. greenish-white; pods large and curved. Thickets, wood borders, etc., on calcareous and limestone soils, local in England and Scotland, rare in Wales. Flo. June–Sept.

Astragalus odoratus Lam. Stems up to 30 cm, erect; leaves 4–12 cm, leaflets up to 14 pairs, lanceolate; racemes dense; flo. yellowish, pendent; pod 8–10 mm, oblong, glabrescent. Introd. Mediterranean region. Established on waste ground, S. England and Midlands. Flo. June–Aug.*

Ornithopus perpusillus L. Bird's-foot. Stems slender; leaves 3–5 mm, pinnate; peduncle with leaf at top; flo. *c.* 4 mm; white, veined red, small; pods knotted. Dry sandy places, widespread, but rare in N. England, Scotland and Ireland. Flo. May–July.

Ornithopus pinnatus (Mill.) Druce. Orange bird's-foot. *O. ebracteatus* Brot. Stems slender; leaflets fewer, 3–4 pairs; peduncle without leaf at apex; flo. slightly larger, 6–8 mm, yellow. Heathy slopes, sandy tracks, etc., Isles of Scilly and Channel Islands, introd. elsewhere. Flo. July–Aug.

Ornithopus compressus L. Similar to *O. perpusillus* but flo. yellow and larger (5–8 mm) and pods scarcely knotted. Introd. S. Europe. Naturalized in grassy places, S. England, very rare. Flo. June–Aug.*

Coronilla varia L. Crown vetch. Spreading plant, 30–60 cm; leaves pinnate, leaflets oblong; peduncles long; flo. many, white and purplish; calyx teeth small; pod slender. Introd. Europe. Established in grassy places, on waste ground, etc., uncommon. Flo. June.*

Coronilla valentina L. ssp. **glauca** (L.) Batt. *C. glauca* L. Shrub up to 1 m; leaflets 2–3 pairs, glaucous; flo. yellow, 7–12 mm, 5–8 in umbels; pod with 5–7 segments. Introd. Mediterranean region. Planted on banks, cliffs, etc., and regenerating, naturalized in S. Devon and Northumberland and doubtless elsewhere. Flo. June–July.*

Hippocrepis comosa L. Horseshoe vetch. Slender, spreading, subglabrous plant; leaves pinnate; peduncles long; flo. yellow, deflexed; pod of crescent-shaped joints. Dry grassy places on calcareous soils, widespread but local in England, rare in Wales. Flo. May–Aug.

Onobrychis viciifolia Scop. Sainfoin. *O. sativa* Lam. Erect, 30–60 cm; leaves long and pinnate; peduncle long; flo. in conical raceme, pink with darker veins; pod 1-seeded. Possibly native on downs, etc., on calcareous soils, S. England, introd. on railway banks, waste ground, etc. Flo. June–Aug.

Vicia hirsuta (L.) S. F. Gray. Hairy tare. Slender, 20–60 cm; leaflets narrow, 6–9 pairs; tendrils branched; peduncles 1–3 cm; flo. small, pale mauve; pod hairy, 2-seeded. Grassy places, common. Flo. May–Aug.

Vicia tetrasperma (L.) Schreb. Smooth tare. Leaflets 4–6 pairs, obtuse; peduncle 1–2-flowered; pod glabrous, 4-seeded. Grassy places or thickets, widespread, but rare in Scotland and absent from Ireland. Flo. May–Aug.

Vicia tenuissima (Bieb.) Schinz & Thell. Slender tare. *V. gracilis* Lois., non Soland. Leaflets 3–4 pairs, linear, acute; peduncle 1–4-flowered; flo. 8 mm; pod 5–8-seeded. Grassy places and arable fields, mostly S. England, local. Flo. June–Aug.

Vicia cracca L. Tufted vetch. Climbing, 60–200 cm; tendrils branched; stipules semi-sagittate; calyx gibbous; leaves sometimes silky. Hedges and thickets, common. Flo. June–Aug.

Vicia orobus DC. Wood bitter-vetch. Erect, stout, 30–60 cm, tendrils 0; leaflets hairy; peduncle short; flo. white and purplish. Rocky woods, local in Wales and Scotland, rare in England and Ireland. Flo. May–June.

Vicia sylvatica L. Wood vetch. Climbing, 60–130 cm; tendrils branched; lower stipules lunate, toothed. Rocky woods and sea cliffs, local, but very rare in S. England. Flo. June–Aug.

Vicia sepium L. Bush vetch. Climbing 30–100 cm; flo. head sessile; stipules semi-sagittate; pod glabrous. Hedges and grassy borders of thickets, very common. Flo. April–Oct.

ASTRAGALUS DANICUS.

ASTRAGALUS GLYCYPHYLLOS.

VICIA HIRSUTA

VICIA TETRASPERMA

VICIA TENUISSIMA

ASTRAGALUS ALPINUS.

ORNITHOPUS PERPUSILLUS.

ORNITHOPUS PINNATUS.

ONOBRYCHIS VICIIFOLIA.

VICIA OROBUS.

VICIA CRACCA.

HIPPOCREPIS COMOSA.

VICIA SYLVATICA.

VICIA SEPIUM

Plate 25

Leguminosae *(continued)*

Vicia lutea L. Yellow vetch. Prostrate, tufted, 10–50 cm; flo. solitary; pod hairy; stipules triangular. Sea coasts, introd. inland, rare. Flo. June–Aug.

Vicia sativa L. Common vetch. Stout, 15–120 cm; flo. 25 mm, usually in pairs; pod erect, 30–80 mm. Introd. Europe. Relic of cultivation, established on arable ground and roadsides, rare. Flo. May–July.

Vicia angustifolia L. Narrow-leaved vetch. Fairly stout; leaflets narrowly oblong; flo. 10–15 mm, often 2 together; calyx gibbous; pod 35–50 mm, spreading, bursting the calyx. Dry banks, meadows and grassy waste places, common. Flo. May–Sept.

Vicia lathyroides L. Spring vetch. Slender, pubescent, 5–20 cm; flo. solitary, 8–10 mm, calyx not gibbous at base, funnel-shaped; leaflets obtuse, mucronate, 6–10 mm; pod 15–30 mm. Dry grassy places. Flo. April–May.

Vicia bithynica (L.) L. Bithynian vetch. Perennial, 30–60 cm; leaflets ovate or linear; pod reticulate, hairy. Bushy places and sea cliffs, local in England and Wales, very rare in Scotland. Flo. July–Aug.

Lathyrus aphaca L. Yellow vetchling. Stipules very large, leaf-like; leaflets o; peduncle usually 1-, sometimes 2-flowered. Dry calcareous and sandy fields, mostly S. England, introd. elsewhere. Flo. May–Aug.

Lathyrus nissolia L. Grass vetchling. Stipules minute; petioles linear, leaf-like. Bushy and grassy places, local in England and Wales, very rare in Scotland. Flo. May–June.

Lathyrus hirsutus L. Hairy vetchling. 30–120 cm; peduncle 2-flowered; leaflets 1 pair, linear-lanceolate; flo. pale blue and red. Introd. Europe. Cultivated and waste ground, mostly S. England. Flo. June–July.*

Lathyrus pratensis L. Meadow vetchling. Stem angular, 60–120 cm, not winged; leaflets 1 pair. Hedges, etc., common. Flo. June–Sept.

Lathyrus tuberosus L. Tuberous pea. Stem angular; leaflets obovate; peduncle 2–5-flowered; roots tuberous. Introd. Europe. Established in fields and waste ground, mostly England, uncommon. Flo. June–Aug.

Lathyrus sylvestris L. Narrow-leaved everlasting pea. Stem 1–2 m, winged; leaflets large, sword-like; stipules large, semi-sagittate. Woods, wet sea cliffs, etc., local. Flo. June–Aug.

Lathyrus latifolius L. Broad-leaved everlasting pea. Stem glabrous, winged; leaflets large, elliptic, glabrous; racemes 5–15-flowered, flo. 2–3 cm, purple-pink. Garden escape. Established on railway banks, waste ground, etc., common. Flo. June–Sept.*

Lathyrus grandiflorus Sibth. & Sm. Similar to *L. latifolius*, but stem pubescent, not winged; racemes 1–4-flowered; flo. with standard violet, wings purple and keel pink. Garden escape. Naturalized in grassy places, etc., uncommon. Flo. June–Sept.*

Lathyrus palustris L. Marsh pea. Stem winged, 60–120 cm; leaflets 2–3 pairs, lanceolate, with tendrils. Fens and boggy meadows, mostly E. England, rare, very rare elsewhere. Flo. June–Aug.

Lathyrus japonicus Willd. Ssp. **maritimus** (L.) P. W. Ball. Sea pea. *L. maritimus* L. Stem angular; leaflets 2–3 pairs, oval; stipules large, ovate, hastate. Sandy beaches and dunes, S. and E. England and Scotland, local and rare, very rare in S. Ireland. Flo. June–Aug.

Lathyrus niger (L.) Bernh. Black pea. *Orobus niger* L. Stem branched, not winged; leaflets 3–6 pairs; peduncle many-flowered; stipules linear subulate. Formerly in rocky woods in Scotland, possibly extinct. Flo. July–Aug.*

Lathyrus montanus Bernh. Bitter vetch. *L. macrorrhizus* Wimm. *Orobus tuberosus* L. Stem winged; leaflets 2–3 pairs; peduncle 2–4-flowered; stipules semi-sagittate. Woods and thickets, widespread, but absent from much of E. England. Flo. May–Aug.

VICIA
LATHYROIDES.

VICIA
SATIVA.

VICIA
BITHYNICA.

VICIA
LUTEA

VICIA
ANGUSTIFOLIA

LATHYRUS
APHACA

LATHYRUS
SYLVESTRIS.

LATHYRUS
NISSOLIA

LATHYRUS
TUBEROSUS

LATHYRUS
PRATENSIS.

LATHYRUS   MONTANUS.

LATHYRUS
PALUSTRIS.

LATHYRUS
JAPONICUS.

— *Plate 26* —

Rosaceae

Prunus spinosa L. Blackthorn, sloe. Shrub with many stout thorns; twigs black; leaves appearing after flo.; fr. erect. Scrub, open woods and hedges, common. Flo. March–April.

Prunus domestica L. Wild plum.
Ssp. **domestica.** Large shrub or small tree without thorns; leaves large; petals greenish in bud; flo. 1–3; fr. oblong, drooping. Introd. S.W. Asia. Hedges, often near houses, rare. Flo. March–May.*

Ssp. **insititia** (L.) C. K. Schneid. Bullace. *P. insititia* L. Shrub with few or no thorns; twigs brown, pubescent; leaves appearing with the flo.; fr. globose, drooping. Hedges, common. Flo. March–May.

Prunus cerasifera Ehrh. Cherry plum. *P. divaricata* Ledeb. Similar to *P. domestica* but twigs glabrous and glossy; flo. usually solitary. Introd. C. Asia. Hedges, common. Flo. March–April.*

Prunus laurocerasus L. Cherry laurel. Small tree; leaves evergreen, obovate-acuminate, dark green, very glossy; flo. many in erect racemes; petals white; fr. ovoid, purple-black. Introd. S.E. Europe. Planted in woods and copses where it sometimes regenerates. Flo. April–June.*

Prunus mahaleb L. Small tree; leaves orbicular to broad-ovate, rounded or subcordate at base, pubescent on midrib beneath, otherwise glabrous; flo. fragrant, in 6–10-flo. racemes; petals white; fr. ovoid, black. Introd. C. Europe. Planted in woods and copses where it sometimes regenerates, rare. Flo. April–May.*

Prunus serotina Ehrh. Rum cherry. Small tree, similar to *P. padus*, but with cylindrical slender racemes; flo. smaller on shorter peduncles; petals white; fr. ovoid, black; calyx persistent. Introd. N. America. Planted in woods and gardens where it sometimes regenerates; also bird-sown into other habitats, rare. Flo. April–June.*

Prunus avium (L.) L. Wild cherry. Small tree with few suckers; leaves acuminate; flo. umbellate; calyx tube constricted; petals obovate; fr. red. Woods and hedges, common. Flo. April–May.

Prunus cerasus L. Dwarf cherry. Shrub with suckers; flo. umbellate; calyx crenate, tube not constricted; petals orbicular; fr. red, sour. Introd. Origin unknown. Hedges, uncommon. Flo. April–May.

Prunus padus L. Bird cherry. Small tree; leaves acuminate; flo. smaller, in long, often drooping raceme; fr. black, bitter. Woods, N. England and Scotland, introd. elsewhere. Flo. May.

Spiraea salicifolia L. Bridewort. Shrub up to 2 m; leaves simple, willow-like, glabrous; flo. pink, in a dense panicle. Introd. E. Europe. Planted and occasionally naturalized. Flo. July–Aug.*

Filipendula ulmaria (L.) Maxim. Meadowsweet. *Spiraea ulmaria* L. Herb up to 120 cm; leaves large, pinnate, usually white beneath; flo. cream. Wet meadows, ditches and riversides, common. Flo. June–Aug.

Filipendula vulgaris Moench. Dropwort. *F. hexapetala* Gilib. *Spiraea filipendula* L. Herb, 20–40 cm; leaves mostly radical; leaflets many, narrow, much cut; petals often 6, red outside. Meadows, etc., on calcareous and limestone soils, local. Flo. May–July.

Sanguisorba officinalis L. Great burnet. Up to 1 m, branched; flo. heads ovoid-oblong, crimson; stamens hardly exserted; fr. smooth, 4-winged. Damp meadows, widespread, but rare in Scotland and Ireland. Flo. June–Sept.

Sanguisorba minor Scop.
Ssp. **minor.** Salad burnet, lesser burnet. *Poterium sanguisorba* L. 30–50 cm; stem leaves few; heads globose; lower flo. male; stamens long exserted; fr. finely reticulate, with 4 even ridges. Dry calcareous pastures, railway banks, etc. Flo. May–Aug.*

Ssp. **muricata** (Gremli) Brig. Salad burnet. *Poterium polygamum* Waldst. & Kit. *P. muricatum* Spach. Larger than ssp. *minor*, 45–130 cm; stem leaves several with narrow leaflets; heads often ovoid; fr. coarsely rugose with 4 irregular ridges. Introd. Mediterranean region. Naturalized on borders of fields, etc. Flo. May–Aug.*

Aremonia agrimonoides (L.) DC. *Agrimonia agrimonoides* L. Differs from *Agrimonia eupatoria* in having flo. in few-flowered cymes, and receptacles without spines. Introd. S.E. Europe. Naturalized in woods, Scotland, local. Flo. June–Aug.*

Agrimonia eupatoria L. Agrimony. Fr. deeply grooved, lower spines spreading. Roadsides, field borders, etc., common. Flo. June–Aug.

Agrimonia procera Wallr. Fragrant agrimony. *A. odorata* auct., non Mill. Leaves stouter, glandular, scented; fr. slightly grooved, lower spines deflexed. Grassy places on heavy soils, widespread, local. Flo. June–Aug.*

Acaena novae-zelandiae Kirk. Pirri-pirri-bur. *A. anserinifolia* auct. Brit. et Austral., non (J. R. & G. Forst.) Druce. Creeping, woody, perennial; leaves pinnate, often bronze; flo. small in heads; sepals 4; petals o; fr. with 4 long barbed spines. Introd. with sheep's wool from Australia and naturalized in grassy places, uncommon. Flo. June–Aug.*

Aphanes arvensis L. Parsley piert. *Alchemilla arvensis* (L.) Scop. Lobes of stipules triangular, ovate, as long as broad; fr. sepals open. Dry cultivated ground, common. Flo. April–Oct.

Aphanes microcarpa (Boiss. & Reut.) Rothm. Lobes of stipules twice as long as broad; fr. sepals closed. Heaths, etc., on acid soils, common. Flo. April–Oct.*

Alchemilla alpina L. Alpine lady's-mantle. Leaflets all separate, white and silky beneath. Mountain pastures and rock crevices, N. England and Scotland, very rare in Ireland. Flo. June–Aug.

Alchemilla conjuncta Bab. Leaves connate at base, white and silky beneath. Rocks, Glen Clova and Arran, introd. elsewhere. Flo. June–July.

The British segregates of *Alchemilla vulgaris* were revised by Walters (1949) and his treatment is followed here.

Alchemilla glaucescens Wallr. *A. minor* auct. Stems and petioles with dense silky hairs; leaves hairy, basal sinus closed. Limestone grassland, Yorkshire, Ross, Sutherland and Leitrim. Flo. June–Sept.*

Alchemilla filicaulis Buser.
Ssp. **filicaulis.** Similar to above, but upper stem and pedicels glabrous; leaves less hairy, stipules purplish. Mountain pastures, etc., uncommon. Flo. June–Sept.*
Ssp. **vestita** (Buser). M. E. Bradshaw. *Alchemilla vestita* (Buser) Raunk. Stems and petioles with spreading hairs; leaves hairy, basal sinus open; stipules purplish. Moors, grassland, etc., widespread. Flo. June–Sept.

Alchemilla subcrenata Buser. Similar to *A. filicaulis* but stipules brownish not purplish; leaves undulate with broad lobes and coarse broad teeth. Grassland, Upper Teesdale and Weardale. Flo. June–Sept.*

Alchemilla minima Walters. Plant small; leaves very small, hairy on folds and on veins beneath, basal sinus open; stipules brown. Limestone grassland, Ingleborough, Yorkshire. Flo. June–Sept.*

Alchemilla monticola Opiz. *A. pastoralis* Buser. Plant medium; stem and petioles with spreading hairs; pedicels glabrous; leaves orbicular, densely hairy on both surfaces, basal sinus closed. Pastures, Upper Teesdale and Weardale, introd. elsewhere. Flo. June–Sept.*

Alchemilla acutiloba Opiz. Lower stem with spreading hairs, glabrous above; leaf lobes with straight sides. Pastures, Upper Teesdale. Flo. June–Sept.*

Alchemilla gracilis Opiz. Similar to *A. monticola* and *A. acutiloba* but differing in the closely appressed hairs of upper leaf surface and narrow inflo. Known only from Northumberland. Flo. June–Sept.*

Alchemilla xanthochlora Rothm. Plant large; stem and petioles with spreading hairs; pedicels and upper sides of leaves glabrous, lobes not overlapping. Grassy places, widespread. Flo. June–Sept.*

Alchemilla glomerulans Buser. Stem and petioles with appressed hairs; leaves hairy, lobes overlapping. Wet mountain rocks, Teesdale and mid Scotland northwards. Flo. June–Sept.*

Alchemilla glabra Neygenf. *A. alpestris* auct. Plant often large; lowest nodes of stem with appressed hairs, glabrous above; leaf lobes rather straight sided, with middle teeth on each side larger. Meadows, open woods, mountains, mostly N. England and Scotland. Flo. June–Sept.

Alchemilla wichurae (Buser) Stefánsson. *A. acutidens* auct. Plant small; stems somewhat more hairy than in *A. glabra*; leaves orbicular in outline, basal sinus closed or nearly so. Grassland on basic soils, Yorkshire to Sutherland. Flo. June–Sept.*

PRUNUS SPINOSA.

P. DOMESTICA
SSP. INSTITIA

P. DOMESTICA.

PRUNUS
CERASUS

PRUNUS PADUS.

PRUNUS
AVIUM.

× 10
FILIPENDULA
ULMARIA.

FILIPENDULA
ULMARIA.

SANGUISORBA
OFFICINALIS.

SANGUISORBA
MINOR

APHANES
ARVENSIS.

ALCHEMILLA
GLABRA.

ALCHEMILLA
FILICAULIS
SSP. VESTITA

ALCHEMILLA
ALPINA.

AGRIMONIA EUPATORIA.

ALCHEMILLA
CONJUNCTA

FILIPENDULA
VULGARIS.

Plate 27

Rosaceae (*continued*)

Alchemilla mollis (Buser) Rothm. Plant robust, very hairy; leaves shallowly lobed, epicalyx equalling the calyx. Garden escape. Naturalized in grassy places, uncommon. Flo. June–Sept.*

Alchemilla tytthantha Juz. *A. multiflora* Buser ex Rothm. Plant robust; leaves hairy on both surfaces; stem with downward directed spreading hairs; flo. small, glabrous. Garden escape. Naturalized in grassy places, S. Scotland, local. Flo. June–Sept.*

Sibbaldia procumbens L. *Potentilla sibbaldii* Haller f. Sibbaldia. Stem woody, depressed; leaves bluish-green; petals small, inconspicuous, yellow. Mountain tops, rocks, etc., mostly N. Scotland. Flo. July.

Potentilla palustris (L.) Scop. Marsh cinquefoil. *Comarum palustre* L. Stems 20–45 cm, from creeping base; leaflets oblong; flo. red-purple. Fens, marshy meadows and wet moorlands, local. Flo. June–July.

Potentilla fruticosa L. Shrubby cinquefoil. Shrub, up to 80 cm, silky; flo. yellow, dioecious. Damp rocky places, Teesdale, Lake District and W. Ireland, very local. Flo. June–Aug.

Potentilla sterilis (L.) Garcke. Barren strawberry. *P. fragariastrum* Pers. Leaflets 3, silky beneath; flo. white; receptacle hairy. Heaths, banks and woodland borders, common. Flo. Feb–May.

Potentilla rupestris L. Rock cinquefoil. Stems 20–50 cm, erect; leaves large and pinnate; flo. white. Rocks, Central Wales and E. Sutherland, rare. Flo. May–June.

Potentilla anserina L. Silverweed. Stoloniferous; leaves pinnate, soft and very silky; flo. solitary. Waste ground, by roadsides and in damp pastures, common. Flo. July–Aug.

Potentilla argentea L. Hoary cinquefoil. Stems decumbent, woody; leaflets 5, slender, digitate, white beneath. Dry grassy places on light soils, mostly England, local, very rare in Scotland. Flo. June–July.

Potentilla recta L. Sulphur cinquefoil. Stems erect, stout, 30–70 cm; leaves long-petioled; leaflets 5, large, oblong; flo. *c.* 3 cm wide, yellow. Garden escape. Naturalized in grassy places, uncommon. Flo. June–July.*

Potentilla norvegica L. Ternate-leaved cinquefoil. Stems 20–50 cm; branched above; leaflets 3; sepals hairy; petals small. Introd. Europe. Grassy places, waste ground, etc., uncommon. Flo. June–Oct.

Potentilla intermedia L. Stem ascending; lower leaflets 5, obovate, upper 3, oblong; petals yellow; achenes rugose. Introd. Europe. Grassy places, waste ground, etc., rare. Flo. June–Sept.*

Potentilla tabernaemontani Aschers. Spring cinquefoil. *P. verna* auct. Stem prostrate, rooting, branched below middle; leaflets 10–15 mm; flo. pale yellow; achenes smooth. Rocks, dry grassy slopes, etc., on calcareous and limestone soils, widespread but mostly northern half of Britain, absent from Ireland. Flo. April–June.

Potentilla crantzii (Crantz) G. Beck ex Fritsch. Alpine cinquefoil. *P. alpestris* auct. Stem ascending, branched above middle; leaflets 1–2 cm; flo. 15–25 mm, achenes smooth; petals bright yellow, sometimes with an orange spot. Mountain rocks, from Central Wales northwards, absent from Ireland, local. Flo. June–July.

Potentilla erecta (L.) Rausch. Tormentil. *P. tormentilla* Stokes.
Ssp. **erecta**. Stems slender, up to 15 cm; stem leaves up to 16 mm, not coarsely dentate, teeth usually short; stipules less than 10 mm in length, divided ½ way to base. Heaths and moors locally plentiful. Flo. June–Sept.
Ssp. **strictissima** (Zimmeter) A. J. Richards. Differs from ssp. *erecta* in having stems more than 15 cm; stem leaves more than 16 mm, coarsely dentate with teeth more than 1.5 mm long; stipules more than 10 mm in length, divided nearly to base. Mountain areas of N. England, Wales, Scotland and Ireland. Flo. June–Sept.

Potentilla × mixta Nolte ex Reichb. *P. erecta × reptans*. *P. × italica* Lehm. Intermediate, though often extremely variable. Occurs with parents and also in their absence.*

Potentilla anglica Laichard. Trailing tormentil. *P. procumbens* Sibth. Stems decumbent, rooting in autumn; radical leaves persistent; cauline leaves cuneate, petiole 7–8 mm; flo. 15–18 mm; petals 5 or 4. Heaths, banks and wood borders, mostly on basic soil, local. Flo. June–Sept.

Potentilla × suberecta Zimmeter. *P. anglica × erecta*. Intermediate. Frequently occurs where parents grow together.*

Potentilla reptans L. Creeping cinquefoil. Stem long, creeping, rooting, unbranched; leaflets mostly obovate, cauline similar; petals 5. Hedge banks, waste and cultivated land, on basic soil, common. Flo. June–Sept.

Fragaria vesca L. Wild strawberry. Runners long and slender; lateral leaflets sessile; receptacle covered by projecting achenes. Grassy banks and wood borders, especially on calcareous soil, common. Flo. April–July.

Fragaria moschata Duchesne. Hautbois strawberry. *F. elatior* Ehrh. Runners few or none; lateral leaflets shortly stalked; flo. 15–25 mm; receptacle bare at base. Introd. C. Europe. Sometimes naturalized in grassy places. Rare. Flo. April–July.*

Fragaria × ananassa Duchesne. Garden strawberry. *F. chiloensis × virginiana*. Fruiting receptacle covered by achenes embedded in fr.; Hortal hybrid. Established on railway banks etc. Flo. May–July.*

POTENTILLA STERILIS.
X 7.

P. STERILIS.

POTENTILLA
TABERNAEMONTANI.

POTENTILLA
CRANTZII.

P. NORVEGICA.

POTENTILLA
ARGENTEA.

POTENTILLA
ERECTA

POTENTILLA
ANGLICA.

POTENTILLA REPTANS.

POTENTILLA
RUPESTRIS.

FRAGARIA
VESCA.

POTENTILLA
PALUSTRIS.

POTENTILLA
FRUTICOSA

SIBBALDIA
PROCUMBENS

POTENTILLA
ANSERINA.

Plate 28

Rosaceae *(continued)*

There are over 400 species of *Rubus* in this country, and the distribution of these both here and on the Continent is becoming better known. The British species were revised by Watson (1958). But in most cases accurate determination of specimens requires the experience of those who have made a special study of the genus. It is not our intention in this present work to figure or to describe more than about a dozen examples of leading groups, in order to illustrate the kind of gradation that is found throughout the genus.

Although the desired handbook has been published, this should not invalidate our small contribution to an understanding of the genus, because in drawing the figures here shown we had valuable help from the late Mr William Watson. He selected and posted most of the samples illustrated, and he very kindly wrote the following descriptions of the selected species. He was, however, not responsible for the specimen figured as *R. caesius*, and he pointed out that the specimen was a hybrid. The clothing of the stems is an essential feature in determining the species, and unfortunately the finer details of this clothing are on the borderline of visibility, and are not easily figured or reproduced.

Even in the few species chosen it will be observed that in the subgenus *Eubatus* there is a gradation. We start with the *Suberecti*, which have no stalked glands or prickles. Indeed, the first sample has the panicle almost unarmed. Then we come to a gradual increase of prickles, which are sometimes all equal or confined to the angles of the stem. And the series continues through an increase of stalked glands, acicles and pricklets to forms which have them all very numerous, unequal and distributed all over the stem. And the last sample of this sub-genus differs also in having only 3 leaflets to each leaf instead of 5–7.

The examples chosen for illustration are not always the same as those given in edition 2 of the *Flora of the British Isles* by Messrs Clapham, Tutin and Warburg. Of those which are different *R. sulcatus* is near to *R. nessensis*, *op. cit.*, p. 374. *R. silvaticus* is near to *R. pyramidalis*, p. 376.

Subgenus CYLACTIS Stone bramble.
1. **Rubus saxatilis** L. On wet limestone. Fr. red. Illus. on pl. 29.

Subgenus CHAMAEMORUS
2. **Rubus chamaemorus** L. Cloud berry. On elevated moors. Fr. ultimately amber. Illus. on pl. 29.

Subgenus IDAEOBATUS
3. **Rubus idaeus** L. Raspberry. In woods on heaths, etc. Fr. felted, red or amber.

Subgenus EUBATUS. Fr. black.
Groups 4–11: Leaves 3–6-nate, or 3–7-nate.
Groups 4–7: Stem without stalked glands or pricklets.

Section *Suberecti*
4. **Rubus sulcatus** Vest ex Tratt. Stem tall, erect, furrowed; root creeping; panicle almost unarmed.

Section *Sylvatici*
5. **Rubus adspersus** Weihe. *R. carpinifolius* Weihe & Nees. Stem arching with strong yellow prickles; panicle racemose in the upper part; sepals patent under the fruit.
6. **Rubus silvaticus** Weihe & Nees. Prickles small; leaflets narrow.

Section *Discolores*
7. **Rubus ulmifolius** Schott. *R. discolor* auct. Leaves closely white-felted beneath; leaflets convex, usually narrow. Stamens equalling the styles.

Groups 8–11: Stem with stalked glands, acicles and pricklets.
Groups 8–9: Stem prickles subequal, seated on the angles.

Section *Vestiti*
8. **Rubus vestitus** Weihe & Nees. Densely hairy all over; prickles long, slender, straight, violet-purple; terminal leaflet round, short-pointed and evenly toothed.

Section *Radulae*
9. **Rubus radula** Weihe ex Boenn. Petals pink, rather small; prickles long and mostly straight; terminal leaflet ovate, gradually acuminate, white-felted beneath.

Groups 10–11: Stem prickles unequal, not confined to the angles of the stem; stalked glands and acicles numerous, some long and gland-tipped.

Section *Apiculati*
10. **Rubus euryanthemus** W. C. R. Wats. Petals white, narrow.

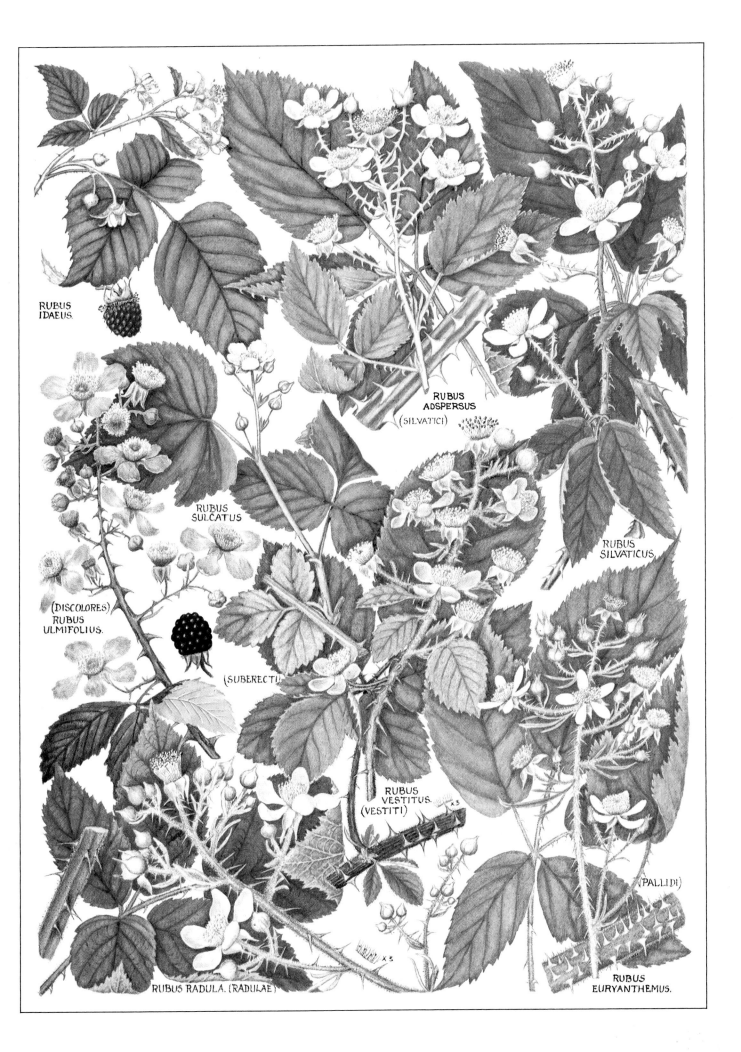

RUBUS
IDAEUS.

RUBUS
ADSPERSUS

(SILVATICI)

RUBUS
SULCATUS

RUBUS
SILVATICUS.

(DISCOLORES)
RUBUS
ULMIFOLIUS.

(SUBERECTI)

RUBUS
VESTITUS.
(VESTITI)

×3

(PALLIDI)

RUBUS RADULA. (RADULAE)

×3

RUBUS
EURYANTHEMUS.

Plate 29

Rosaceae *(continued)*

Section *Hystrices*
11. **Rubus dasyphyllus** (Rogers) E. S. Marshall. Petals pink; leaves thick, soft beneath, principal teeth turned outwards; stalked glands very long.

Groups 12–13: Leaves all ternate.

Section *Glandulosi*
12. **Rubus glandulosus** Bellardi. *R. bellardii* Weihe & Nees. Petals white; leaflets subequal, regular, elliptical, evenly toothed.

Subgenus GLAUCOBATUS
13. **Rubus caesius** L. Dewberry. On wet or calcareous soils. Fr. black, pruinose. The figure represents a hybrid.

Numbers 7, 8, 11, 13 desiderate or tolerate a loamy, clayey or calcareous soil; others restricted to soils that are siliceous or peaty or rich in humus.

Rubus saxatilis L. See text opposite pl. 28.

Rubus chamaemorus L. See text opposite pl. 28.

Dryas octopetala L. Mountain avens. Pedicel and calyx glandular; petals often 8; style feathery, persistent. Basic rocks, N. Wales, Teesdale, N. Scotland and Ireland, local. Flo. June–July.

Geum urbanum L. Wood avens. Flo. erect, yellow; head of achenes sessile; style persistent as a hooked awn. Woods, hedges and shady lanes, common. Flo. June–Aug.

Geum rivale L. Water avens. Flo. nodding, red; head of achenes stalked; style persistent as a hooked awn. Wet rocks and shady banks, mostly N. and N.W. Britain, local or rare elsewhere. Flo. May–Aug.

Geum × intermedium Ehrh. *G. rivale × urbanum*. Intermediate. Found in association with the parents. Widespread.

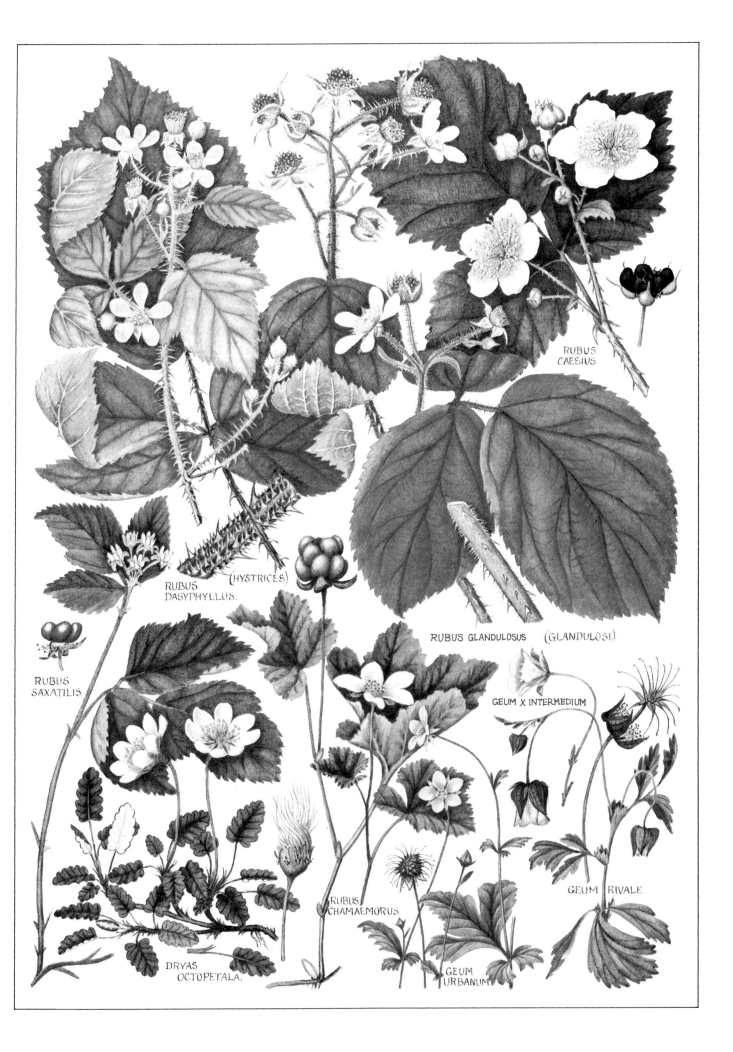

RUBUS
CAESIUS.

(HYSTRICES)

RUBUS
DASYPHYLLUS.

RUBUS GLANDULOSUS   (GLANDULOSI.)

RUBUS
SAXATILIS.

GEUM X INTERMEDIUM

GEUM RIVALE

RUBUS
CHAMAEMORUS

DRYAS
OCTOPETALA.

GEUM
URBANUM.

Plate 30

Rosaceae (continued)

Rosa pimpinellifolia L. Burnet rose. *R. spinosissima* auct. Stem creeping, with many small straight prickles; leaflets 3–5 pairs, glabrous; fr. purple. Sand dunes, cliffs and heaths, particularly near the sea, widespread. Flo. May–July.

Rosa rugosa Thunb. Japanese rose. Stem very prickly and rough; leaflets 2–4 pairs, elliptic; dark green and rugose above, felted below; flo. large, deep pink or white; fr. large red; sepals erect, persistent. Introd. Japan. Often planted for hedging and occurring in woods, thickets, on dunes and waste ground as a bird-sown introd., widespread. Flo. June–Aug.*

Rosa arvensis Huds. Field rose. Stem trailing, purplish; flo. white; fr. small; styles united in an exserted column. Wood borders, etc., common in S. and W. England, Wales and Ireland, rare in N. England and introd. in Scotland. Flo. June–July.

Rosa stylosa Desv. Stem stout, erect; pedicels long, hispid; disk conical; styles united in an exserted column. Woods and hedges on basic soils, mostly S. England and S. Ireland, locally common. Flo. June–July.

Rosa canina L. Dog rose. *R. systyla* Bast. Pedicels 1–2 cm, subglabrous; sepals falling early; stigmas conical, narrower than disk. Hedges, etc., widespread and common. Flo. June–July.

Rosa dumalis Bechst. *R. coriifolia* Fr. *R. afzeliana* auct. *R. glauca* Vill. ex Lois., non Pourr. Pedicels short, 1 cm, hidden in bracts; sepals persistent; stigmas flat, concealing disk. Hedges, etc., N. England and Scotland, very rare in S. England. Flo. June–July.

Rosa rubiginosa L. Sweet briar. *R. eglanteria* auct. Leaflets roundly oval, very glandular below and scented; pedicels short, glandular, hispid; sepals persistent; flo. usually deep pink. Wood borders, etc., mostly on calcareous soils, widespread. Flo. June–July.

Rosa tomentosa Sm. Downy rose. Stems arching, prickles curved; leaves pubescent, often densely so; pedicels up to 2 cm, glandular; sepals constricted at base; flo. 4 cm, pink; disk large, 4–6 times orifice. Woods borders, thickets, etc., mostly on calcareous soil, widespread, but rare in Scotland. Flo. June–July.

Rosa sherardii Davies. *R. omissa* Déségl. Stems slightly arching, prickles moderately curved; leaves rather glaucous; pedicels $\frac{1}{2}$–$1\frac{1}{2}$ cm; sepals short, slightly constricted, persistent; flo. often deep pink; styles villous; disk 3–$3\frac{1}{2}$ times orifice. Hedges, etc., frequent in Wales and N. England, local in Ireland, very rare in S. England. Flo. June–July.

Rosa villosa L. *R. mollis* Sm. Stems erect, prickles straight and slender; leaflets roundly oval, tomentose; sepals erect, persistent; pedicels short, hispid; fr. globose, hispid; flo. deep pink. Hedges, etc., frequent in N. Britain, local in W. Midlands and Wales, introd. in S. England. Flo. June–July.*

Rosa obtusifolia Desv. Leaves roundly ovate, pubescent or glandular beneath; pedicels short; sepals short, lobes broad. Hedges and thickets, England and Wales, local, rare in Ireland. Flo. June–July.*

Rosa micrantha Borrer ex Sm. Stems arching; leaflets ovate, glandular beneath; pedicels long, hispid; sepals falling early; flo. pink; styles glabrous. Woods and thickets, local in England and Wales, rare in Scotland and Ireland. Flo. June–July.

Rosa agrestis Savi. *R. sepium* Thuill., non Lam. Stems arching; leaflets narrow, tapering to base; pedicels smooth; styles subglabrous; fr. smooth; sepals falling early. Chiefly on calcareous soils, mostly S. England and Ireland, very local. Flo. June–July.

Rosa elliptica Tausch. *R. inodora* auct. Similar to *R. agrestis*, but stems erect; leaflets obovate, tapering below only; styles hairy; sepals more persistent. Hedges, Somerset to Huntingdonshire, very rare.*

ROSA
PIMPINELLIFOLIA

ROSA
TOMENTOSA

ROSA
SHERARDII

ROSA RUBIGINOSA

ROSA
MICRANTHA

R. DUMALIS

ROSA
CANINA. &

ROSA DUMALIS

ROSA STYLOSA.

ROSA ARVENSIS

Plate 31

Rosaceae *(continued)*

Sorbus torminalis (L.) Crantz. Wild service tree. *Pyrus torminalis* (L.) Ehrh. Leaves oval, deeply lobed, green beneath; fr. elongated, brown. Woods on clay and limestone soils, England. Flo. May–June.

Sorbus intermedia agg. Leaves elliptic with rounded ascending lobes, felted beneath; veins 7–11 pairs.*

Sorbus arranensis Hedlund. Leaves lobed at base about ½ way to midrib; greyish felted beneath; veins 7–9 pairs; fr. ovoid. Arran. Flo. May–June.

Sorbus pseudofennica E. F. Warb. *S arranensis × aucuparia.* Intermediate. Small tree; leaves ovate-oblong, but some with free basal leaflets. Arran. Flo. May–June.*

Sorbus leyana Wilmott. Leaves broader, cuneate at base; basal lobe nearly ½ way to midrib; petals and fr. a little larger than in previous species. S. Wales. Flo. May–June.*

Sorbus minima (A. Ley) Hedlund. Least white beam. *Pyrus minima* A. Ley. Leaves elliptic, twice as long as broad, base lobed about ½ way to midrib; petals 4 mm; fr. small 6–8 mm, subglobose. Limestone crags, S. Wales. Flo. May–June.

Sorbus intermedia (Ehrh.) Pers. *Pyrus intermedia* Ehrh. Leaves elliptic, lobed at base ¼–⅓ way to midrib, yellowish felted beneath; fr. very oblong. Introd. N. Europe. Planted, but freely regenerating. Flo. May.*

Sorbus anglica Hedlund. Cheddar white beam. *S. mougeotti* Soy.-Will. & Godr. var. *anglica* (Hedlund) C. E. Salmon. Leaves broadly ovate, about 1½ times as long as broad; lobed ⅛–¼ way to midrib, greyish felted beneath; fr. subglobose, with a few lenticels. Limestone rocks, Devon to Shropshire and Wales, also in Kerry. Flo. May.*

Sorbus aria agg. Leaves ovate or obovate, toothed or slightly lobed, white felted beneath; veins 7–14 pairs.

Sorbus aria (L.) Crantz. Common white beam. *Pyrus aria* (L.) Ehrh. Leaves oval, usually curved to base; veins 10–14 pairs; fr. longer than broad, scarlet; lenticels small. Woods on calcareous and limestone soils, S. England, though frequently planted elsewhere. Flo. May–June.

Sorbus × pinnatifida (Sm.) Düll. *S. aria × aucuparia. S. × thuringaca* (Ilse) Fritsch. Leaves oblong, sometimes with 1–3 pairs of free leaflets at base; serrate; green and glabrous above, greyish-green felted beneath; veins 10–12 pairs; fr. subglobose, scarlet; lenticels few, inconspicuous. Sometimes found where the parents grow together, also occurs as a planted tree. Flo. May–June.*

Sorbus × rotundifolia (Bechst.) Hedlund. *S. aria × torminalis. S. × vagensis* Wilmott. Tree, with wide crown and spreading branches; leaves ovate, deeply lobed, with acuminate lobes finely, and sometimes doubly, serrate, teeth small, yellowish-green above, greenish-grey felted beneath; fr. brownish, longer than broad. Woods on limestone soil. Wye Valley. Flo. May–June.*

Sorbus leptophylla E. F. Warb. Shrub similar to *S. aria* but leaves yellow or dark green above; teeth curved on outer margins; veins *c.* 11 pairs. Limestone rocks, S. Wales. Flo. May.*

Sorbus wilmottiana E. F. Warb. Shrub or small tree, similar to *S. aria* but leaves bright green above, teeth curved on outer margins; veins *c.* 8–9 pairs; fr. crimson. Woods on limestone soil, Cheddar Gorge. Flo. May–June.*

Sorbus eminens E. F. Warb. Shrub or small tree similar to *S. aria* but leaves bright green above, teeth symmetrical; veins *c.* 10–11 pairs. Woods on limestone soil, Wye Valley and Avon Gorge. Flo. May–June.*

Sorbus hibernica E. F. Warb. Irish white beam. Leaves oval, shortly cuneate at the base; veins 9–11 pairs; teeth triangular, acute, turned outwards; fr. broader than long. Woods on limestone soil, Ireland. Flo. May.*

Sorbus porrigentiformis E. F. Warb. *S. porrigens* Hedlund. *pro parte.* Leaves obovate, rounded above, tapering below, 1½ times as long as broad, greyish felted beneath; veins 8–10 pairs; fr. broader than long, crimson, with few large lenticels. Woods on limestone soil, S. Devon to Mendips, Wye Valley and Wales. Flo. May–June.

Sorbus lancastriensis E. F. Warb. Shrub similar to *S. aria* but teeth of leaves symmetrical and pointing outwards; veins *c.* 8–10 pairs; fr. crimson with a number of large lenticels towards the base. Limestone rocks, Lancashire and Cumbria. Flo. May–June.*

Sorbus rupicola (Syme) Hedlund. Rock white beam. Leaves obovate, rounded above, length *c.* double the breadth, white felted beneath; veins 7–9 pairs; fr. broader than long, with many small lenticels. Limestone rocks, S. Devon to Scotland and N. and W. Ireland. Flo. May–June.*

Sorbus vexans E. F. Warb. Small tree, similar to *S. aria* but leaves obovate, with cuneate base; veins *c.* 8–10 pairs; fr. longer than broad, with few lenticels. Rocky woods near coast, Somerset and S. Devon. Flo. May.*

Sorbus latifolia agg. Broad-leaved white beam. Leaves with triangular lobes; veins 7–9 pairs; fr. orange, subglobose or longer than broad.

Sorbus bristoliensis Wilmott. Leaves obovate; anthers pink; fr. longer than broad, bright orange, with small lenticels. Rocky woods on limestone soil, Avon Gorge. Flo. May–June.*

Sorbus subcuneata Wilmott. Leaves elliptic, tapered at the base, white-felted beneath; anthers cream; fr. subglobose, brownish-orange. Open oakwoods, Somerset and Devon. Flo. May–June.*

Sorbus devoniensis E. F. Warb. Leaves ovate, round at base, with shallow triangular lobes; greyish-green felted beneath; fr. subglobose. Woods, Devon, E. Cornwall and Ireland. Flo. May–June.*

Sorbus aucuparia L. Rowan, mountain ash. *Pyrus aucuparia* (L.) Ehrh. Leaves pinnate, all leaflets separate; flo. many, smaller than in other species. Woods and scrub, etc., on light soils, native in W. and N. Britain, probably introd., though readily regenerating, elsewhere. Flo. May–June.

Pyrus pyraster Burgsd. Pear. *P. communis* auct. Flo. on very short rachis; petals broad, very concave, white; fr. 2–4 cm, sometimes tapered into stalk. England, widespread but uncommon. Flo. April–May.

Pyrus cordata Desv. Lesser pear. Leaves rather small, round, subglabrous; flo. on longer rachis, smaller; petals narrow, obovate, pink; fr. very small, 1–2 cm, obovoid or round. Hedges near Plymouth, Devonshire, very rare. Flo. April–May.

Malus sylvestris Mill. Crab apple. *Pyrus malus* L. Small tree; flo. in an umbel; styles united below. Woods, common. Flo. May.

Malus domestica Borkh. Cultivated apple. *Malus sylvestris* Mill. ssp. *mitis* (Wallr.) Mansf. *Pyrus malus* L. var. *mitis* Wallr. Similar to *M. sylvestris* but young twigs tomentose, glabrous later; buds hairy; leaves obtuse, pubescent beneath; pedicels, calyx, etc., woolly; fr. largish, sometimes sweet. Introd. S.E. Europe. Naturalized in hedges, woods, etc. Flo. May.*

Mespilus germanica L. Medlar. Small thorny tree; stalks pubescent; leaves large; sepals persistent, linear. Introd. S.E. Europe. Naturalized in hedges, mostly England, rare. Flo. May–June.*

Crataegus laevigata (Poir.) DC. Midland hawthorn. *C. oxyacanthoides* Thuill. Leaf lobes broader than long, without auxillary hairs beneath; styles 2. Woods on heavy soils, S. and E. England, the Midlands and Wales, rare in N. England and Ireland, and introd. in Scotland. Flo. May–June.

Crataegus × media Bechst. *C. laevigata × monogyna.* Intermediate. Common where the parents grow together.*

Crataegus monogyna Jacq. Hawthorn. Leaf lobes longer than broad, very variable, with hairs in axils beneath; style 1. Hedges, etc., common, though often planted. Flo. May–June.

Cotoneaster integerrimus Medic. Wild cotoneaster. Leaves 15–40 mm or more, rounded at base; petals erect, pink. Rocks, Great Orme's Head, Caernarvon, very rare. Flo. April–June.

SORBUS
ARRANENSIS.

SORBUS
AUCUPARIA.

SORBUS
PORRIGENTI·
~FORMIS

SORBUS
MINIMA

SORBUS
ARIA

SORBUS
LATIFOLIA

MALUS SYLVESTRIS

SORBUS
TORMINALIS.

PYRUS
PYRASTER.

PYRUS
CORDATA

CRATAEGUS
MONOGYNA

CRATAEGUS LAEVIGATA

COTONEASTER
INTEGERRIMUS

Plate 32

Rosaceae *(continued)*

Cotoneaster microphyllus Wall. ex Lindl. Small-leaved cotoneaster. Stem prostrate; leaves 5–8 mm, or less, obovate; petals white and spreading. Introd. India. Bird-sown from gardens and naturalized on banks, in chalk pits, etc., uncommon. Flo. May–June.*

Cotoneaster simonsii Bak. Himalayan cotoneaster. Stem erect; leaves 12–25 mm, green and glabrous above, sparsely pubescent beneath, cuneate at base; petals erect, pink. Introd. India. Bird-sown from gardens and naturalized on cliffs, heaths, etc., uncommon. Flo. May–July.*

Cotoneaster horizontalis Decne. Wall cotoneaster. Similar to *C. simonsii*, but procumbent with horizontal spreading stems; leaves small, dark green, glabrous above. Introd. China. Bird-sown from gardens and naturalized on cliffs, old walls, etc., uncommon. Flo. May–July.*

Amelanchier lamarckii F. Schroeder. Juneberry. *A. grandiflora* Rehder, *A. confusa* auct., non Hyl. *A. laevis* auct. eur., non Wieg. Small tree or shrub to 12 m, similar to *Prunus padus*, but flo. in erect racemes. Introd. Naturalized on heaths and commons, etc., mostly S. England. Flo. June–July.*

Saxifragaceae

Saxifraga oppositifolia L. Purple saxifrage. Stems many, prostrate; leaves many, opposite; flo. rose-purple or pink, solitary. Mountain rocks, mostly N. Britain and Ireland. Flo. April–June.

Saxifraga nivalis L. Alpine saxifrage. Leaves in basal rosette, broadly obovate; stem naked; flo. in a close head. High mountain rocks, mostly Scotland, rare. Flo. July–Aug.

Saxifraga stellaris L. Starry saxifrage. Stems with small rosettes of subsessile leaves; sepals reflexed. Wet mountain rocks and streamsides, local. Flo. June–July.

Saxifraga hirculus L. Marsh saxifrage. Erect, leafy, with prostrate basal branches; lower leaves petiolate; flo. yellow, ovary free. Wet moorland, etc. N. England, Scotland and Ireland, rare.

Saxifraga aizoides L. Yellow saxifrage. Prostrate with ascending branches; leaves sessile; flo. several, yellow, ovary partly inferior. Wet mountain rocks, mostly N. England, Scotland and Ireland, local. Flo. June–Aug.

Saxifraga umbrosa L. London pride. Leaves oval with obtuse teeth, terminal tooth shorter and broader; petiole shorter than blade, very ciliate. Introd. S. Europe. Rocks, etc., Yorkshire, introd. before 1800.

Saxifraga spathularis Brot. St Patrick's-cabbage. *S. umbrosa* auct., non L. Leaves oval, with triangular equal teeth; petiole longer than blade, sparsely ciliate. Mountain rocks, Ireland. Flo. June–Aug.*

Saxifraga × urbium D. A. Webb. London pride. *S. spathularis × umbrosa*. *S. umbrosa* L. var. *crenatoserrata* Bab. Leaves subacute with equal triangular teeth; flo. stem less glandular, sterile. Garden escape. Naturalized in grassy places. Flo. June–Aug.*

Saxifraga hirsuta L. Kidney saxifrage. *S. geum* L. *S. lactiflora* Pugsley. Leaves orbicular or reniform, cordate, crenate; petiole slender, much longer than blade. Rocks, S.W. Ireland. Flo. May–July. Figure is probably that of *S. × polita* auct. = *S. hirsuta × spathularis*.

Saxifraga cymbalaria L. Annual up to 30 cm; stems and leaves fleshy; leaves rounded, crenate or dentate; petals shiny, buttercup-yellow, up to 5 mm long. Garden escape. Established in damp places, by walls, etc., widespread but uncommon. Flo. June–Sept.*

Saxifraga tridactylites L. Rue-leaved saxifrage. Annual, plant small, glandular; leaves 3–5-lobed, upper entire. Dry grassy places on light soils and wall tops. Flo. April–June.

Saxifraga granulata L. Meadow saxifrage. Stem with large bulbils at base; leaves cordate, with rounded lobes. Meadows, England, except the S.W., where it is introd., rare in Wales and mostly introd. in Ireland. Flo. April–June.

Saxifraga cernua L. Drooping saxifrage. Stem erect, with small red bulbils in axils; flo. terminal or none. Rock ledges on mountain tops, Perthshire, Inverness and Argyll, very rare. Flo. July.

Saxifraga rivularis L. Highland saxifrage. Stems weak, trailing, ascending in flo.; leaves reniform, 3–7-lobed. Wet rocks on high mountains, Scotland, very rare. Flo. July–Aug.

Saxifraga cespitosa L. Tufted saxifrage. Plant small, compact; leaf lobes oblong, obtuse; glandular hairs short, dense. Mountain rocks, N. Wales and Scotland, very rare. Flo. May–July.

Saxifraga hartii D. A. Webb. Similar to *S. cespitosa*, but plant looser, leaves larger and densely covered with short glandular hairs, lobes subacute; petals larger, pure white. Sea cliffs, Arranmore Island, Donegal. Flo. May–June.*

Saxifraga decipiens Ehrh. Irish saxifrage. *S. rosacea* Moench. Plant rather compact, with erect barren branches, and few longer glandular hairs. Wet mountain rocks, mostly W. Ireland, local, very rare in N. Wales. Flo. May–July.

Saxifraga hypnoides L. Mossy saxifrage. Barren branches long and prostrate, often with axillary tufts; leaf lobes acute, aristate. Wet calcareous rocks, Somerset and Wales to N. Scotland, and Ireland. Flo. May–July.
Var. **platypetala** Sm. Axillary leaf buds few or o; petals broad, contiguous, flat.

Chrysosplenium oppositifolium L. Opposite-leaved golden saxifrage. Upper leaves opposite; basal leaf petiole equalling blade. Wet shady places, local. Flo. March–May.

Chrysosplenium alternifolium L. Alternate-leaved golden saxifrage. Upper leaves alternate or only 1; basal petioles longer than blade. In similar habitats to *C. oppositifolium*, but less frequent. Flo. March–June.

Parnassiaceae

Parnassia palustris L. Grass-of-Parnassus. Flo. solitary; stamens 5, and 5 staminoides, fringed with stalked glands. Wet moorlands and fixed dunes, widespread but absent from S.W. England and now very rare in S. England and the Midlands. Flo. July–Sept.

SAXIFRAGA
OPPOSITIFOLIA.

CHRYSOSPLENIUM
OPPOSITIFOLIUM.

CHRYSOSPLENIUM
ALTERNIFOLIUM.

SAXIFRAGA.
STELLARIS.

SAXIFRAGA
RIVULARIS.

SAXIFRAGA
UMBROSA.

SAXIFRAGA
TRIDACTYLITES.

SAXIFRAGA NIVALIS.

SAXIFRAGA
CERNUA.

SAXIFRAGA
HIRSUTA.

SAXIFRAGA
CESPITOSA.

SAXIFRAGA
GRANULATA

SAXIFRAGA
AIZOIDES.

SAXIFRAGA
DECIPIENS

SAXIFRAGA HIRCULUS.

S. HYPNOIDES
VAR. PLATYPETALA

SAXIFRAGA HYPNOIDES.

PARNASSIA
PALUSTRIS.

Plate 33

Grossulariaceae

Ribes rubrum L. Red currant. *R. vulgare* Lam. *R. sylvestre* (Lam.) Mert. & Koch. Leaves not strong smelling; inflo. drooping; receptacle with a raised rim; sepals broader than long. Woods, streamsides, etc., local. Flo. April–May.

Ribes spicatum Robson. Downy currant. *R. petraeum* auct. Inflo. erect; receptacle deeper, without raised rim; sepals circular. Woods on limestone soil, N. England to N. Scotland. Flo. May.

Ribes nigrum L. Black currant. Leaves strong smelling; inflo. drooping, campanulate; fr. black. Woods, streamsides, etc., local. Flo. April–May.

Ribes sanguineum Pursh. Flowering currant. Leaves bluntly lobed, pubescent beneath; flo. pink; fr. dark bluish-black, pruinose,. Garden outcast or bird-sown from gardens. Naturalized by streams, etc., uncommon. Flo. April–May.*

Ribes alpinum L. Mountain currant. Flo. dioecious in erect spikes; male numerous, small; female few; fr. red. Limestone rocks, mainly N. England and Wales. Flo. April–May.

Ribes uva-crispa L. Gooseberry. *R. grossularia* L. Stems spinous at the nodes; flo. 1 or 2; fr. usually bristly. Woods and hedges, native, or bird-sown from gardens. Flo. March–April.

Crassulaceae

Crassula tillaea L.-Garland. Mossy stonecrop. *Tillaea muscosa* L. Plant small and reddish with minute, crowded, oval leaves; flo. very small, axillary. Bare places on heaths on sandy or gravelly soils, S. Devon to Norfolk, local. Flo. June–July.

Crassula aquatica (L.) Schönl. *Tillaea aquatica* L. Leaves linear, not crowded; flo. minute, axillary. Wet mud, Yorkshire, extinct. Discovered in Inverness-shire in 1969, very rare. Flo. June–July.

Crassula helmsii (Kirk) Cockayne. *Tillaea helmsii* Kirk. *T. recurva* (Hook. f.). Hook. F. Perennial, succulent herb, to 30 cm, robust and erect in water, prostrate and smaller on wet mud; leaves 4–15 mm, opposite, sessile, linear-lanceolate to ovate, glabrous, fleshy; flo. solitary, axillary; petals 4, 1.7×1.2 mm, white to pale pink. Introd. Australasia. Cultivated by aquarists, naturalized in ponds as an outcast. Flo. Aug.–Oct.*

Sedum telephium L. Orpine. *S. purpureum* auct.
Ssp. **telephium**. Leaves flat, rounded at base; flo. reddish-purple, rarely white. Dry woods, rocks, etc., widespread, but rare in N. Scotland, and introd. in Ireland. Flo. July–Sept.*
Ssp. **fabaria** (Koch) Kirschleger. *Sedum fabaria* Koch. Leaves all tapering at base, sometimes shortly stalked. Dry woods, hedge banks, etc., mostly England, Wales and Scottish Highlands, uncommon. Flo. July–Sept.

Sedum spurium Bieb. *S. stoloniferum* auct., non S. G. Gmel. Stems procumbent, creeping, forming dense mats with numerous ascending branches; leaves opposite, flat, obtuse; flo. pink in flat terminal cymes. Garden escape. Naturalized on hedge banks, waste ground, etc., widespread. Flo. July–Sept.*

Sedum dasyphyllum L. Thick-leaved stonecrop. Stems procumbent or ascending; leaves roundly obovoid, glandular. Introd. S. Europe. Walls and limestone rocks, uncommon. Flo. June July.

Sedum anglicum Huds. English stonecrop. Prostrate with short, erect, forked flo. stems; leaves spurred. Rocks, especially granite, and sandy soil, mostly near coast, local. Flo. June–Aug.

Sedum album L. White stonecrop. Prostrate, with erect much-branched flo. stems; leaves not spurred. Limestone rocks, Mendips and S. Devon, introd. on walls elsewhere. Flo. June–Aug.

Sedum acre L. Biting stonecrop. Creeping with ascending flo. stems with few short branches; leaves hot tasting. Limestone rocks and walls, railway tracks and on basic soils, common. Flo. June–July.

Sedum sexangulare L. Tasteless stonecrop. Similar to *S. acre*, with smaller flo. Introd. Europe. Walls, etc., uncommon. Flo. July–Aug.*

Sedum forsteranum Sm. Rock stonecrop. *S. rupestre* L. *pro parte*.
Ssp. **forsteranum**. Leaves linear, erect, tufted at ends of branches; flo. stems slender, tall, usually green, sometimes glaucous, branched; inflo. convex in flo. Damp rocks and cliffs, Devon to Wales, local. Flo. June–July.
Ssp. **elegans** (Lej.) E. F. Warb. *Sedum elegans* Lej. *S. rupestre* L. ssp. *elegans* (Lej.) Syme. Similar to ssp. *forsteranum* but glaucous and more robust; flat-topped inflo. Dry rocks and cliffs, Devon to Wales. Flo. June–July.*

Sedum rupestre L. Reflexed stonecrop. *S. reflexum* L. Leaves stout, recurved, equally distributed, not tufted; flo. larger. Introd. Europe. Old walls and rocks, local. Flo. June–Aug.

Sedum villosum L. Hairy stonecrop. Annual, erect, glandular, shortly branched; petals ovate, pink. Wet mountain rocks, Yorkshire to N. Scotland. Flo. June–July.

Umbilicus rupestris (Salisb.) Dandy. Navelwort. *Cotyledon umbilicus-veneris* auct. Leaves peltate; petals united in a tube; stamens 10. Rock crevices and walls, common on acid soils. Flo. June–Aug.

Rhodiola rosea L. Roseroot. *Sedum rosea* (L.) Scop. *S. rhodiola* (L.) DC. Rootstock thick and fleshy; flo. dioecious with 4 linear petals. Rock crevices, Wales to Scotland, and Ireland, local. Flo. May–Aug.

RIBES
SPICATUM.

RIBES
ALPINUM.

RIBES UVA-CRISPA.

RIBES
RUBRUM

RIBES NIGRUM.

SEDUM
DASYPHYLLUM

SEDUM
TELEPHIUM
SSP.
FABARIA

CRASSULA TILLAEA.

CRASSULA AQUATICA

SEDUM ANGLICUM.

SEDUM ALBUM.

SEDUM
VILLOSUM.

SEDUM
RUPESTRE

UMBILICUS
RUPESTRIS.

SEDUM ACRE.

SEDUM FORSTERANUM.

RHODIOLA
ROSEA

Plate 34

Droseraceae

Drosera rotundifolia L. Round-leaved sundew. Leaves orbicular, spreading, long-petioled; petiole hairy; flo. stem from centre. Wet moors and peat bogs, widespread. Flo. June–Aug.

Drosera anglica Huds. Great sundew. Leaves up to 3 cm, tapering into petiole; petiole glabrous; flo. stem from centre. Wet peat bogs, local. Flo. July–Aug.

Drosera × obovata Mert. & Koch. *D. anglica × rotundifolia.* Similar to *D. intermedia* but with a straight scape up to 3 times as long as the leaves. This sterile hybrid sometimes occurs where the parents grow together.*

Drosera intermedia Hayne. Oblong-leaved sundew. *D. longifolia* auct. Leaves 1 cm, obovate, tapering into petiole; flo. stem from base of rosette. Damp peaty moors, widespread. Flo. June–Aug.

Sarraceniaceae

Sarracenia purpurea L. Pitcherplant. Plant stout, up to 40 cm, with large erect clusters of root-leaves, splashed with green and purple; leaves tubular with a flap at the apex, the whole forming a 'pitcher', often containing water in which small insects drown; flo. purple, *c.* 6 cm wide, solitary or in few-flowered racemes, nodding on leafless stems; top of style umbrella-shaped. Introd. N. America. Naturalized in bogs, Roscommon and Westmeath, Ireland. Flo. June–July.*

Haloragaceae

Hippuris vulgaris L. Mare's-tail. Leaves narrow, linear, whorled; submerged leaves longer, more flaccid; flo. sessile; perianth almost o; stamen 1. Pools and slow streams, local. Flo. June–July.

Myriophyllum verticillatum L. Whorled water-milfoil. Leaves mostly 5 in a whorl, pectinate; floral bracts leaf-like, variable; lower flo. female. Ponds and slow streams, uncommon. Flo. July–Aug.

Myriophyllum spicatum L. Spiked water-milfoil. Leaves usually 4 in a whorl; flo. spike long, erect; bracts very short; upper flo. male with red petals. Ponds and slow streams, common. Flo. June–July.

Myriophyllum alterniflorum DC. Alternate water-milfoil. Leaves 3 or 4 in a whorl; flo. spike short, drooping in bud; petals yellowish. Lakes and slow streams and peaty water, rare. Flo. May–Aug.

Callitrichaceae

Callitriche stagnalis Scop. Common water-starwort. Leaves usually roundly obovate, about twice as long as broad, at least 3-veined; submerged leaves never linear; bracts usually deciduous; fr. nearly round, freely produced. Ponds, ditches, etc., very common. Flo. May–Sept.

Callitriche platycarpa Kütz. Various-leaved water-starwort. *C. polymorpha* auct. Leaves usually obovate or rhomboid, about 3 times as long as broad, 1-veined in submerged plants; bracts usually persistent; fr. small, nearly round, sparsely produced; styles long, deflexed, persistent. In similar habitats to *C. stagnalis.* Widespread and common, but rarely occurring above 150 m. Flo. May–Sept.

Callitriche obtusangula Le Gall. Blunt-fruited water-starwort. Leaves rhomboid-spathulate, forming rosettes; bracts persistent; fr. *c.* 1.5 mm, globose, grooved; styles long, persistent. Ponds, ditches, streams, etc., S. England, Wales and Ireland, local, rarer in the N. Flo. May–Sept.

Callitriche cophocarpa Sendtn. *C. polymorpha* Lönnr. Closely related to *C. obtusangula* but differs in a number of minor characters including smaller fr., *c.* 1 mm, suborbicular with deepish grooves. Perhaps introduced. Ponds, streams, etc., very rare or overlooked. Flo. May–Sept.*

Callitriche palustris L. *C. verna* auct. Similar to *C. platycarpa,* but fr. small, 1 mm, turgid, narrowed below in side view, edges keeled, converging above in end view; styles short, 2 mm, erect, soon falling off. The figure was drawn from a Devon specimen, but it is now said that all the available British material formerly referred to this species belongs to *C. platycarpa.*

Callitriche hamulata Kütz. *C. intermedia* Hoffm. Intermediate water-starwort. Leaves linear, widened and emarginate at apex; bracts deciduous; fr. small, sessile, black, about as long as broad; styles reflexed. Lakes, ditches, slow streams, etc., probably widespread. Flo. April–Sept.

Callitriche brutia Petagna. *C. pedunculata* DC. A complex plant closely related to *C. hamulata,* differs in being smaller, with shorter leaves, and brown (not black) fr. borne on slender peduncles. In similar situations to *C. hamulata.* Flo. May–Sept.

Callitriche hermaphroditica L. *C. autumnalis* L. Autumnal water-starwort. Leaves linear 10–20 mm long, widest at base; fr. large, 2 mm, of 4 separate winged lobes. Lakes and streams, mostly N. Britain. Flo. May–Sept.

Callitriche truncata Guss. Ssp. **occidentalis** (Rouy) Schotsman. Short-leaved water-starwort. Leaves linear, 5–10 mm, only slightly wider at base; fr. small, 1 mm, edges not winged. Ponds and ditches, mostly in S. half of England, rare and decreasing. Flo. May–Sept.

Ceratophyllaceae

Ceratophyllum demersum L. Rigid hornwort. Leaves once or twice forked; fr. with 2 spines at base. Ponds and dikes, widespread, mostly England and Ireland, local or rare in Wales and Scotland. Flo. June–Aug.

Ceratophyllum submersum L. Soft hornwort. Leaves 3 times forked; fr. without spines. In ponds and dikes, mostly S. and E. England, rare, and much confused with *C. demersum.* Flo. July–Sept.

Lythraceae

Lythrum portula (L.) D. A. Webb. Water-purslane. *Peplis portula* L. Stems prostrate, rooting; petals often 6, small, soon falling. Wet mud, especially on acid soils, local. Flo. June–Sept.

Lythrum salicaria L. Purple-loosestrife. Perennial, 60–120 cm; flo. 10–15 mm, clustered; styles and stamens of variable length. River banks, ditches and marshes, common. Flo. June–Aug.

Lythrum hyssopifolia L. Grass-poly. Annual, 10–25 cm; flo. 5 mm, solitary in axils. In pools that dry up in summer, mostly E. England, very rare and uncertain in appearance. Flo. June–July.

DROSERA
ROTUNDIFOLIA

DROSERA
INTERMEDIA

LYTHRUM
HYSSOPIFOLIA

DROSERA
ANGLICA

HIPPURIS
VULGARIS

LYTHRUM PORTULA

C. DEMERSUM

C.
OBTUSANGULA

MYRIOPHYLLUM
VERTICILLATUM.

C. BRUTIA

CALLITRICHE
HAMULATA

LYTHRUM
SALICARIA.

CALLITRICHE
HERMAPHRODITICA

MYRIOPHYLLUM
ALTERNIFLORUM.

CALLITRICHE
STAGNALIS.

MYRIOPHYLLUM
SPICATUM

CALLITRICHE
PALUSTRIS.

CALLITRICHE
PLATYCARPA

CALLITRICHE
TRUNCATA

CERATOPHYLLUM
SUBMERSUM

Plate 35

Onagraceae

Epilobium angustifolium L. Rose bay willowherb. *Chamaenerion angustifolium* (L.) Scop. Flo. horizontal; stamens long and drooping; petals a little unequal. Woodland clearings, waste and burnt ground, widespread and common. Flo. July–Sept.

Epilobium hirsutum L. Great willowherb. Stem up to 150 cm, terete, hairy; leaves sessile, hairy; stigma 4-lobed. Ditches and streamsides, common. Flo. July–Aug.

Epilobium parviflorum Schreb. Hoary willowherb. Stem up to 80 cm, terete, hairy; leaves oblong, sessile, softly hairy; stigma 4-lobed. Ditches and damp ground, common. Flo. June–Aug.

Epilobium montanum L. Broad-leaved willowherb. Stem up to 60 cm, slender, terete; leaves stalked, ovate, acute; stigma 4-lobed. Woods, hedges and cultivated ground, common. Flo. June–Aug.

Epilobium lanceolatum Seb. & Mauri. Spear-leaved willowherb. Stem with 4 slight ridges; leaves stalked, lanceolate; stigma 4-lobed. Dry banks, in woods and rock cuttings, S. England, the Midlands and Wales, introd. in Ireland. Flo. July–Sept.

Epilobium roseum Schreb. Pale willowherb. Stem up to 60 cm, with 2 raised lines; leaves stalked, tapering below; stigma entire, equalling style. Damp waste and cultivated ground, local. Flo. July–Aug.

Epilobium ciliatum Raf. American willowherb. *E. adenocaulon* Hausskn. Stem up to 1 m with 4 raised lines and glandular hairs; leaves rounded below; flo. small, pale; stigma entire, shorter than style. Introd. N. America. Woods, streamsides, walls, etc., widespread. Flo. June–Sept.*

Epilobium tetragonum L. Square-stalked willowherb. *E. adnatum* Griseb. *E. lamyi* F. W. Schultz. Leaves oblong, shining, sessile; stigma entire; fr. 7–10 mm, plant with small autumn rosettes. Ditches and damp places, common. Flo. July–Aug. *E. lamyi* is now regarded as conspecific with *E. tetragonum*.

Epilobium obscurum Schreb. Short-fruit willowherb. Stem up to 60 cm, with stolons and 4 raised lines; leaves short, sessile; stigma entire; fr. 4–6 cm. Ditches and wet shady places, common. Flo. July–Aug.

Epilobium palustre L. Marsh willowherb. Stem terete, with slender stolons; leaves linear-lanceolate; buds drooping; stigma entire. Peaty moorland bogs, marshes, etc., local. Flo. July–Aug.

Epilobium anagallidifolium Lam. Alpine willowherb. *E. alpinum* auct. Stem up to 10 cm, stoloniferous; leaves small, elliptical; flo. drooping. By mountain springs, N. Yorkshire northwards. Flo. July–Aug.

Epilobium alsinifolium Vill. Chickweed willowherb. Stem 5–20 cm, with white stolons; leaves ovate, dentate; flo. drooping. By mountain streams, Wales and N. Yorkshire northwards. Flo. July–Aug.

Epilobium brunnescens (Cockayne) Raven & Engelhorn. New Zealand willowherb. *E. pedunculare* var. *brunnescens* Cockayne. Stems slender, creeping; leaves suborbicular; fr. 2–4 cm, glabrous. Garden escape. Spreading by streamsides, on wet rocky places, moors, etc., mostly S.W. and N. England, Wales, Scotland and Ireland. Flo. June–July.*

Hybrids are frequent in the genus *Epilobium*; they are usually intermediate between the parent species and almost always sterile.

Fuchsia magellanica Lam. Fuchsia. *F. gracilis* Lindl. *F. riccartonii* auct. Shrub, up to 2 m; leaves toothed, oval-acuminate; flo. small, solitary, pendulous; sepals bright red; petals plum-purple; stigma and stamens exserted; fr. black. Cultivated for hedging purposes and naturalized in S.W. England, Wales and W. Ireland. Flo. June–Sept.*

Ludwigia palustris (L.) Ell. Hampshire-purslane. Stem prostrate below; flo. axillary, subsessile; stamens 4; petals 0. Shallow pools, New Forest, introd. elsewhere, rare. Flo. June.

The taxa of *Oenothera* found in Wales were monographed by Rostański and Ellis (1979), this also covered species found elsewhere in the British Isles and the following treatment is based on their revision.

Oenothera stricta Ledeb. ex. Link. Fragrant evening-primrose. *O. odorata* auct. europ., non Jacq. Stem up to 60 cm, erect, simple or branched, reddish; stem leaves oblong-lanceolate, sessile, bracts lanceolate-ovate with solitary flo. in each axil; flo. yellow; petals 12–35 mm long; capsule oblong or cylindrical. Garden escape. Naturalized on coastal dunes, waste ground, etc., mostly S. England and Wales, rare. Flo. June–Sept.*

Oenothera glazioviana Micheli ex Mart. Large-flowered evening-primrose. *O. erythrosepala* Borbás. *O. grandiflora* auct. *O. lamarckiana* auct. Stem up to 100 cm, erect, simple or branched, green, sometimes reddish below, with red bulbous-based hairs; stem leaves elliptic-lanceolate, subsessile; sepals red-striped, rarely green; flo. yellow; petals 30–50 mm long; capsule cylindrical tapering upwards, with red bulbous-based hairs. Garden escape. Naturalized in waste places, established on railway banks, etc., widespread and common. Flo. June–Sept.*

Oenothera biennis L. Common evening-primrose. Stem up to 100 cm, green, sometimes reddish below, without red bulbous-based hairs, but with green bulbous-based hairs; stem leaves elliptic or elliptic-lanceolate; sepals always green; flo. yellow; petals 10–50 mm long, broader than long; capsule cylindrical with glandular hairs. Garden escape. Naturalized on dunes, waste ground, etc., established on railway banks, widespread, but uncommon. Flo. June–Sept.*

Oenothera × fallax Renner emend. Rostański. *O. biennis × glazioviana*. *O. × velutirubata* Renner. Intermediate between the parents but stem with red bulbous-based hairs; leaves often crinkled with white or pink midribs; sepals red-striped; petals up to 28 mm long, broader than long; capsule cylindrical, densely glandular with some stiff hairs.*

Oenothera rubricaulis Klebahn. *O. muricata* L., 1767, *nom. confusum*. Similar to *O. glazioviana* but sepals always green; petals 10–22 mm long, often narrower than long. Garden escape. Naturalized on coastal dunes, W. Lancashire and probably elsewhere, rare. Flo. July–Sept.*

Oenothera cambrica Rostański. Similar to *O. biennis* but leaves lanceolate, flat; sepals always green; petals 20–30 mm long, as broad as long or slightly narrower; lower capsules without glandular hairs. Garden escape. Naturalized on coastal dunes, waste ground, etc., widespread, and possibly common but confused with *O. biennis* and *O. parviflora*. Flo. June–Sept.*

Circaea lutetiana L. Enchanter's-nightshade. Rhizomes overwintering; plant hairy; leaf base truncate, margin slightly denticulate; bracteoles 0; flo. widely spaced. Shady places, common. Flo. July.

Circaea alpina L. Alpine enchanter's-nightshade. Rhizomes overwinter; plant subglabrous; leaf base cordate, margin strongly dentate; flo. bracteolate, clustered when open. Shady places, Wales, N.W. England and N. Scotland, very local.

Circaea × intermedia Ehrh. Upland enchanter's-nightshade. *C. alpina × lutetiana*. Intermediate in most characters and always sterile. More widely dispersed in Wales, N.W. England, Scotland and N. Ireland, in areas where *C. alpina* is absent or extinct.*

EPILOBIUM
ANGUSTIFOLIUM

EPILOBIUM
HIRSUTUM

EPILOBIUM
ALSINIFOLIUM

EPILOBIUM
ANAGALLIDIFOLIUM

EPILOBIUM
PARVIFLORUM

EPILOBIUM
MONTANUM

E. TETRAGONUM

EPILOBIUM
PALUSTRE

EPILOBIUM
ROSEUM

EPILOBIUM
TETRAGONUM

EPILOBIUM OBSCURUM

EPILOBIUM
LANCEOLATUM

CIRCAEA
LUTETIANA

LUDWIGIA
PALUSTRIS.

CIRCAEA ALPINA.

Plate 36

Cucurbitaceae

Bryonia dioica Jacq. White bryony. *B. cretica* L. ssp. *anglica* Tutin. Climbing by tendrils; leaves 5-lobed; flo. greenish-white, male with 5 stamens, female with 3 bifid stigmas; fr. red. Hedges, etc., mostly S.E. and mid England, introd. in S.W. England and Scotland, absent from Ireland. Flo. May–Aug.

Umbelliferae

The Umbelliferae were monographed by Tutin (1980) and the nomenclature given here follows that treatment.

Hydrocotyle vulgaris L. Marsh pennywort. Stem creeping, rooting; leaves orbicular; flo. in small sessile whorls; fr. laterally compressed. Peaty bogs, pond verges, etc., common. Flo. July–Aug.

Eryngium maritimum L. Sea-holly. Very glaucous; radical leaves suborbicular; bracts very broad, lobes spine-pointed; flo. blue. Sandy sea-shores, widespread. Flo. July–Sept.

Eryngium campestre L. Field eryngo. Pale green; radical leaves pinnate; bracts with narrow lobes; flo. white. Grassy places, mostly near S.W. coast of England, very local and rare. Flo. July–Sept.

Astrantia major L. Astrantia. Radical leaves broadly lobed; bracts lanceolate; umbels simple; outer flo. male. Introd. Europe. Naturalized in grassy places, especially in Shropshire, rare.

Sanicula europaea L. Sanicle. Radical leaves roundly lobed; flo. in 2–3 partial umbels; outer male; calyx long and sharp; fr. with hooks. Woods on basic soils, common. Flo. May–Aug.

Physospermum cornubiense (L.) DC. Bladderseed. *Danaa cornubiensis* (L.) Burnat. Leaf segments stalked, laciniate; umbel rays and pedicels long; fr. broad. Woods, Cornwall, rare in S.W. Devon and Buckinghamshire. Flo. July–Aug.

Smyrnium olusatrum L. Alexanders. Leaves broad and celery-like; fr. becoming black; commissure narrow. Introd. Europe. Cliffs and hedge banks, particularly near the sea, S. and mid England, Wales and Ireland. Flo. April–May.

Smyrnium perfoliatum L. Similar to *S. olusatrum*, but with roundish upper leaves clasping the stem. Introd. S. Europe. Naturalized in grassy places, rare. Flo. May–June.*

Conium maculatum L. Hemlock. Stem up to 150 cm, spotted; foliage poisonous; fr. suborbicular; vittae o. Damp roadsides, hedges and river banks, common. Flo. June–Sept.

Bupleurum fruticosum L. Shrubby hare's-ear. Evergreen shrub up to 250 cm; stems slender, sometimes purplish; leaves bluish-green, alternate, oblong-lanceolate, entire, mucronate; flo. small, greenish-yellow in terminal umbels; bracts and bracteoles reflexed. Garden escape. Naturalized in a few localities, mostly S. England and S. Midlands. Flo. July–Aug.*

Bupleurum rotundifolium L. Thorow-wax. Stem up to 30 cm; leaves elliptic-ovate to suborbicular, upper perfoliate; bracteoles broadly ovate. Cornfields on basic soils, S. England, very rare or extinct. Flo. June–July.*

Bupleurum subovatum Link. False thorow-wax. *B. lancifolium* auct., non Hornem. *B. intermedium* auct. Annual. Similar to *B. rotundifolium* but smaller, and with leaves 3 times as long as wide, instead of twice as long as wide; fr. strongly tuberculate. Introd. S. Europe. Casual in gardens and waste places, introd. with bird seed or with chicken food, common. Flo. June–Oct.*

Bupleurum baldense Turra. Small hare's-ear. *B. opacum* (Ces.) Lange. *B. aristatum* auct. Plant up to 10 cm; bracteoles ovate, concealing the sessile flowers. Dry banks near the sea, Devon, Sussex and Channel Isles. Flo. June–July.

Bupleurum tenuissimum L. Slender hare's-ear. Annual; slender, wiry, erect, up to 50 cm; bracts and bracteoles subulate. Salt marshes, England and Wales. Flo. July–Sept.

Bupleurum falcatum L. Sickle-leaved hare's-ear. Perennial; stem hollow; upper leaves and bracteoles linear-lanceolate. Formerly in hedges and waste places, in Essex, but now lost. Flo. July–Oct.

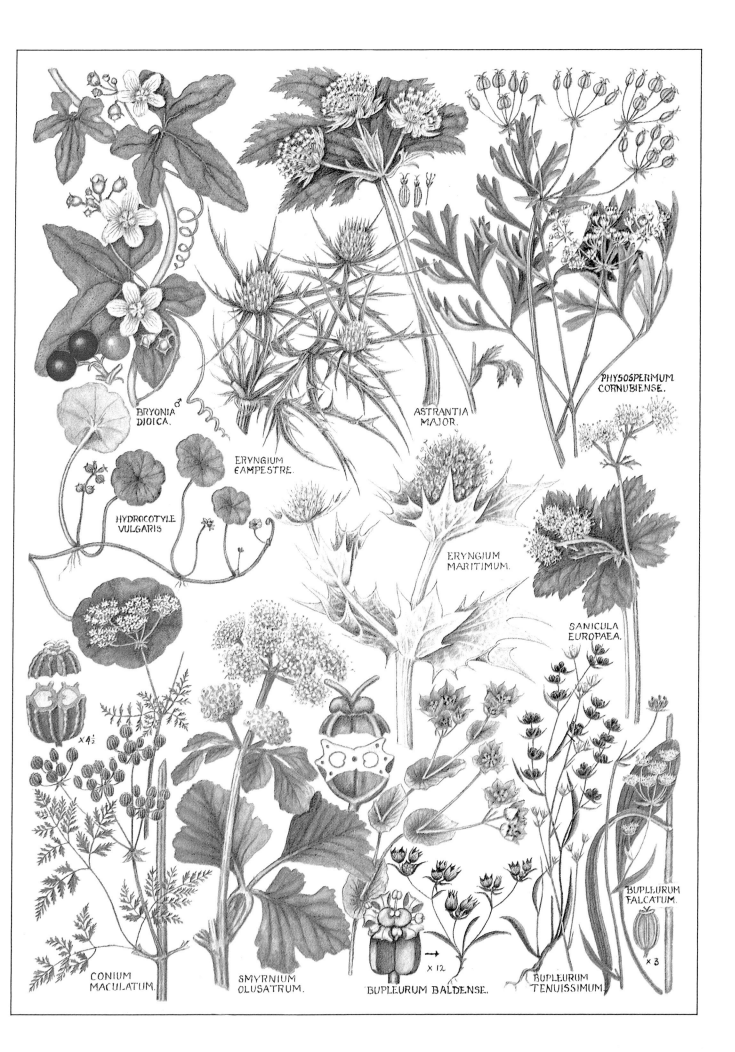

BRYONIA
DIOICA.

ASTRANTIA
MAJOR.

PHYSOSPERMUM
CORNUBIENSE.

ERYNGIUM
CAMPESTRE.

HYDROCOTYLE
VULGARIS

ERYNGIUM
MARITIMUM.

SANICULA
EUROPAEA.

× 4½

× 12

BUPLEURUM
FALCATUM.

× 3

CONIUM
MACULATUM.

SMYRNIUM
OLUSATRUM.

BUPLEURUM BALDENSE.

BUPLEURUM
TENUISSIMUM.

Plate 37

Umbelliferae *(continued)*

Trinia glauca (L.) Dumort. Honewort. Stem up to 20 cm; leaf segments linear; male umbels *c.* 15 mm, female *c.* 5 cm. Dry limestone hills, S. Devon, N. Somerset and W. Gloucestershire. Flo. May–July.

Apium graveolens L. Wild celery. Leaves with broad segments, lower segments stalked; umbels subsessile. Wet places and ditches, mostly near the sea, widespread. Flo. June–Aug.

Apium nodiflorum (L.) Lag. Fool's water-cress. *Helosciadum nodiflorum* (L.) Koch. Ascending from a creeping base; leaves pinnate; umbels often nearly sessile. Muddy ditches and pond verges, common in S. England, the Midlands and Ireland, local in Wales and N. England, rare in Scotland. Flo. July–Aug.

Apium nodiflorum × repens. Intermediate between the parents, often with a coarse stem and peduncled umbels, though the peduncles vary greatly in length. Very rare. Sometimes occurs in absence of the parents.*

Apium repens (Jacq.) Lag. Creeping marshwort. Stem entirely creeping; leaf segments broadly oval; umbels peduncled. Wet places, Oxfordshire, local and rare. Flo. July–Aug.

Apium inundatum (L.) Reichb. f. Lesser marshwort. *Helosciadum inundatum* (L.) Koch. Floating; segments of submerged leaves capillary, of upper 3-lobed; umbel rays up to 10 mm. Ponds and dikes, widespread but rather local. Flo. June–July.

Apium × moorei (Syme) Druce. *A. inundatum × nodiflorum*. Similar to, but larger than, *A. inundatum*, but with linear segments to lower leaves. This sterile hybrid sometimes occurs where the parents grow together. Locally common in Ireland, rare in England.*

Bunium bulbocastanum L. Great pignut. *Carum bulbocastanum* (L.) Koch. Perennial; root a black tuber 1–2.5 cm diam.; leaf segments narrow; fr. oblong. Banks, grassy places, etc., on calcareous soils, Hertfordshire, Buckinghamshire, Bedfordshire and Cambridgeshire, local. Flo. June–July.

Cicuta virosa L. Cowbane. Plant strong-smelling; stem up to 120 cm, hollow; leaf segments linear-lanceolate; bracteoles many. Ditches and marshes, rare, except in Ireland where it is local. Flo. July–Aug.

Ammi majus L. Bullwort. Stem up to 1 m, glaucous; leaves pinnate or bipinnate, serrate; bracts several, pinnate; bracteoles linear; fr. oblong-ovoid. S. Europe. Waste ground, rare. Flo. July–Sept.*

Ammi visnaga (L.) Lam. Similar to *A. majus* but rays thicken and become erect following flowering, and bracts are deflexed. Introd. Mediterranean region. Waste ground, rare. Flo. July–Sept.*

Petroselinum crispum (Mill.) Nyman. Garden parsley. *Carum petroselinum* (L.) Benth. Leaves deltoid, tripinnate; bracts with hyaline margins; flo. yellowish. Garden escape. Naturalized on walls and rocks, especially limestone. Flo. June–Aug.*

Petroselinum segetum (L.) Koch. Corn parsley. *Carum segetum* Benth. Leaves linear, simply pinnate, segments ovate; bracts subulate; flo. white, anthers purple. Grassy places, particularly near the sea, mostly S. England, Wales and Ireland. Flo. Aug.–Sept.

Carum verticillatum (L.) Koch. Whorled caraway. Perennial; stem solid; leaf segments capillary and whorled; bracts lanceolate; anthers pink. Damp acid meadows, mostly W. England to W. Scotland and Ireland, local and rare. Flo. July–Aug.

Carum carvi L. Caraway. Biennial; stem 30–60 cm, striate, hollow; leaf segments linear; fr. used for flavouring. Introd. Europe. Naturalized in grassy places, on waste ground, etc., rather rare. Flo. June–July.

Sium latifolium L. Greater water-parsnip. Stem up to 200 cm, hollow, grooved; petioles sheathing; leaf segments regularly serrate. Fens and marshes, mostly E. England, local. Flo. July–Aug.

TRINIA
GLAUCA.

CICUTA
VIROSA.

APIUM
GRAVEOLENS

CARUM
VERTICILLATUM

CARUM
CARVI

PETROSELINUM
SEGETUM.

BUNIUM
BULBOCASTANUM.

SIUM
LATIFOLIUM.

A.REPENS.

×3

APIUM
INUNDATUM.

APIUM NODIFLORUM.

×3

Plate 38

Umbelliferae *(continued)*

Berula erecta (Huds.) Coville. Lesser water-parsnip. *Sium erectum* Huds. *S. angustifolium* L. Stem up to 80 cm; leaf segments *c*. 5 cm, irregularly serrate; flo. 2 mm. Marshes and ditches, local. Flo. July–Sept.

Sison amomum L. Stone parsley. Umbels small, with few rays and few minute flo.; plant aromatic. Hedge banks, S. England and Midlands, common on basic soils, local in Wales. Flo. July–Sept.

Falcaria vulgaris Bernh. Longleaf. Leaves with long linear or strap-shaped segments, regularly serrate; flo. small, yellow. Introd. Europe. Naturalized in a few places, S. and E. England, rare. Flo. July–Sept.*

Aegopodium podagraria L. Ground-elder. Stem up to 75 cm, hollow, with white rhizomes; leaflets broad; fr. without vittae. Waste places, and as a garden weed, common. Flo. May–July.

Conopodium majus (Gouan) Loret. Pignut. *C. denudatum* Koch. *Bunium flexuosum* Stokes. Root tuberous; petioles sheathing; leaf segments and fr. narrow; styles short. Woods and shaded sides of fields, common. Flo. May–June.

Pimpinella major (L.) Huds. Greater burnet-saxifrage. *P. magna* L. Stem up to 1 m, ridged, glabrous, purple below; leaves broad, simply pinnate; styles equalling petals. Grassy places and road-sides, local. Flo. July–Aug.

Pimpinella saxifraga L. Burnet-saxifrage. Stem up to 50 cm, subterete, rough; leaflets ovate or in linear segments; styles much shorter than petals. Grassy places, except on acid soils, common. Flo. July–Aug.

Myrrhis odorata (L.) Scop. Sweet cicely. Plant up to 1 m, aromatic; male flo. on shorter rays; fr. 15–25 mm, oblong with 10 ridges. Grassy places and hedge banks, N. England and S. Scotland, introd. elsewhere. Flo. May–June.

Chaerophyllum temulentum L. Rough chervil. Stem hairy, purple-spotted, swollen below nodes; leaves dark green, hairy. Hedge banks, common, except mid Wales, Scotland and Ireland where it is local. Flo. June–July.

Chaerophyllum aureum L. Golden chervil. Stem glabrous, swollen; leaves yellow-green, glabrous above; fr. *c*. 10 mm. Introd. Europe. Naturalized locally in S. Scotland and elsewhere. Flo. July.*

Scandix pecten-veneris L. Shepherd's-needle. Umbels of 1–2 rays only; bracteoles ciliate; fr. with long beak, 30–70 mm. Cultivated land, mostly S. and E. England, local and decreasing. Flo. April–July.

Anthriscus caucalis Bieb. Bur chervil. *A. vulgaris* Pers., non Bernh., *A. neglecta* Boiss. & Reut. Stem glabrous; peduncle short; rays few; flo. minute; fr. oval, muricate. Hedges and waste places, often near the sea, local, rare in Scotland. Flo. June–July.

Anthriscus cerefolium (L.) Hoffm. Garden chervil. Stem pubescent above nodes; peduncles very short, pubescent; flo. 2 mm; fr. 10 mm, smooth. Introd. E. Europe. Naturalized in waste places, rare. Flo. May–June.*

Anthriscus sylvestris (L.) Hoffm. Cow parsley. Stem pubescent; peduncle long; rays many; flo. 3–4 mm; fr. oblong, smooth. Hedgebanks, widespread, except in N. Scotland and W. Ireland. Flo. April–June.

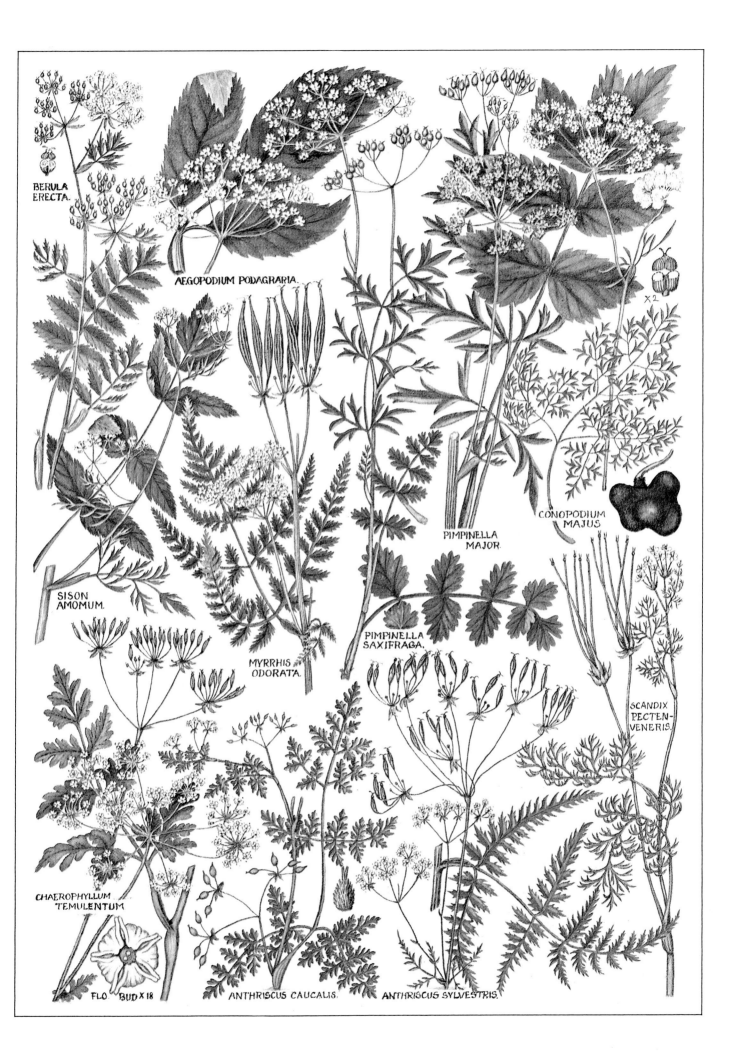

BERULA
ERECTA.

AEGOPODIUM PODAGRARIA.

X 2

CONOPODIUM
MAJUS.

PIMPINELLA
MAJOR.

SISON
AMOMUM.

MYRRHIS
ODORATA.

PIMPINELLA
SAXIFRAGA.

SCANDIX
PECTEN-
VENERIS.

CHAEROPHYLLUM
TEMULENTUM.

FLO. BUD X 18

ANTHRISCUS CAUCALIS.

ANTHRISCUS SYLVESTRIS.

Plate 39

Umbelliferae *(continued)*

Seseli libanotis (L.) Koch. Moon carrot. Leaf lobes oblong; peduncle long; rays, bracts and fr. pubescent; fr. ovoid. Grassy places on calcareous soils, Sussex to Cambridgeshire, local. Flo. July–Aug.

Foeniculum vulgare Mill. Fennel. Stem 120–150 cm, striate, glaucous; leaf segments long, capillary, scented. Sea cliffs, Wales and Norfolk southwards, rare in Scotland, on waste ground inland. Flo. July–Oct.

Crithmum maritimum L. Rock samphire. Stem up to 40 cm; leaves fleshy; rays stout; fr. corky. Sea cliffs, widely distributed. Flo. June–Sept.

Oenanthe fistulosa L. Tubular water-dropwort. Stem a hollow tube; leaf segments linear; blade shorter than hollow petiole; rays 2·5. Shallow pools, dikes and marshes, mostly S. England, Midlands, Wales and Ireland. Flo. July–Sept.

Oenanthe pimpinelloides L. Corky-fruited water-dropwort. Tubers distant, obovate; stem solid; leaf blade longer than petiole; fr. cylindrical. Meadows, mostly S. England. Flo. June–Aug.

Oenanthe silaifolia Bieb. Narrow-leaved water-dropwort. Roots thickened from base; stem hollow, ribbed; rays thick in fr.; fr. constricted below. Damp meadows, mostly E. and S. England and Midlands, rare. Flo. June.*

Oenanthe crocata L. Hemlock water-dropwort. Stem 120–150 cm, hollow, grooved; leaves with broad segments; umbels 15–20 cm wide; rays 15–25, slender. Boggy places and beds of streams, widespread but rare in E. England. Flo. June–July.

Oenanthe lachenalii C. C. Gmel. Parsley water-dropwort. Roots cylindrical; stem solid; rays 7–12, slender; fr. ovoid, reddish. Salt marshes and fens, widespread. Flo. June–Sept.

Oenanthe aquatica (L.) Poir. Fine-leaved water-dropwort. *O. phellandrium* Lam. Segments of submerged leaves capillary; peduncles short; rays 7–12; fr. 3–4 mm. Ponds, dikes and fen ditches, widespread. Flo. June–Sept.

Oenanthe fluviatilis (Bab.) Colem. River water-dropwort. Segments of submerged leaves cut into narrow lobes; peduncles short; fr. 5–6 mm. Ponds and streams, N. to Yorkshire, local in Ireland. Flo. July–Sept.

Aethusa cynapium L. Fool's parsley.
Ssp. **cynapium**. Stem 30–80 cm, hollow, striate; bracteoles mostly several times as long as longer pedicels; outer pedicels *c.* twice as long as fr. Gardens, roadsides, etc., common and widespread except in N. England and Scotland where it is local. Flo. June–Sept.
Ssp. **agrestis** (Wallr.) Dostál. Differs from ssp. *cynapium* in being smaller, and having bracteoles as long as longer pedicels and outer pedicels shorter than fr. Distribution as ssp. *cynapium*. Flo. June–Sept.*

Silaum silaus (L.) Schinz & Thell. Pepper-saxifrage. *Silaus flavescens* Bernh. Stem 30–100 cm, solid, striate; bracteoles linear with scarious edges; flo. yellowish. Meadows and grassy places, mostly England, local in Wales and rare in S. Scotland, and absent from N. Scotland and Ireland. Flo. June–Aug.

Meum athamanticum Jacq. Spignel. Stem 30–60 cm, hollow; leaves finely divided, aromatic; fr. ovoid, ridges acute. Mountain meadows, Wales, N. England and Scotland, local. Flo. June–July.

OENANTHE CROCATA.

OENANTHE
LACHENALII

OENANTHE
FISTULOSA

SESELI
LIBANOTIS

MEUM ATHAMANTICUM.

AETHUSA
CYNAPIUM.

OENANTHE
PIMPINELLOIDES.

OENANTHE
FLUVIATILIS

SILAUM
SILAUS

OENANTHE
AQUATICA.

FOENICULUM
VULGARE

CRITHMUM
MARITIMUM.

Plate 40

Umbelliferae *(continued)*

Ligusticum scoticum L. Scots lovage. Stem red below; leaf segments 2–5 cm, broad; fr. ridges prominent, acute. Rocky coasts, Northumberland northwards, and Ireland. Flo. July–Aug.

Selinum carvifolia (L.) L. Cambridge milk-parsley. Stem ridges prominent, acute; leaf segments lanceolate, mucronate, minutely serrate; fr. ovoid, ridges winged. Damp meadows, Cambridgeshire, very local, formerly in Nottinghamshire and Lincolnshire. Flo. July–Oct.*

Angelica sylvestris L. Wild angelica. Stem hollow, purple; petioles inflated, sheathing; leaf segments ovate, serrate; flo. pink and white. Streamsides, damp meadows, etc., widespread, common. Flo. July–Sept.

Angelica archangelica L. Garden angelica. *Archangelica officinalis* Hoffm. Stem hollow, green; leaf segments decurrent; flo. greenish-white. Introd. Europe. Naturalized on river banks, local. Flo. June–July.*

Caucalis platycarpos L. Small bur-parsley. *C. lappula* Grande. *C. daucoides* L. 1767, non L. 1753. Leaves 2–3, pinnate; flo. 2 mm; bracts 0; outer flo. long-pedicelled, male. Introd. Mediterranean region. Formerly on waste ground, etc. Last recorded in 1962. Flo. June–July.

Peucedanum officinale L. Hog's fennel. Stem solid; leaf segments long, 3–8 cm, narrow, linear, entire. Banks by Thames estuary, local. Flo. July–Sept.

Peucedanum palustre (L.) Moench. Milk-parsley. Stem hollow; leaf segments with lanceolate lobes, finely serrate. Fens and marshes, Somerset and Sussex to S. Yorkshire, rare. Flo. July–Sept.

Peucedanum ostruthium (L.) Koch. Masterwort. Stem hollow; leaf segments few, broad, serrate; fr. suborbicular. Garden escape. Naturalized in moist meadows, Midlands and Yorkshire to N. Scotland, and N.E. Ireland. Flo. July–Aug.*

Pastinaca sativa L. Wild parsnip.
Ssp. **sativa**. Stem hollow, furrowed; hairs on stem and upper leaf surfaces few, short and straight; leaf-lobes narrow, acute. Outcast from cultivation. Waste ground, etc. Flo. July–Aug.*
Ssp. **sylvestris** (Mill.) Rouy & Camus. Similar to ssp. *sativa* but hairs on stem and upper leaf surface profuse, long and flexuous; leaf-lobes broad, obtuse. Grassy places on base-rich soils, England and Wales, introd. elsewhere. Flo. July–Aug.

Heracleum sphondylium L. Hogweed.
Ssp. **sphondylium**. Leaf segments broadly ovate, irregularly cut, petals pink or white, those of outer flo. enlarged. Grassy places, waste ground, etc., common and widespread. Flo. June–Sept.

Ssp. **sibiricum** (L.) Simonkai. Differs from ssp. *sphondylium* in having greenish-white petals and those of outer flo. not or scarcely enlarged. Known only from E. Norfolk but may occur elsewhere in East Anglia. Flo. June–Sept.*

Heracleum mantegazzianum Somm. & Lev. Giant hogweed. Differs from *H. sphondylium* in its enormous size (stems up to 3 m tall, red-spotted); leaves and very large panicles. Garden escape. Naturalized by rivers, etc., widespread. Flo. June–Sept.*

Heracleum mantegazzianum × sphondylium. Intermediate. Common and widespread where the parents occur together.*

Tordylium maximum L. Hartwort. Stem 90–130 cm; leaves simply pinnate; lobes ovate to lanceolate; fr. with thick whitish ridges. Bushy slopes, Essex, formerly in Oxford, Buckinghamshire, Middlesex, etc., very rare. Flo. June–July.*

Coriandrum sativum L. Coriander. Stem solid, 30–60 cm; lower leaves pinnate; lobes ovate; upper leaves bipinnate; umbels small; fr. orbicular. Garden escape. Waste places. Flo. June.*

Daucus carota L. Wild carrot.
Ssp. **carota**. Leaf-lobes lanceolate, acute, leaves not fleshy; umbels concave in fr.; spines hooked at tip, separate below. Grassy places near the coast and on calcareous soil. Flo. June–Aug.
Ssp. **gummifer** Hook. f. *D. gummifer* Lam., non All., *D. gingidium* auct. Leaf-lobes more ovate, obtuse, leaves thick and fleshy; umbels flatter; spines straight at tip, confluent at base. Cliffs by the sea, S. and W. England, Wales and Ireland. Not very distinct.*

Levisticum officinale Koch. Lovage. Stout, strongly aromatic, perennial up to 200 cm; stems glabrous; leaves pinnate; leaflets obovate-cuneate, deeply toothed; flo. small, yellow, in terminal umbels; fr. with 10 narrowly winged ribs. Garden escape. Naturalized in wet places, thickets, etc., Scotland. Flo. July–Aug.*

Torilis arvensis (Huds.) Link. Spreading hedge-parsley. *T. infesta* (L.) Spreng. Umbels long-pedicelled; rays 3–5; bracts 0–1; fr. spines curved, not hooked; style glabrous. Probably introd. Cultivated fields, mostly S. England and Midlands, scarce. Flo. July–Sept.

Torilis japonica (Houtt.) DC. Upright hedge-parsley. *Caucalis anthriscus* (L.) Huds. Umbels long-pedicelled; rays 5–12; bracts 4–10; fr. spines hooked; style hairy. Hedgerows, widespread and common. Flo. July–Aug.

Torilis nodosa (L.) Gaertn. Knotted hedge-parsley. Stem prostrate; umbels nearly sessile, short-rayed; bracts 0; carpels with straight or hooked spines. Dry places, mostly on calcareous and alluvial soils, mostly S. and E. England, Midlands and Wales. Flo. May–July.

ANGELICA
SYLVESTRIS.

LIGUSTICUM
SCOTICUM.

PEUCEDANUM
PALUSTRE.

×4

×6

PEUCEDANUM
OFFICINALE.

PASTINACA
SATIVA

HERACLEUM
SPHONDYLIUM.

DAUCUS CAROTA.

TORILIS
JAPONICA

CAUCALIS PLATYCARPOS.

TORILIS
ARVENSIS.

TORILIS NODOSA.

Plate 41

Buxaceae

Buxus sempervirens L. Box. Leaves coriaceous; flo. clusters 1 female and several male with 4 stamens. Woods, scrub, etc., on calcareous and limestone soils, Gloucestershire to Kent, local; introd. elsewhere. Flo. April–May.

Araliaceae

Hedera helix L. Ivy. Flowers tomentose, 5-merous; styles united; fr. black, globose. Climbing in woods, hedges, etc., common. Flo. Oct.–Nov.

Cornaceae

Cornus suecica L. Dwarf cornel. *Chamaepericlymenum suecicum* (L.) Aschers. & Graebn. Stem creeping with erect shoots; flo. surrounded by 4 white bracts. Mountains, Scotland, local, and rare in N. England. Flo. July–Aug.

Cornus sanguinea L. Dogwood. *Swida sanguinea* (L.) Opiz. *Thelycrania sanguinea* (L.) Fourr. Shrub up to 4 m; twigs red; petals 4, valvate; calyx teeth very small. Hedges on calcareous and other soils, S. England, local in Wales and Ireland, probably introd. in N. England and Scotland. Flo. June–July.

Adoxaceae

Adoxa moschatellina L. Moschatel. Rhizome creeping, white; lateral flo. with 5 petals, facing N.S.E. and W. as clock tower; upper flo. with 4 petals facing sky; fr. green. Shady lanes and banks, widespread. Flo. April. A symbol of Christian watchfulness.

Caprifoliaceae

Sambucus nigra L. Elder. Shrub or small tree; leaflets 5; stipules 0 or small; flo. 5 together, creamy-white; fr. 6–8 mm, glossy black. Hedges and waste places, common except in N. Scotland. Flo. June–July.

Sambucus ebulus L. Dwarf elder. Stem up to 120 cm, herbaceous; stipules prominent, ovate; flo. 3 together, pinkish-white. Waste places, roadsides, etc., local. Flo. July–Aug.

Sambucus canadensis L. American elder. Smaller than *S. nigra*; leaflets 7, bright green; flo. white; fr. 4–5 mm, purple-black. Bird-sown from gardens and naturalized in woods and hedges, mostly N. England and Scotland. Flo. June–July.*

Sambucus racemosa L. Red-berried elder. Shrub; leaves ovate-lanceolate; stipules replaced by large glands; flo. creamy-white in dense panicle-like cymes; fr. globose, scarlet. Bird-sown from gardens and naturalized in woods and hedges, particularly N.E. England and E. Scotland. Flo. April–May.*

Viburnum lantana L. Wayfaring-tree. Leaves oval, wrinkled, pubescent; fr. oval, becoming black; flo. all equal. Hedges, common in S. England especially on calcareous soils, introd. elsewhere. Flo. May–June.

Viburnum opulus L. Guelder-rose. Leaves lobed, glabrous above; outer flo. enlarged and sterile; fr. globose, scarlet. Woods and damp hedgerows, widespread. Flo. June–July.

Symphoricarpos albus (L.) S. F. Blake. Snowberry. *S. rivularis* Suksd. *S. racemosus* Michx. Small shrub; twigs slender; leaves orbicular, entire; flo. *c.* 6 mm, pink, campanulate, 3–6 in terminal spikes; fr. globular, *c.* 1 cm, white. Garden escape. Naturalized in hedges. Flo. June–Aug.*

Symphoricarpos microphyllus Kunth. Larger than *S. albus*; leaves ovate, grey-pubescent beneath; flo. 1 cm, pinkish, in terminal and axillary clusters; fr. pink or white shaded pink. Garden escape, naturalized in hedges and thickets, Cambridgeshire and elsewhere, rare. Flo. July–Aug.*

Symphoricarpos orbicularis Moench. Similar to *S. albus* but leaves elliptic or ovate; flo. 4 mm, yellowish-white, flushed pink; fr. reddish. Bird-sown from gardens and naturalized in hedges and thickets, S. England, rare. Flo. June–July.*

Linnaea borealis L. Twinflower. Stems slender, pubescent, creeping, forming a mat; flo. pendulous, pink; fr. an achene. Woods and shady places, mostly Scotland, rare. Flo. June–Aug.

Lonicera periclymenum L. Honeysuckle. Climbing to 6 m; upper leaves free, often downy beneath; flo. yellow, numerous. Woods and hedgerows, widespread and common. Flo. June–Sept.

Lonicera xylosteum L. Fly honeysuckle. Stem slender, climbing; leaves broadly ovate, pubescent; flo. *c.* 1 cm, long, in pairs on peduncles 1–2 cm; fr. red. Possibly native in Sussex garden escape, elsewhere, rare. Flo. May.

Lonicera caprifolium L. Perfoliate honeysuckle. Stem glabrous, climbing; leaves ovate, green above, glaucous below; upper leaves united at their bases; flo. pale yellow, in terminal whorls, sometimes with additional axillary whorls; bracts large; fr. orange-red. Garden escape. Naturalized in hedges and thickets, rare. Flo. May–June.*

Lonicera japonica Thunb. Stem pubescent; leaves oblong-ovate; flo. white, tinged purple, becoming yellowish; fr. black. Bird-sown from gardens and naturalized in hedges, thickets, etc., mostly S.W. England and S. Wales. Flo. June–Oct.*

Lonicera nitida Wills. Evergreen; stem pubescent, purplish; leaves ovate to oblong-lanceolate, glossy green; flo. white in pairs in leaf-axils; fr. purple, transparent. Bird-sown from gardens and naturalized in hedges, thickets, etc., mostly S. and W. England. Flo. April–May.*

Leycesteria formosa Wall. Himalayan honeysuckle. Shrub, leaves opposite, ovate-acuminate; flo. *c.* 2 cm, purplish, funnel-shaped, sessile, in whorls enclosed by large claret-coloured leaf-like bracts; fr. *c.* 25 mm, dark purplish-brown. Bird-sown from gardens and naturalized in woods and hedges, widespread but local. Flo. June–Sept.*

HEDERA HELIX

BUXUS
SEMPERVIRENS.

CORNUS
SUECICA

CORNUS
SANGUINEA

ADOXA
MOSCHATELLINA.

SAMBUCUS
EBULUS.

VIBURNUM
OPULUS

VIBURNUM LANTANA.

×2½

SAMBUCUS NIGRA.

LONICERA
PERICLYMENUM.

LINNAEA BOREALIS.

LONICERA XYLOSTEUM.

Plate 42

Rubiaceae

Rubia peregrina L. Wild madder. Stems climbing by downward prickles; leaves shining; flo. yellowish, 5-cleft; fr. black. Hedgerows near the sea, mostly S. and S.W. England, Wales and W. Ireland. Flo. June–Aug.

Cruciata laevipes Opiz. Crosswort. *C. ciliata* Opiz. *C. chersonensis* auct. *Galium cruciata* (L.) Scop. Stem up to 60 cm; leaves 4 in whorl, 3-veined, hairy; flo. yellow; fr. small, smooth. Banks and shady places, especially on calcareous soils, locally common, but rare in W. Wales and N. Scotland, and introd. in Ireland. Flo. May–June.

Galium boreale L. Northern bedstraw. Stems 20–40 cm; leaves 4 in whorl, 3-veined; flo. white; fr. bristles hooked. Moist rocky places, N. England, Scotland and Ireland. Flo. July–Aug.

Galium verum L. Lady's bedstraw. Stems up to 80 cm, ascending to erect; leaves many, narrow, 1-veined, downy beneath; flo. yellow; fr. smooth. Dry grassy places, widespread and common. Flo. July–Sept.

Galium mollugo L. Hedge bedstraw. Stems 30–100 cm, trailing on hedges or upright; leaf margins rough with forward prickles; flo. branches spreading; fr. 1–2 mm. Banks, pastures, etc., especially on calcareous soils, common in S. England, local in the Midlands, N. England and Wales, rare in Scotland and Ireland. Flo. June–Sept.

Galium × pomeranicum Retz. *G. mollugo × verum. G. × ochroleucum* Wolf ex Schweigg. & Koerte. Intermediate between the parents, with pale yellow flo., sometimes occurs where they grow together.*

Galium album Mill., *G. erectum* Huds. 1778, non 1762. Similar to *G. mollugo* but with larger flowers and denser inflo. Hedge banks, etc., on calcareous soils. Local, but confused with *G. mollugo*. Flo. June–Sept.

Galium saxatile L. Heath bedstraw. *G. harcynicum* Weig. Stems procumbent, matted, 4-angled, glabrous; flo. branches shorter than internodes; fr. with tubercles. Peaty heaths, etc., widespread and common. Flo. June–Aug.

Galium pumilum Murr. Slender bedstraw. Stems few, often hairy below; leaves 10–15 mm, lanceolate, margin revolute, ciliate; flowering branches usually longer than internodes; pedicels 1–1.5 mm; fr. faintly granular. Grassy places on limestone and calcareous soils, S. England, northwards to Lincoln, local. Flo. June–Aug.

Galium timeroyi Jord. ssp. ***fleurotii*** (Jord.) Duvigneaud. *G. fleurotii* Jord. similar to *G. pumilum* but with many stems which are densely hairy; leaves 6–10 mm; pedicels 0.8–1 mm. Grassy places on limestone soil, Cheddar Gorge. Flo. June–Aug.*

Galium sterneri Ehrend. Limestone bedstraw. *G. pumilum* Murr. ssp. *septentrionale* Sterner ex Hyland. Similar to *G. pumilum* but more prostrate; leaves oblanceolate to linear; flo. cymes more compact, forming a pyramidal panicle (panicle open in *G. pumilum*); fr. covered with tubercles.

Calcareous and limestone slopes and rocks, mid Wales to N. Scotland, also in W. and N.E. Ireland, local. Flo. June–Aug.*

Galium palustre L. Common marsh-bedstraw. Stem up to 120 cm, nearly smooth, supported by other plants; black when dry; flo. 3–4 mm wide; fr. rugose. Wet meadows, common. Flo. June–Aug.
Var. ***elongatum*** C. Presl. More robust, less branched, flo. 4–5 mm.

Galium debile Desv. Slender marsh-bedstraw. Stem nearly smooth; leaves narrow, linear, subglabrous, margin slightly rough; flo. pinkish-white; fr. granular. Pond verges, ditch banks, etc., Devon and the New Forest, formerly in Channel Islands, very local. Flo. May–July.

Galium uliginosum L. Fen bedstraw. Stems slender; leaf margins rough with backward prickles; leaves 6–8 in whorl, mucronate; green when dry; fr. granular. Fens and boggy meadows, local. Flo. July–Aug.

Galium parisiense L. ssp. ***anglicum*** (Huds.) Clapham. Wall bedstraw. *G. anglicum* Huds. Small, stems slender with backward prickles; leaves with forward prickles; flo. very small, greenish-white; fr. small, granular. Walls and dry places, mostly S. and E. England, rare. Flo. June–July.

Galium aparine L. Cleavers. Climbing, 60–120 cm, stems and leaves with deflexed prickles; fr. large, 4–6 mm, with hooked prickles. Hedge banks, etc., common. Flo. June–Aug.

Galium tricornutum Dandy. Corn cleavers. *G. tricorne* Stokes *pro parte*. Plant up to 50 cm; stems and leaf margins very rough with backward prickles; fr. large, 3–4 mm, granular, recurved. Arable fields on calcareous soil, mostly S. and E. England, local, and decreasing. Flo. June–Sept.

Galium spurium L. False cleavers. *G. vaillantii* DC. Similar to *G. aparine* but branches with more numerous (3–9) flo., greenish, with only 2 floral bracts instead of a whorl; fr. glabrous or with hooked hairs. Arable fields, S. and E. England, very rare and decreasing. Flo. July.*

Galium odoratum (L.) Scop. Woodruff. *Asperula odorata* L. Rhizomatous; stem up to 35 cm; flo. funnel-shaped, tube equalling limb, white, fragrant; fr. with hooked hairs. Woods, mostly on calcareous soil, widespread. Flo. May–June.

Asperula cynanchica L. Squinancy wort. Stock woody, slender, brown; branches prostrate; leaves less than 1 mm wide, texture thin; flo. few, funnel-shaped, pale pink; fr. tubercled. Dry calcareous and limestone soils, mostly S. and E. England, S. Wales and W. Ireland, local. Flo. July–Aug.

Asperula occidentalis Rouy. Similar to *A. cynanchica* but stock slender, orange; leaves 1–2 mm wide, fleshy; flo. sessile. Coastal dunes, S. Wales and W. Ireland. Flo. June–Aug.*

Sherardia arvensis L. Field madder. Stems prostrate; flo. in involucre, pink, tube much exceeding limb; sepals 4, 2 bifid crowning the fr. Arable land, common in S. Britain, local in Ireland and in N. Scotland where it is mainly confined to the E. coast dunes. Flo. June–July.

RUBIA
PEREGRINA.

CRUCIATA
LAEVIPES.

GALIUM
PALUSTRE

GALIUM
VERUM

GALIUM
ALBUM

GALIUM
ULIGINOSUM

GALIUM BOREALE.

×3
GALIUM
MOLLUGO

×5

GALIUM
SAXATILE

×3

GALIUM
APARINE.

GALIUM
PUMILUM

SHERARDIA
ARVENSIS.

GALIUM
ODORATUM

GALIUM TRICORNUTUM

GALIUM
PARISIENSE

GALIUM
DEBILE.

ASPERULA
CYNANCHICA.

Plate 43

Valerianaceae

Valeriana dioica L. Marsh valerian. Plant stoloniferous; stem 15–30 cm; lower leaves entire; flo. dioecious, pale pink. Marshes, England and Wales, local, rare in Scotland. Flo. May–June.

Valeriana officinalis L. Common valerian. *V. sambucifolia* Mikan f. Stolons short or o; stem up to 150 cm; leaves all pinnate, very variable. Damp woods, chalk downs, widespread and common. Flo. June–Sept.

Valeriana pyrenaica L. Pyrenean valerian. Stolons absent; stem up to 1 m, downy, erect; basal leaves large, petiolate, cordate, toothed; upper leaves pinnate; lower pairs of leaflets oblong-acuminate; terminal leaflet broadly ovate-cordate; leaflets deeply and irregularly serrate; flo. pale pink, rarely white, in terminal corymbs; fr. glabrous. Garden escape. Naturalized in woods, mostly S.W. and N. England and in Scotland. Flo. June–July.*

Centranthus ruber (L.) DC. Red valerian. Stem up to 60 cm; leaves ovate; flo. rose-red, sometimes white, with slender tube and long spur. Garden escape. Naturalized on walls, rocks and banks, mostly S. England, the Midlands, Wales and S. and E. Ireland. Flo. June–Aug.*

Valerianella locusta (L.) Latterade. Common cornsalad. *V. olitoria* (L.) Poll.
Ssp. **locusta**. Stem slender, 8–40 cm; leaves up to 7 cm long; fr. suborbicular, corky; calyx o or 1 minute point. Cultivated ground, hedge banks, etc., mostly S. England, common. Flo. April–June.
Ssp. **dunensis** (D. E. Allen) P. D. Sell. Differs from ssp. *locusta* in its smaller size (stem 1–3 cm), more compact and cushion-like habit and leaves only up to 3.5 cm long. Maritime dunes from Cornwall to N. Scotland. Flo. April–June.*

Valerianella carinata Lois. Keeled-fruited cornsalad. Fr. oblong, nearly square in section, not corky; calyx faintly 1-toothed, sterile cells nearly confluent, as figure. Cultivated ground, banks, walls, etc., mostly S. and S.W. England, local. Flo. April–June.

Valerianella rimosa Bast. Broad-fruited cornsalad. Inflo. lax; calyx teeth minute; sterile cells together larger than fertile one, and confluent. Cultivated ground, mostly S. England, rare and decreasing. Flo. July–Aug.

Valerianella dentata (L.) Poll. Narrow-fruited cornsalad. Inflo. lax; calyx 4-lobed, 3 lobes very small; fr. not corky. Fields, mostly S. and E. England, local. Flo. June–July.

Valerianella eriocarpa Desv. (fr. only). Hairy-fruited cornsalad. Fr. pilose; calyx deeply 5-lobed and strongly net-veined. Introd. Europe. Banks, walls, etc., mostly S. England, rare and decreasing. Flo. May–June.

Dipsacaceae

Dipsacus fullonum L. Teasel. *D. sylvestris* Huds. Stem 50–200 cm; involucre long, erect; bracteoles exceeding purple flo. and ending in flexible or stiff spine. Fields, hedge banks, stream banks, waste ground, etc., mostly S. and E. England. Flo. July–Aug.

Dipsacus pilosus L. Small teasel. Stems 30–120 cm; bracteoles shorter than white flo., heads subglobose. Ditches, and by calcareous streams, mostly England, local. Flo. Aug.

Knautia arvensis (L.) Coult. Field scabious. *Scabiosa arvensis* L. Stem 30–90 cm; bracts ovate; bracteoles o; calyx teeth 8; petals 5. Dry banks and pastures, widespread and common. Flo. May–Sept.

Scabiosa columbaria L. Small scabious. Stem up to 70 cm; bracts and bracteoles linear; calyx teeth 5; petals 5. Banks and pastures, mostly on calcareous soils, widespread, but very rare in Scotland and absent from Ireland. Flo. July–Aug.

Succisa pratensis Moench. Devil's-bit scabious. *Scabiosa succisa* L. Stem 15–60 cm; bracteoles elliptic; calyx teeth 4; petals 4, blue-purple. Fens, damp meadows, etc., common. Flo. June–Sept.

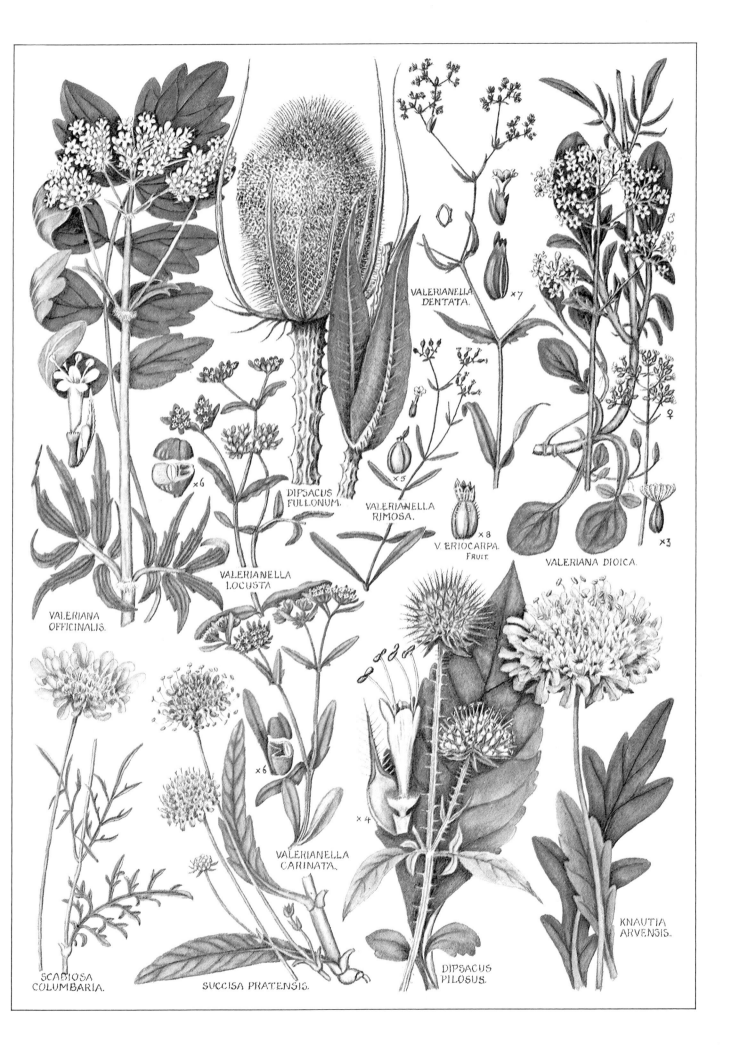

VALERIANELLA
DENTATA.

×7

DIPSACUS
FULLONUM.

VALERIANELLA
RIMOSA.

×5

V. ERIOCARPA.
Fruit.

×8

VALERIANA DIOICA.

×3

VALERIANA
OFFICINALIS.

VALERIANELLA
LOCUSTA

×6

VALERIANELLA
CARINATA.

×6

×4

DIPSACUS
PILOSUS.

KNAUTIA
ARVENSIS.

SCABIOSA
COLUMBARIA.

SUCCISA PRATENSIS.

Plate 44

Compositae

Eupatorium cannabinum L. Hemp-agrimony. Stem up to 120 cm; inflo. of many small heads; each with oblong bracts and 5–6 reddish florets. Ditches and streamsides, common, but local in N. England and Scotland. Flo. July–Sept.

Solidago virgaurea L. Goldenrod. Stem 10–70 cm; flo. bracts in many rows; flo. golden; achenes ribbed. Heaths, dry banks and cliffs, common. Flo. July–Sept.

Solidago altissima L. Tall goldenrod. *S. canadensis* auct., non L. Stem pubescent, 90–150 cm; leaves lanceolate, 3-veined, unequally toothed, roughish above, pubescent below; flo. small, golden-yellow in numerous recurved racemes, forming a large pyramidal panicle. Garden escape. Naturalized by rivers, streams and lakes, and established on waste ground, etc., very common. Flo. Aug.–Nov.*

Solidago gigantea Ait. ssp. ***serotina*** (O. Kuntze) McNeill. *S. serotina* Ait. Early goldenrod. Similar to *S. altissima*, but stem glabrous below, up to 100 cm; leaves 3-veined, glabrous below except on midrib; flo. larger, ray florets exceeding disk florets, golden-yellow, in compact, erect, corymbose panicles. Garden escape. Naturalized by rivers, streams and lakes, and established on waste ground, etc., common. Flo. July–Nov.*

Solidago graminifolia (L.) Salisb. *S. lanceolata* L. Stems glabrous, up to 100 cm; leaves linear-lanceolate, 3–5-veined, entire, glabrous except on veins beneath; flo. small, ray florets not exceeding disk florets, golden-yellow, in erect corymbose panicles. Garden escape. Naturalized on hedge banks, etc., rare. Flo. July–Sept.*

Bellis perennis L. Daisy. Plants forming a close mat; achenes without pappus. Grassy places, very common. Flo. March–Oct.

Aster tripolium L. Sea aster. Stem up to 60 cm; leaves fleshy; ray florets mauve or absent. Salt marshes, common. Flo. July–Sept.

Aster linosyris (L.) Bernh. Goldilocks aster. *Crinitaria linosyris* (L.) Less. Stem up to 50 cm; leaves linear; flo. all tubular, golden and fertile. Limestone cliffs, S. Devon, Somerset, Wales, Lancashire, rare. Flo. Aug.–Sept.

Several alien species of *Aster* are spreading as garden escapes.

Conyza canadensis (L.) Cronq. Canadian fleabane. *Erigeron canadensis* L. Stem 10–60 cm; leaves linear; heads many, small, *c.* 5 mm across, white. Introd. N. America. Cultivated and waste ground, mostly England and Wales. Flo. Aug.–Sept.

Conyza sumatrensis (Retz.) E. Walker. *C. floribunda* Kunth. *Erigeron sumatrensis* Retz. Similar to *C. canadensis* but with stems up to 250 cm; side branches usually longer than central one; leaves rough; heads many, *c.* 6 mm across, yellowish. Introd. C. America. Naturalized and locally plentiful in dry waste places, etc., Channel Islands. Flo. Aug.–Sept.*

Erigeron acer L. Blue fleabane. Stem 10–40 cm; heads many, small; ray florets small, mauve; pappus red. Dry sandy and calcareous banks, fields, etc., mostly S. and E. Britain. Flo. July–Aug.

Erigeron borealis (Vierh.) Simmons. Alpine fleabane. *E. alpinus* auct., non L. Stem 10–20 cm; leaves mostly basal; heads solitary, *c.* 20 mm; rays mauve. Rock ledges, *c.* 1000 m, mid Scotland. Flo. July–Aug.

Erigeron karvinskianus DC. var. ***mucronatus*** (DC.) Aschers. Mexican fleabane. *E. mucronatus* DC. Stem slender, up to 20 cm; basal leaves obovate-cuneate, 3-lobed or coarsely toothed at apex; upper leaves linear-lanceolate; rays in 2 rows, white above, purple below. Garden escape. Naturalized in stony places and on walls, S. and S.W. England, Wales and the Channels Islands, local. Flo. July–Aug.*

Erigeron glaucus Ker-Gawl. Perennial with woody rootstock; stem up to 20 cm; leaves fleshy, spathulate, a basal rosette; flo. few in a solitary head; ray florets lilac; disk yellow. Garden escape. Naturalized in maritime areas, S. England, rare. Flo. June–Aug.*

Filago vulgaris Lam. Common cudweed. *F. germanica* auct. Flo. in spherical clusters of 10–30 heads, not overtopped by leaves. Sandy and acid heaths, etc., widespread but rare in Scotland. Flo. July–Aug.

Filago lutescens Jord. Red-tipped cudweed. *F. apiculata* auct. Flo. in clusters of 10–15 heads, overtopped by leaves; flo. bracts red-tipped. Sandy fields, S. and E. England, rare. Flo. July–Aug.

Filago pyramidata L. Broad-leaved cudweed. *F. spathulata* C. Presl. Branches horizontal; clusters of about 12 5-angled heads, overtopped by leaves; flo. bracts yellow-tipped. Sandy fields, mostly S. and W. England, rare. Flo. July–Aug.

Filago minima (Sm.) Pers. Small cudweed. Flo. in small clusters of 3–6 heads, not overtopped by leaves; tips of flo. bracts blunt, yellowish. Bare places on sandy and gravelly soils, common. Flo. June–Sept.

Filago gallica L. Narrow-leaved cudweed. Flo. in small clusters of 2–6 heads, overtopped by leaves; tips of flo. bracts yellowish. Introd. Europe. Formerly naturalized in dry grassy places in S. and E. England, but now found only in Channel Islands. Flo. July–Aug.

Antennaria dioica (L.) Gaertn. Mountain everlasting. Dioecious and stoloniferous; stem 10–20 cm; leaves woolly, white beneath; flo. bracts often pink. Heaths and mountains, mostly N. Britain, Wales and W. Ireland. Flo. June–July.

Anaphalis margaritacea (L.) Benth. Pearly everlasting. Dioecious; stem 30–100 cm, and leaves very woolly; flo. yellowish with woolly bracts. Garden escape. Naturalized in meadows, by streams and on wall tops, mostly Wales and Scotland. Flo. Aug.*

Gnaphalium uliginosum L. Marsh cudweed. Stem 5–20 cm with woolly branches; flo. bracts pale brown, overtopped by leaves. Damp places and waysides, common. Flo. July–Aug.

Gnaphalium luteoalbum L. Jersey cudweed. Plant covered with dense white tomentum; stem up to 40 cm, branched leaves oblong; flo. bracts yellowish not overtopped by leaves. Ditches, cultivated ground, etc., native in Channel Islands, introd. in E. England, very rare. Flo. June–Aug.*

Gnaphalium undulatum L. Similar to *G. luteoalbum*, but plant foetid and more robust, stem up to 80 cm; leaves green and rough above, tomentose below. Introd. S. Africa. Waste ground, heaths, etc., widely naturalized in the Channel Islands and an early colonizer of burnt ground. Flo. July–Sept.*

Gnaphalium sylvaticum L. Heath cudweed. Stem 8–30 cm; leaves linear-lanceolate; heads in a long leafy spike; bracts brown and green. Woods and heaths on acid soil, local. Flo. July–Sept.

Gnaphalium norvegicum Gunn. Highland cudweed. Leaves lanceolate; heads in a short spike, $\frac{1}{4}$ length of stem; bracts dark brown. Mountains at 1100 m, Central Scotland, rare. Flo. Aug.

Gnaphalium supinum L. Dwarf cudweed. Stems creeping, ascending 2–10 cm; heads very few; bracts dark brown. Mountains, Scotland, rare. Flo. July–Aug.

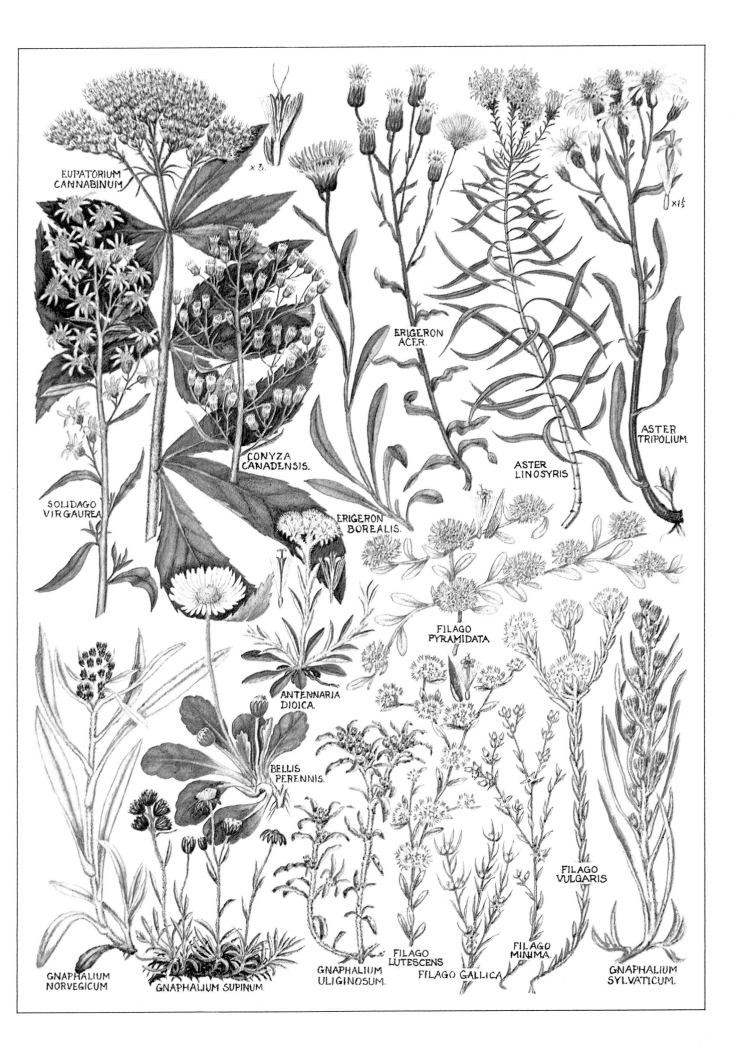

EUPATORIUM
CANNABINUM

× 3.

ERIGERON
ACER.

CONYZA
CANADENSIS.

SOLIDAGO
VIRGAUREA

ERIGERON
BOREALIS.

ASTER
LINOSYRIS

ASTER
TRIPOLIUM.

× 1½

FILAGO
PYRAMIDATA

ANTENNARIA
DIOICA.

BELLIS
PERENNIS.

FILAGO
VULGARIS

GNAPHALIUM
NORVEGICUM

GNAPHALIUM SUPINUM.

GNAPHALIUM
ULIGINOSUM.

FILAGO
LUTESCENS

FILAGO GALLICA

FILAGO
MINIMA.

GNAPHALIUM
SYLVATICUM.

Plate 45

Compositae *(continued)*

Inula helenium L. Elecampane. Stem 60–160 cm; flo heads 6–8 cm across, golden; bracts broad. Garden escape. Fields and waste places, uncommon. Flo. July–Aug.

Inula conyza DC. Ploughman's-spikenard. *I. squarrosa* (L.) Bernh. Stem tough, 20–100 cm; inner flo. bracts purplish; outer florets tubular or very short ligulate. Dry calcareous grassland, mostly E. and S. England, Midlands and Wales, local in N. England, rare in Scotland. Flo. July–Sept.

Inula salicina L. Irish fleabane. Stem up to 50 cm; leaves elliptical, cordate at base; flo. few, *c.* 3 cm; ligules narrow, golden. Beside Lough Derg, Ireland. Flo. July–Aug.*

Inula crithmoides L. Golden samphire. Stems and narrow leaves bright green, thick and fleshy; flo. golden. Salt marshes and wet rocks by the sea, S. and W. England, Wales and Ireland, very rare in Scotland. Flo. July–Aug.

Telekia speciosa (Schreb.) Baumg. *Buphthalmum speciosum* Schreb. Plant robust, hairy, strongly aromatic, superficially resembling *Inula helenium*; stem 90–150 cm; leaves alternate, glabrous above, hairy below; lower leaves triangular-cordate, double toothed, stalked; upper leaves ovate, sessile, with simple teeth; florets subtended by linear filiform scales (absent in *Inula*); flo. heads large with orange-yellow ray florets and very large prominent disk; bracts ovate, mucronate. Garden escape. Naturalized in wet places, mostly Scotland, though long known at Woodwalton Fen, Huntingdon. Flo. July–Sept.*

Pulicaria dysenterica (L.) Bernh. Common fleabane. Stem up to 70 cm, woolly; leaf base cordate; flo. heads 2.5 cm; outer florets spreading, golden. Wet meadows and ditches, rather common, but local in mid Wales and Ireland and very rare in Scotland. Flo. Aug.–Sept.

Pulicaria vulgaris Gaertn. Small fleabane. Stem 20–60 cm; leaf base rounded; flo. heads 2–3 cm, pale yellow; outer florets erect. Moist sandy places where water stands in winter, pond verges, etc., S. England, very rare. Flo. Aug–Sept.

Bidens cernua L. Nodding bur-marigold. Leaves simple, lanceolate, serrate; flo. heads nodding; sometimes (var. *radiata* DC.) with broad, yellow rays. Ponds and ditches, mostly S. and mid Britain and Ireland. Flo. July–Sept.

Bidens tripartita L. Trifid bur-marigold. Leaves usually tripartite, stalked; terminal leaflet broad; flo. heads erect, yellow. Ponds and ditches, widespread and common, though local in parts of N. England and rare in Scotland. Flo. July–Sept.

Bidens frondosa L. Beggarticks. Leaves usually pinnate with 3–6 separate leaflets; flo. heads erect on long stalks; disk florets yellow; achenes blackish, densely tubercled. Introd. N. America. By canals and rivers, mostly W. Midlands and S. Wales. Flo. July–Oct.*

Bidens connata Mühl. Similar to *B. frondosa* but leaves unlobed with irregular teeth, awns of achenes with stiff antrorse bristles. *B. cernua, B. tripartita* and *B. frondosa* have retrorse bristles. Introd. N. America. Canal sides, London area, and likely to spread. Flo. July–Sept.*'

Galinsoga parviflora Cav. Gallant soldier. 10–60 cm, much branched; leaves ovate; flo. heads small; rays short, white; disk yellow; pappus of silvery scales, not awned. Introd. S. America. Cultivated and waste ground, mostly England and Wales, especially London area. Flo. May–Sept.*

Galinsoga quadriradiata Ruiz & Pav. Shaggy soldier. *G. ciliata* (Raf.) Blake. Closely resembles *G. parviflora* but stem thickly clothed with spreading hairs; pappus scales awned. Introd. S. America. In similar situations to *G. parviflora*, mostly England and Wales, especially London area. Flo. May–Sept.*

Ambrosia artemisiifolia L. Ragweed. *A. elatior* L. Annual; stem erect, shortly hairy, up to 80 cm; leaves short, stalked, in pairs, pinnatifid, dark green above, grey-felted beneath; flo. small, greenish-yellow; male flo. short-stalked in clusters on drooping terminal spikes; female flo. solitary, or in small clusters in axils of upper leaves. Introd. N. America. Established on waste ground, though often only casual. Flo. July–Oct.*

Ambrosia psilostachya DC. Similar to *A. artemisifolia*, but stem up to 60 cm; leaves smaller, thicker, less pinnatifid and more heavily grey-felted beneath. Introd. N. America. Naturalized on dunes, Lancashire and Ayrshire. Flo. July–Oct.*

Achillea millefolium L. Yarrow. Stoloniferous; stem up to 45 cm; leaves finely divided; flo. heads *c.* 5 mm, white or pink. Grassy places, common. Flo. June–Aug.

Achillea ptarmica L. Sneezewort. Stoloniferous; stem up to 60 cm; leaves linear-lanceolate; flo. heads few, *c.* 15 mm, white. Wet meadows and moors, common. Flo. Jul.

Otanthus maritimus (L.) Hoffmans. & Link. Cottonweed. *Diotis maritima* (L.) Desf. ex Cass. Stem woolly, 15–30 cm; leaves woolly, white; flo. heads yellow, bracts woolly. Formerly on sandy seashores in England and N. Wales, now survives in a single locality in Ireland. Flo. Aug.–Sept.

Anthemis tinctoria L. Yellow chamomile. Perennial; stem up to 60 cm; ray florets golden; disk scales lanceolate, subulate. Garden escape. Naturalized in fields, etc., mostly England. Flo. July–Aug.

Anthemis cotula L. Stinking chamomile. Annual; stem up to 60 cm; foetid; flo. heads *c.* 25 mm; ray florets white; disk scales linear; achenes tubercled. Cultivated and waste ground, common in England, but local in Wales and very rare in Scotland and Ireland. Flo. July–Sept.

Anthemis arvensis L. Corn chamomile. Annual; slightly scented; flo. heads *c.* 25 mm; ray florets white; disk scales lanceolate, cuspidate; achenes rugose at top. Cultivated ground, local, and very rare in Ireland. Flo. June–July.

Anthemis punctata Vahl. Ssp. ***cupaniana*** (Tod. ex Nyman) R. Fernandes. Perennial with a woody rootstock, whole plant silvery-grey; stems up to 60 cm, robust, much branched; ray florets white, large. Garden escape. Naturalized in coastal areas of S. England. Flo. June–Aug.*

Chamaemelum nobile (L.) All. Chamomile. *Anthemis nobilis* L. Perennial; sweetly aromatic; flo. heads *c.* 25 mm; rays white; disk scales oblong; achenes 3-ribbed. Grassy places and sandy soils, mostly S. Britain and S. Ireland, probably introd. elsewhere. Flo. June–July.

INULA
CONYZA.

INULA
CRITHMOIDES.

PULICARIA
VULGARIS

PULICARIA
DYSENTERICA.

OTANTHUS
MARITIMUS

INULA
HELENIUM

ACHILLEA
MILLEFOLIUM

ACHILLEA
PTARMICA.

BIDENS
CERNUA.
VAR.
RADIATA.

BIDENS
TRIPARTITA

×4

×4

ANTHEMIS
TINCTORIA

ANTHEMIS
ARVENSIS.

ANTHEMIS COTULA.

CHAMAEMELUM NOBILE.

Plate 46

Compositae *(continued)*

Chrysanthemum segetum L. Corn marigold. Annual; stem to 45 cm; thickened below the flo.; rays yellow; bracts with broad scarious margins. Cultivated fields, common. Flo. June–Aug.

Leucanthemum vulgare Lam. Oxeye daisy. *Chrysanthemum leucanthemum* L. Perennial; stem to 60 cm; leaves simple; flo. heads solitary; rays white. Pastures and grassy places on basic soils, widespread and common. Flo. June–Aug.

Tanacetum parthenium (L.) Schultz Bip. Feverfew. *Chrysanthemum parthenium* (L.) Bernh. Perennial; stem up to 60 cm; leaves pinnate; flo. heads many; rays white. Cultivated ground and waste places. Flo. July–Aug.

Tanacetum vulgare L. Tansy. *Chrysanthemum vulgare* (L.) Bernh. Perennial; stem up to 100 cm, tough; leaves fragrant, lower bipinnate; heads golden; rays o. Hedge banks, etc., common. Flo. July–Sept.

Matricaria maritima L. Sea mayweed. *Tripleurospermum maritimum* (L.) Koch. Leaf segments short, fleshy; disk nearly flat, without scales; achenes with oil glands at top. Maritime shingle, rocks, etc. Flo. July–Sept.*

Matricaria perforata Mérat. Scentless mayweed. *Tripleurospermum maritimum* ssp. *inodorum* (L.) Hyland. ex Vaarama. Leaf segments long and mucronate; oil glands on achenes nearly circular. Cultivated land, etc., widespread and common. Flo. July–Sept.

Chamomilla recutita (L.) Rauschert. Scented mayweed. *Matricaria chamomilla* L. Annual; fragrant; flo. heads *c.* 20 mm; disk conical, without scales; rays white, soon reflexed. Cultivated land, mostly S. and mid England, casual in Scotland and Ireland, local. Flo. June–July.

Chamomilla suaveolens (Pursh) Rydb. Pineappleweed. *M. suaveolens* (Pursh) Buchen. *M. matricarioides* (Less.) Porter. Annual; aromatic; flo. heads greenish; disk conical, hollow; rays o. Introd. N. America. Farm tracks and waste places, common. Flo. June–July.

Cotula coronopifolia L. Buttonweed. Aromatic, stem ascending; leaves toothed or pinnatifid, with sheathing base; heads *c.* 8 mm, yellow; rays o; marginal achenes winged. Introd. S. Africa. Established on waste ground, etc., rare. Flo. July–Aug.*

Artemisia vulgaris L. Mugwort. Aromatic; stem up to 120 cm, tough, grooved, reddish; leaves dark green above, white beneath. Waysides and waste places, common. Flo. July–Sept.

Artemisia verlotiorum Lamotte. Chinese mugwort. Similar to *A. vulgaris*, but with long rhizomes and lower part of scape semi-woody and naked; leaflets longer and narrower, darker green, less white beneath and very aromatic; inflo. much more leafy. Introd. China. Naturalized by rivers, streams and roadsides and established on waste ground, common in the London area especially near the R. Thames. Flo. Oct.–Dec.*

Artemisia norvegica Fr. Norwegian mugwort. Plant tufted, greyish, hairy, up to 6 cm; basal leaves stalked with toothed cuneate lobes; upper leaves sessile, pinnate; flo. heads yellow, *c.* 12 mm across, usually solitary, but sometimes 2–4 together, nodding; bracts with greenish midrib and wide dark brown margins. Mountains at *c.* 800 m, W. Ross, very rare. Flo. July–Sept.*

Artemisia absinthium L. Wormwood. Stem silky, up to 80 cm; leaf segments blunt, silky both sides; bracts silky; heads hemispherical. Waste places, especially by the sea, local. Flo. July.

Artemisia maritima L. Sea wormwood. Aromatic; stem up to 50 cm, downy; leaf segments blunt, woolly above and beneath. Salt marshes, dunes, etc., mostly S. and E. England and S. Wales, rare in N. England, Scotland and Ireland. Flo. Aug–Sept.

Artemisia campestris L. Field wormwood. Scentless; stem up to 60 cm., glabrous; leaf segments narrow, linear, acute; bracts reddish. Sandy heaths, E. Anglia, rare and decreasing. Flo. Aug.–Sept.

Tussilago farfara L. Coltsfoot. Perennial with deep rhizomes; flo. rays very many, female, bright yellow. Cultivated and waste ground on basic soils, a troublesome weed. Flo. March.

Petasites albus (L.) Gaertn. White butterbur. Perennial with thick rhizomes; leaves roundish, cordate, up to 30 cm wide, glabrous above, white pubescent beneath; leaf stems hairy; flo. heads many, white, scented, long stalked, appearing before the leaves; bracts narrow, pale green, glabrous. Garden escape. Naturalized in woods and plantations, by roadsides, etc., widespread, but mostly N.E. Scotland. Flo. March–May.*

Petasites japonicus (Sieb. & Zucc.) Maxim. Giant butterbur. Low creeping perennial; leaves roundish, cordate, deeply toothed, glabrous, bright green, up to 80 cm wide; flo. heads many, whitish, in dense corymbs, appearing before the leaves; bracts broad, oblong, pale green. Garden escape. Naturalized by lakes, etc., widespread, rare but increasing. Flo. March–April.*

Petasites fragrans (Vill.) C. Presl. Winter heliotrope. Perennial with deep rhizomes; scapes with 6–8 heads of pale lilac flo.; leaves surviving winter. Garden escape. Established in hedge banks, etc., widespread. Flo. Feb.

Petasites hybridus (L.) Gaertn., Mey. & Scherb. Butterbur. Perennial with deep thick rhizomes; leaves up to 90 cm wide; flo. heads many, pink. Streamsides and wet meadows, common. Flo. April.

Homogyne alpina (L.) Cass. Purple coltsfoot. Leaves 3–4 cm across, reniform, dark green above, paler beneath; leaf stalks hairy; flo. heads similar to those of *Tussilago farfara*, solitary, purplish, on stem up to 30 cm. Introd. Europe. Naturalized in mountains, Clova and Outer Hebrides. Flo. May–Aug.*

Doronicum pardalianches L. Leopard's-bane. Leaves ovate amplexicaul; scape up to 45 cm, with 3–8 heads, *c.* 45 mm, yellow. Garden escape. Plantations, rare. Flo. May–July.*
A similar plant with leaves narrowed into petiole and 1–3 heads up to 70 mm wide is *D. plantagineum* L., plantain-leaved leopard's-bane, sometimes found outcast from gardens.*

*TANACETUM
PARTHENIUM

LEUCANTHEMUM
VULGARE

TANACETUM
VULGARE

CHRYSANTHEMUM
SEGETUM

TUSSILAGO
FARFARA.

PETASITES HYBRIDUS

*PETASITES
FRAGRANS.

CHAMOMILLA
RECUTITA

ARTEMISIA
MARITIMA.

ARTEMISIA
VULGARIS.

ARTEMISIA
CAMPESTRIS.

ARTEMISIA
ABSINTHIUM

MATRICARIA
PERFORATA

*CHAMOMILLA SUAVEOLENS

Plate 47

Compositae *(continued)*

Senecio vulgaris L. Groundsel.
Ssp. **vulgaris.** Flo. heads with involucre cylindrical; bracts linear, outer black-tipped; rays o. Cultivated ground, common. Flo. Feb.–Nov.
Ssp. **denticulatus** (O. F. Muell.) Sell. *S. denticulatus* O. F. Muell. Similar to ssp. *vulgaris* but usually less robust and with ray florets. Maritime dunes, cliffs, etc., mostly England. Flo. March–Oct.

Senecio sylvaticus L. Heath groundsel. Leaves softly pubescent; flo. heads with involucre conical, glandular; rays revolute. Woods, heaths, etc., on sandy soils, common. Flo. July–Sept.

Senecio × viscidulus Scheele. *S. sylvaticus × viscosus.* Intermediate between the parents, sometimes occurs where they grow together.*

Senecio viscosus L. Sticky groundsel. Stem stout, very glandular; heads with involucre ovoid, conical; rays revolute. Waste ground, locally common. Flo. July–Sept.

Senecio squalidus L. Oxford ragwort. Stem up to 30 cm; leaves glabrous, toothed or pinnatifid; heads *c.* 25 mm; rays rather broad. Introd. S. Europe. Spreading on railways, established on walls and waste ground, locally abundant, but local or rare in Scotland, and local in Ireland. Flo. May–Sept.

Senecio × londinensis Lousley. *S. squalidus × viscosus.* Intermediate between the parents, sometimes occurs where they grow together.*

Senecio fluviatilis Wallr. Broad-leaved ragwort. *S. sarracenicus* auct. Stoloniferous; stem up to 150 cm; leaves elliptical, glabrous, 10–20 cm; heads numerous, *c.* 2–3 cm; involucre pubescent. Introd. Europe. Streamsides, widespread, but uncommon. Flo. Aug.*

Senecio jacobaea L. Common ragwort. Stem 40–100 cm; leaves glabrous with lobes broadly toothed and blunt. Neglected pastures, common. Flo. July–Oct.

Senecio aquaticus Hill. Marsh ragwort. Stem 25–80 cm, purplish; upper leaves pinnatifid with forward-pointing lobes, lower undivided or pinnatifid. Wet meadows, widespread and common. Flo. July–Aug.

Senecio × ostenfeldii Druce. *S. aquaticus × jacobaea.* Intermediate between the parents, often occurs where they grow together, especially in Scotland and Wales.*

Senecio cambrensis Rosser. Intermediate between *S. squalidus* and *S. vulgaris.* Stems up to 50 cm, robust; rays bright yellow, short and broad. Waste ground, etc., N. Wales, Shropshire and Cheshire, very local but spreading. Flo. May–Sept.*

Senecio doria L. Stem up to 150 cm; leaves elliptical, fleshy, glaucous, entire or toothed; heads *c.* 2 cm; rays few, 4–6. Garden escape. Established on a few streamsides, rare. Flo. July–Sept.*

Senecio erucifolius L. Hoary ragwort. Stem 30–100 cm; leaves with linear-acute lobes, cottony beneath. Grassy places on calcareous and heavy soils, mostly S. and E. England. Flo. July–Aug.

Senecio paludosus L. Fen ragwort. Stem up to 200 cm; leaves long lanceolate, serrate, cottony beneath; rays many. Fen ditches, E. England, very rare, almost extinct. Flo. May–June.

Senecio congestus (R. Br.) DC. Marsh fleawort. *S. palustris* (L.) Hook., non Velloso. Stem stout, woolly, 30–100 cm; leaves broadly lanceolate; involucre without shorter scales; heads 2–3 cm, crowded. Formerly widespread in fens, ditches, E. England, now extinct. Flo. June.*

Senecio integrifolius (L.) Clairv. Field fleawort.
Ssp. **integrifolius.** *S. campestris* (Retz.) DC. Stem 10–30 cm, wiry, cottony; lower leaves broadly ovate; heads *c.* 2 cm, 1–6 short-stalked. Downs and grassland on calcareous soil, mostly S. England, local. Flo. June–July.
Ssp. **maritimus** (Syme) Chater. *S. campestris* var. *maritimus* Syme. *S. spathulifolius* auct., non Turcz. Stem 20–60 cm, robust; lower leaves ovate-spathulate; heads *c.* 2.5 cm, 3–12. Maritime cliffs, Anglesey, rare. Flo. June–July.

Senecio bicolor Tod. ssp. **cineraria** (DC.) Chater. Silver ragwort. *S. cineraria* DC. Stem up to 60 cm, shrubby and woolly; leaves pinnatifid, white felted beneath; heads many. Garden escape. Naturalized on sea cliffs, S. and S.W. England, Wales and Ireland. Flo. June–Aug.

Senecio × albescens Burbidge & Colgan. *S. bicolor* ssp. *cineraria × erucifolius.* Intermediate. Sometimes occurs with the parents.*

Carlina vulgaris L. Carline thistle. Leaves and outer bracts spinous; inner bracts whitish, spreading like rays; florets purple. Calcareous grassland, local. Flo. July–Sept.

Arctium lappa L. Great burdock. *A. majus* Bernh. Leaf petioles solid; heads few, 3–4 cm, long stalked, open in fr.; bracts green. Waste places, mostly S. and mid Britain. Flo. July–Sept.

Arctium pubens Bab. *A. nemorosum* auct. *A. vulgare* auct. Petioles hollow; heads 2–3 cm, stalked and webbed, wide open in fr.; all bracts subulate, equalling the flo. Woods, scrub, etc., local. Flo. July–Sept.

Arctium minus Bernh. Lesser burdock. Smaller plant; heads short-stalked or sessile, 1.5–2.5 cm, ovate, closed in fr.; bracts distinctly shorter than flo., subulate. Waste places, by roadsides, etc. Flo. July–Sept.

S. VULGARIS
SSP. DENTICULATUS

SENECIO
SYLVATICUS

SENECIO
SQUALIDUS

SENECIO
JACOBAEA

×6

SENECIO
ERUCIFOLIUS

SENECIO
VULGARIS

SENECIO
AQUATICUS

SENECIO
BICOLOR

SENECIO
VISCOSUS

ARCTIUM
PUBENS

SENECIO
INTEGRIFOLIUS

ARCTIUM
LAPPA

SENECIO
INTEGRIFOLIUS SSP. MARITIMUS

SENECIO
PALUDOSUS

×2

CARLINA VULGARIS

ARCTIUM MINUS

Plate 48

Compositae *(continued)*

Carduus pycnocephalus L. Plymouth thistle. Wings on stems interrupted below heads; leaves cottony beneath; heads *c.* 24 mm, florets exceeding bracts. Introd. S. Europe. Long established on Plymouth Hoe, Devonshire casual elsewhere. Flo. June–Aug.*

Carduus tenuiflorus Curt. Slender thistle. Stem winged and spinous throughout; leaves less cottony; heads *c.* 15 mm; florets not exceeding bracts. Sea cliffs, rare inland, widespread, but rare in N. England and Scotland. Flo. June–Aug.

Carduus nutans L. Musk thistle. Stem wings interrupted; heads *c.* 4 cm, nodding; inner bracts contracted above base. Grassy places, riversides, etc., on calcareous and alluvial soils, mostly S. England, Midlands and Wales, local in N. England and rare in Scotland and perhaps extinct in Ireland. Flo. May–Aug.

Carduus crispus L. Welted thistle. *C. acanthoides* auct. Stem wings almost continuous; heads *c.* 20 mm, erect; inner bracts not contracted above base. Waste places, widespread but rare in Scotland and Ireland. Flo. June–Aug.

Cirsium vulgare (Savi) Ten. Spear thistle. *Carduus lanceolatus* L. Stem leaves 15–30 cm, decurrent, with few lobes; heads 3–4 cm; involucre ovate, hairy. Waste ground, etc., very common. Flo. July–Sept.

Cirsium eriophorum (L.) Scop.
Ssp. **britannicum** Petrak. Woolly thistle. Leaves 30–60 cm, not decurrent, lobes deep and bifid; heads 4–8 cm, globose, woolly. Grassy places on calcareous soil, mostly S. and E. England and Midlands, local. Flo. Aug.

Cirsium palustre (L.) Scop. Marsh thistle. *Carduus palustris* L. Stem 30–130 cm; leaves decurrent, pinnatifid, spinous; heads *c.* 20 mm, clustered. Wet places, common. Flo. June–Sept.

Cirsium dissectum (L.) Hill. Meadow thistle. *Carduus pratensis* Huds. Stoloniferous; stem up to 80 cm, simple, cottony; leaves mostly basal, toothed or lobed, prickles soft. Wet meadows, heaths and bogs, mostly S. and mid Britain and Ireland. Flo. June–July.

Cirsium tuberosum (L.) All. Tuberous thistle. Similar to *C. dissectum*, but with tuberous roots and no stolons; basal leaves deeply lobed. Pastures, etc., on calcareous soils, Wiltshire, Glamorgan and Cambridgeshire, local and rare. Flo. Aug.*

Cirsium helenioides (L.) Hill. Melancholy thistle. *C. heterophyllum* (L.) Hill. Stoloniferous; stem up to 120 cm; leaves broad, cordate, not prickly, white beneath. Wet places on mountains, mid Wales to Scotland, very rare in Ireland. Flo. July–Aug.

Cirsium acaule Scop. Dwarf thistle. *C. acaulon* auct. Stemless or nearly so; flo. heads sessile on basal leaf rosette. Downs, grassy places, etc., on calcareous and limestone soils, Yorkshire southwards, local. Flo. July–Aug.

Cirsium arvense (L.) Scop. Creeping thistle. Roots creeping and white; stem up to 100 cm without wings; heads dioecious, bracts appressed. Waste places, etc., very common. Flo. July–Sept.

Cirsium oleraceum (L.) Scop. Cabbage thistle. Stem up to 120 cm, wingless; leaves ovate, uppermost yellowish exceeding flo. heads. Introd. Europe. Locally established in plantations, mostly N. England and Scotland, rare. Flo. July.*

CARDUUS
NUTANS.

CIRSIUM
PALUSTRE.

CARDUUS
TENUIFLORUS.

CARDUUS
CRISPUS

CIRSIUM
VULGARE.

CIRSIUM
HELENIOIDES

CIRSIUM
ERIOPHORUM.

CIRSIUM
ARVENSE.

CIRSIUM
DISSECTUM.

CIRSIUM
ACAULE

Plate 49

Compositae *(continued)*

Silybum marianum (L.) Gaertn. Milk thistle. Stem up to 120 cm; leaves large, green, variegated, edged with milk-white veins; heads *c*. 5 cm. Introd. S. Europe. Waste places, etc., local. Flo. June–July.*

Saussurea alpina (L.) DC. Alpine saw-wort. 8–30 cm; stem and underside of leaves cottony; flo. blue, scented. Alpine rocks, Scotland to N. Wales and Ireland. Flo. Aug.–Sept.

Serratula tinctoria L. Saw-wort. Stem 30–70 cm, slender, grooved; leaves mostly pinnate; margin finely toothed. Moist meadows and moors, England and Wales, very rare in Scotland and Ireland. Flo. June–Aug.

Centaurea jacea L. Brown knapweed. Leaves lanceolate, mostly subentire; bract appendages pale brown, rounded and jagged. Introd. Europe. Pastures, S. England, very rare. Flo. Aug.–Sept.

Centaurea nigra L. Common knapweed. *C. obscura* Jord. Stem swollen below the heads; bract appendages, blackish, concealing base. Grassy places on heavy soils, especially N. Britain, common. Flo. July–Sept.

Centaurea debeauxii Gren. & Godron. ssp. **nemoralis** (Jord.) Dostal. Slender knapweed. *C. nemoralis* Jord. Stem slender, not swollen below heads; bract appendages brown; outer flo. often enlarged. Grassy places on calcareous and light soils, especially S. England, common, widespread. Flo. July–Sept.

Centaurea scabiosa L. Greater knapweed. Leaves pinnatifid; bracts pale green, not fully covered by dark fringe. Grassy places, mostly on calcareous soils, but frequently introd. by railways. Flo. July–Sept.

Centaurea cyanus L. Cornflower. Stem, and upper linear-lanceolate leaves cottony; bract fringe silvery; flo. blue. Cornfields and waste ground, rare and decreasing. Flo. June–Aug.

Centaurea paniculata L. Jersey knapweed. Leaves pinnatifid, lobes linear, cottony; bract teeth small, pale; flo. purple. Introd. Mediterranean region. Fields, etc., Jersey. Flo. July.*

Centaurea aspera L. Rough star-thistle. Leaves narrow; bract fringe reflexed, yellowish, palmately spinous. Waste ground, Channel Islands. Flo. July–Aug.

Centaurea calcitrapa L. Red star-thistle. Flo. red-purple; bracts ending in long spreading spurs and smaller spines. Gravelly and sandy places, mostly S. England, casual elsewhere, rare and decreasing. Flo. July–Sept.

Centaurea solstitialis L. Yellow star-thistle. Stem broadly winged; bracts palmately spinous; terminal spine and flo. yellow. Introd. S. Europe. Cultivated land, mostly S. and E. England. Flo. July–Sept.*

Onopordum acanthium L. Cotton thistle. Stem up to 150 cm, broadly winged; leaves elliptic, woolly, spinous; heads nearly globose. Doubtfully native. Roadsides, waste places, etc., England and Wales. Flo. July–Aug.

SERRATULA TINCTORIA..

CENTAUREA NIGRA.

CENTAUREA ASPERA.

ONOPORDUM ACANTHIUM

SAUSSUREA ALPINA.

C. DEBEAUXII ssp.NEMORALIS

CENTAUREA SCABIOSA

CENTAUREA JACEA.

CENTAUREA CYANUS.

CENTAUREA CALCITRAPA.

Plate 50

Compositae *(continued)*

Arnoseris minima (L.) Schweigg. & Koerte. Lamb's succory. *A. pusilla* Gaertn. Leaves radical; stems hollow, widening above; bracts united; flo. yellow. Cultivated sandy soils, S. and E. England, rare. Flo. June–Aug.

Lapsana communis L. Nipplewort.
Ssp. **communis.** Stem up to 125 cm, branched and leafy; involucre 5–7 mm long; ligule less than twice as long as involucre. Waste ground, etc., common, except in N. Scotland. Flo. July–Sept.
Ssp. **intermedia** (Bieb.) Hayek. *L. intermedia* Bieb. Similar to ssp. *communis* but stem up to 80 cm; involucre 7–10 mm long; ligule more than twice as long as involucre. Introd. Caucasus. Naturalized in grassy places, Bedfordshire and N. Wales, rare. Flo. July–Sept.*

Picris hieracioides L. Hawkweed oxtongue. Stem up to 1 m, with hooked bristles; stiff bristles on leaves; beak of fr. short. Grassy places, mostly on calcareous soils, S. Britain, very rare in Ireland. Flo. July–Sept.

Picris echioides L. Bristly oxtongue. *Helmintia echioides* (L.) Gaertn. Stem up to 80 cm; leaves and bracts with hairs on white tubercles; fr. long beaked. Grassy places on calcareous and clay soils and on sea cliffs, mostly S. and E. England and Wales, very rare in Ireland, and introd. in Scotland. Flo. June–Sept.

Crepis foetida L. Stinking hawk's-beard. Stem 20–60 cm, branched and leafy below; buds drooping; bracts downy; inner fr. long beaked. Waste ground on calcareous soil, S. England, rare. Flo. June–Aug.

Crepis polymorpha Pourr. Beaked hawk's-beard. *C. taraxacifolia* Thuill. *C. vesicaria* ssp. *taraxacifolia* (Thuill.) Thell. *C. vesicaria* ssp. *haenseleri* (Boiss. ex DC.) P. D. Sell. Stem 20–80 cm; branched above; heads many, erect in bud; fr. beaked. Waste ground, fields, by roadsides, etc., common in S. and E. England and the Midlands, local in Wales and Ireland, and rare, but increasing in N. England and Scotland. Flo. June–July.

Crepis setosa Haller f. Bristly hawk's-beard. Stem 20–60 cm; leaves pinnate, hispid; bracts bristly; flo. pale yellow; fr. beaked. Introd. Europe. Mostly in clover fields, very rare. Flo. July–Aug.*

Crepis capillaris (L.) Wallr. Smooth hawk's-beard. *C. virens* L. Stem 20–80 cm; leaves pinnate, upper sagittate, glabrous; heads *c.* 15 mm; fr. 10-ribbed. Grassy places, common. Flo. June–Sept.

Crepis nicaeensis Balb. Leaves pinnate or sagittate, roughly hairy; heads 25 mm; bracts glandular; disk ciliate. Introd. S. Europe. Cultivated land, rare. Flo. June–July.*

Crepis biennis L. Rough hawk's-beard. Stem up to 100 cm; leaves hispid, pinnate, broad; heads *c.* 3 cm; inner bracts downy within. Grassy places, mostly on calcareous soils, native in S. and E. England, probably introd. elsewhere, local. Flo. June–July.

Crepis mollis (Jacq.) Aschers. Northern hawk's-beard. Stem 30–60 cm; leaves entire; outer bracts short, appressed, glandular; fr. 20-ribbed. Woods, N. England and Scotland, local. Flo. July–Aug.

Crepis paludosa (L.) Moench. Marsh hawk's-beard. Stem up to 80 cm; leaves tapering to point; bracts woolly, glandular; pappus brown. Wet meadows, S. Wales to N. Scotland and Ireland. Flo. July–Sept.

Cichorium intybus L. Chicory. Stem up to 1 m, branched and tough; heads clustered in axils; flo. blue. Fields, by roadsides, etc., mostly on calcareous and alluvial soils, widespread, but probably introd. in Scotland and Ireland. Flo. July–Sept.

Hypochoeris glabra L. Smooth cat's-ear. Stem 10–40 cm; leaves radical; heads *c.* 15 mm, bracts glabrous; inner fr. beaked. Sandy heaths and dunes, mostly southern half of Britain, local; rare in Scotland and Ireland, opening in morning sun only. Flo. June–Oct.

Hypochoeris radicata L. Cat's-ear. Stem up to 60 cm; forked and bracteate; leaves radical, hispid; heads 3–4 cm across. Grassy places, etc., very common. Flo. May–July.

Hypochoeris maculata L. Spotted cat's-ear. Stem up to 60 cm; leaves hispid, purple spotted; heads broad; involucre blackish, hispid. Calcareous banks and cliffs, mostly E. England, very local; very rare in the Channel Islands, Cornwall, N. Wales and Lancashire. Flo. July–Aug.

CICHORIUM
INTYBUS.

LAPSANA
COMMUNIS.

PICRIS
ECHIOIDES

PICRIS
HIERACIOIDES.

× 2

ARNOSERIS
MINIMA.

HYPOCHOERIS
MACULATA.

HYPOCHOERIS
RADICATA.

HYPOCHOERIS GLABRA.

CREPIS
POLYMORPHA

CREPIS
PALUDOSA.

CREPIS
FOETIDA.

CREPIS
MOLLIS.

CREPIS CAPILLARIS

CREPIS BIENNIS.

Plate 51

Compositae *(continued)*

Genus HIERACIUM

The extremely critical British *Hieracia* were revised by Pugsley (1948). The following notes are only abbreviated extracts from Mr. Pugsley's summary of sections, together with short descriptions of 23 sample species, 15 of them figures, in order to show the kind of gradation recognized among them.

Section 1. *Amplexicaulia*

Leaves mostly in a radical rosette, densely clothed with many stalked glands; stem with a few amplexicaul leaves; heads large; ligules with pilose tips. Unlike the rest of the genus the 3 species in this section seem to be fairly recently introd. e.g. *Hieracium amplexicaule* L.

Section 2. *Alpina*

Leaves in a radical rosette, with long pilose hairs and sparingly clothed with stalked glands; stem leaves o or bract-like; heads solitary, rather large; involucre (floral bracts) incumbent in bud, densely clothed with long pilose hairs; ligules pilose at tip. 15 species including:

Hieracium holosericeum Backh. Leaves light green, narrow, obtuse, subentire, clothed with silky pilose hairs. Mostly N. Scotland. The scarcer *H. alpinum* L. has leaves darker green, more obovate, with less silky heads.

Section 3. *Subalpina*

Leaves in a radical rosette, pilose, and with a few fine yellow glands; stem leaves 1-few, small, lanceolate; inflo. of 2–5 large heads, often very glandular or pilose. 22 species including:

Hieracium lingulatum Báckh. Radical leaves long, lanceolate, subentire, rough with stiff pilose hairs; head large, blackish, pilose; flo. bracts broad, erect in bud. Central to N. Scotland.

Section 4. *Cerinthoidea*

Stem and leaves without glands, in rosette, clothed with long denticulate hairs, rather glaucous; stem leaves semi-amplexicaul; heads large, with densely pilose incumbent bracts; ligules with pilose tips. 14 species including:

Hieracium anglicum Fr. Radical leaves ovate, denticulate, narrowed below to petiole; stem leaves 2, upper bract-like; heads 1–4 with long glandular peduncles; flo. bracts densely clothed with long black-based hairs and few glands; styles livid. Scotland, N. England and Ireland, widespread.

Section 5. *Oreadea*

Leaves in rosette, narrowed below (except nos. 1–3), often glaucous, without glands but with long rigid hairs (setae); stem leaves not amplexicaul; heads less pilose than in sections 2–4; flo. bracts erect; ligules mostly glabrous tipped; styles yellow. 19 species including:

Hieracium lasiophyllum Koch. Leaves oblong, obtuse, little-toothed, rounded below, upper surface rough with setae; flo. bracts greyish-green. England (W. Midlands), Wales, Scotland and Ireland.*

Hieracium eustomon (E. F. Linton) Roffey. Leaves broadly oval, rounded below, toothed, with setae on margin only; flo. bracts dark green. Devon, W. Somerset and Wales.*

Hieracium schmidtii Tausch. Leaves oval, toothed, usually tapering below, with stiff hairs on margin only; 1 stem leaf; flo. bracts dark green. England, Wales, Scotland, Ireland.

Hieracium argenteum Fr. Plant more slender; leaves narrower, lanceolate, glaucous, toothed, with fewer stiff hairs; 2 stem leaves; flo. bracts dark green. N. England, Wales, Scotland and Ireland.*

Section 6. *Suboreadea*

Leaves in rosette, glaucous, sometimes purple-spotted, rather broad, rounded or angled below; stem leaves o–3, narrowed below, with hairs less rigid than in section 5; bracts usually erect in bud; styles yellow. 17 species including:

Hieracium britannicum F. J. Hanb. Leaves ovate-lanceolate, scarcely glaucous, unspotted, sharply toothed; stem leaf o or 1; flo. bracts long, narrow, greyish-green; ligules glabrous. Wales, and from Cheddar, Derbyshire dales, Teesdale to Scotland and Ireland.

Section 7. *Vulgata*

Subsection *Bifida*. Leaves in rosette, mostly glabrous above; peduncles and flo. bracts not very glandular, but more or less pilose and with stellate hairs. 13 species of limited distribution, N. England and Scotland.

Subsection *Stellatifolia*. Leaves in a rosette, these and the flo. bracts clothed with stellate hairs. 2 species of limited distribution, England and Wales.

Subsection *Glandulosa*. Leaves in rosette, usually more or less clothed with long pilose hairs; flo. bracts clothed with dark, strong glandular hairs; stem leaves o–1. 21 species including:

Hieracium pellucidum Laest. Leaves dark green, subglabrous above, purplish beneath, broadly oval, with broad-toothed base; heads small; flo. bracts blackish-green; styles livid. England, Wales and Ireland.*

Hieracium exotericum Jord. ex Bor. Leaves light green, softly pilose on both surfaces, oval with broad toothed base; styles yellow. England, Wales, Ireland, rare in Scotland.*
Forma **grandidens** (Dahlst.) Pugsley. Leaves more deeply toothed; styles livid.

Subsection *Sagittata*. Leaves mostly in rosette, pilose, with spreading teeth at base; flo. bracts densely glandular and sometimes with long or stellate hairs. 12 species, Scotland, N. England, Wales.

Subsection *Caesia*. Plants with more stem leaves, glaucous, narrowed below; flo. bracts with dense stellate hairs and a few glandular. 23 species mostly Scotland and N. England.

Subsection *Eu-vulgata*. Plants with several stem leaves, tapering to petiole; flo. bracts densely glandular and with stellate hairs. 22 species, mostly England and Wales, including:

Hieracium vulgatum Fr. Radical leaves narrow with sharp ascending teeth, purplish beneath; stem leaves 2–5; flo. bracts greyish-green, incumbent in bud, with pilose hairs and a few short glands. Scotland, N. and mid England, Wales, Ireland.

HIERACIUM
HOLOSERICEUM.

HIERACIUM
LINGULATUM.

HIERACIUM
PILOSELLA.

HIERACIUM
ANGLICUM.

HIERACIUM
SCHMIDTII

HIERACIUM
EXOTERICUM
F.
GRANDIDENS

HIERACIUM
BRITANNICUM.

HIERACIUM
VULGATUM.

Plate 52

Compositae *(continued)*

Hieracium maculatum Sm. Radical leaves narrow, dark green, spotted, dentate, with stiff hairs on both surfaces; stem leaves 3–5; flo. bracts greyish-green, with short glandular and few longer pilose hairs. England.

Hieracium diaphanum Fr. *H. anglorum* (Ley) Pugsley. Plant robust; radical leaves often few, ovate, dentate; stem leaves 3–5; heads small; flo. bracts with dense, dark glandular hairs and a few stellate. England, rare in Ireland.*

Hieracium lachenalii C. C. Gmel. Plant robust; radical leaves few, with rough hairs, ovate, sharply dentate; stem leaves 4–12; flo. bracts deep olive-green, with stellate hairs; ligules with pilose tips. England and Wales.

Section 8. *Alpestria*
Stem leaves numerous, rounded below, amplexicaul; heads few, often on branches from upper leaf axils; flo. bracts dark, obtuse, finely glandular, without stellate hairs; ligules glabrous. 18 species, N. Scotland.

Section 9. *Prenanthoidea*
Radical leaves 0; stem leaves numerous, green, reticulate below, semi-amplexicaul; heads many, small; peduncles and flo. bracts densely clothed with dark glandular hairs; styles livid. 2 species.

Section 10. *Tridentata*
Plants often tall; stem leaves many, green, serrate, with thickened edges and narrowed base; flo. bracts incumbent in bud, less clothed than in sections 1–9, often micro-glandular; ligules glabrous. 32 species mostly of very limited distribution, but including:

Hieracium trichocaulon (Dahlst.) Johans. *H. tridentatum* Fr. Leaves elliptic-lanceolate with sharp erect teeth, subglabrous; heads many, small, pale; flo. bracts olive-green with pale edges, with some pilose hairs and some glandular. England and Wales.

Section 11. *Foliosa*
Leaves all on the stem, numerous, paler and reticulate beneath; upper semi-amplexicaul, margins thickened; heads rather large, numerous; flo. bracts with glandular hairs and some pilose. 16 species, mostly Scotland and N. England, including:

Hieracium latobrigorum (Zahn) Roffey. Leaves dull or yellowish-green, shortly or sparingly dentate, lower tapering below, upper rounded; peduncles with stellate hairs; flo. bracts dark olive-green, with dark glandular hairs and micro-glands; styles yellow. Local in Scotland, rare in England.

Section 12. *Umbellata*
Leaves numerous, not reticulate beneath, margins recurved, base narrow, attenuate; inflo. subumbellate; outer flo. bracts with reflexed tips, nearly glabrous. 3 species including:

Hieracium umbellatum L.
Ssp. **umbellatum**. Leaves numerous, dark green, paler beneath, linear-lanceolate with few small spreading teeth; flo. bracts blackish-green; styles yellow. England, Wales, Scotland and Ireland.
Ssp. **bichlorophyllum** (Druce & Zahn) P. D. Sell & C. West. *H. bichlorophyllum* (Druce & Zahn) Pugsley. Leaves numerous, clear green, paler beneath, oblong-lanceolate, subentire or with 1–2 broad shallow teeth; inflo. with longer branches; flo. bracts olive-green; styles yellow. S.W. England, Wales and Ireland.*

Section 13. *Sabauda*
Stems hirsute; leaves numerous, lower lanceolate, upper ovate, often densely pilose beneath, not reticulate; flo. bracts appressed or the outer lax, dark green with fine glands and pilose or subglabrous; styles livid. 11 species mostly England and Wales.

Hieracium perpropinquum (Zahn) Druce. *H. bladonii* Pugsley. Lower stem clothed with long whitish hairs; leaves dark green, broadly lanceolate, with sharp ascending teeth; peduncles with stellate and pilose hairs; flo. bracts with some glandular hairs and long whitish hairs at base; outer bracts loose. England, Wales and Scotland.

Section 14. *Pilosellina*
Plants with stolons, basal rosettes and 1-headed flo. stems; ligules pale yellow, red beneath.

Hieracium pilosella L. Mouse-ear hawkweed. *Pilosella officinarum* C. H. & F. W. Schultz. Stolons long and creeping; leaves setose above and on the margins, white beneath with soft hairs; flo. bracts clothed with dense stellate, glandular and pilose hairs. Common. Illus. on pl. 51.

Hieracium peleteranum Mérat. *Pilosella peleterana* (Mérat) C. H. & F. W. Schultz. Stolons short and thick; leaves deep green, with dense pilose hairs above, grey beneath with stellate hairs; flo. bracts tapering, clothed with long, pale black-based hairs. Channel Islands and Cornwall to Merioneth and Derbyshire, very local.

Section 15. *Pratensina*
Plants with stolons and few stem leaves; leaves entire with long stiff hairs; heads many.

Hieracium aurantiacum L. *Pilosella aurontiaca* (L.) C. H. & F. W. Schultz. Fox-and-cubs.
Ssp. **aurantiacum**. Plant with few stolons; leaves obovate; flo. brick-red or reddish-orange. Garden escape. Naturalized in grassy places, rare.*
Ssp. **carpathicola** Naeg. & Peter. *Hieracium brunneocroceum* Pugsley. Plant with many long quick-growing stolons; leaves oblong or oblanceolate; flo. brownish-orange. Garden escape. Naturalized in grassy places, common.*

Hieracium caespitosum Dumort. ssp. **colliniforme** (Peter) P. D. Sell, *Pilosella caespitosa* (Dumort.) P. D. Sell & C. West ssp. *colliniformis* (Naeg. & Peter) P. D. Sell & C. West. Stem hairy; heads 12–30 in a compact corymb; flo. yellow with dark styles. W. Midlands to N. Scotland, rare.*

HIERACIUM
LACHENALII

HIERACIUM
UMBELLATUM

HIERACIUM
LATOBRIGORUM

HIERACIUM
PERPROPINQUUM

HIERACIUM
TRICHOCAULON.

HIERACIUM
MACULATUM.

HIERACIUM PELETERANUM

Plate 53

Compositae (*continued*)

Leontodon taraxacoides (Vill.) Mérat. Lesser hawkbit. *L. leysseri* (Wallr.) Beck. Stem slender, subglabrous, head solitary, drooping in bud; outer fr. with crown of scales, inner with pappus. Dry grassy places, locally common, but rare in N. England and very rare in Scotland. Flo. June–Sept.

Leontodon hispidus L. Rough hawkbit. Stem hairy; head solitary, densely hairy, drooping in bud; fr. with 2 rows of pappi. Grassy places, especially on calcareous soils, locally common, but very rare in Scotland and N. Ireland. Flo. June–Sept.

Leontodon autumnalis L. Autumn hawkbit. Stem glabrous, branched, scaly; leaves usually glabrous, often pinnatifid; fr. with 1 row of pappus. Grassy places, common. Flo. July–Oct.

The microspecies of *Taraxacum* found in the British Isles were revised by Richards (1972).

Taraxacum officinale Weber. Dandelion. Leaves with tooth-like lobes; outer flo. bracts long, recurved; heads large; fr. light brown. Fields, lawns, waste places, by roadsides, etc., very common. Flo. March–July.

Taraxacum palustre (Lyons) DC. *T. paludosum* (Scop.) Schlecht. ex Crep. Leaves narrow, subentire or teeth few; heads small; flo. bracts broadly ovate, closely appressed. Marshes, fens, wet meadows, etc., rare. Flo. May–July.

Taraxacum spectabile Dahlst. Leaves large, dark green, midrib red; flo. bracts loosely appressed; ligules red at back. Marshes, wet meadows, by streamsides, on mountains, etc., local. Flo. May–July.*

Taraxacum laevigatum (Willd.) DC. *T. erythrospermum* Andrz. ex Bess. Leaves deeply divided, segments narrow, with intermediate smaller ones; outer flo. bracts spreading, inner with a dorsal appendage at apex; fr. red. Dry places, common. Flo. May–July.

Lactuca virosa L. Great lettuce. Stem up to 2 m; lower leaves with broad segments; beak equalling smooth black fr. Waste ground, banks, etc., especially near the sea, locally common, but rare in Scotland and absent from Ireland. Flo. July–Aug.

Lactuca serriola L. Prickly lettuce. *L. scariola* L. Stem up to 150 cm; lower leaves with narrow distant curved segments; beak equalling fr. Dunes and waste places, mostly S. and E. England. Flo. July–Aug.

Lactuca saligna L. Least lettuce. Stem up to 1 m; upper leaves linear, lower pinnate, segments narrow, acute; inflo. narrow; beak long. Banks near S. and E. coasts of England, very rare, and decreasing. Flo. July–Aug.*

Mycelis muralis (L.) Reichb. Wall lettuce. *Lactuca muralis* (L.) Gaertn. Stem up to 80 cm; leaves thin, lobes irregular; inflo. wide, spreading; beak of fr. very short. Calcareous rocks, walls and woods, widespread, but local in N. England and rare in Scotland and Ireland. Flo. July–Aug.

Cicerbita alpina (L.) Wallr. Alpine sow-thistle. *Lactuca alpina* (L.) A. Gray. Stem up to 200 cm, glandular above; leaves with large terminal lobe; involucre glandular; flo. blue. Clova Mountains, very rare. Flo. July–Aug.

Cicerbita macrophylla (Willd.) Wallr. Ssp **uralensis** (Rouy) P. D. Sell. Blue sow-thistle. *Lactuca macrophylla* (Willd.) A. Gray. Stem up to 150 cm, with creeping rhizome; glabrous below, glandular above; lower leaves large, lyrate, with triangular terminal lobe; upper leaves smaller, often sessile; involucre glandular, hairy; flo. lilac-blue in a simple or compound terminal raceme. Garden escape. Naturalized in grassy places and established on waste ground, widespread throughout Britain and Ireland. Flo. July–Aug.*

Sonchus oleraceus L. Smooth sow-thistle. Leaves not spinous, basal auricles acute, spreading; involucre glabrous; fr. 6-ribbed, rugose. Cultivated land, common. Flo. June–Aug.

Sonchus asper (L.) Hill. Prickly sow-thistle. Leaves spinous, basal auricles round and clasping; involucre glabrous; fr. 6-ribbed, smooth. Cultivated land, common. Flo. June–Aug.

Sonchus arvensis L. Perennial sow-thistle. Stoloniferous; leaf spines soft, basal auricles round; inflo. with yellow glands; flo. golden; fr. 10-ribbed. Cultivated land, common. Flo. Aug.–Sept.

Sonchus palustris L. Marsh sow-thistle. Stem up to 3 m; lower leaves deeply pinnatifid, basal lobes acute; inflo. with blackish glands; flo. lemon yellow. Fens and ditches, E. England, rare. Flo. July–Aug.

LEONTODON
HISPIDUS.

LEONTODON
TARAXACOIDES.

TARAXACUM
LAEVIGATUM.

LEONTODON
AUTUMNALIS.

TARAXACUM
OFFICINALE.

MYCELIS
MURALIS.

TARAXACUM
PALUSTRE.

CICERBITA
ALPINA.

LACTUCA
VIROSA.

LACTUCA
SERRIOLA.

SONCHUS
ASPER

SONCHUS OLERACEUS

SONCHUS PALUSTRIS.

SONCHUS
ARVENSIS.

Plate 54

Compositae *(continued)*

Tragopogon pratensis L. Goat's-beard.
Ssp. **pratensis**. Flo. rather pale yellow, equalling pale-edged involucre; anthers yellow; outer fr. smooth, 15–20 mm. Waste places, mostly S. England, Midlands and Wales, local. Flo. June–July.*
Ssp. **minor** (Mill.) Wahlenb. *Tragopogon minor* Mill. Flo. bright yellow, shorter than red-edged involucre; anthers brownish; outer fr. rugose, 10–12 mm. Grassy places, waste places, etc., common. Flo. June–July.

Tragopogon porrifolius L. Salsify. Similar to *T. pratensis* but stem much thickened at top; flo. purple. Escape from cultivation. Naturalized in rough grassy places, etc., mostly S. England. Flo. June–Aug.*

Scorzonera humilis L. Viper's-grass. Leaves lanceolate, acuminate; flo. pale yellow, exceeding involucre, woolly below. Marshy fields, Dorset, and formerly in a meadow in Warwickshire, very rare. Flo. May–July.*

Campanulaceae

Lobelia dortmanna L. Water lobelia. Aquatic; leaves radical submerged, linear, of 2 tubes; flo. pale lilac. Gravelly lakes, Wales, Lake District, Scotland and Ireland. Flo. July.

Lobelia urens L. Heath lobelia. Terrestrial; stem 20–60 cm, angular, leafy, with acrid juice; flo. blue. Heathy fields and woods, Cornwall, S. Devon, Hampshire, Kent, and formerly in S. Wales, rare. Flo. Aug.

Jasione montana L. Sheep's-bit. Stem up to 45 cm, base leafy, pilose; heads solitary; flo. blue, petals narrow. Grassy places on dry sandy and acid soils, widespread, rare in N. England and Scotland. Flo. May–Aug.

Wahlenbergia hederacea (L.) Reichb. Ivy-leaved bellflower. *Campanula hederacea* L. Stems slender, trailing; leaves thin, glabrous; flo. solitary, pale blue; capsule opening at top. Acid moors and peat bogs, mostly W. England and Wales, rare in S. and N. England and Ireland, very rare in Scotland. Flo. July–Aug.

Phyteuma orbiculare L. Round-headed rampion. *P. tenerum* ssp. *anglicum* R. Schulz. Lower leaves ovate; bracts triangular; flo. deep blue-purple, in globose heads. Pastures on calcareous soil, mostly S.E. England, rare. Flo. July.

Phyteuma spicatum L. Spiked rampion. Lower leaves cordate; bracts linear; flo. spikes cream. Woods and verges, E. Sussex, local. Flo. July.

Campanula glomerata L. Clustered bellflower. Stem up to 40 cm, downy; leaves rounded below; flo. sessile, terminal, deep blue-purple. Downs, alluvial grassland and railway banks, mostly S. and E. England, rare in S.W. England, Wales and Scotland. Flo. May–Sept.

Campanula lactiflora Bieb. Stem hispid, 90–130 cm, branched above; leaves sessile, ovate-lanceolate, deeply serrate, pale beneath; flo. large, open-campanulate, variable in colour from milky-white tinged with blue to pale and dark blue, in loose leafy panicles; calyx lobes broad-ovate, acute, about half as long as the corolla. Garden escape. Naturalized by rivers, mostly Scotland. Flo. June–Sept.*

Campanula trachelium L. Nettle-leaved bellflower. Stem 50–100 cm, hispid; upper leaves shortly petioled, teeth coarse and blunt; peduncles 2–3-flowered. Shady places and woods on calcareous and clay soils, mostly S. half of Britain, local. Flo. July–Sept.

Campanula latifolia L. Greater bellflower. Stem 50–120 cm; upper leaves sessile, serrate; peduncles with 1 large blue-purple flo. Open woods and hedge banks, mostly N. England and Scotland, rare in S. England and Wales, introd. in Ireland. Flo. July.

Campanula rapunculoides L. Creeping bellflower. Stoloniferous; stem up to 60 cm; calyx tube with stiff appressed hairs; flo. blue-purple. Garden escape. Naturalized in grassy places, on hedge and railway banks and established on waste ground, widespread. Flo. July–Aug.

Campanula rotundifolia L. Harebell, bluebell (in Scotland). Stoloniferous; stem 10–30 cm, decumbent below; radical leaves orbicular, upper linear. Dry grassy places, common, except S.W. England and Ireland where it is local. Flo. July–Sept.

Campanula persicifolia L. Peach-leaved bellflower. Leaves long, linear-lanceolate, glabrous; flo. few, a broad open cup *c.* 35 mm wide. Formerly native in a few localities in S. and W. England but now extinct. Occurs still in grassy places as a garden escape, rare. Flo. June–Aug.*

Campanula rapunculus L. Rampion bellflower. Stem up to 90 cm; lower leaves truncate at base; flo. small *c.* 15 mm; upper peduncles 1-flowered, lower 2–3-flowered. Garden escape. Naturalized on sandy soil, S. England, rare. Flo. July–Aug.

Campanula patula L. Spreading bellflower. Stem 20–50 cm; lower leaves narrowed into petiole; flo. *c.* 25 mm; calyx lobes toothed at base. Shady places, S. England, Midlands and Wales, rare. Flo. July–Aug.

Campanula alliariifolia Willd. Stem up to 120 cm, downy; radical leaves large, ovate-cordate to reniform, pubescent above, densely grey tomentose beneath, coarsely and irregularly toothed; upper leaves much smaller; flo. creamy-white, 3–5 cm long, borne singly on short pedicels in the axils of the leaf-like bracts, the whole forming a loose terminal 1-sided raceme; calyx teeth separated by oblong to lanceolate appendages; stigmas 3. Garden escape. Established on railway banks, mostly Devon and Cornwall. Flo. July–Sept.*

Campanula medium L. Canterbury-bell. Stem hispid, 30–90 cm; leaves sessile, ovate-lanceolate, crenate; flo. large, inflated-campanulate, dark blue to white; calyx teeth separated by broad reflexed appendages. Garden escape. Established in chalky railway cuttings, mostly S. England and Midlands. Flo. May–July.*

Legousia hybrida (L.) Delarb. Venus's looking-glass. *Specularia hybrida* (L.) A. DC. Stem 10–30 cm, hispid; leaves oblong, wavy; flo. small, erect, purple; capsule long. Cultivated land, on calcareous soil, mostly S. and E. England, rare and decreasing. Flo. June–Sept.

TRAGOPOGON
PRATENSIS
SSP. MINOR

CAMPANULA PATULA.

×3
JASIONE
MONTANA

PHYTEUMA
SPICATUM

WAHLENBERGIA
HEDERACEA.

×2

CAMPANULA
GLOMERATA

CAMPANULA
LATIFOLIA.

CAMPANULA
RAPUNCULUS.

PHYTEUMA
ORBICULARE

LEGOUSIA
HYBRIDA.

CAMPANULA
ROTUNDIFOLIA

LOBELIA
URENS.

LOBELIA
DORTMANNA.

CAMPANULA TRACHELIUM.

CAMPANULA
RAPUNCULOIDES.

Plate 55

Ericaceae

Vaccinium vitis-idaea L. Cowberry. Leaves evergreen, leathery, dotted beneath, margins revolute; flo. pale pink; fr. scarlet. Moors and woods on acid soils, mostly N. Britain and Ireland. Flo. May–July.

Vaccinium myrtillus L. Bilberry. Leaves deciduous, ovate, acute, serrate, green; flo. subglobose; fr. black. Heaths and moors, widespread but rare in S. and E. England and the Midlands. Flo. April–June.

Vaccinium × intermedium Ruthe. *V. myrtillus × vitis-idaea.* Semi-evergreen; leaves elliptic, slightly serrate, with faint glandular dots beneath; fr. purplish, rarely produced. Occurs with the parents on Cannock Chase, Staffordshire, and in N. Derbyshire, and Yorkshire.*

Vaccinium uliginosum L. Bog bilberry. Leaves deciduous, oval, obtuse, entire, bluish-green, net-veined; fr. black. Moors, N. England and Scotland, local. Flo. May–June.

Vaccinium oxycoccus L. Cranberry. *Oxycoccus palustris* Pers. Stems slender; leaves small, ovate, with sides parallel; pedicels downy; fr. subglobose, red. Bogs and wet heaths, mostly N. half of Britain and Ireland, local. Flo. June–Aug.

Vaccinium microcarpum (Rupr.) Hook. f. Small cranberry. *Oxycoccus microcarpus* Turcz. ex Rupr. Leaves triangular-ovate, widest near base; pedicels glabrous; fr. more elongate. Bogs, C. and N. Scotland. Flo. July.*

Vaccinium macrocarpon Ait. American cranberry. *Oxycoccus macrocarpos* (Ait.) Pursh. Similar to *V. oxycoccus* but leaves oblong, up to twice as long and less glaucous beneath; flo. up to twice as large and up to 10 in a raceme (up to 4 in *V. oxycoccus*); fr. twice as large, red, edible. Bird-sown from gardens, etc., and naturalized on moors and heaths, mostly N. England and Scotland. Flo. June–Aug.*

Arbutus unedo L. Strawberry-tree. Shrub up to 9 m; leaves leathery, glabrous; flo. cream; fr. a scarlet warty berry. Rocky places and scrub, S.W. Ireland, introd. elsewhere. Flo. Sept.–Oct.

Arctostaphylos uva-ursi (L.) Spreng. Bearberry. Stem trailing; leaves thick, shining, evergreen; flo. pink-tipped; fr. red. Moors, Scotland, N. England and W. Ireland, local. Flo. June.

Arctous alpinus (L.) Nied. Alpine bearberry. *Arctostaphylos alpinus* (L.) Spreng. Stem trailing; leaves thin, wrinkled, not evergreen; flo. white; fr. black. Moors, N. Scotland. Flo. May.

Andromeda polifolia L. Bog rosemary. Stem woody, prostrate below; leaves evergreen, glaucous beneath; fr. a subglobose capsule. Bogs, mid Scotland to mid England, mid Wales and Ireland. Flo. April–May.

Gaultheria shallon Pursh. Shallon. Evergreen shrub, up to 1 m, spreading by underground stems; leaves alternate, ovate, acute, toothed; flo. urceolate, *c.* 8 mm, pinkish, in panicles; fr. *c.* 1 cm, black, hairy, Planted for pheasant cover and naturalized on sandy heaths and peaty bogs, widespread but uncommon. Flo. May–June.*

Pernettya mucronata (L. f.) Gaudich ex Spreng. Prickly heath. Erect evergreen shrub, up to 2 m, stems freely suckering; leaves alternate, ovate, acute, mucronate, leathery, toothed; flo. campanulate, *c.* 8 mm, white, axillary, nodding; fr. 15 mm, white, pink, crimson, deep purple or black. Garden escape. Naturalized on heaths and banks, widespread but rare. Flo. May–June.*

Calluna vulgaris (L.) Hull. Heather. Leaves minute, evergreen; calyx large, pink like corolla, with 4 ovate bracteoles. Moors, woodland banks, etc., common. Flo. Aug.–Sept.

Erica ciliaris L. Dorset heath. Leaves 3 in whorl, glandular, white beneath; stamens included; anthers not awned. Heaths, Cornwall, Devon, Dorset and Galway, local. Flo. Aug.–Sept.

Erica × watsonii Benth. *E. ciliaris × tetralix.* Intermediate between the parents, occurs commonly where they grow together.*

Erica tetralix L. Cross-leaved heath. Leaves 4 in whorl, glandular, margins revolute to midrib; anthers awned. Boggy heaths, common. Flo. July–Aug.

Erica mackaiana Bab. Mackay's heath. Leaves wider, margin revolute, glabrous above, white beneath; calyx glabrous except apex; anthers awned. Wet moors, Galway and Donegal. Flo. Aug.–Sept.

Erica × stuartii (Macf.) E. F. Linton. *E. mackaiana × tetralix. E. × praegeri* Ostenf. Intermediate between the parents, sometimes occurs where they grow together.*

Erica cinerea L. Bell heather. Stem with short leafy shoots; leaves 3 in whorl; stamens included; anthers awned. Dry heaths, common. Flo. July–Aug.

Erica vagans L. Cornish heath. Leaves 4–5 in whorl; flo. whitish; pedicels long; stamens exserted; anthers not awned. Heaths, Lizard Head, Cornwall, perhaps also native in Fermanagh. Flo. Aug.–Sept.

Erica erigena R. Ross. Irish heath. *E. mediterranea* auct. *E. hibernica* (Hook. & Arn.) Syme. Stem 50–150 cm; leaves 4–5 in whorl; flo. pale pink; anthers ½ exserted, not awned. Heaths, W. Ireland. Flo. March–May.

Ledum palustre L. ssp. **groenlandicum** (Oeder) Hultén. Labrador-tea. *L. groenlandicum* Oeder. *L. latifolium* Jacq. *L. palustre* auct. brit., non L. Stem up to 1 m; leaves elliptic, densely felted beneath; pedicels slightly pubescent; capsule oblong. Garden escape. Naturalized in bogs, etc., mostly N. Britain, rare. Flo. June–July.

Rhododendron ponticum L. Rhododendron. Large evergreen shrub; leaves elliptic to oblong; dark green; flo. large, widely campanulate, purple flecked with brown. Planted, but now naturalized in woods, on heaths, etc., on peaty and sandy soils. Flo. May–June.*

Phyllodoce caerulea (L.) Bab. Blue heath. *Bryanthus caeruleus* (L.) Dippel. Stem 12–15 cm, hairy above; leaves evergreen, linear; flo. purple. Moorlands, Perthshire, very rare. Flo. June–July.

Daboecia cantabrica (Huds.) C. Koch. St. Dabeoc's heath. *Boretta cantabrica* (Huds.) Kuntz. Stem 20–50 cm, glandular above; leaves alternate, evergreen, white beneath; flo. rose-purple. Heaths, Mayo and W. Galway. Flo. June–Aug.

Loiseleuria procumbens (L.) Desv. Trailing azalea. *Azalea procumbens* L. Procumbent cushion-like shrubs; leaves evergreen, leathery; calyx reddish; corolla pink. Mountains, Scotland. Flo. May–July. Illus. on pl. 56.

Empetraceae

Empetrum nigrum L.
Ssp. **nigrum**. Crowberry. Stem prostrate; leaves 3–4 times as long as broad; flo. mostly dioecious. Moors, S.W. England, Wales, N. England, Scotland and Ireland. Flo. May–June.
Ssp. **hermaphroditum** (Hagerup) Böcher. Mountain crowberry. *E. hermaphroditum* Hagerup. Stem not prostrate; leaves 2–3 times as long as broad; flo. hermaphrodite. Mountains, N. Wales, N. England and Scotland. Flo. May–June.*

VACCINIUM
MYRTILLUS.

VACCINIUM
VITIS-IDAEA

VACCINIUM
ULIGINOSUM

ARBUTUS
UNEDO

E. MACKAIANA

VACCINIUM
OXYCOCCUS

ERICA
TETRALIX

ERICA CILIARIS

×7

ANDROMEDA
POLIFOLIA.

ARCTOSTAPHYLOS
UVA-URSI.

ERICA
VAGANS

L. PALUSTRE
SSP. GROENLANDICUM

ERICA CINEREA.

PHYLLODOCE
CAERULEA

×5

DABOECIA
CANTABRICA.

EMPETRUM NIGRUM

ARCTOUS ALPINUS.

ERICA
ERIGENA

×4

CALLUNA VULGARIS.

Plate 56

Pyrolaceae

Pyrola rotundifolia L. Round-leaved wintergreen.
Ssp. **rotundifolia**. Flo. white, *c.* 12 mm across; pedicels 4–6 mm; calyx lobes triangular, lanceolate, acute; style 7–8 mm, curved; stigma with 5 small erect lobes. Fens, damp woods, on rock ledges, etc., local in mid Scotland; very rare in England, S. Wales and Ireland. Flo. July–Sept.
Ssp. **maritima** (Kenyon) E. F. Warb. Similar to ssp. *rotundifolia*, but pedicels shorter; calyx lobes ovate; style smaller and more curved. Dune slacks, N. Wales and Lancashire, rare.*

Pyrola media Sw. Intermediate wintergreen. Flo. pinkish-white, 10 mm; style straight, with 5 lobes above a thick ring. Woods and moors, mostly N. England, Scotland and N. and W. Ireland, very local. Flo. June–Aug.

Pyrola minor L. Common wintergreen. Flo. pink, globose, *c.* 6 mm; style very short; stigma with 5 spreading lobes. Woods, moors and dunes, mostly N. half of Britain, local. Flo. June–Aug.

Orthilia secunda (L.) House. Serrated wintergreen. *Pyrola secunda* L. *Ramischia secunda* (L.) Garcke. Flo. greenish-white, secund; style exserted; stigma with 5 spreading lobes. Woods and damp rocks, Scotland, N. England, Wales and Ireland, very local except in N. Scotland. Flo. July–Aug.

Moneses uniflora (L.) A. Gray. One-flowered wintergreen. *Pyrola uniflora* L. Flo. solitary, white, drooping; disk large; stigma with 5 spreading lobes. Pine woods, Scotland, local and rare. Flo. June–Aug.

Monotropaceae

Monotropa hypopitys L. Yellow bird's-nest. Saprophyte; flo. ovoid, with stiff hairs inside; petals 7–10 mm. The name means 'under pine wood', mostly S. England, and W. Ireland, local. Flo. June–Aug.

Monotropa hypophegea Wallr. Saprophyte; flo. glabrous inside; petals up to 12 mm; fr. subglobose. The name means 'under beech wood', also on dunes mostly S. England, local. Flo. June–Aug*

Plumbaginaceae

Limonium vulgare Mill. Common sea lavender. *Statice limonium* L. Leaves large, pinnately veined; spikelets crowded; calyx lobes with teeth between them. Muddy salt marshes, locally common in S. and E. England, rather rare in Wales and N. England, very rare in Scotland. Flo. July–Sept.

Limonium humile Mill. Lax-flowered sea lavender. *Statice rariflora* Drej. Leaves pinnately veined; flo. separated on branches; calyx lobes with teeth between them. Muddy salt marshes, widespread but uncommon. Flo. July–Aug.

Limonium × ***neumanii*** C. E. Salmon. *L. humile* × *vulgare*. Intermediate. Occurs where the parents grow together.*

Limonium bellidifolium (Gouan) Dumort. Matted sea lavender. Leaves small, obovate; stems spreading with many barren branches; calyx without teeth between. Drier saltings, Norfolk and Suffolk, and formerly in Lincolnshire. Flo. July.

Limonium auriculae-ursifolium (Pourr.) Druce. Alderney sea lavender. *Statice lychnidifolia* Girard. Plant robust; leaves large, obovate, glaucous, 5-veined; calyx without teeth between. Seaside rocks, Jersey and Alderney. Flo. June–Sept.*

Limonium binervosum (G. S. Sm.) C. E. Salmon. Rock sea lavender. Leaves obovate or oblanceolate, 3-veined below; calyx without teeth between; spikelets in 2 rows. Sea cliffs, England, Wales and Ireland, very rare in Scotland. Flo. July–Sept.

Limonium companyonis (Gren. & Billot.) O. Kuntze. Closely related to *L. binervosum* but more branched with broadly obovate leaves and taller spikes. Chalk cliffs, E. Sussex, very rare. Flo. July–Sept.*

Limonium recurvum C. E. Salmon. Leaves obovate; petiole 3-veined; barren branches 0; spikes dense; calyx teeth shallow, blunt. Cliffs, Portland, Dorset, very rare. Flo. July–Sept.*

Limonium transwallianum (Pugsley) Pugsley. Leaves narrow, oblanceolate, 1-veined; flo. small, 4 mm; calyx teeth deep; petals narrow, blue. Sea cliffs, Pembrokeshire. Flo. July–Sept.

Limonium paradoxum Pugsley. Branches short, erect, from near base; leaves 1-veined; flo. in small round heads. Sea cliffs, St David's Head, Wales and Donegal. Flo. July–Sept.*

Armeria maritima (Mill.) Willd. Thrift. *Statice armeria* L.
Ssp. **maritima**. Leaves narrow, linear, 1-veined; calyx teeth acute or very shortly awned. Sea cliffs, rocks and salt-marshes, widespread and common. Flo. March–Sept.
Var. **planifolia** Syme. Leaves a little broader, often 3-veined. Scottish mountains.*
Ssp. **elongata** (Hoffm.) Bonnier. Leaves up to 15 cm; scape tall, 50 cm. Heaths, around Grantham, Lincolnshire and formerly in Leicestershire.*

Armeria alliacea (Cav.) Hoffmans. & Link. Jersey thrift. *A. plantaginea* Willd. *A. arenaria* (Pers.) Schult. Leaves 3–5-veined, margin membranous; calyx teeth with long awns. Dunes, Jersey. Flo. June–July.*

Armeria alliacea × ***maritima***. Intermediate. Occurs in Jersey.*

LOISELEURIA
PROCUMBENS.

PYROLA
MEDIA.

PYROLA
MINOR.

LIMONIUM
HUMILE.

×3

LIMONIUM
VULGARE.

×3

×3

×3

ORTHILIA
SECUNDA.

LIMONIUM BINERVOSUM.

LIMONIUM
TRANSWALLIANUM.

MONOTROPA
HYPOPITYS.

ARMERIA
MARITIMA.

×1½

PYROLA
ROTUNDIFOLIA.

MONESES UNIFLORA

LIMONIUM
BELLIDIFOLIUM.

×3

Plate 57

Diapensiaceae

Diapensia lapponica L. Diapensia. Stems forming a mat; leaves mostly in rosette, nearly linear, flo. pale yellow. Mountains at *c.* 800 m, Inverness-shire. Discovered in 1951. Flo. July.

Primulaceae

Hottonia palustris L. Water-violet. Stems and leaves submerged; pedicels glandular; flo. lilac with yellow eye; fr. globose. Ponds and ditches, mostly E. England, rare elsewhere. Flo. May–June.

Primula vulgaris Huds. Primrose. Scape short or o; pedicels long; leaves narrowed gradually below; throat of corolla narrow. Woods and shady banks, widespread and common. Flo. Feb–May.

Primula veris L. Cowslip. Scape 20–30 cm; pedicels short; leaves abruptly narrowed below; flo. small. Meadows on basic and calcareous soils, locally common, but rare in Scotland and N. Ireland. Flo. April–May.

Primula × tommasinii Gren. & Godr. *P. veris × vulgaris. P. × variabilis* Goupil, non Bast. This hybrid occurs with parent species. Variable, and compared with *P. elatior* more hairy; flo. larger, yellower, with narrower throat. Widespread.*

Primula elatior (L.) Hill. Oxlip. Leaves abruptly narrowed below; flo. facing one way; throat without folds, more open than in the hybrid. Woods on boulder clay, Essex, Hertfordshire, Buckinghamshire, Bedfordshire, Huntingdonshire and E. Anglia. Flo. April–May.

Primula × media Petermann. *P. elatior × veris.* Intermediate between the parents, sometimes occurs where they grow together in East Anglia.*

Primula × digenea A. Kerner. *P. elatior × vulgaris.* A very variable hybrid, leaves usually intermediate between the parents; flo. similar to *P. vulgaris*, but usually paler yellow, and often with an orange eye; pedicels long, erect, pubescent; peduncle and calyx with long woolly hairs. Frequent where the parents grow together.*

Primula farinosa L. Bird's-eye primrose. Leaves crenulate, mealy beneath; flo. petals not contiguous, lobes oblong, pale lilac, heterostylous. Damp meadows, N. England and S. Scotland, local. Flo. May–July.

Primula scotica Hook. Scottish primrose. Leaves not crenulate, mealy beneath; petals contiguous, obcordate; red-purple styles all alike. Maritime meadows, N. Scotland. Flo. May–June.

Cyclamen hederifolium Ait. Cyclamen. *C. neapolitanum* Ten. Root a corm; leaves angled; peduncles erect and nodding in flo., coiled in fr.; corolla lobes reflexed. Possibly native in woods in Kent, and formerly in Sussex, introd. elsewhere, rare. Flo. Aug.–Sept.

Lysimachia thyrsiflora L. Tufted loosestrife. *Naumbergia thyrsiflora* (L.) Reichb. Stem erect 30–60 cm; leaves glandular; flo. small, yellow; peduncles axillary at middle of stem. Verges of ponds and canals, mostly N. England and S. Scotland, introd. elsewhere. Flo. June.

Lysimachia vulgaris L. Yellow loosestrife. Rhizomes stout; stem erect up to 120 cm; leaves glandular; flo. not glandular. Ditches, fens and riversides, widespread. Flo. July–Aug.

Lysimachia punctata L. Dotted loosestrife. Stem up to 80 cm; leaves ovate, margins ciliate; calyx, *c.* 32 mm, and corolla glandular, ciliate. Garden escape. Naturalized in wet places. Flo. July–Sept.*

Lysimachia ciliata L. Fringed loosestrife. Stem 30–90 cm; leaves ovate-acuminate; petiole ciliate; petals very glandular at base; spreading by rhizomes. Garden escape. Naturalized by streams, ditches, etc., and established on waste ground, common. Flo. June–July.

Lysimachia terrestris (L.) Britton, Sterns & Poggenb. Lake loosestrife. Stem erect, bearing bulbils in axils of narrow leaves; flo. yellow and purple. Garden escape. Shores of Lake Windermere, and possibly elsewhere. Flo. July–Sept.*

Lysimachia nemorum L. Yellow pimpernel. Stems weak and prostrate; leaves ovate, glabrous; flo. pedicels slender. Woods, especially on stiff soils, widespread and common. Flo. May–Sept.

Lysimachia nummularia L. Creeping jenny. Stems matted; leaves suborbicular; gland dotted; flo. large; calyx ovate. Damp grassy places, in wet woods, etc., local, but rare in Ireland and a garden escape in S.W. England and N. Scotland.

Trientalis europaea L. Chickweed wintergreen. Rhizomes slender; stem 10–20 cm; leaves mostly in whorl at top; flo. white. High moors and pine woods, mostly Scotland and N. England, rare in Suffolk. Flo. June–July.

PRIMULA VULGARIS

HOTTONIA
PALUSTRIS.

PRIMULA
ELATIOR

PRIMULA
VERIS.

PRIMULA
SCOTICA.

PRIMULA
FARINOSA

P.VERIS X 4

DIAPENSIA
LAPPONICA.

x2

LYSIMACHIA
THYRSIFLORA.

LYSIMACHIA
VULGARIS.

CYCLAMEN
HEDERIFOLIUM.

TRIENTALIS
EUROPAEA.

LYSIMACHIA
NEMORUM

*LYSIMACHIA
CILIATA

LYSIMACHIA
NUMMULARIA

Plate 58

Primulaceae *(continued)*

Glaux maritima L. Sea-milkwort. Stems trailing; flo. small, axillary, sessile; corolla o; calyx petaloid, pink. Estuarine mud, salt marshes, etc., widespread. Flo. June–Aug.

Anagallis arvensis L. Scarlet pimpernel.
Ssp. **arvensis**. Flo. petals overlapping, fringed with glandular hairs, usually scarlet, rarely pink or blue; fr. pedicels longer than leaves. Cultivated and waste land, dunes, etc., widespread and common, but rare in mid and N. Scotland.*
Ssp. **foemina** (Mill.) Schinz & Thell. Blue pimpernel. Petals obovate, not overlapping, glands few; fr. pedicels not longer than leaves. Cultivated land, mostly S. England, rare.

Anagallis tenella (L.) L. Bog pimpernel. Stem prostrate; leaves nearly orbicular; flo. erect, funnel-shaped, pink. Wet peaty heaths, mostly S. England, W. Scotland and W. Ireland. Flo. June–Aug.

Anagallis minima (L.) E. H. L. Krause. Chaffweed. *Centunculus minimas* L. Stem 3–7 cm; flo. sessile, axillary, minute, pinkish, chaff-like. Bare sandy ground, mostly S. England, W. Wales, W. Scotland and Ireland. Flo. June–July.

Samolus valerandi L. Brookweed. Stem 5–40 cm, erect; leaves obtuse, glabrous; flo. white, pedicels bent. Wet ground, mostly near the sea, locally common, but very rare in E. Scotland. Flo. June–Aug.

Oleaceae

Fraxinus excelsior L. Ash. Tall tree; flo. in small racemes, without sepals or petals; stamens crimson; fr. winged. Woods, mostly on calcareous soils, but frequently planted elsewhere, and readily regenerating. Flo. April–May.

Ligustrum vulgare L. Wild privet. Shrub, up to 3 m; young shoots puberulous; leaves lanceolate; corolla limb equalling tube. Thickets, etc., on calcareous soils, mostly S. England. Flo. June–July.
The commonly planted shrub with glabrous shoots, ovate leaves and longer corolla limb is *L. ovalifolium* Hassk.

Buddlejaceae

Buddleja davidii Franch. Butterfly-bush. Shrub, up to 5 m; branchlets downy; leaves lanceolate, acuminate, serrate, up to 30 cm long, green above, white-felted below; flo. small, campanulate, lilac to deep purple, rarely white, with an orange eye, in dense long narrow drooping spikes, up to 30 cm long. The flowers are very attractive to butterflies. Garden escape. Naturalized in chalk pits, and established on waste ground, old walls, etc., widespread and common. Flo. June–Oct.*

Apocynaceae

Vinca minor L. Lesser periwinkle. Stems rooting freely; leaves lanceolate, 25–40 mm; calyx lobes glabrous; flo. *c.* 30 mm, blue-mauve, solitary; fr. rarely found. Woods, local. Flo. March–May and autumn.

Vinca major L. Greater periwinkle.
Ssp. **major**. Plant larger than *V. minor*; flo. stems not rooting; leaves ovate, 25–60 mm; calyx lobes ciliate; flo. 2–3, 40–50 mm wide, blue-mauve. Garden escape. Naturalized in hedge banks, woods, etc., widespread. Flo. April–June.*
Ssp. **hirsuta** (Boiss.) Stearn. *Vinca herbacea* auct., non Waldst. & Kit. Similar to ssp. *major*, but leaves narrower, lanceolate; flo. deep violet, with much narrower lobes. Garden escape. Naturalized in woods and plantations, etc., Devon, Essex, Kent and Glamorgan. Flo. April–June.*

Gentianaceae

Cicendia filiformis (L.) Delarb. Yellow centaury. *Microcala filiformis* (L.) Hoffmanns. & Link. Slender, erect, 3–12 cm; leaves small; flo. small, *c.* 5 mm, yellow. Sandy places, especially near the sea, S. England, W. and N. Wales and S.W. Ireland, local or rare. Flo. Aug.–Sept.

Exaculum pusillum (Lam.) Caruel. Guernsey centaury. *Cicendia pusilla* (Lam.) Griseb. Stems several, short, slender; leaves linear; flo. small, *c.* 3 mm, pink. Sandy places, Guernsey, very rare. Flo. July–Sept.

Centaurium pulchellum (Sw.) Druce. Lesser centaury. *Erythraea pulchella* (Sw.) Fr. Plant erect, without basal rosette; flo. pedicelled, not clustered; lobes 3–4 mm, deep pink. Damp grassy places on stiff soils, often near the sea, mostly S. England. Flo. June–Sept.

Centaurium tenuiflorum (Hoffmans. & Link) Fritsch. Slender centaury. Similar to *C. pulchellum* but branches more strict and erect. Corolla tube constricted above, petals narrower. Damp grassy places, Dorset, formerly in Channel Islands and Isle of Wight. Flo. June–Sept.*

Centaurium erythraea Rafn. Common centaury. *C. umbellatum* auct. Erect from basal rosette; flo. subsessile; clusters subumbellate; stamens inserted at top of tube. Common in dry grassy places, wood borders, etc., especially on calcareous soil, also on dunes, widespread. Flo. June–Oct.
Var. **subcapitatum** (Corb.) Gilmour. Dwarf, capitate, resembling the following species, but with stamens inserted at top of corolla tube.

Centaurium capitatum (Willd.) Borbás. Tufted centaury. Dwarf plant branched from basal rosette; flo. capitate; stamens inserted at base of corolla tube. Dry calcareous downs near the sea, mostly S. England and S. Wales, rare. Flo. July–Aug.

Centaurium littorale (D. Turner) Gilmour. Seaside centaury. Erect from basal rosette; leaves linear, basal, spathulate; flo. few, sessile, lobes 6–7 mm. Dunes near the sea, mostly Wales, N. England and S. Scotland. Flo. July–Aug.

Centaurium scilloides (L. f.) Samp. Perennial centaury. *C. portense* (Brot.) Butcher. Stems decumbent, often barren; leaves obovate; flo. pedicelled; corolla lobes 8–9 mm. Cliffs, Pembrokeshire and W. Cornwall. Flo. July–Aug.

Blackstonia perfoliata (L.) Huds. Yellow-wort. *Chlora perfoliata* L. Stems up to 45 cm, erect; very glaucous; cauline leaves connate in pairs; flo. bright yellow. Pastures, downs, etc., on calcareous soils and dunes, mostly England and Ireland, local in Wales and very rare in Scotland. Flo. June–Oct.

ANAGALLIS
ARVENSIS.

ANAGALLIS TENELLA.

A. ARVENSIS
SSP. FOEMINA

ANAGALLIS
MINIMA.

GLAUX
MARITIMA.

SAMOLUS
VALERANDI

LIGUSTRUM
VULGARE.

CENTAURIUM
PULCHELLUM.

EXACULUM PUSILLUM.

FRAXINUS
EXCELSIOR.

VAR
SUBCAPITATUM.

CICENDIA
FILIFORMIS.

CENTAURIUM
ERYTHRAEA.

BLACKSTONIA
PERFOLIATA.

CENTAURIUM CAPITATUM.

CENTAURIUM
LITTORALE.

VINCA MINOR.

CENTAURIUM SCILLOIDES

Plate 59

Gentianaceae *(continued)*

Gentiana pneumonanthe L. Marsh gentian. Stem suberect, up to 40 cm; leaves linear; flo. large, 3–4 cm, blue, narrowed below. Wet heaths, mostly S. and E. England, very local and decreasing. Flo. July–Sept.

Gentiana verna L. Spring gentian. Leaves ovate, in rosettes; flo. solitary, 2–2.5 cm, deep blue, lobes spreading; tube cylindric. Grassy places on limestone soil, at altitudes of 300–800 m, N. England and W. Ireland, very local. Flo. April–June.

Gentiana nivalis L. Alpine gentian. Annual; erect, up to 15 cm; leaves 2–5 mm; flo. small, deep blue; tube cylindric. Rocks, Perthshire and Angus at *c*. 900 m. Flo. July–Sept.

The British taxa of *Gentianella* were revised by Pritchard (1959 & 1960) and the following account is based on his treatment.

Gentianella campestris (L.) Börner. Field gentian. *Gentiana campestris* auct. Stem 10–25 cm; sepals 4, outer 2 larger overlapping inner; flo. bluish-purple. Dunes, meadows, etc., on acid soils, N. England, Scotland and Ireland, very rare in S. England. Flo. July–Sept.
Var. **baltica** (Murb.) H. Sm. *Gentiana baltica* auct. Annual; stem subsimple; cotyledons persisting. No longer regarded as distinct.

Gentianella germanica (Willd.) Börner. Chiltern gentian. *Gentiana germanica* Willd. Stem 5–35 cm, branched; calyx lobes 5, lanceolate unequal; corolla 2–3.5 cm, lilac, tapering below. Grassy places on calcareous soil, S. England, local. Flo. Aug.–Sept.

Gentianella amarella (L.) Börner. Autumn gentian. *Gentiana amarella* L.
Ssp. **amarella**. Stem 3–50 cm, subsimple; stem leaves ovate-lanceolate; calyx lobes 5 subequal; corolla *c*. 2 cm, cylindric, purple. Pastures and downs on calcareous soil, dunes, mostly England, Wales, N. and E. Scotland. Flo. Aug.–Oct.
Ssp. **hibernica** Pritchard. Similar to ssp. *amarella*, but basal leaves usually linear-lanceolate; corolla slightly larger, dull purple, rarely pale blue or white. Pastures on sandy or gravelly soils, Ireland. Flo. Aug.–Oct.*
Ssp. **septentrionalis** (Druce) Pritchard. *Gentianella septentrionalis* (Druce) E. F. Warb., *Gentiana septentrionalis* (Druce) Druce. Annual; stem 10–30 cm; calyx lobes unequal; corolla creamy-white suffused with purplish-red outside, whitish within. Dunes by the sea and limestone meadows near the sea, N. Scotland. Flo. July–Aug.*
Ssp. **druceana** Pritchard. Similar to ssp. *amarella* and ssp. *septentrionalis*, but middle and upper stem leaves ovate-lanceolate to lanceolate; flo. colour and shape similar to ssp. *septentrionalis*. Shell-sand dune slacks and limestone pastures, mid and N. Scotland, local. Flo. Aug.–Oct.*

Gentianella × pamplinii (Druce) E. F. Warb. *Gentianella amarella × germanica. Gentiana × pamplinii* Druce. Intermediate between the parents. Occurs rarely where they grow together.*

Gentianella amarella × uliginosa. Intermediate between the parents. Occurs frequently where they grow together.*

Gentianella anglica (Pugsley) E. F. Warb. *Gentiana anglica* Pugsley.
Ssp. **anglica**. Stem 4–20 cm, branched from base; basal leaves narrowly spathulate, obtuse; stem leaves lanceolate, acute; corolla *c*. 15 mm long, about 1½ times as long as calyx teeth; calyx teeth unequal. Grassland on calcareous soil, Devon to Lincolnshire, local. Flo. April–June.
Ssp. **cornubiensis** Pritchard. Similar to ssp. *anglica*, but slightly smaller; basal leaves broadly spathulate; stem leaves linear or linear-lanceolate, obtuse; corolla slightly larger; calyx teeth subequal. Sea cliffs, W. Cornwall, local. Flo. March–June.

Gentianella uliginosa (Willd.) Börner. Dune gentian. *Gentiana uliginosa* Willd. Annual, 10–12 cm; often branched from base; cotyledons persisting; calyx lobes unequal; leaves lanceolate; flo. 4–5-merous. Dunes, S. Wales. Flo. July–Oct.*

Menyanthaceae

Menyanthes trifoliata L. Bogbean. Aquatic; leaves large, tri-foliate and flo. pale pink, fimbriate, both held above water. Fens and wet bogs, local. Flo. May–July.

Nymphoides peltata (S. G. Gmel.) O. Kuntze. Fringed water-lily. *Limnanthemum peltatum* S. G. Gmel. Leaves orbicular, floating; petioles long; flo. yellow, fringed, fimbriate at base. Slow streams and ponds, mostly S. and E. England, local, sometimes grown for ornamental purposes. Flo. July–Aug.

Polemoniaceae

Polemonium caeruleum L. Jacob's-ladder. 30–90 cm; leaves pinnate; lower petioles winged; flo. deep blue; filaments hairy below. Shady places on carboniferous limestone, Staffordshire, Derbyshire, and Northumberland, elsewhere as a garden escape. Flo. June–July.

Boraginaceae

Cynoglossum officinale L. Hound's-tongue. Stem woody, leaves softly hairy; fr. with hooked bristles and thickened border. Downs, wood borders, etc., on dry soils, especially near the sea, mainly S. half of Britain, and in Ireland. Flo. June–Aug.

Cynoglossum germanicum Jacq. Green hound's-tongue. *C. montanum* auct. non L. Stem slender, green; leaves subglabrous above; fr. bristly without a thickened border. Shady places, mostly S. England, rare. Flo. May–July.

Omphalodes verna Moench. Stoloniferous perennial; stem pubescent, up to 30 cm; basal leaves cordate; stem leaves broadly lanceolate to ovate; flo. sky-blue, *c*. 15 mm across, similar to a large forget-me-not, but throat closed by obtuse scales, in few-flowered cymes on erect stems; calyx 5-toothed, hairy; nutlets smooth with ciliate margins. Garden escape. Naturalized in hedge banks and woods, rare. Flo. March–May.*

Asperugo procumbens L. Madwort. Stems procumbent and bristly; leaves oblong, hispid; flo. small, axillary, becoming blue. Introd. Europe. Fields, waste places, etc., very rare. Flo. May–July.*

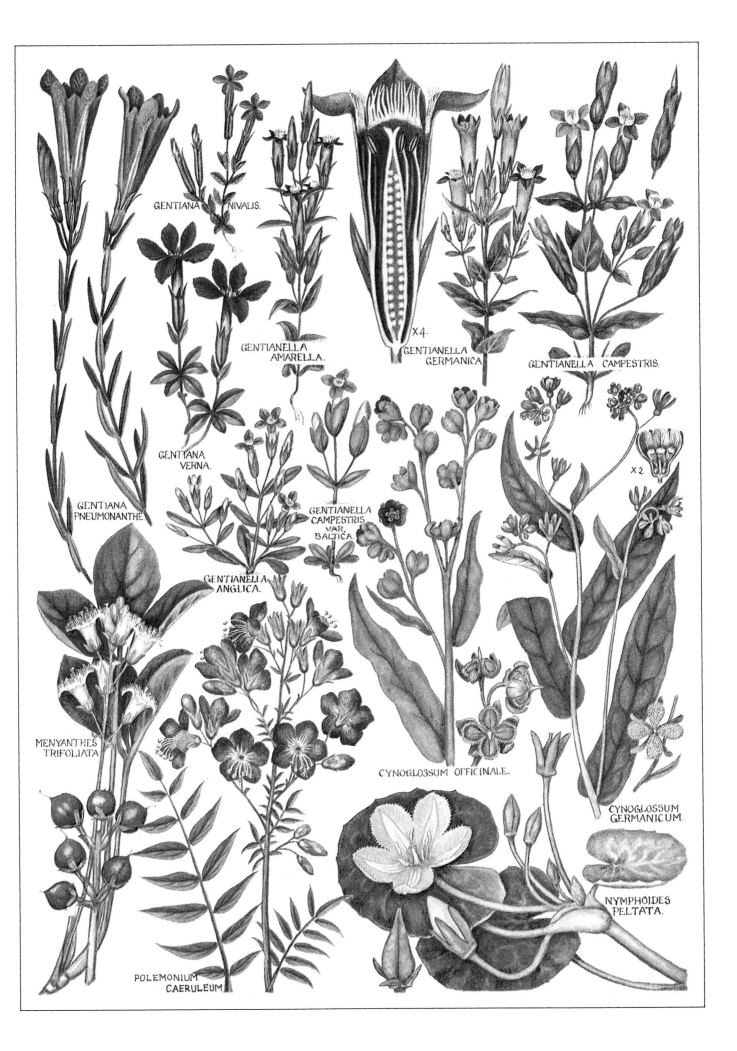

GENTIANA NIVALIS.

GENTIANELLA
AMARELLA.

GENTIANELLA
GERMANICA

GENTIANELLA CAMPESTRIS.

X4.

GENTIANA
VERNA.

GENTIANA
PNEUMONANTHE.

GENTIANELLA
CAMPESTRIS
VAR.
BALTICA.

GENTIANELLA
ANGLICA.

X2

CYNOGLOSSUM OFFICINALE.

CYNOGLOSSUM
GERMANICUM.

MENYANTHES
TRIFOLIATA

NYMPHOIDES
PELTATA.

POLEMONIUM
CAERULEUM.

Plate 60

Boraginaceae *(continued)*

Symphytum officinale L. Common comfrey. Stem winged with decurrent leaves; calyx teeth twice as long as tube; flo. cream or purple. By rivers and canals, etc., common. Flo. May–June.

Symphytum asperum Lepech. Rough comfrey. Stems covered with short hooked bristles; upper leaves shortly stalked; flo. becoming blue. Introd. Caucasus. Established in waste places, very rare. Flo. June–July.

Symphytum × uplandicum Nyman. *S. asperum × officinale.* Russian comfrey. *S. peregrinum* auct. Stem tall, branched, bristly, not winged; calyx teeth acuminate, twice length of tube; flo. blue. Naturalized in rough grassy places, on waste ground, by roadsides, etc., common. Flo. June–Aug.*

Symphytum orientale L. White comfrey. Leaves ovate, softly pubescent, petioled; calyx teeth obtuse, ½ length of tube; flo. white. Garden escape. Naturalized in grassy places, by roadsides, etc., mostly S. and W. England. Flo. April–May.*

Symphytum caucasicum Bieb. Stems rough, hairy, angular, 45–70 cm; leaves ovate-lanceolate, acuminate, slightly decurrent, softly hairy above, grey-felted beneath; flo. blue, campanulate, in terminal twin racemes; calyx teeth obtuse, hispid. Garden escape. Naturalized in woods and plantations, mostly S. England. Flo. May–June.*

Symphytum tuberosum L. Tuberous comfrey. Root tuberous; stems 30–50 cm; calyx teeth acute, 3 times length of tube; flo. cream. Woods, mainly N. England and Scotland, introd. elsewhere. Flo. June–July.

Symphytum bulbosum Schimp. Similar to *S. tuberosum* but its slender spreading rhizome bears large brown tubers at intervals and the corolla scales are lanceolate, exserted. Garden escape. Naturalized by streamsides, etc., Dorset and Surrey and probably elsewhere, rare. Flo. April–May.*

Symphytum grandiflorum DC. Creeping comfrey. Similar to *S. tuberosum* but with slender rhizomes and smaller leaves; calyx deeply divided; teeth linear-lanceolate, obtuse; flo. cream or yellowish-white. Garden escape. Naturalized in woods and hedge banks, mostly S. and E. England, rare. Flo. April–May.*

Borago officinalis L. Borage. Leaves large, ovate, hispid; flo. 20 mm, deep blue; anthers exserted, black. Garden escape. Established on waste ground, etc., uncommon. Flo. June–July.*

Pentaglottis sempervirens (L.) Tausch. Green alkanet. *Anchusa sempervirens* L. Leaves broad, ovate, hispid; peduncles axillary, forked; flo. bright blue. Garden escape. Naturalized in woods, grassy places, by roadsides, etc., widespread. Flo. May–Aug.

Trachystemon orientalis (L.) G. Don. Abraham-Isaac-Jacob. Stem hispid, thick, *c.* 30 cm; radical leaves ovate, long-stalked; flo. bluish-violet, similar to those of *Borago officinalis*, but smaller with a longer corolla tube. Garden escape. Naturalized in hedge banks and woods, mostly S. and E. England, rare. Flo. March–May.*

Lycopsis arvensis L. Bugloss. Leaves oblong, hispid with tuberous hairs; inflo. forked; flo. bright blue; corolla tube with double bend. Arable land, cornfields, etc., mostly on light soils, especially near the sea, widespread, but very rare in W. Ireland. Flo. June–July.

Pulmonaria longifolia (Bast.) Bor. Narrow-leaved lungwort. *P. angustifolia* auct., non L. Leaves narrow, lanceolate, not always blotched; flo. pink then bright blue. Woods on clay, Hampshire, Dorset and Isle of Wight, introd. elsewhere, rare. Flo. April–June.

Pulmonaria officinalis L. Lungwort. Leaves broadly ovate, always with pale blotches; flo. pale purple. Garden escape. Naturalized in woods, S. half of Britain, rare. Flo. April–May.

Mertensia maritima (L.) S. F. Gray. Oysterplant. Stem procumbent; leaves fleshy, glaucous, rough with hard points; flo. pink becoming bluish. Seashores, Isle of Man, N. England, Scotland and N. Ireland, rare and decreasing. Flo. June–July.

Brunnera macrophylla (Adams) I. M. Johnston. *Myosotis macrophylla* Adams. *Anchusa myosotidiflora* Lehm. Stem up to 50 cm; basal leaves cordate, stem leaves ovate, sessile; flo. *c.* 4 mm, blue, in cymes in terminal panicles. Garden escape. Naturalized in thickets, etc., mostly S. England, rare. Flo. April–May.*

Myosotis scorpioides L. Water forget-me-not. *M. palustris* (L.) Hill. Cyme not bracteate; calyx hairs appressed; teeth short, triangular; flo. 5–10 mm, style equalling calyx tube. Pond and stream verges, etc., common and widespread. Flo. May–Oct.

Myosotis secunda A. Murr. Creeping forget-me-not. *M. repens* auct. Stoloniferous; cyme bracteate; calyx hairs appressed; teeth ½ calyx length; fr. pedicels long, 3–5 times calyx. Wet places on heaths, etc., particularly on peaty soils, widespread, but very rare in E. Anglia. Flo. May–Aug.

Myosotis stolonifera (DC.) Gay. ex Leresche & Levier. Pale forget-me-not. *M. brevifolia* C. E. Salmon. Leaf length not exceeding twice its breadth, bluish-green; calyx teeth obtuse; flo. paler. Wet hilly places, N. England, S. Scotland, rare. Flo. June–Aug.

Myosotis laxa Lehm, ssp. **caespitosa** (C. F. Schultz) Hyland. ex Nordh. *M. caespitosa* C. F. Schultz. Tufted forget-me-not. Stems, leaves and calyx with appressed hairs; cyme bracteate; flo. small, *c.* 4 mm; style short, ½ calyx tube. Marshes and wet places, common. Flo. May–Aug.

Myosotis sicula Guss. Jersey forget-me-not. Stem 5–15 cm, subglabrous below; calyx subglabrous; teeth oblong, obtuse, ½ length of calyx. Dunes, Jersey, rare. Flo. April–June.*

Myosotis alpestris F. W. Schmidt. Alpine forget-me-not. Stem and leaves with spreading hairs; flo. large, 6–8 mm; calyx with spreading and few hooked hairs. Limestone grassland in Teesdale and rock ledges and slopes in Perthshire, rare. Flo. July–Aug.

Myosotis sylvatica Hoffm. Wood forget-me-not. Stems and leaves with spreading hairs; calyx ¾ cleft, with straight and hooked hairs; flo. 6–10 mm. Woods, except S.W. England, S. Wales, N. Scotland and Ireland, elsewhere grassy places, as naturalized garden escape. Flo. May–July.

Myosotis arvensis (L.) Hill. Field forget-me-not. Stem and leaves with spreading hairs; calyx with many hooked hairs; flo. *c.* 5 mm; style short. Woods, cultivated land, dunes, etc., widespread. Flo. April–Sept.

Myosotis discolor Pers. Changing forget-me-not. *M. versicolor* Sm. Inflo. in fr. not much longer than leafy stem; calyx closed in fr.; flo. yellow becoming blue. Grassy places on light soils, widespread. Flo. May–June.

Myosotis ramosissima Rochel. Early forget-me-not. *M. hispida* Schlecht. *M. collina* auct. Inflo. in fr. much longer than leafy stem; calyx open in fr.; flo. bright blue. Dry banks and wall tops, mainly S. half of Britain and in Ireland. Flo. April–June.

SYMPHYTUM
TUBEROSUM.

SYMPHYTUM
ASPERUM

PULMONARIA
OFFICINALIS.

SYMPHYTUM
OFFICINALE.

PENTAGLOTTIS
SEMPERVIRENS.

PULMONARIA
LONGIFOLIA.

MERTENSIA
MARITIMA

LYCOPSIS
ARVENSIS.

MYOSOTIS
ALPESTRIS

MYOSOTIS LAXA
SSP. CAESPITOSA

MYOSOTIS
RAMOSISSIMA

MYOSOTIS
SCORPIOIDES

MYOSOTIS SECUNDA.

MYOSOTIS
STOLONIFERA

MYOSOTIS
ARVENSIS.

MYOSOTIS
DISCOLOR.

MYOSOTIS
SYLVATICA.

Plate 61

Boraginaceae *(continued)*

Buglossoides purpureocaerulea (L.) I. M. Johnston. Purple gromwell. *Lithospermum purpureocaeruleum* L. Stems long, creeping and trailing, flo. portion erect, forked, supported by shrubs; flo. deep blue. Thickets on chalk and limestone soils, mostly S.W. England and S. Wales, rare, elsewhere as a garden escape. Flo. May–July.

Buglossoides arvensis (L.) I. M. Johnston. Field gromwell. *Lithospermum arvense* L. Annual; up to 50 cm; leaves obtuse, lateral nerves obscure; nutlets rugose, grey or brownish. Cultivated land, S. and E. England, rare elsewhere. Flo. May–July.

Lithospermum officinale L. Common gromwell. Perennial; up to 70 cm; leaves acute, lateral nerves obvious; nutlets smooth and white. Bushy places, mostly on calcareous soil, widespread. Flo. June–July.

Echium vulgare L. Viper's-bugloss. Upper leaves rounded at base; lower with no obvious lateral veins; flo. blue, 4 stamens exserted. Downs, dry pastures, etc., on calcareous soil, dunes, sea cliffs, etc., widespread in England and Wales, local in Scotland and Ireland. Flo. June–Aug.

Echium plantagineum L. Purple viper's-bugloss. *E. lycopsis* L. pro parte. Upper leaves cordate at base; lower with obvious lateral veins; flo. purple, 2 stamens exserted. Sea cliffs and dunes, Cornwall, Isles of Scilly and Jersey, elsewhere as a garden escape. Flo. June–Aug.*

Convolvulaceae

Calystegia sepium (L.) R. Br. Hedge bindweed.
Ssp. **sepium.** Stems long, glabrous, climbing; flo. up to 50 mm wide, white, rarely pink (f. *colorata* Lange); bracteoles cordate, not inflated. Hedges, marshes, ditches and gardens, etc., widespread, but less common in Scotland. Flo. June–Aug.*
Ssp. **roseata** Brummitt. Stems usually hairy; leaf apex often more attenuate; flo. pink. Hedges, marshes and ditches in coastal and sub-coastal areas in the west from Cornwall to mid Scotland. Flo. June–Aug.*

Calystegia × lucana (Ten.) G. Don. *C. sepium × silvatica.* Intermediate between the parents and often frequent where they grow together, especially in S. England and Midlands.*

Calystegia pulchra Brummitt & Heywood. Hairy bindweed. *C. dahurica* auct., non (Herbert) G. Don. Stems long, climbing; peduncles hairy; bracteoles slightly inflated; flo. bright pink, usually with white bands on the throat, intermediate in size between *C. sepium* and *C. silvatica.* Garden escape. Naturalized in hedge banks and thickets, etc., usually near habitation, rather common. Flo. June–Aug.*

Calystegia silvatica (Kit.) Griseb. Large bindweed. *C. sylvestris* (Willd.) Roem. & Schult. Similar to *C. sepium* but bracteoles greatly inflated; flo. up to 70 mm. Garden escape. Naturalized in hedges and thickets and established on waste ground, widespread. Flo. June–Aug.

Calystegia soldanella (L.) R. Br. Sea bindweed. Stem prostrate, 40–60 cm; leaves reniform; flo. pink. Sandy seashores, widespread, but rare in Scotland. Flo. June–Aug.

Convolvulus arvensis L. Field bindweed. Stem climbing; flo. bracts very small, low in peduncle; flo. *c.* 30 mm, pink and white. Cultivated ground, widespread and common, but rare in N. Scotland. Flo. June–Aug.

Cuscuta europaea L. Greater dodder. Parasitic, string-like, climbing; heads 10–15 mm; corolla scales small; styles shorter than ovary. On *Urtica dioica* and *Humulus lupulus,* S. England, rare. Flo. July–Sept.

Cuscuta epithymum (L.) L. Dodder. Parasitic, thread-like, red; heads smaller, pink; corolla scales nearly closing tube; styles longer than ovary. On *Calluna, Erica* and *Ulex* (sometimes white flo.) on *Trifolium, Lotus,* etc., mostly S. and E. England. Flo. July–Sept.

Solanaceae

Nicandra physalodes Gaertn. Annual. Plant tall, foetid; stems glabrous; leaves oval, lobed; flo. 3–4 cm across, solitary, blue or pale violet with white throat; fr. a brown berry, enclosed in bladdery calyx. Introd. S. America. Waste ground, etc., rare. Flo. June–Sept.*

Solanum dulcamara L. Bittersweet. Perennial; shrubby; leaves cordate, upper hastate; flo. *c.* 15 mm, blue-purple, rarely white; fr. scarlet. Hedgerows, copses, common, but local in Scotland. Flo. June–Aug.

Solanum nigrum L. Black nightshade.
Ssp. **nigrum.** Annual; stem with appressed eglandular hairs; leaves ovate; flo. *c.* 10 mm; fr. black. Cultivated ground, widespread and common in England and Wales, rare in Scotland, introd. in Ireland. Flo. June–Sept.
Ssp. **schultesii** (Opiz) Wessely. Differs from ssp. *nigrum* in having glandular hairy stems, at least some of the hairs ascending or spreading. Introd. S. Europe. Waste ground, mostly S. England. Flo. June–Sept.*

Solanum sarrachoides Sendtn. Similar to *S. nigrum* but very hairy and sepals inflating to enclose green fr. Introd. Central America. Established on waste ground, mostly S. England. Flo. July–Sept.*

Lycium barbarum L. Duke of Argyll's teaplant. *L. halimifolium* Mill. Stem with a few straight spines; leaves lanceolate, grey-green; petals short. Garden escape. Naturalized in hedges and thickets and established on waste ground, widespread. Flo. June–Aug.

Lycium chinense Mill. China teaplant. *L. barbarum* auct., non L. Usually without spines; leaves a little wider, bright green; corolla lobes equalling tube. Garden escape. Naturalized in hedges, etc., especially near the sea, rare. Flo. June–Aug.*

Atropa bella-donna L. Deadly nightshade. Stem up to 150 cm; leaves in unequal pairs; flo. dull purple; fr. black; whole plant very poisonous. Native in woods and thickets on calcareous soil, England and Wales, elsewhere on waste ground, etc., as an introd. Flo. June–Aug.

Salpichroa origanifolia (Lam.) Baill. Perennial with woody pubescent sprawling stems; leaves up to 2.5 cm, ovate-rhomboid; flo. 1 cm, white, solitary, nodding, urceolate; fr. white or yellowish, edible. Garden escape. Naturalized in grassy places particularly near the sea, Channel Islands, Isle of Wight, Hampshire, and elsewhere, rare. Flo. June–Sept.*

Datura stramonium L. Thorn-apple. Leaves very broad, coarsely toothed; flo. erect, *c.* 6 cm, funnel-shaped, white; capsule large, covered with spines, very poisonous. Introd., cosmopolitan weed. Waste ground, etc., rare. Flo. June–July.*

Hyoscyamus niger L. Henbane. Stem up to 80 cm; leaves hairy and clammy; flo. with many dark purple veins; fr. enclosed in calyx. Waste places especially near the sea, mostly S. half of Britain. Flo. May–Aug.

BUGLOSSOIDES
PURPUREO-
CAERULEA

LITHOSPERMUM
OFFICINALE.

BUGLOSSOIDES
ARVENSIS

ECHIUM
VULGARE.

CALYSTEGIA
SILVATICA

CUSCUTA
EPITHYMUM.

CUSCUTA
EUROPAEA.

CONVOLVULUS
ARVENSIS.

CALYSTEGIA SOLDANELLA

SOLANUM
DULCAMARA

SOLANUM
NIGRUM.

LYCIUM BARBARUM

ATROPA BELLA-DONNA

HYOSCYAMUS NIGER.

Plate 62

Solanaceae *(continued)*

Physalis alkekengi L. Cape-gooseberry. Perennial with a creeping root; stem pubescent, 40–60 cm; leaves in pairs, entire, variable in shape from ovate-acute to ovate-deltoid, acuminate, on long stems; flo. rotate, dirty white, solitary, axillary; calyx ovate, inflated, reddish-yellow, enclosing the orange-red fr. which resembles a small cherry. Garden escape. Established on waste ground, mostly S. and E. England. Flo. June–Aug.*

Scrophulariaceae

Verbascum thapsus L. Great mullein. Leaves decurrent, clothed with soft woolly hairs; sepals ovate, upper filaments with white hairs, lower sub-glabrous. Dry banks, walls, etc., common in England and Wales, often casual in Scotland and Ireland. Flo. June–Aug.

Verbascum phlomoides L. Orange mullein. Similar to *V. thapsus* but corolla larger, and flat and filaments shorter, leaves non-decurrent; flo. larger, orange-yellow. Garden escape. Established on waste ground, mostly S. England. Flo. June–Aug.*

Verbascum pulverulentum Vill. Hoary mullein. Leaves not decurrent, clothed with mealy white wool; sepals lanceolate; all filaments with white hairs. Roadsides, Norfolk and Suffolk, introd. elsewhere. Flo. July–Aug.

Verbascum speciosum Schrad. Plant clothed with thick white woolly hairs; corolla yellow, larger than in *V. pulverulentum*; sepals lanceolate; all filaments with white hairs. Garden escape. Naturalized on banks, waste ground, etc., rare. Flo. July–Aug.*

Verbascum lychnitis L. White mullein. Leaves green above, white woolly beneath; sepals linear; all filaments with white hairs; flo. white or yellow. Calcareous banks and quarries, mostly S. England. Flo. July–Aug.

Verbascum nigrum L. Dark mullein. Leaves dark green above, pubescent beneath; filaments with purple hairs. Calcareous banks S. England, rare in Wales, introd. in Scotland and Ireland. Flo. June–Sept.

Verbascum chaixii Vill. Similar to *V. nigrum*, but leaves rounded at base; flo. 2–4 in axils of branches. Garden escape. Established on waste ground, etc., rare.*

Verbascum virgatum Stokes. Twiggy mullein. Stem and leaves green but glandular; flo. large, clustered in axils; subsessile filaments with purple hairs. Waste ground, etc., Cornwall and Devon, introd. elsewhere. Flo. June–Sept.

Verbascum blattaria L. Moth mullein. Plant green, glandular above; flo. solitary, axillary, pedicelled; filaments with purple hairs. Waste places, mostly S. and E. England. Flo. June–Sept.*

A number of hybrids in *Verbascum* have been recorded from Britain. They are usually intermediate between the putative parents and are mostly rare. The following have, however, been reported from a number of localities: *Verbascum × thapsi* L., *V. lychnitis × thapsus*, *V. × foliosum* Franch, *V. × spurium* Koch; *V. × semialbum* Chaub.; *V. nigrum × thapsus*, *V. × collinum* Schrad., non Salisb.; *V. × schiedeanum* Koch., *V. lychnitis × nigrum*.

Cymbalaria muralis Gaertn., Mey. & Scherb. Ivy-leaved toadflax. *Linaria cymbalaria* (L.) Mill. Stems weak, trailing; leaves 5-lobed, glabrous; flo. 8–12 mm, mauve, lip white and yellow, spur 2–3 mm long. Garden escape. Established on old walls, widespread. Flo. May–Sept.

Cymbalaria pallida (Ten.) Wettst. Similar to *C. muralis* but stem and leaves pubescent; flo. 15–30 mm, pale blue, spur 6–9 mm long. Garden escape. Established on old walls, rocks, etc., widespread but rare. Flo. May–Sept.*

Cymbalaria hepaticifolia (Poir.) Wettst. Similar to *C. pallida* but stem and leaves glabrous; flo. 15–18 mm, spur 4–5 mm long. Garden escape. Established on old walls, rocks, etc., widespread, but mostly Scotland. Flo. May–Sept.*

Kickxia elatine (L.) Dumort. Sharp-leaved fluellen. *Linaria elatine* (L.) Mill. Stem prostrate; leaves with basal lobes; pedicels glabrous; flo. spur straight. Cornfields and arable land, England and Wales, rare in Ireland. Flo. July–Oct.

Kickxia spuria (L.) Dumort. Round-leaved fluellen. *Linaria spuria* (L.) Mill. Stem prostrate; leaves ovate or orbicular; pedicels hairy; flo. spur curved. Cornfields and arable land, mid. S. and E. England, very rare in Wales, and casual elsewhere. Flo. July–Oct.

Chaenorhinum minus (L.) Lange. Small toadflax. *Linaria minor* (L.) Desf. Stem erect, up to 25 cm, glandular; flo. solitary, axillary, mauve spur short. Cultivated land, railways, in chalk pits, rather common, but rare in Scotland. Flo. May–Sept.

Linaria pelisseriana (L.) Mill. Jersey toadflax. Stem erect, 15–30 cm; flo. few, violet with white lip, spur long and straight. Heaths, Jersey, introd. elsewhere. Flo. May–July.*

Linaria purpurea (L.) Mill. Purple toadflax. Perennial; erect, 15–30 cm; flo. deep violet, spur long and curved. Garden escape. Old walls, waste ground, etc., common. Flo. June–Sept.

Linaria repens (L.) Mill. Pale toadflax. Stems from rhizome erect, 30–70 cm; flo. pale mauve with purple veins, spur short. Stony or calcareous land, railway tracks, etc., local. Flo. June–Sept.

Linaria × sepium Allman. *L. repens × vulgaris*. Flo. yellowish, striped with purple; foliage intermediate between the parents; variable. Sometimes occurs where the parents grow together.*

Linaria vulgaris Mill. Common toadflax. Stem from rhizome erect, up to 80 cm; leaves linear, rarely lanceolate; flo. large, yellow, lip orange. Waste ground, banks, etc., common in England, Wales and S. Scotland, local in N. Scotland and Ireland. Flo. July–Oct.

Linaria supina (L.) Chazelles. Prostrate toadflax. Stem glaucous; branches prostrate and ascending; flo. *c.* 15 mm, few, close, yellow with orange lip. Sandy places near Par, Cornwall and Plymouth, Devon, elsewhere on railway tracks as an introd. Flo. June–Sept.*

Linaria arenaria DC. Sand toadflax. Stems, 10–15 cm, much branched, sticky with glands; flo. small, bright yellow, spur slender. Introd. Europe. Naturalized on dunes, N. Devon. Flo. May–Sept.

Antirrhinum majus L. Snapdragon. Bracts short, ovate; calyx lobes ovate, much shorter than corolla. Garden escape. Established on old walls and rock cuttings, common. Flo. July–Sept.*

Misopates orontium (L.) Raf. Lesser snapdragon. *Antirrhinum orontium* L. Bracts linear; calyx lobes long, linear, equalling pink corolla. Cultivated land, mostly S. and E. England and Wales, introd. in Scotland and Ireland. Flo. July–Sept.

VERBASCUM VIRGATUM

VERBASCUM NIGRUM

V. PULVERULENTUM

*LINARIA PURPUREA

KICKXIA SPURIA × 4

LINARIA VULGARIS

VERBASCUM THAPSUS

K. SPURIA

KICKXIA ELATINE.

VERBASCUM LYCHNITIS.

LINARIA REPENS

CHAENORHINUM MINUS.

*CYMBALARIA MURALIS

*LINARIA ARENARIA

MISOPATES ORONTIUM

Plate 63

Scrophulariaceae *(continued)*

Scrophularia auriculata L. Water figwort. *S. aquatica* auct., non L. Stems narrowly 4-winged; leaves crenate; bracts small; staminode orbicular. Ponds and wet ditches, common in England, local in Wales and Ireland, rare in Scotland. Flo. June–Sept.

Scrophularia umbrosa Dumort. Green figwort. *S. aquatica* L., *nom. ambig. S. ehrhartii* Stevens. *S. alata* Gilib. Stem broadly 4-winged; leaves serrate; bracts leafy; flo. fewer; staminode 2-lobed. Wet shady places, widespread but rare. Flo. July–Sept.

Scrophularia nodosa L. Common figwort. Root knobbed; stem 4-angled, not winged; leaves coarsely serrate at base. Woods and hedge banks, widespread and common. Flo. June–Sept.

Scrophularia scorodonia L. Balm-leaved figwort. Stem and leaves pubescent; leaves very rugose, doubly serrate; teeth mucronate. Hedge banks, Cornwall, S. Devon, Channel Islands and S. Wales. Flo. June–Aug.

Scrophularia vernalis L. Yellow figwort. Glandular, hairy; sepals subacute, without a border; flo. greenish-yellow; staminode o. Introd. S. Europe. Naturalized in shady places, widespread but rare. Flo. April–June.*

Mimulus guttatus DC. Monkeyflower. Glabrous except for pubescent calyx; flo. yellow with red spots; lower lip much the longest. Garden escape. Naturalized by streams, etc., widespread. Flo. June–Aug.

Mimulus guttatus × luteus. Intermediate between the parents but very robust. Occurring often in the absence of either parent. Stream banks and river-shingle, mostly N. England, Wales and Scotland.*

Mimulus × burnetii S. Arnott. *M. cupreus × guttatus.* Similar to *M. guttatus* but more robust and flo. copper-coloured with red spots. Occurring often in the absence of either parent. Stream banks and river-shingle, N. England and Scotland.*

Mimulus luteus L. Blood-drop-emlets. Glabrous throughout; flo. with large red blotches; lower lip but little longer than upper. Garden escape. In similar situations to *M. guttatus*, mostly N. England and Scotland. Flo. June–Sept.*

Mimulus moschatus Dougl. ex Lindl. Musk. Plant glandular, hairy; formerly fragrant; calyx teeth subequal; flo. 10–20 cm, yellow. Garden escape. Naturalized by sides of streams, widespread. Flo. July–Aug.*

Limosella aquatica L. Mudwort. Leaves spathulate; calyx longer than corolla tube; corolla white or mauve; lobes triangular. On mud at margin of pools, rare and decreasing. Flo. June–Oct.

Limosella australis R. Br. Welsh mudwort. *L. subulata* Ives. Leaves all subulate; calyx short; corolla white with longer orange tube; lobes ovate. Margins of pools, Wales, very rare. Flo. June–Oct.*

Sibthorpia europaea L. Cornish moneywort. Very slender; stems and leaves hairy; upper lobes of corolla yellowish, lower pink. Shady stream banks, very rare in S. England, and local in S.W. England, Wales and S. Ireland. Flo. July–Oct.

Digitalis purpurea L. Foxglove. Stems 50–130 cm; leaves 15–30 cm; flo. pink-purple, pollinated by bumble bees. Woodland clearings, heaths and banks, widespread and common. Flo. June–Sept.

Erinus alpinus L. Fairy foxglove. Perennial; plant small, tufted; stems many; leaves obovate, the basal ones forming a rosette; corolla *c*. 6 mm across, slender, purple or white; capsule ovoid. Garden escape. Naturalized in rocky woods and established on old walls, mostly N. England, Scotland and Ireland. Flo. April–Oct.*

Veronica filiformis Sm. Slender speedwell. Stems slender, creeping; leaves suborbicular, pubescent; pedicels long; flo. bright blue. Garden escape, spreading without setting fr. Meadows, by streams, also as a pest of lawns in many places, widespread and common. Flo. March–May.

Veronica hederifolia L. Ivy-leaved speedwell.
Ssp. **hederifolia.** Stems decumbent, hairy; leaves sharply toothed; sepals cordate; flo. bright blue. Wood borders, etc., local. Flo. March–May.
Ssp. **lucorum** (Klett & Richter) Hartl. *V. sublobata* M. Fischer. Similar to ssp. *hederifolia* but leaves lobed and flo. smaller, pink or white. Cultivated ground, shady places, etc., widespread and common. Flo. March–May.*

Veronica polita Fr. Grey field-speedwell. Leaves grey-green, pubescent, equalling pedicels; sepals ovate; capsule lobes erect. Cultivated ground, widespread and common, but rare in Scotland. Flo. March–Nov.

Veronica agrestis L. Green field-speedwell. Leaves yellow-green; sepals oblong, spreading beside capsule lobes; flo. blue and white or pink. Cultivated land, local. Flo. March–Nov.

Veronica persica Poir. Common field-speedwell. *V. buxbaumii* Ten. Leaves bright green; flo. large; pedicels long; capsule lobes divergent, keeled. Introd. Europe. Cultivated ground, etc., very common. Flo. March–Oct.

Veronica crista-galli Stev. Similar to *V. hederifolia* and *V. persica*, but with small blue flo. and calyces in which the four sections are united in pairs almost to the apex. Introd. Caucasus. Naturalized on banks, verges, etc., England, Wales and Ireland, rare. Flo. March–April.*

Veronica praecox All. Breckland speedwell. Stem erect; leaves conspicuously dentate; pedicels not twice as long as calyx; fr. longer than broad. Sandy fields, E. Anglia, introd. elsewhere. Flo. March–April.*

Veronica triphyllos L. Fingered speedwell. Leaves with 3–7 finger-like lobes; sepals spathulate; flo. deep blue. Sandy fields, mostly E. Anglia, very rare. Flo. April–June.

Veronica verna L. Spring speedwell. Stems erect, 3–15 cm; leaves pinnate, 3–7 lobed; sepals linear-lanceolate, unequal; flo. lilac, small. Dry pastures, Suffolk, and formerly in Norfolk, rare. Flo. May–June.

Veronica peregrina L. American speedwell. Erect, 5–20 cm; leaves ovate, subentire; bracts longer than blue flo.; style almost wanting. Introd. Europe. Cultivated land, shady places, etc., widespread but mostly Scotland and N.W. Ireland, uncommon. Flo. April–July.*

Veronica repens Clarion ex DC. Stems creeping; leaves broadly ovate, subentire; flo. few, 3–6, pink; pedicels longer than bracts. Garden escape. N. England, very rare. Flo. April–May.*

SCROPHULARIA
UMBROSA

SCROPHULARIA
NODOSA

SCROPHULARIA
SCORODONIA.

SCROPHULARIA
AURICULATA

MIMULUS GUTTATUS

SIBTHORPIA EUROPÆA

X 10

LIMOSELLA
AQUATICA

VERONICA
HEDERIFOLIA.

VERONICA
TRIPHYLLOS

V. PERSICA.

DIGITALIS
PURPUREA

VERONICA
POLITA.

VERONICA
AGRESTIS.

V. FILIFORMIS.

VERONICA VERNA.

— *Plate 64* —

Scrophulariaceae *(continued)*

Veronica arvensis L. Wall speedwell. Leaves ovate-triangular, toothed, pubescent; bracts mostly leaf-like; spike elongating; flo. bright blue. Dry banks, walls, etc., common. Flo. March–Sept.

Veronica serpyllifolia L. Thyme-leaved speedwell.
Ssp. ***serpyllifolia.*** Stem creeping; leaves ovate, glabrous; spike erect; flo. whitish; fr. shorter than calyx. Cultivated land, heaths, etc., common. Flo. March–Oct.
Ssp. ***humifusa*** (Dickson) Syme. Leaves suborbicular; inflo. glandular; flo. larger, blue. Mountains, N. England, Wales and Scotland.*

Veronica alpina L. Alpine speedwell. Leaves subglabrous; flo. few, small, dull blue; fr. longer than broad. Mountain rocks, Scotland, local. Flo. July–Aug.

Veronica fruticans Jacq. Rock speedwell. *V. saxatilis* Scop. Stem wiry; leaves glabrous; corolla large, bright blue with red eye; fr. longer than calyx. High mountain rocks, mid Scotland. Flo. July–Aug.

Veronica spicata L. Spiked speedwell. *V. hybrida* L. Stem 10–60 cm, erect; lower leaves oval, stalked; upper leaves lanceolate, not stalked; flo. dark blue. Dry grassland, E. Anglia, and limestone rocks, Avon Gorge, Wales and N.W. England, rare. Flo. July–Sept.

Veronica officinalis L. Heath speedwell. Stem creeping; leaves ovate, hairy; flo. lilac; spike rather dense; pedicels short. Dry heaths, banks, etc., common. Flo. May–Aug.

Veronica chamaedrys L. Germander speedwell. Stem hairy on 2 sides; leaves hairy; flo. large and blue; capsule shorter than calyx. Cultivated ground, grassy places, etc., common. Flo. March–Aug.

Veronica montana L. Wood speedwell. Stem hairy all round; leaves yellow-green; flo. lilac; capsule exceeding calyx. Woods on damp or stiff soils, local. Flo. April–July.

Veronica scutellata L. Marsh speedwell. Leaves linear-lanceolate; flo. spikes lax, alternate; flo. pale lilac. Wet meadows and moors, widespread. Flo. June–Aug.

Veronica anagallis-aquatica L. Blue water-speedwell. Stem green; leaves long; spikes long; flo. blue; fr. pedicels ascending. Pond verges and watery places, mostly S. and E. England, rare elsewhere. Flo. June–Aug.

Veronica catenata Pennell. Pink water-speedwell. *V. aquatica* Bernh., non S. F. Gray. Stem purple; leaves and spikes shorter; flo. pink; fruiting pedicels spreading. In similar watery places to *V. anagallis-aquatica*, mostly S. and E. England, local in Wales and Ireland, very rare in Scotland. Flo. June–Aug.

Veronica beccabunga L. Brooklime. Stems creeping, fleshy; leaves obtuse; spikes opposite; flo. bright blue; capsule suborbicular. Streams and watery places, widespread and common. Flo. May–Sept.

The identification of species of *Euphrasia* is not easy even for the specialist. This is due to genetical, ecotypical and geographical variation and the presence of hybrid swarms where the geographical ranges of certain species overlap, further complicated by the necessity of using minor morphological characters to distinguish between closely related species. The European species of the genus were revised by Yeo (1978) and the following taxa follow the nomenclature and arrangement of that treatment.

Euphrasia rostkoviana Hayne
Ssp. ***montana*** (Jordan) Wettst. Mountain sticky eyebright. *E. montana* Jordan. Stem up to 36 cm, simple, or with 1–3 pairs of branches from near middle; basal internodes longer than leaves; corolla very large, up to 12.5 mm across, upper lip often lilac, lower lip white. Mountain pastures, Lake District and northern Pennines, local in Wales. Flo. July–Aug.*
Ssp. ***rostkoviana.*** Large-flowered sticky eyebright. Similar to ssp. *montana*, but with up to 5 pairs of branches from near base of stem; basal internodes shorter than leaves. Very variable. Meadows and rough pastures, mostly Wales and Ireland, less widespread in N. Britain. Flo. July–Aug.*

Euphrasia rivularis Pugsley. Snowdon eyebright. Stem slender, flexuous, up to 10 cm, simple or with up to 2 pairs of branches; leaves small, orbicular to elliptical, glandular, hairy; corolla large, up to 9 mm across, upper lip lilac, relatively larger lower lip, white or pale lilac; capsule broad and short. By streams and in damp pastures in mountain areas of Lake District and N. Wales. Flo. June–July.*

Euphrasia anglica Pugsley. English sticky eyebright. Plant densely clothed with glandular hairs; stem rather robust, up to 20 cm, simple or with 1–4 pairs of long branches from near base; leaves greyish-green; corolla up to 8 mm across, white or pale lilac. Heaths and rough pastures, S. England, local in Midlands, Wales and Ireland. Flo. May–Sept.

Euphrasia vigursii Davey. Cornish eyebright. Similar to *E. anglica* but stem and leaves dark purplish; branches higher up stem; corolla up to 8.5 mm across, lilac to deep reddish-purple. Local on heaths, Cornwall and S. Devon. Flo. June–Sept.*

Euphrasia arctica Lange ex. Rostrup.
Ssp. ***arctica.*** *E. borealis* sensu Wettst. Stem erect, flexuous, up to 25 cm, simple, or with up to 2 pairs of flexuous branches; lower leaves eglandular, orbicular; corolla up to 11 mm across, upper lip lilac, lower lip usually white. Pastures, Orkney and Shetland. Flo. June–July.*
Ssp. ***borealis*** (Townsend) P. F. Yeo. Greater eyebright. *E. brevipila* sensu Wettst. Stem robust, erect, up to 25 cm, simple, or with up to 5 pairs of usually long branches; lower leaves glandular, oblong, obtuse; corolla up to 9 mm across, upper lip lilac, lower lip lilac or white. Meadows and pastures, widespread in N. England and S. Scotland, rare in W. England, Midlands and Wales. Flo. July–Aug.

Euphrasia nemorosa (Pers.) Wallr. Common eyebright. *E. curta* (Fries) Wettst. Stem purplish, erect, up to 35 cm, simple, or with up to 9 pairs of branches often bearing secondary branches; leaves dark green, lower elliptical to oblong or ovate usually with deeply impressed veins; corolla up to 7.5 mm across, white to lilac. Very variable. Downs, meadows, open woods, etc., common in England and Wales, widespread but local in Scotland and Ireland. Flo. Aug.–Sept.

Euphrasia pseudokerneri Pugsley. Chalk hill eyebright. Similar to *E. nemorosa* but stem green, not more than 20 cm; lower leaves pale green, oblong-ovate, finely toothed; corolla up to 9 mm across. Chalk and limestone grassland, S. and E. England and W. Ireland. Flo. July–Sept.*

Euphrasia confusa Pugsley. Little kneeling eyebright. Stem flexuous, up to 20 cm, simple or with 2–8 pairs of long, slender, flexuous branches bearing many secondary branches; lower leaves ovate to ovate-lanceolate; corolla up to 9 mm across, white to purple. Variable. Widespread on short turf on a variety of soils and in a wide range of habitats, but local in Ireland and rare in C. and S.E. England. Flo. July–Sept.

Euphrasia frigida Pugsley. Stem flexuous or erect, up to 20 cm, simple, or with up to 2 pairs of branches; upper cauline internodes very long, those of the inflorescence much shorter; lower leaves oblong to suborbicular, setose and often densely glandular; corolla up to 7 mm across, white to lilac, rarely purple. Rock ledges and short turf at altitudes above 320 m, N. England, Scotland and W. Ireland. Flo. July–Aug.*

Euphrasia foulaensis Townsend ex Wettst. Similar to *E. frigida* but dwarf and more compact, and with up to 3 pairs of branches; leaves small, dark green, not densely glandular; corolla *c.* 6 mm across, violet, sometimes white. Cliff-tops and salt marshes, N. Scotland. Flo. July–Aug.*

Euphrasia micrantha Reichb. Common slender eyebright. *E. gracilis* (Fries) Drejer. Plant strongly tinged with purple; stem slender, erect, up to 25 cm, simple or with up to 7 pairs of branches; lower leaves glabrous or minutely scabrid, ovate to obovate; corolla up to 7 mm across, mostly lilac to purple. Acid heaths, mostly N. and W. Britain and mainly coastal in Ireland; absent or very rare in S.E. England and East Anglia. Flo. July–Sept. Hairy plants from W. Scotland similar to *E. micrantha* but with very small leaves and small corolla have been described as *E. rhumica* Pugsley. They are probably of hybrid origin.

Euphrasia scottica Wettst. Slender Scottish eyebright. Similar to *E. micrantha* but stem flexuous, green or tinged with red, simple or with up to 4 pairs of branches; cauline internodes 2–5 times as long as leaves; leaves light green above, purple beneath; corolla usually white, occasionally violet. Hilly areas, N. Britain, Wales and Ireland. Flo. July–Aug.

Euphrasia heslop-harrisonii Pugsley. Similar to *E. scottica* but cauline internodes shorter, not more than 2–3 times as long as leaves; leaves not purple beneath; capsules slightly larger and often curved. Maritime turf and salt marshes, N. and N.W. Scotland. Flo. Aug.*

Euphrasia salisburgensis Funck var. ***hibernica*** Pugsley. Irish eyebright. Stem slender, erect, up to 12 cm, simple or with 1–7 pairs of slender branches; lower leaves narrow-oblong, green, but usually tinged purple, glabrous or minutely scabrous; corolla narrow, up to 7 mm across, white, rarely purple, lower lip usually small; capsule glabrous. Limestone rocks and dunes, W. Ireland. Flo. July–Aug.

VERONICA
FRUTICANS.

VERONICA ARVENSIS.

VERONICA
ALPINA.

VERONICA
SERPYLLIFOLIA.

VERONICA
SPICATA.

VERONICA
OFFICINALIS.

VERONICA
MONTANA.

VERONICA
CATENATA.

VERONICA
SCUTELLATA.

VERONICA
BECCABUNGA.

VERONICA
CHAMAEDRYS.

VERONICA
ANAGALLIS-AQUATICA.

EUPHRASIA
MICRANTHA.

EUPHRASIA
SCOTTICA.

EUPHRASIA
NEMOROSA.

EUPHRASIA CONFUSA.

EUPHRASIA
ARCTICA

EUPHRASIA ANGLICA.

EUPHRASIA
SALISBURGENSIS

Plate 65

Scrophulariaceae *(continued)*

Euphrasia tetraquetra (Brëb.) Arrond. Broad-leaved eyebright. *E. occidentalis* Wettst. Stem robust, erect, up to 15 cm, simple, or with up to 5 pairs of branches; internodes shorter than leaves creating dense spikes in inflo.; leaves broad, fleshy and glabrous; corolla up to 7 mm across, white to lilac. Short turf in maritime situations, rarely inland on limestone grassland, mostly in S. and W. Britain, local in N.E. Britain and Ireland. Flo. May–Aug.*

Euphrasia cambrica Pugsley. Dwarf Welsh eyebright. A distinctive dwarf mountain species with flexuous stem up to 8 cm (usually less), simple, or with up to 2 pairs of flexuous branches; lower leaves broadly ovate to suborbicular or deltate; corolla up to 6 mm across, upper lip white or lilac, lower lip very small, white or yellowish; capsule large. Mountain grassland, N. Wales. Flo. July.*

Euphrasia ostenfeldii (Pugsley) P. F. Yeo. *E. curta* var. *ostenfeldii* Pugsley. Stem erect or flexuous, up to 12 cm, simple, or with up to 4 pairs of branches; lower leaves suborbicular to oblong-ovate; corolla up to 6 cm across; capsule rather large. Grassy, stony and sandy places, usually near the sea, from N. Wales to N. Scotland. Flo. Aug. *E. eurycarpa* Pugsley, similar to *E. ostenfeldii*, but a dwarf hairy plant with rounded leaves from the Inner Hebrides, is probably of hybrid origin.*

Euphrasia marshallii Pugsley. Stem erect, up to 15 cm, with 1–5 pairs of rather long erect branches; lower leaves large, densely hairy, oblong-ovate or elliptical; corolla up to 7 mm across, white, rarely lilac; capsule large and broad. Maritime grassland, N. Scotland. Flo. July–Aug.*

Euphrasia rotundifolia Pugsley. Similar to *E. marshallii* but stem simple or with 1–3 pairs of short branches; lower leaves orbicular to oblong-ovate, rounded at base. Maritime grassland, N. Scotland. Flo. July–Aug.*

Euphrasia campbelliae Pugsley. Stem erect, up to 10 cm, simple or with up to 2 short erect branches; lower leaves obovate to elliptical, green above, sometimes purplish beneath, and with white bristles on margins; corolla up to 7 mm. Maritime heaths, Isle of Lewis, Outer Hebrides. Flo. July.*

Odontites verna (Bellardi) Dumort. Red bartsia. *Bartsia odontites* (L.) Huds.
Ssp. **verna**. *Odontites rubra* Gilib. Branches ascending; leaves lanceolate, toothed; bracts exceeding pink flo. Arable fields, etc., common in Scotland, less so in England. Flo. June–July.*
Ssp. **serotina** (Dumort.) Corb. Branches horizontal; leaves narrow, subentire; bracts not longer than flo. Arable fields, etc., widespread. Flo. July–Aug.

Parentucellia viscosa (L.) Caruel. Yellow bartsia. *Bartsia viscosa* L. Plant 10–45 cm; viscid with glandular hairs; flo. yellow, lower lip longer. Damp grassy places, mostly near S. and W. coasts, England, Wales and S.W. Ireland. Flo. June–Sept.

Bartsia alpina L. Alpine bartsia. Rhizome short; plant pubescent; bracts purplish; flo. dull purple, lips subequal. Mountain pastures, Yorkshire to Perthshire, rare. Flo. June–Aug.

Pedicularis palustris L. Marsh lousewort. Annual up to 60 cm, much branched below; leaf pinnae many; calyx pubescent; flo. pink and crimson. Damp heaths, etc., widespread, but rare in S. England. Flo. May–Sept.

Pedicularis sylvatica L. Lousewort.
Ssp. **sylvatica**. Perennial, 8–20 cm; branches few basal; leaf pinnae many calyx glabrous; flo. few. Damp heaths, bogs, marshes, etc., widespread but local. Flo. April–July.
Ssp. **hibernica** D. A. Webb. Similar to ssp. *sylvatica*, but stem only up to 10 cm, and calyx hairy. In similar situations to ssp. *sylvatica*. Ireland, widespread. Flo. April–July.*

Rhinanthus angustifolius C. C. Gmel. *R. major* auct., non L. Plant robust; leaves long, teeth many, acute; bracts acuminate; inflo. crowded; corolla 20–22 mm, tube slightly curved; purple teeth longer than broad. Cornfields, arable ground, grassy places, etc., widespread but rare, and much confused with large forms of *R. minor*. Flo. June–Sept.

Rhinanthus minor L. Yellow rattle.
Ssp. **minor**. Less robust; branches short; leaves crenate, intercalary none; corolla 15 mm, straight; purple teeth broader than long; lowest bract teeth less deep. Pastures on basic soils, widespread, common. Flo. May–June.
Ssp. **stenophyllus** (Schur.) Swartz. *Rhinanthus stenophyllus* (Schur.) Druce. Flo. branches many; intercalary leaves 2–4, linear-lanceolate, teeth often prominent. Common in Scotland and W. England, often on limestone soils. An autumnal variant of *R. minor* ssp. *minor*. Flo. June–Aug.
Ssp. **calcareus** (Wilmott) E. F. Warb. *Rhinanthus calcareus* Wilmott. Flo. branches many, slender; intercalary leaves 2–4, small, linear, teeth appressed. Pastures on chalk and limestone soils, mostly S. and W. England. Flo. July–Aug.*
Ssp. **monticola** (Sterneck) Swartz. *Rhinanthus monticola* Sterneck. *R. spadiceus* Wilmott. Lower internodes crowded, bearing short flowerless branches; calyx often violet-tinted. Mountain pastures, N. England and Scotland. Flo. July–Aug.
Ssp. **borealis** (Sterneck) P. D. Sell. *Rhinanthus borealis* (Sterneck) Druce. Stem simple, 10–20 cm; leaves broad, blunt, pubescent; calyx hairy. Mountains, Scotland and Kerry. Now considered to fall within the range of *R. minor* ssp. *minor*. Flo. July–Aug.
Ssp. **lintoni** (Wilmott) P. D. Sell. *Rhinanthus lintoni* Wilmott. *R. drummondhayi* auct. Stem 10–20 cm, subsimple, slender; leaves narrow, tapering; calyx pubescent, elongate. Mountains, Scotland. Flo. July–Aug.

Melampyrum cristatum L. Crested cow-wheat. Flo. in dense spike, yellow and purple tinted; bracts with wider, pink, finely pectinate base, lower with long points. Woods, S. and E. England, rare. Flo. June–Sept.

Melampyrum arvense L. Field cow-wheat. Flo. pink and yellow in lax spike; bracts finely pinnate, points less long. Cornfields, S. and E. England, rare and decreasing. Flo. June–Sept.

Melampyrum pratense L. Common cow-wheat. Flo. in separate leaf axils; calyx small; corolla 10–15 mm, yellow in woods, or white splashed with pink on moors, common. Flo. June–Aug.

Melampyrum sylvaticum L. Small cow-wheat. Flo. in separate leaf axils; calyx lobes long, equalling smaller yellow corolla. Mountain woods, N. England, Scotland and N. Ireland, rare. Flo. June–Aug.

PARENTUCELLIA
VISCOSA.

BARTSIA
ALPINA

PEDICULARIS
SYLVATICA.

ODONTITES VERNA
SSP. SEROTINA

PEDICULARIS
PALUSTRIS.

RHINANTHUS
ANGUSTIFOLIUS

MELAMPYRUM
PRATENSE.

R. MINOR
SSP. STENOPHYLLUS

RHINANTHUS MINOR
SSP. MONTICOLA

RHINANTHUS MINOR
SSP. BOREALIS

RHINANTHUS
MINOR.

RHINANTHUS MINOR
SSP. LINTONI

MELAMPYRUM
CRISTATUM

MELAMPYRUM
SYLVATICUM

MELAMPYRUM
ARVENSE.

Plate 66

Orobanchaceae

Orobanche purpurea Jacq. Yarrow broomrape. *O. caerulea* Vill. Stem simple, bluish; flo. dull bluish-purple, with 1 bract and 2 bracteoles; stigma lobes white, united. Parasitic on *Achillea millefolium*, Channel Islands, common; S. and E. England, rare. Flo. June–July.

Orobanche ramosa L. Hemp broomrape. Stem with a few basal branches; flo. *c.* 15 mm, cream with purple edges; 1 bract and 2 bracteoles. Parasitic on *Cannabis*, Channel Islands, introd. in S.E. England, very rare. Flo. July–Sept.

Orobanche rapum-genistae Thuill. Greater broomrape. Stem 20–80 cm; flo. large, yellowish; bract 1 only; stamens basal; stigma lobes yellow, distant. Parasitic on *Ulex* and *Cytisus*, mostly England and Wales, rare and decreasing. Flo. May–July.

Orobanche alba Steph. ex Willd. Thyme broomrape. Stem 8–25 cm, red; flo. deep red (in Britain); stigma lobes red, contiguous. Parasitic on *Thymus*, mostly near S. coast of Cornwall, W. coast of Scotland and N.E. and W. coasts of Ireland. Flo. June–Aug.

Orobanche caryophyllacea Sm. Bedstraw broomrape. Flo. large, yellowish, purple-tinted, densely glandular; stamens subbasal; stigma lobes distant, purple. Parasitic on *Galium mollugo*, E. Kent, very rare. Flo. July.

Orobanche elatior Sutton. Knapweed broomrape. *O. major* auct. Stem 15–70 cm; flo. pale yellow, tinted purple, glandular; stigma lobes yellow; stamens inserted 5 mm above base. Parasitic on *Centaurea scabiosa*, S. and E. England, local. Flo. July.

Orobanche reticulata Wallr.
Ssp. **pallidiflora** (Wimm. & Grab.) Hegi. Thistle broomrape. Stem 15–45 cm, glandular; flo. yellowish with purple edges; stamens 3–4 mm above base; stigmas purple. Parasitic on *Cirsium*, Yorkshire, very rare. Flo. June–Aug.*

Orobanche amethystea Thuill. Carrot broomrape. Flo. many, dull yellow-veined purple; central lobe larger; stigma lobes purple, partly united. Parasitic, mostly on *Daucus carota*, S. and W. coasts of England, very rare. Flo. June–July.*

Orobanche loricata Reichb. Oxtongue broomrape. *O. picridis* F. W. Schultz ex Koch. Flo. pale, whitish-yellow, tinted purple, glandular; filaments very hairy below, inserted 4 mm above base. Parasitic on *Picris* and *Crepis*, S. England, very rare. Flo. June–July.

Orobanche hederae Duby. Ivy broomrape. Corolla straight, cream, veined purple; stamens inserted 3 mm above base; stigma lobes yellow, united. Parasitic on *Hedera*, S. England, Wales, and Ireland, mostly coastal. Flo. June–July.

Orobanche minor Sm. Common broomrape. *O. apiculata* Wallr. Stem 10–30 cm, spike lax, yellow, tinted purple; corolla curved and equal throughout; stigma lobes purple, contiguous; filaments subglabrous. Parasitic on species of Leguminosae and Compositae, mostly S. and E. England, S. Wales and S. Ireland. Flo. June–Aug.

*****Lathraea squamaria** L. Toothwort. Root parasite without green colour; stem up to 30 cm; calyx glandular; flo. cream, short-stalked. Parasitic, mostly on roots of *Corylus* and *Ulmus*, widespread. Flo. March–May.

*****Lathraea clandestina** L. Purple toothwort. Similar to *L. squamaria* but stems mostly underground, branched, forming clumps; flo. reddish-purple to violet, long-stalked. Parasitic on roots of *Populus* or *Salix* species. Garden escape. Verges of ponds and streams, mostly S. and E. England, rare. Flo. April–May.*

Lentibulariaceae

Utricularia vulgaris L. Greater bladderwort. Aquatic with bladders on green capillary leaves; corolla up to 25 mm, deep yellow, upper lip equalling palate, lower lip deflexed. Ponds, local and decreasing. Flo. July–Aug.

Utricularia australis R. Br. *U. neglecta* Lehm. *U. major* auct. Aquatic with bladders on green leaves; upper lip of flo. longer than palate, lower lip margins flat. Ponds, widespread, but local. Flo. July–Aug.

Utricularia intermedia Hayne. Intermediate bladderwort. Aquatic with bladders mostly on colourless leaves under mud; corolla up to 12 mm, pale yellow streaked red. Peaty water, mostly N. England, Scotland and W. Ireland, very local. Flo. rare, July–Sept.

Utricularia minor L. Lesser bladderwort. Aquatic with bladders on small colourless and green leaves; corolla up to 8 mm, pale yellow. Boggy pools and ditches, widespread, but local. Flo. July–Sept.

Pinguicula vulgaris L. Common butterwort. Flo. up to 12 mm across, deep violet with white throat; lobes of lip spreading; spur 5–6 mm, acute. Wet rocks and bogs, mostly N. England, Scotland and N. Ireland. Flo. May–June.

Pinguicula grandiflora Lam. Large-flowered butterwort. Flo. large, 20–25 mm across, deep violet with white throat; lobes of lip broad, overlapping spur 10 mm. Bogs, S.W. Ireland, formerly naturalized in S.W. England. Flo. May–June.

Pinguicula lusitanica L. Pale butterwort. Flo. 6–7 mm across, pale yellow, tinged lilac; spur cylindrical; capsule globose. Wet heaths and peaty bogs, mostly S.W. England, W. Scotland, and W. Ireland. Flo. June–Sept.

*The most recent treatment places the genus *Lathraea* in the family Scrophulariaceae.

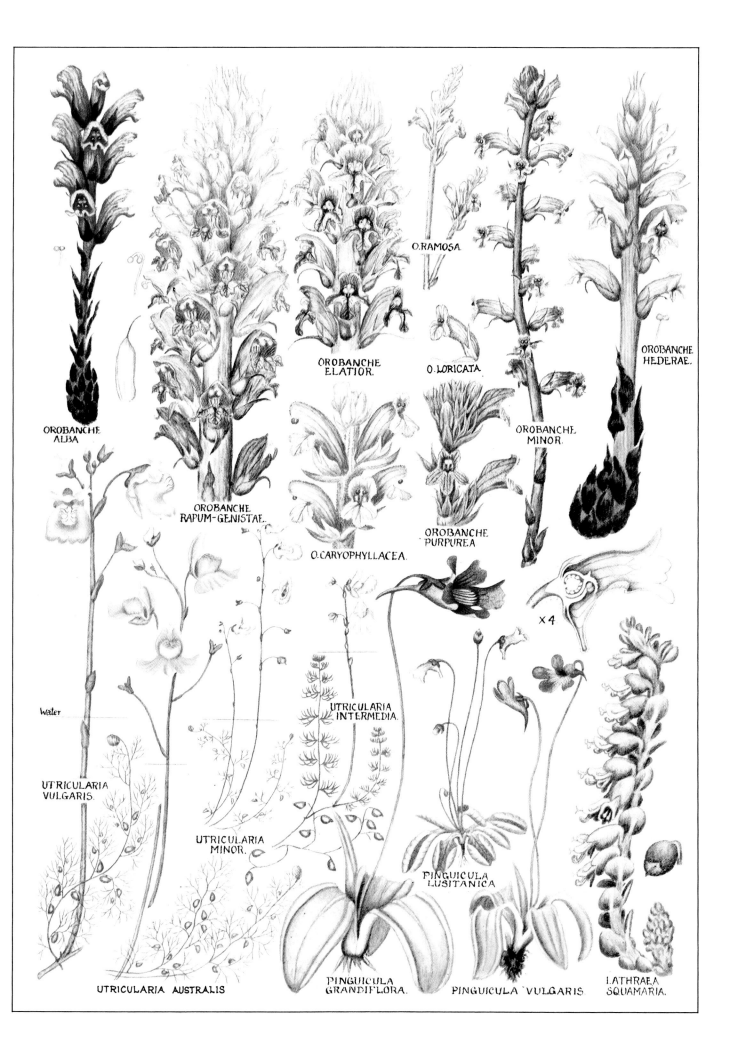

OROBANCHE
ALBA

OROBANCHE
RAPUM-GENISTAE.

OROBANCHE
ELATIOR.

O.RAMOSA.

O.LORICATA.

OROBANCHE
HEDERAE.

OROBANCHE
MINOR.

O.CARYOPHYLLACEA.

OROBANCHE
PURPUREA

×4

Water

UTRICULARIA
VULGARIS.

UTRICULARIA
INTERMEDIA.

UTRICULARIA
MINOR.

PINGUICULA
LUSITANICA

UTRICULARIA AUSTRALIS

PINGUICULA
GRANDIFLORA.

PINGUICULA VULGARIS

LATHRAEA
SQUAMARIA.

Plate 67

Verbenaceae

Verbena officinalis L. Vervain. Stem 30–50 cm, tough, hispid; branches few, spreading; flo. few, pale lilac. Waste ground, roadsides, etc., mostly England and Wales, very rare in Scotland, introd. in Ireland. Flo. July–Sept.

Labiatae

Mentha suaveolens Ehrh. Round-leaved mint. *M. rotundifolia* auct., non (L.) Huds. Leaves nearly round, much wrinkled; bracts lanceolate; flo. in compact spike. Ditches, roadsides, etc., mostly S. and W. England, local, rare in Wales, Scotland and Ireland. Flo. Aug.–Sept.

Mentha longifolia auct., non (L.) Huds. Horse mint. Leaves lanceolate, woolly white beneath; bracts subulate; flo. spike dense. Commonly naturalized from gardens. Now regarded as merely a hairy form of *M. spicata*. Flo. Aug.–Sept.

Mentha spicata L. Leaves sessile, lanceolate, glabrous; flo. in spike; bracts linear; lower stamens exserted. Garden escape. Established on waste ground, etc., common. Flo. Aug.–Sept.

Mentha × villosa Huds. *Mentha spicata × suaveolens*. *M. alopecuroides* Hull. Very robust; leaves large, broadly ovate, softly wrinkled; bracts subulate; flo. in a spike. Garden escape. Waste ground, etc., common.*

Mentha × piperita L. *M. aquatica × spicata*. Peppermint. Stem red; leaves ovate, stalked, subglabrous, purple-tinted; spike interrupted below; stamens included. Ditches, etc., local. Flo. Aug.–Sept.

Mentha aquatica L. Water mint. Stem and ovate leaves robust, hairy; inflo. of 2–3 whorls, lower separate; stamens exserted. Ditches and wet places. Widespread and common. Flo. Aug–Sept.

Mentha × smithiana R. A. Graham. *M. aquatica × arvensis × spicata*. *M. rubra* Sm., non Mill. Stems often red; leaves broadly ovate, obtuse, subglabrous; bracts leaf-like; calyx teeth twice as long as broad; stamens exserted. Streamsides, marshes, etc., mostly S. Britain, local. Flo. Aug.–Sept.

Mentha × gentilis L. *M. arvensis × spicata*. *M × cardiaca* (S. F. Gray) Bak. Leaves ovate-lanceolate, hairy; bracts leaf-like; pedicels and calyx subglabrous; teeth twice as long as broad; flo. small, 3 mm; stamens not exserted. Damp places, common. Flo. Aug.–Sept.

Mentha × verticillata L. Whorled mint. *M. aquatica × arvensis*. *M. × sativa* L. Robust; leaves ovate, hairy; bracts leaf-like; pedicels and calyx hairy; teeth twice as long as broad; stamens not exserted. Damp cultivated and waste ground, pond and river sides, etc., common. Flo. Aug.–Sept.*

Mentha arvensis L. Corn mint. Leaves ovate, hairy; whorls axillary, distant; bracts leaf-like; calyx teeth triangular, hairy, as long as broad; stamens exserted. Cornfields and cultivated ground, common. Flo. Aug.–Sept.

Mentha requienii Benth. Corsican mint. Stems 3–10 cm, creeping, rooting at nodes to form large mats; leaves 3–5 mm, ovate, entire, strongly scented; flo. few in leaf-axils, very small, lilac. Garden escape. Established on paths, bare ground, etc., mostly S. England. Flo. June–Aug.*

Mentha pulegium L. Penny royal. Stem prostrate below; leaves small, oval, 8–10 mm; whorls distant; bracts leaf-like; flo. swollen below mouth. Damp sandy places, often near the sea, mostly S. England and S. Ireland, very rare and decreasing. Flo. Aug.–Sept.

Lycopus europaeus L. Gipsywort. Stem 3–8 cm; leaves lobed or dentate; calyx spine pointed; flo. white, spotted purple. Ditches, river banks, etc., widespread and common, but local in N. England and Scotland. Flo. June–Sept.

Origanum vulgare L. Marjoram. Stem wiry, branched as shown; bracts leaf-like, small; bracteoles purple; flo. pale rose. Dry fields, scrub, etc., mostly on calcareous soils, widespread, common in England, Wales and S. Ireland, local in Scotland and N. Ireland. Flo. July–Sept.

VERBENA
OFFICINALIS.

MENTHA
SUAVEOLENS

×3

MENTHA
LONGIFOLIA.

×3

MENTHA
X PIPERITA

×2

×3

MENTHA
SPICATA.

MENTHA PULEGIUM.

MENTHA AQUATICA.

×3

MENTHA
GENTILIS

MENTHA
SMITHIANA.

MENTHA
ARVENSIS

LYCOPUS
EUROPAEUS

ORIGANUM
VULGARE.

Plate 68

Labiatae *(continued)*

Thymus serpyllum L. Breckland thyme. Creeping stems many, long; flo. stems hairy all round; leaves 4–6 mm; flo. in 1 head. Sandy heaths, etc., E. England, very local. Flo. June–Aug.

Thymus praecox Opiz ssp. **britannicus** (Ronn.) Holub. Wild thyme. *T. drucei* Ronn. Creeping stems many, dense; flo. stems hairy on 2 sides only; leaves 5–8 mm; flo. in 1 head. Dry banks and heaths, widespread and common. Flo. June–Aug.*

Thymus pulegioides L. Large thyme. *T. chamaedrys* Fr. Creeping stems few; stem angles sharp and hairy; leaves up to 10 mm; inflo. with separate whorl below. Grassy places on calcareous and other dry soils, mostly S. and E. England. Flo. July–Aug.

Clinopodium vulgare L. Wild basil. *Calamintha clinopodium* Benth. Stems up to 60 cm; flo. rose-red in terminal and axillary heads; bracteoles subulate, ciliate. Banks, scrub, etc., mostly on calcareous soils. Widespread, common in S. half of Britain, local in N. England and Scotland. Flo. July–Sept.

Acinos arvensis (Lam.) Dandy. Basil thyme. *Calamintha acinos* (L.) Clairv. Stem 10–30 cm, ascending; flo. violet in small whorls; calyx curved, swollen below. Dry grassy places mostly on calcareous soils, S. England and Wales, local elsewhere. Flo. Aug.–Sept.

Melissa officinalis L. Balm. Stems many, up to 60 cm; leaves ovate, wrinkled; calyx with 2 unequal lips; flo. white. Garden escape. Naturalized, mostly S. England. Flo. May–July.

Calamintha nepeta (L.) Savi. Lesser calamint. Stem up to 50 cm; leaves small, greyish, hairy; calyx teeth nearly alike, internal hairs protruding; flo. mauve. Dry banks on calcareous soils, mostly S. England, rare. Flo. July–Aug.

Calamintha sylvatica Bromf.
Ssp. **sylvatica**. Wood calamint. Stem up to 50 cm; leaves large; flo. 15–20 mm; flo. purple, blotched. Chalky banks, Isle of Wight, very rare. Flo. July–Sept.
Ssp. **ascendens** (Jord.) P. W. Ball. Common calamint. *C. ascendens* Jord. *C. officinalis* auct. Stem up to 30 cm; leaves larger, calyx with lower teeth much longer; flo. pale lilac, spotted. Banks, etc., on calcareous soils, England and Ireland, local. Flo. July–Sept.

Salvia verbenaca L. Wild clary. *S. horminoides* Pourr. Leaves coarsely toothed or lobed; upper teeth of calyx united; flo. often shorter than calyx, violet with 2 white spots. Dry grassy places, roadsides, etc., mostly S. and E. England, rare elsewhere, local. Flo. June–Sept.

Salvia pratensis L. Meadow clary. Upper leaves and bracts ovate; corolla large, up to 25 mm, 3 times length of calyx, deep violet. Calcareous soils, S. and S.E. England, local, introd. elsewhere. Flo. June–July.

Salvia verticillata L. Whorled clary. Bracts small, brown, reflexed; calyx with 3 upper teeth distinct; flo. *c.* 12 mm, violet, with a ring of hairs within. Introd. S. Europe. Waste places, mostly S. England, uncommon. Flo. June–July.*

Nepeta cataria L. Cat-mint. Stem 40–90 cm; leaves pubescent, white beneath; inflo. dense; flo. white. Hedge banks, thickets, etc., often on calcareous soils, mostly S. England, rare in Wales, N. England and Scotland, introd. in Ireland. Flo. July–Sept.

Glechoma hederacea L. Ground-ivy. *Nepeta glechoma* Benth. Stem creeping; leaves reniform, soft; flo. blue-purple, sometimes small and female. Woods and shady places, widespread and common, but rare in N. Scotland. Flo. April–June.

Scutellaria galericulata L. Skullcap. Stem up to 40 cm, from rhizome; leaves rounded or cordate below; flo. 10–20 mm, blue-violet. Edges of ponds and streams, widespread. Flo. July–Sept.

Scutellaria × hybrida Strail. *S. galericulata × minor*. *S. × nicholsonii* Taub. Intermediate between the parents. Sometimes occurs where they grow together, mostly S. England.*

Scutellaria hastifolia L. Stem 20–40 cm, from rhizome; leaves hastate below; flo. in terminal spike, 15–25 mm, blue-violet. Introd. Europe. Woods, W. Norfolk, rare. Flo. July–Sept.*

Scutellaria minor L. Lesser skullcap. Stem up to 15 cm, from rhizome; leaves round below; flo. in leaf axils *c.* 8 mm, pale pink. Wet heaths, etc., common. Flo. July–Sept.

THYMUS
SERPYLLUM.

THYMUS
PULEGIOIDES.

CLINOPODIUM
VULGARE.

CALAMINTHA
NEPETA.

CALAMINTHA SYLVATICA
SSP. ASCENDENS

CALAMINTHA
SYLVATICA.

ACINOS ARVENSIS

MELISSA
OFFICINALIS

SALVIA
PRATENSIS.

SALVIA
VERBENACA

GLECHOMA
HEDERACEA

NEPETA CATARIA.

SCUTELLARIA
MINOR.

SCUTELLARIA
GALERICULATA.

Plate 69

Labiatae *(continued)*

Prunella vulgaris L. Selfheal. Leaves ovate, subentire, rounded below; upper teeth of calyx united; flo. blue-violet, rarely pink. Pastures, widespread and common. Flo. June–Sept.

Prunella laciniata (L.) L. Cut-leaved selfheal. Upper leaves lobed or pinnate, cuneate below; upper teeth of calyx more distinct; flo. creamy-white. Downs, grassy slopes, etc., on calcareous and limestone soils, mostly S. England, local. Flo. June–Aug.

Prunella × hybrida Knaf. *P. laciniata × vulgaris.* Intermediate. Occurs with the parents where they grow together.*

Melittis melissophyllum L. Bastard balm. Stem 20–60 cm; leaves strong smelling; flo. large, white, blotched red-purple. Woods and banks, S.W. England and W. Wales, local. Flo. May–June.

Marrubium vulgare L. White horehound. Stem and leaves hoary or woolly; calyx with 10 subulate hooked teeth; flo. whitish. Downs and chalk cliffs near the sea, S. England, introd. elsewhere. Flo. July–Oct.

Stachys germanica L. Downy woundwort. Plant stoloniferous, clothed with long white hairs; flo. in dense spike, pale rose. Shady banks on calcareous soil, Oxfordshire, very rare. Flo. July–Aug.

Stachys palustris L. Marsh woundwort. Stem up to 100 cm, from rhizome; leaves lanceolate; bracteoles equalling pedicels; flo. pale lilac. Ditches and streams, widespread and common. Flo. July–Sept.

Stachys × ambigua Sm. *S. palustris × sylvatica.* Intermediate between the parents, though sometimes resembling *S. palustris* more than *S. sylvatica.* Widespread, often in the absence of parents.*

Stachys sylvatica L. Hedge woundwort. Leaves ovate, petioles long; bracteoles equalling pedicels; flo. claret-red. Hedge banks, waste ground, etc., widespread and common. Flo. July–Sept.

Stachys alpina L. Limestone woundwort. Stem up to 100 cm; leaves often purplish; bracteoles exceeding pedicels; flo. red with yellow eye, downy. Woods, Gloucestershire and Denbighshire, rare. Flo. July–Aug.

Stachys officinalis (L.) Trev. Betony. *S. betonica* Benth. *Betonica officinalis* L. Stem up to 45 cm; leaves distant; flo. mostly in dense head, red-purple, without internal hairs. Hedge banks, shady places, etc., widespread and common, though local or rare in Scotland. Flo. June–Sept.

Stachys arvensis (L.) L. Field woundwort. Annual, 10–25 cm, branched at base; flo. *c.* 6 mm, pale pink. Cultivated fields, common in W. England, local or rare elsewhere. Flo. June–Aug.

Stachys annua (L.) L. Annual, 10–30 cm; leaves oblong, 2–6 cm; flo. *c.* 12 mm, pale yellow. Introd. Europe. Cultivated ground, casual and rare. Flo. June–Sept.*

Galeopsis ladanum L. Stem softly hairy, not thickened at nodes; leaf width 1–3 cm; side 3–8 toothed; flo. small, lilac. Introd. Europe. Cultivated and waste land, casual and rare. Flo. July–Sept.*

Galeopsis angustifolia Ehrh. ex Hoffm. Red hemp-nettle. Stem soft, not thickened at nodes; leaves linear-lanceolate, *c.* 12 mm wide; teeth few; flo. large, 15–25 mm, pale rose. Cultivated land, common. Flo. July–Sept.

Galeopsis segetum Neck. Downy hemp-nettle. *G. dubia* Leers. Stem not thickened at nodes; leaves very soft, downy; flo. large, pale yellow. Arable ground, N. Wales, sporadic elsewhere, very rare. Flo. July–Aug.

Galeopsis tetrahit L. Common hemp-nettle. Stem thickened at nodes, hispid; flo. 15–20 mm, rose-purple and yellow; mid lobe of lip flat, entire, margin pale. Woods, hedge banks and cultivated ground, widespread and common. Flo. July–Sept.

Galeopsis bifida Boenn. Thickened at nodes, more evenly hispid; flo. *c.* 15 mm; mid lobe of lip convex notched, deeply coloured to margin. In similar situations to *G. tetrahit,* common. Flo. July–Sept.*

Galeopsis speciosa Mill. Large-flowered hemp-nettle. Thickened at nodes, evenly hispid; flo. 20–35 mm, pale yellow, and lip mostly violet. Arable land, especially on peaty soil of Fen District, rare. Flo. July–Sept.

Leonurus cardiaca L. Motherwort. Stem up to 100 cm; lower leaves 5-lobed, upper 3-lobed; flo. in dense whorls, white or pink, purple-spotted. Introd. Europe. Cultivated and waste ground, rare. Flo. July–Sept.*

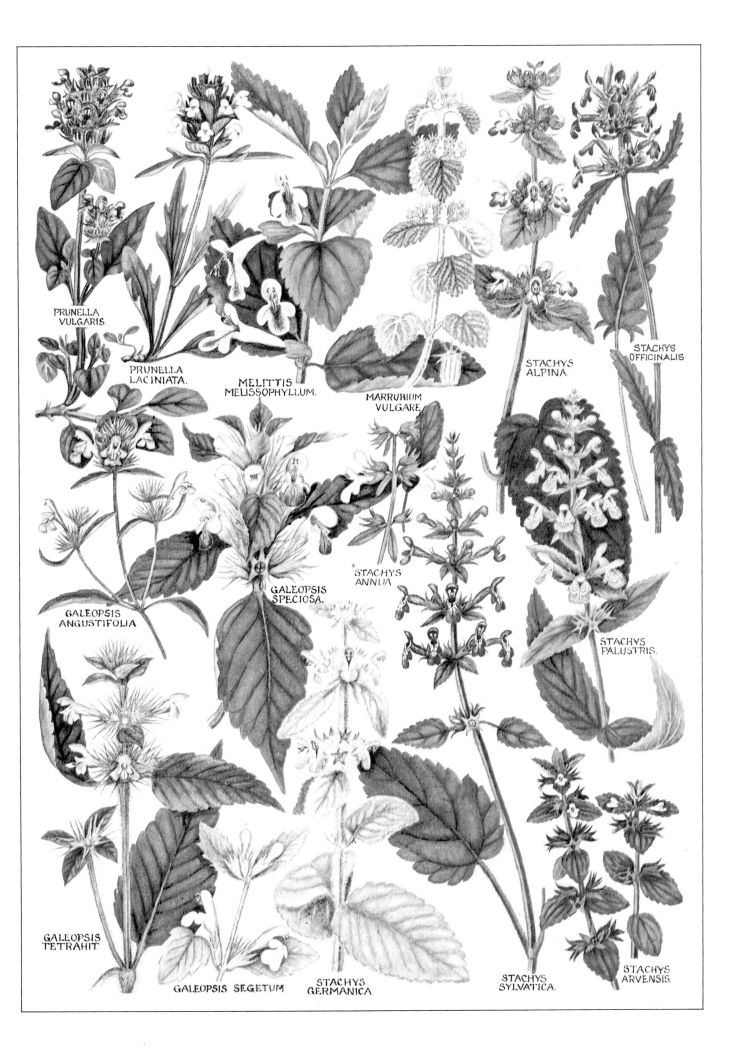

PRUNELLA
VULGARIS.

PRUNELLA
LACINIATA.

MELITTIS
MELISSOPHYLLUM.

MARRUBIUM
VULGARE.

STACHYS
ALPINA.

STACHYS
OFFICINALIS

GALEOPSIS
ANGUSTIFOLIA

GALEOPSIS
SPECIOSA.

STACHYS
ANNUA

STACHYS
PALUSTRIS.

GALEOPSIS
TETRAHIT

GALEOPSIS SEGETUM

STACHYS
GERMANICA

STACHYS
SYLVATICA.

STACHYS
ARVENSIS.

— *Plate 70* —

Labiatae *(continued)*

Ballota nigra L. Black horehound.
Ssp. **nigra**. Stem 40–80 cm, hairy, strong-smelling; calyx tube short; calyx teeth lanceolate, 2–4 mm long; flo. pale purple. Introd. E. Europe. Waste ground, etc., very rare. Flo. June–Sept.*
Ssp. **foetida** Hayek. Differs from ssp. *nigra* in its longer calyx tube and broadly ovate calyx teeth, becoming abruptly acuminate, 1–2 mm long; flo. pale purple. Hedge banks, waste ground, etc., common, in England and Wales, local in Scotland and Ireland. Flo. June–Sept.

Lamium amplexicaule L. Henbit dead-nettle. Bract leaves sessile, like an involucre; calyx short and closing; corolla pink with crimson hood. Cultivated ground, mostly England and Wales, local or rare elsewhere. Flo. April–Aug.

Lamium moluccellifolium Fr. Northern dead-nettle. *L. intermedium* Fr. Upper bracts sessile; calyx deeply cut, spreading; corolla *c.* 12 mm, pink. Cultivated ground, Scotland and Ireland, rare elsewhere. Flo. June–Sept.

Lamium hybridum Vill. Cut-leaved dead-nettle. *L. incisum* Willd. Leaves all stalked, truncate at base, teeth deeply cut; corolla short, ring of hairs within faint or o. Cultivated ground, local. Flo. April–June.

Lamium purpureum L. Red dead-nettle. Leaves cordate at base, teeth rounded; corolla pink, with ring of hairs inside. Cultivated ground, hedge banks, etc., widespread and common. Flo. March–Aug.

Lamium maculatum L. Spotted dead-nettle. Leaves usually blotched with white; corolla pink, with ring of hairs. Garden escape. Waste ground, uncommon. Flo. May–Aug.*

Lamium album L. White dead-nettle. Flo. large and white, lateral lobes of lower lip with small teeth. Waste ground and roadsides, widespread and common, though local in mid Wales and Ireland and rare in N. Scotland. Flo. April–June and autumn.

Lamiastrum galeobdolon (L.) Ehrend. & Polatschek. Yellow archangel. *Galeobdolon luteum* Huds., *Lamium galeobdolon* (L.) L.

Ssp. **galeobdolon**. Stolons widely spreading; inflo. up to 8-flowered; flo. yellow; uppermost bracts 1–2 times as long as broad. Woods, N. Lincoln only, very rare. Flo. May–July.*
Ssp. **montanum** (Pers.) Ehrend. & Polatschek. Similar to ssp. *galeobdolon* but inflo. 10–15-flowered and uppermost bracts up to $3\frac{1}{2}$ times as long as broad. Woods and shady places on heavy soils, widespread but local in England, Wales and Ireland, rare in Scotland. Flo. May–July.

Teucrium botrys L. Cut-leaved germander. Stem 10 cm; leaves all pinnatifid; calyx gibbous; flo. pale purple. Arable ground, slopes, etc., on calcareous soil, mostly S. England, rare. Flo. July–Sept.

Teucrium scordium L. Water germander. Plant up to 60 cm, stoloniferous; stems and leaves softly hairy; flo. pale purple. Wet places, and hollows on dunes, S.W. and E. England, very rare, and decreasing, and Ireland, very local. Flo. July–Sept.

Teucrium chamaedrys L. Wall germander. Stem up to 30 cm; leaves dark green, cuneate below, uppermost smaller; flo. purple. Garden escape. Established on walls and ruins, mostly S. England, rare. Flo. July–Sept.

Teucrium scorodonia L. Wood sage. Stem 15–30 cm; leaves wrinkled; flo. yellowish-green, in pairs. Woods and heaths, common. Flo. July–Sept.

Ajuga reptans L. Bugle. Stolons leafy; stem up to 25 cm, hairy on 2 sides; uppermost leaves shorter than blue flo. Damp shady places, widespread and common. Flo. May–July.

Ajuga pyramidalis L. Pyramidal bugle. Stem up to 15 cm, hairy all round; upper leaves longer than pale mauve flo. Rock crevices, N. England, Scotland and Ireland, rare. Flo. May–July.

Ajuga genevensis L. Rhizomatous; stem hairy all round; upper leaves shorter than deep blue flo. Introd. Europe. Formerly established on dunes in Cornwall and pastures in Berkshire but now extinct. Flo. May–July.

Ajuga chamaepitys (L.) Schreb. Ground-pine. Stem 5–20 cm; leaves of 3 narrow lobes; flo. short, in pairs, yellow. Chalky fields, S. and E. England, local. Flo. May–Sept.

LAMIUM HYBRIDUM.

LAMIUM PURPUREUM.

LAMIUM MOLUCCELLIFOLIUM.

BALLOTA NIGRA.

LAMIUM AMPLEXICAULE.

LAMIASTRUM GALEOBDOLON.

TEUCRIUM BOTRYS.

LAMIUM ALBUM.

TEUCRIUM SCORODONIA.

×2

A. GENEVENSIS.

TEUCRIUM CHAMAEDRYS.

AJUGA PYRAMIDALIS.

TEUCRIUM SCORDIUM.

AJUGA CHAMAEPITYS.

AJUGA REPTANS.

Plate 71

Plantaginaceae

Plantago major L. Greater plantain. Leaves abruptly contracted below to a petiole; spike of flo. brownish; capsule many-seeded. Cultivated ground, lawns, etc., widespread and common. Flo. May–Sept.

Plantago media L. Hoary plantain. Leaves gradually narrowed below, subsessile, pubescent; flo. whitish; stamens purple. Grassy places on calcareous and basic soils, mostly England, rare in Wales and introd. in Scotland and Ireland. Flo. June–Sept.

Plantago lanceolata L. Ribwort plantain. Leaves lanceolate, ribbed; scape furrowed; spike ovate; flo. brown. Grassy places, roadsides, etc., widespread and common. Flo. April–Aug.

Plantago maritima L. Sea plantain. Leaves long, linear, fleshy; flo. brown; stamens pale yellow. Salt marshes, mountains, etc., widespread. Flo. June–Aug.

Plantago coronopus L. Buck's-horn plantain. Leaves pinnatifid and pubescent, but very variable. Dry grassy places on sandy and gravelly soils, especially near the sea, widespread in S. Britain, local elsewhere. Flo. May–Aug.

Plantago arenaria Waldst. & Kit. *P. psyllium* L. *nomen. ambig. P. indica* auct., non L. Stem long, leafy and branched; leaves linear, opposite. Introd. Europe. Cultivated and waste ground and dunes, etc., rare. Flo. July–Aug.*

Littorella uniflora (L.) Aschers. Shoreweed. *L. lacustris* L. Submerged, with slender stolons; male flo. stalked, female sessile with long slender stigmas. Verges of lakes, widespread, but local. Flo. June–Aug.

Illecebraceae

Illecebrum verticillatum L. Coral-necklace. Branches prostrate; sepals thick, white, hooded and awned; petals minute, white. Moist sandy places, S. and W. England, introd. elsewhere, very local. Flo. July–Sept.

Corrigiola litoralis L. Strapwort. Plant glaucous or reddish; leaves tapering below, stipulate; flo. clustered, white-tipped with red. Native on gravelly banks in S. Devon, and formerly in Cornwall, elsewhere adventive on railway tracks, very rare. Flo. July–Aug.

Herniaria ciliolata Melderis. Fringed rupturewort. *H. ciliata* Bab., non Clairv. Leaves ovate, usually ciliate; sepals tipped with a bristle; fr. obtuse, equalling sepals. Coastal sand and rocks, Lizard Head, Cornwall and Channel Islands, rare. Flo. July–Aug.*

Herniaria glabra L. Smooth rupturewort. Leaves narrowed below; fr. acute, longer than sepals, which are glabrous. Dry sandy places, mostly E. Anglia, rare. Flo. July–Sept.

Scleranthus annuus L. Annual knawel. Stems erect; calyx lobes acute, with narrow white margin, spreading in fr. Sandy fields, etc., widespread, but rare in N. Scotland. Flo. June–Aug.

Scleranthus perennis L. Perennial knawel.
Ssp. **perennis**. Stems ascending to erect, woody below; sepals oblong, blunt, with broad white margins; closed in fr. Rocks, Radnorshire, very rare. Flo. June–Aug.*
Ssp. **prostratus** P. D. Sell. Similar to ssp. *perennis* but with long procumbent or slightly ascending stems and smaller leaves and fr. Sandy heaths, Norfolk and Suffolk, very rare. Flo. June–Aug.

Amaranthaceae

Amaranthus retroflexus L. Common amaranth. Stout, erect, pubescent, leafless above; leaves ovate; flo. in dense spikes; sepals 5. Introd. N. America. Cultivated and waste ground, uncommon. Flo. July–Sept.*

Chenopodiaceae

Chenopodium polyspermum L. Many-seeded goosefoot. Leaves ovate, green; flo. spikes small, leafless; sepals 5, not keeled; testa of seed has pits with sinuous margin. Cultivated ground, mostly S. England, rare elsewhere. Flo. July–Sept.

Chenopodium vulvaria L. Stinking goosefoot. *C. olidum* Curt. Whole plant smelling of stinking fish; leaves rhomboid-oval, mealy; flo. spikes dense; sepals not keeled; seed testa with faint furrows. Waste places, often near the sea, mostly S. England, very rare. Flo. Aug.–Sept.

Chenopodium album L. Fat-hen. Stem often reddish; leaves thick, variable, dentate, mealy; inflo. branched; sepals keeled; testa of seed faintly striate or reticulate. Arable land, common. Flo. July–Aug.

Chenopodium suecicum J. Murr. *C. viride* auct. Similar to *C. album*, but stem green; leaves thin, bright glaucous green; seed testa regularly pitted, obtusely keeled. In similar situations to *C. album*, possibly common but overlooked. Flo. July–Aug.*

Chenopodium opulifolium Schrad. ex Koch & Ziz. Grey goosefoot. Stem *c.* 60 cm; leaves broad, obtuse, dentate, mealy below; sepals keeled; testa furrowed and finely papillose. Introd. Europe. Waste places, etc., mostly S. England. Flo. Aug.–Sept.*

PLANTAGO
CORONOPUS

PLANTAGO
MAJOR.

PLANTAGO
LANCEOLATA

PLANTAGO
MEDIA

×7

×6

CHENOPODIUM
POLYSPERMUM

CHENOPODIUM
VULVARIA

×7

HERNIARIA GLABRA

CHENOPODIUM ALBUM

PLANTAGO
MARITIMA

×4

SCLERANTHUS
PERENNIS.

ILLECEBRUM
VERTICILLATUM

×10

SCLERANTHUS
ANNUUS.

×10.

CORRIGIOLA LITORALIS.

LITTORELLA UNIFLORA.

— *Plate 72* —

Chenopodiaceae (*continued*)

Chenopodium ficifolium Sm. Fig-leaved goosefoot. Lower leaves with pair of ascending lobes; sepals white with green keel; seed testa furrowed. Cultivated and waste land, locally common, S. and E. England, rare elsewhere. Flo. July–Sept.

Chenopodium murale L. Nettle-leaved goosefoot. Stem leafy almost to top; leaves sharply toothed; flo. branches short; testa with dense minute pits. Cultivated and waste ground, mostly England. Flo. Aug.

Chenopodium hybridum L. Maple-leaved goosefoot. Lower leaves subcordate, teeth few and large; flo. spikes spreading; sepals hardly keeled; testa with large pits. Cultivated land, S. and E. England, rare. Flo. Aug.–Sept.*

Chenopodium urbicum L. Upright goosefoot. Leaves glabrous, triangular, dentate; flo. spikes short, erect; clusters small; seeds black; testa reticulate. Cultivated land, mostly S. and E. England, very rare and much confused with forms of *C. rubrum*. Flo. Aug.–Sept.*

Chenopodium rubrum L. Red goosefoot. Stem often red; leaves rhomboidal, coarsely toothed; sepals of lateral flo. 3–4, free to middle; seed red-brown; testa pitted. Cultivated and waste ground, pond verges, etc., common in S. and E. England, local or rare elsewhere. Flo. Aug.

Chenopodium botryodes Sm. Leaves subentire, triangular; sepals of lateral flo. 2–4, united almost to apex, keeled at top. Salt marshes, S. and E. England. Flo. Sept.

Chenopodium glaucum L. Oak-leaved goosefoot. Leaves small, oak-shaped, green above, white beneath; flo. spikes many, small; seeds reddish. Cultivated and waste ground, etc., mostly S. England, rare. Flo. Sept.

Chenopodium bonus-henricus L. Good-King-Henry. Perennial, 30–50 cm; leaves broad, green; inflo. pyramidal; stigmas long. Introd. Europe. Roadsides, farmyards, etc., widespread but local. Flo. May–Aug.

Beta vulgaris
Ssp. **maritima** (L.) Arcangeli. Sea beet. *B. maritima* L. Stems mostly decumbent; leaves thick, green and glossy; fruiting sepals corky. Seashores, widespread. Flo. July–Sept.
Cultivated forms of *B. vulgaris*, with erect stem and thick root, sometimes occur as outcasts.

Atriplex littoralis L. Grass-leaved orache. Leaves linear, entire or toothed; flo. spike long, leafless above; fruiting sepals rhomboid, tuberculate. Seashores, widespread and common. Flo. July–Aug.

Atriplex prostrata Boucher. *A. hastata* auct., non L. Leaves triangular, abruptly contracted below; sepals mostly truncate below, less than half united. Waste ground, widespread and common, especially near the sea. Flo. Aug.–Sept.

Atriplex patula L. Common orache. Leaves tapering to pedicel, lobes ascending; sepals smooth or little tuberculate. Cultivated and waste ground, common. Flo. Aug.–Sept.

Atriplex glabriuscula Edmondst. Babington's orache. Stems spreading; leaves triangular, subentire; inflo. leafy; sepals 5–10 mm, tubercled, united along the base.
Var. **babingtonii** (Woods) Moss. Leaves much toothed; sepals 5 × 5 mm. Sea-shores, common. Flo. July–Sept.

Atriplex longipes Drej. Similar to *A. prostrata* but axillary bracteoles with stalks up to 20 mm long. Coasts of Britain, widespread, but confused with *A. prostrata* and *A. glabriuscula*. Flo. July–Sept.*

Atriplex praecox Hülphers. Similar to *A. prostrata* but smaller, 8–10 cm tall; basal leaves lanceolate to rhombic-ovate, cuneate to attenuate at base. Maritime shingle, mostly N.W. Scotland, rare. Flo. June–July.*

Atriplex laciniata L. Frosted orache. *A. sabulosa* Rouy. Plant silvery-white, decumbent; leaves rhomboid-ovate, very mealy; flo. spikes short. Sandy seashores, local. Flo. July–Sept.

Halimione portulacoides (L.) Aellen. Sea-purslane. *Atriplex portulacoides* L. Perennial, dense, shrubby plant; leaves mostly opposite, entire; sepals 3-lobed. Salt marshes, etc., locally abundant. Flo. July–Sept.

Halimione pedunculata (L.) Aellen. *Atriplex pedunculata* L. Annual, erect; leaves alternate, entire; sepals 3-lobed; fr. pedicelled. Salt marshes, S. and E. England, but not seen for nearly 50 years. Flo. July–Sept.

Sarcocornia perennis (Mill.) A. J. Scott. Perennial glasswort. *Salicornia perennis* Mill. Perennial, much branched, in large tussocks; fertile segments 4–8; central separating 2 lateral. Salt marshes, mostly S. and E. England. Flo. Aug.–Sept.*

Salicornia dolichostachya Moss. Annual; spikes long, 10–40 cm; segments 15–30; central flo. larger, almost separating the lateral. Tidal salt marshes, widespread. Flo. Aug.–Sept.*

Salicornia europaea L. Glasswort. *S. stricta* Dumort. Bright green; spikes long, blunt, segments 6–16; flo. nearly equal, central, not separating the lateral. Muddy, tidal marshes, widespread. Flo. Aug.–Sept.

Salicornia ramosissima Woods. Prostrate glasswort. *S. prostrata* auct. Stems usually becoming prostrate and reddish; flo. branches short and tapering, segments 2–6, oval; central flo. large but not separating lateral ones; young plants sometimes erect and variable in angle of branching. Muddy salt marshes, widespread, but local. Flo. Aug.–Sept.

Salicornia pusilla Woods. Fragile glasswort. *S. disarticulata* Moss. Stems erect; flo. branches very short, segments 1–2, all separating when ripe; flo. solitary not in threes. Drier parts of salt marshes, S. and E. England and S. Ireland. Flo. Aug.–Sept.*

× 10

CHENOPODIUM
BOTRYODES

CHENOPODIUM
RUBRUM

CHENOPODIUM
MURALE.

CHENOPODIUM
GLAUCUM

CHENOPODIUM
FICIFOLIUM.

CHENOPODIUM
BONUS-HENRICUS.

ATRIPLEX
GLABRIUSCULA

× 5

ATRIPLEX
PATULA

ATRIPLEX
LITTORALIS

B. VULGARIS
SSP. MARITIMA

HALIMIONE
PORTULACOIDES.

× 2

ATRIPLEX
LACINIATA.

HALIMIONE PEDUNCULATA.

SALICORNIA
EUROPAEA.

SALICORNIA RAMOSISSIMA.

ATRIPLEX
PROSTRATA

Plate 73

Chenopodiaceae *(continued)*

Suaeda vera Forsk. ex. J. F. Gmel. Shrubby sea-blite. *S. fruticosa* auct., non Forst. Perennial shrub; leaves rounded at ends; stigmas 3; seeds smooth. Maritime shingle, mostly S. and E. England. Flo. July–Sept.

Suaeda maritima (L.) Dumort. Annual sea-blite. Annual, mostly spreading or prostrate, glaucous and reddish; leaves acute; stigmas 2; seeds reticulate. Sea-shores, widespread and common. Flo. July–Sept.

Salsola kali L.
Ssp. **kali.** Prickly saltwort. Prostrate and prickly; stem striped; leaves succulent, spinous; flo. axillary; sepals thick and green. Sandy seashores, widespread. Flo. July–Sept.
Ssp. **ruthenica** (Iljin) Soó. Spineless saltwort. *S. pestifer* A. Nels. *S. tragus* auct., non L. Similar to ssp. *kali* but stem erect, slender, grey-green; perianth segments winged. Introd. E. Europe. Rubbish tips, waste ground, etc., mostly England, rare. Flo. July–Oct.

Polygonaceae

The taxa of the Polygonaceae found in the British Isles were monographed by Lousley and Kent (1981) and their treatment is followed here.

Fallopia convolvulus (L.) Á. Löve. Black-bindweed. *Polygonum convolvulus* L. Stem 30–120 cm, twining; flo. subsessile or pedicels 1–3 mm; outer sepals keeled. Cultivated ground, widespread. Flo. July–Oct.

Fallopia dumetorum (L.) J. Holub. Copse-bindweed. *Polygonum dumetorum* L. Stem up to 3 m, twining; flo. pedicels 8 mm long; outer sepals broadly winged. Hedges and thickets, S. England, rare. Flo. July–Oct.

Fallopia aubertii (Louis Henry) J. Holub. Russian-vine. *Polygonum aubertii* Louis Henry. *P. baldschuanicum* auct., non Regel. Similar to *F. dumetorum* but rampant woody climber up to 10 m; leaves cordate to hastate, bronzy-red when young; flo. small in axillary and terminal panicles; perianth segments white, turning pink. Garden escape. Hedges, ditches, etc., mostly England and Wales. Flo. Aug.–Oct.*

Polygonum aviculare L. Knotgrass. *P. heterophyllum* Lindm. Stems mostly prostrate; leaves lanceolate, very unequal; ochreae silvery, torn; sepals pinkish, united at base only. Cultivated and waste ground, etc., widespread and common. Flo. July–Aug.

Polygonum rurivagum Jord. ex Bor. Leaves unequal, linear-lanceolate, acute; ochreae long, 7–10 mm; fr. 2.5–3.5 mm. Cultivated ground on calcareous soil, S. and W. England, rare. Flo. Aug.–Nov.*

Polygonum arenastrum Bor. *P. aequale* Lindm. Stems matted; leaves small, blunt, nearly equal; sepals green and white, united halfway; fr. 2–3 mm. Paths and farm gateways, etc., widespread. Flo. July–Nov.

Polygonum boreale (Lange) Small. Leaves oblong-ovate to spathulate; petioles projecting from ochreae; fr. 3–5 mm. Arable land, N. Scotland, very local. Flo. June–Oct.*

Polygonum oxyspermum Mey. & Bunge ex Ledeb. ssp. **raii** (Bab.) D. A. Webb & A. O. Chater. Ray's knotgrass. *P. raii* Bab. Stems prostrate, woody; leaf margins flat; ochreae silvery, torn, with simple veins; fr. 5–6 mm, exceeding sepals. Maritime sand and shingle, widespread, but rare. Flo. June–Sept.

Polygonum maritimum L. Sea knotgrass. Stems prostrate, woody; leaf margins revolute; ochreae with many-branched veins; fr. 4 mm. Maritime sand and shingle, S.W. England, Channel Islands and S. Ireland, very rare. Flo. July–Oct.*

Polygonum hydropiper L. Water-pepper. Plant acrid; stems suberect, 30–80 cm, nodding; flo. greenish; sepals with yellow glands. Damp places, etc., widespread and common. Flo. July–Sept.

Polygonum mite Schrank. Lax-flowered persicaria. *P. laxiflorum* Weihe. Similar to *P. hydropiper* but not acrid, suberect; ochreae much fringed; flo. interrupted pink, without glands. Ditches and wet places, England and Wales, rare and decreasing, introd. in N. Ireland. Flo. July–Sept.

Polygonum minus Huds. Small water-pepper. Stems 10–30 cm, leaves narrow, 2–15 mm wide; ochreae much-fringed; flo. smaller, pink; fr. only 2–3 mm. Edges of pools and streams, widespread but local. Flo. July–Sept.

Polygonum persicaria L. Redshank. Leaves often dark-blotched; ochreae fringed; inflo. dense, obtuse; flo. pink, without glands. Cultivated and damp ground, widespread and common. Flo. June–Oct.

Polygonum lapathifolium L. Pale persicaria. Leaves often black-blotched or downy; ochreae unfringed except uppermost; inflo. dense, obtuse; flo. greenish-white, sometimes glandular. Cultivated and waste ground, pond verges, etc., widespread and common, though rare in N. Scotland. Flo. June–Oct.

Polygonum nodosum Pers. *P. maculatum* (S. F. Gray) Dyer ex Bab. Undersides of leaves dotted with glands; ochreae shortly fringed; inflo. lax and acute; flo. pink; peduncle glandular. Damp ground, etc., local. The specimen figured was exceptionally large, but determined by an expert. Now considered to fall within the range of variation of *P. lapathifolium*. Flo. July–Sept.

Polygonum amphibium L. Amphibious bistort. Aquatic; leaves usually ovate-oblong, floating; flo. in a stout spike, pink. Pools and slow streams, and damp places, widespread and common. Flo. July–Sept.

Polygonum bistorta L. Common bistort. Rhizome twisted; stem simple, erect; young leaves folded lengthwise; flo. pink. Moist meadows, widespread, but local, and introd. in Ireland. Flo. June–Aug.

Polygonum campanulatum Hook. f. Lesser knotweed. Similar to *P. bistorta*, but leaves very tomentose, whitish to buff, with herring-bone pattern beneath. Garden escape. Naturalized in ditches, wet places, etc., especially Scotland and Ireland, rare. Flo. July–Sept.*

Polygonum viviparum L. Alpine bistort. Rhizome creeping; stem erect 10–30 cm; spike slender; flo. pink mixed with red bulbils. Mountain pastures, N. England, Wales and Scotland, rare in Ireland. Flo. June–Aug.

Reynoutria japonica Houtt. Japanese knotweed. *Polygonum cuspidatum* Sieb. & Zucc. Rhizome deep; plant very large; leaves broadly ovate, truncate at base; inflo. of many-flowered axillary panicles; flo. white. Garden escape. Waste ground, etc., widespread and common. Flo. Aug.–Oct.*

Reynoutria sachalinensis (F. Schmidt) Nakai. Giant knotweed. *Polygonum sachalinense* F. Schmidt. Similar to *R. japonica* but taller and stouter; leaves ovate-acute, cordate at base; inflo. shorter and more compact; flo. white. Garden escape. Waste ground, etc., widespread. Flo. Aug.–Oct.*

Polygonum polystachyum Wall. ex Meisn. Himalayan knotweed. Rhizome creeping; stems stout, erect; leaves oblong-lanceolate, acuminate, truncate or cuneate at the base; sometimes hairy beneath, with red veins; flo. white in lax leafy panicles. Garden escape. Waste ground, etc., widespread. Flo. Aug–Oct.*

Polygonum amplexicaule D. Don. Red bistort. Stems erect; leaves large, ovate, cordate; lower leaves stalked, upper leaves sessile, clasping stem; flo. dark red in dense cylindrical spikes. Garden escape. Naturalized in thickets, hedge banks, etc., widespread, but rare. Flo. Aug.–Oct.*

Polygonum sagittatum L. Stems weak with many short, hooked prickles; leaves oblong-sagittate, glabrous; flo. white in small spikes. Introd. E. Asia and N. America. Naturalized in ditches in S. Ireland, very rare. Flo. July–Sept.*

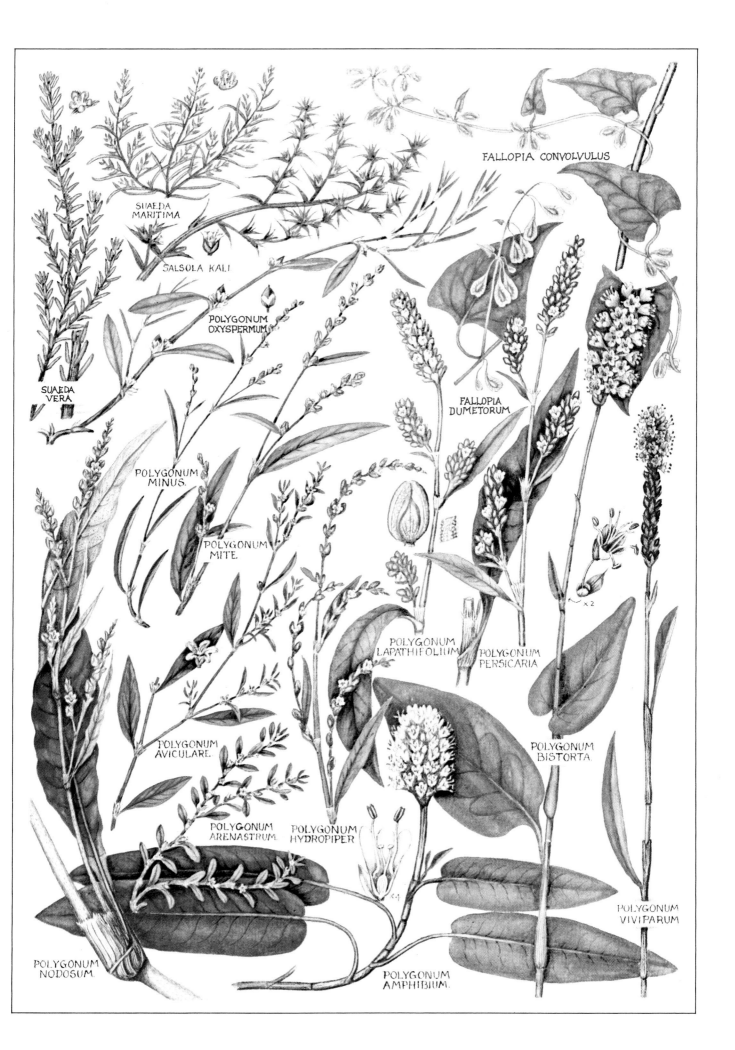

FALLOPIA CONVOLVULUS

SUAEDA
MARITIMA

SALSOLA KALI

POLYGONUM
OXYSPERMUM

SUAEDA
VERA

FALLOPIA
DUMETORUM

POLYGONUM
MINUS.

POLYGONUM
MITE.

×2

POLYGONUM
LAPATHIFOLIUM

POLYGONUM
PERSICARIA

POLYGONUM
AVICULARE.

POLYGONUM
BISTORTA.

POLYGONUM
ARENASTRUM.

POLYGONUM
HYDROPIPER

×4

POLYGONUM
VIVIPARUM

POLYGONUM
NODOSUM.

POLYGONUM
AMPHIBIUM.

Plate 74

Polygonaceae *(continued)*

Fagopyrum esculentum Moench. Buckwheat. *F. sagittatum* Gilib. Stem up to 60 cm, branched; leaves cordate at base; flo. pink or white; fr. 6 mm, much exceeding sepals. Cultivated alien, casual, on waste ground, etc., common. Flo. July–Sept.*

Koenigia islandica L. Iceland-purslane. Annual; stem mostly 1–6 cm; leaves small, 3–5 mm long, obovate; ochreae short; flo. small, clustered; fr. trigonous. Mountains, Mull and Skye. Flo. June–Aug.*

Muehlenbeckia complexa (A. Cunn.) Meisn. Woody sprawling or climbing shrub with many reddish wiry stems, hanging down walls or cliffs; leaves 4–8 mm, dark green above, pale below, broad-oblong, coriaceous; flo. small, segments greenish, cut ⅔ to base, in axillary or terminal spikes; fr. succulent, waxy-white. Garden escape. Established on walls and rocks, Isles of Scilly, Cornwall and Channel Islands. Flo. Aug.–Sept.*

Oxyria digyna (L.) Hill. Mountain sorrel. Stem up to 30 cm; leaves radical, reniform; inflo. leafless; inner sepals enlarging in fr. Damp mountain rocks, N. Wales, Lake District, Scotland and S. Ireland. Flo. July–Sept.

Rumex triangulivalvis (Danser) Rech. f. Willow-leaved dock. *R. salicifolius* auct. Graceful perennial; stem up to 50 cm; leaves linear-lanceolate, gradually narrowing at both ends; panicle open with few ascending branches; as each panicle passes into fr. a secondary flo. shoot grows up from a lower axil and eventually exceeds the primary panicle; whorls congested above, distant below, the latter with long linear leafy bracts. Introd. N. America. Waste ground, etc., mostly S. and E. England, uncommon. Flo. June–Sept.*

Rumex frutescens Thouars. *R. cuneifolius* Campd. Perennial with long woody rhizome; stem up to 30 cm; leaves obovate, obtuse, margins crenate and crisped, coarse and leathery; panicle congested; valve 4–5 mm long. Introd. S. America. Naturalized on maritime dunes, Cornwall, Devon and S. Wales, very rare. Flo. July–Aug.*

Rumex conglomeratus Murr. Clustered dock. Leaves oblong, sometimes narrowed centrally; valves oblong, entire, all with tubercles. Marshes, ditches, etc., widespread and common. Flo. July–Oct.

Rumex rupestris Le Gall. Shore dock. Leaves oblong, blunt, glaucous; valves oblong, entire, 4 mm, all with long tubercles, 2–3 mm. Sandy shores, S.W. England, Wales and Channel Islands, rare. Flo. June–Aug.

Rumex sanguineus L. var. ***viridis*** Sibth. Wood dock. *R. condylodes* Bieb. Leaves ovate-lanceolate, with green or red veins; valves oblong, entire, only 1 with a globular tubercle. Woods, shady places, etc., common, except in Scotland where it is local or rare. Flo. June–Aug.

Rumex maritimus L. Golden dock. Upper leaves linear-lanceolate; valves acute, with long, slender teeth and slender pedicels; plant golden in fr. Wet ground near pools, mostly England, rare. Flo. June–Sept.

Rumex palustris Sm. Marsh dock. Similar to *R. maritimus* but valves and tubercles obtuse with shorter teeth; pedicles shorter, thicker. Wet ground by pools, mostly S. and E. England, local. Flo. June–Sept. (fr. only illus.).

Rumex pulcher L. Fiddle dock. Branches nearly horizontal; leaves oblong or fiddle-shaped; valves ovate, toothed, all tubercled. Grassy places, mostly S. and E. England, local. Flo. June–July.

Rumex obtusifolius L. Broad-leaved dock. Lower leaves very broad, ovate-oblong; valves triangular, toothed, 1 or 3 with tubercle. Cultivated and waste ground, field margins, etc., widespread and common. Flo. July–Oct.

Rumex crispus L. Curled dock. Branches erect; leaves oblong-lanceolate, margins crisped; valves ovate, subentire, 1 or all 3-tubercled. Cultivated and waste ground, etc., widespread. Flo. June–Oct.

Rumex cristatus DC. Greek dock. *R. graecus* Boiss. & Heldr. Similar to *R. patientia* but basal leaves smaller and valves roundish-cordate, with many irregular teeth up to 1 mm long. Introd. S. Italy, etc. Established on waste ground, England and Wales, rare. Flo. June–July.*

Rumex longifolius DC. Northern dock. *R. domesticus* Hartm., *R. aquaticus* auct., non L. Stem 60–120 cm; leaves very long, margin undulate; valves broadly cordate, entire; tubercles 0. Wet places, N. England and Scotland. Flo. July–Aug.

Rumex patientia L. Patience dock. Very tall; leaves ovate-acute; valves broadly ovate, subentire, without teeth, 1 with tubercle. Introd. E. Europe. Waste ground, mostly S. England. Flo. May–June.*

Rumex hydrolapathum Huds. Water dock. Stem stout, up to 200 cm; leaves ovate-lanceolate; valves 5–7, triangular, shortly dentate and tubercled. Margins of canals and pools, common in S. England and Midlands, local in W. England, Wales and Ireland, rare in Scotland. Flo. July–Sept.

Rumex aquaticus L. Scottish dock. Stem 100–185 cm; leaves broad, cordate; valves ovate-triangular, entire, 5–8 mm; tubercles 0; pedicels slender. Watery places, Loch Lomond, W. Scotland, very local. Flo. July–Aug.*

Rumex alpinus L. Monk's-rhubarb. Rhizome creeping; leaves rounded, as broad as long; valves ovate, entire; tubercles 0. Introd. Europe. Near farms, by streamsides, roadsides, etc., N. Midlands to Scotland, local. Flo. July–Aug.*

Rumex scutatus L. French sorrel. Leaves 1.5–5.5 cm, rounded, as broad as long, basal lobes diverging; flo. bisexual. Garden escape. Naturalized on screes and rocky roadsides, mostly N. England and Scotland, uncommon. Flo. June–July.*

Rumex acetosa L. Common sorrel. Leaves oblong, hastate with downward lobes; flo. unisexual, outer sepals reflexed. Pastures, etc., widespread and common. Flo. May–June.

Rumex hibernicus Reching. f. similar to *R. acetosa* but much smaller, with a thin rootstock; basal leaves 10–15 mm long with short, acute, slightly divergent basal lobes; panicle dense. Maritime dunes, W. Ireland and W. Scotland, very local. Flo. May–June.*

Rumex acetosella L. Sheep's sorrel. Stem 15–30 cm; leaves lanceolate, hastate, lobes spreading; flo. unisexual, outer sepals erect. Heaths, etc., on acid soils, widespread and common. Flo. May–Aug.

Rumex tenuifolius (Wallr.) A. Löve. Similar to *R. acetosella* but leaves very narrow, margins inrolled; fr. 1 mm. Poor sandy soils, widespread and possibly common but confused with small forms of *R. acetosella*. Flo. May–Sept.*

Hybrids are frequent in *Rumex* sect. *Rumex* and are often intermediate between the parents. Many are rare but the following appear to be widespread: *R.* × *schulzei* Hausskn., *R. conglomeratus* × *crispus*; *R.* × *abortivus* Ruhmer, *R. conglomeratus* × *obtusifolius*; *R. sagorskii* Hausskn., *R. crispus* × *sanguineus*; *R.* × *pratensis* Mert. & Koch, *R. crispus* × *obtusifolius*.

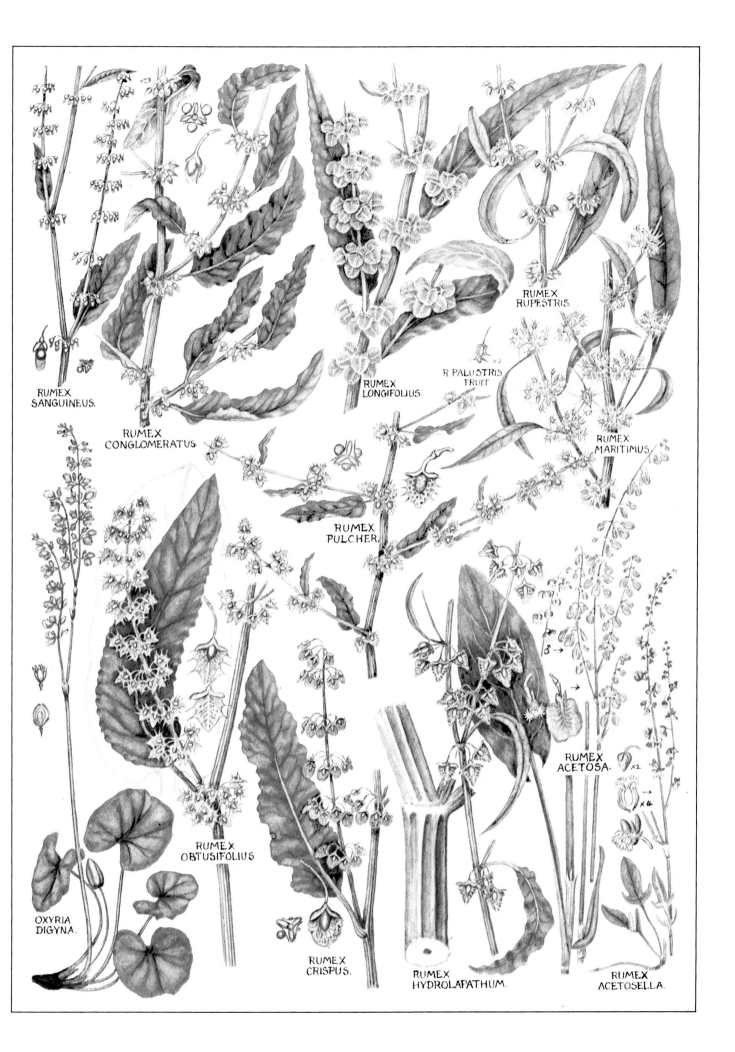

RUMEX
SANGUINEUS.

RUMEX
CONGLOMERATUS.

RUMEX
LONGIFOLIUS.

RUMEX
RUPESTRIS.

R. PALUSTRIS.
FRUIT

RUMEX
MARITIMUS.

RUMEX
PULCHER.

RUMEX
OBTUSIFOLIUS

RUMEX
ACETOSA.

OXYRIA
DIGYNA.

RUMEX
CRISPUS.

RUMEX
HYDROLAPATHUM.

RUMEX
ACETOSELLA.

Plate 75

Elaeagnaceae

Hippophae rhamnoides L. Sea-buckthorn. Thorny shrub, 1–3 m; leaves clothed with silvery scales; flo. small, green; fr. globose, orange. Dunes, mostly E. and S.E. coasts of Britain. Flo. March–April.

Loranthaceae

Viscum album L. Mistletoe. Shrubby parasite, 60 cm; leaves thick; flo. mostly unisexual; petals yellowish; fr. white. Parasitic on branches of *Malus*, *Populus* and other trees, mostly S. and E. England. Flo. Feb.–April.

Santalaceae

Thesium humifusum DC. Bastard-toadflax. Slender, prostrate, root parasite; flo. small, with 3 bracteoles, cream. On various roots on calcareous soil, mostly S. and E. England. Flo. June–Aug.

Euphorbiaceae

Euphorbia peplis L. Purple spurge. Procumbent, purple; leaves lopsided with narrow stipules; bracts leaf-like; glands entire, rounded. Sandy shores, S.W. England and Channel Islands, very rare. Flo. July–Sept.

Euphorbia helioscopia L. Sun spurge. Up to 50 cm, erect; leaves obovate, narrowed below; bracts leaf-like; glands entire, green; capsule smooth. Cultivated land, common. Flo. May–Oct.

Euphorbia platyphyllos L. Broad-leaved spurge. Leaves oblong, base cordate; upper bracts different, deltoid; glands oval; capsule with warts. Arable land, mostly S. England, rare. Flo. June–Aug.

Euphorbia serrulata Thuill. Upright spurge. *E. stricta* L. *nom. ambig.* Similar to *E. platyphyllos*; leaves smaller, clasping; bracts changing gradually to leaves; capsule smaller, 1–2 mm, warts more prominent, cylindrical. Woods on limestone soil, W. Gloucestershire and Monmouthshire, very rare. Flo. June–Sept.*

Euphorbia hyberna L. Irish spurge. Perennial up to 60 cm, downy; leaves large, up to 10 cm; bracts ovate, rounded below; glands entire; capsule 5–6 mm, with prominent warts. Shady woods and streambanks, S.W. Ireland, locally common, S.W. England, very rare. Flo. April–July.

Euphorbia dulcis L. Sweet spurge. Perennial; leaves oblanceolate; upper bracts deltoid, truncate below; glands entire, green becoming purple; capsule 2–3 mm, warts prominent. Garden escape. Established by roadsides, etc., widespread, mostly Scotland, rare. Flo. June–Aug.*

Euphorbia amygdaloides L. Wood spurge. Stem 30–70 cm, pubescent; upper bracts yellowish, united in pairs; glands with horns. Woods, shady places, common in S. England, local or rare elsewhere, very rare in Ireland. Flo. March–June.

Euphorbia corallioides L. Coral spurge. Tall, 30–100 cm; leaves lanceolate, woolly; bracts pilose; glands entire; capsule woolly. Introd. Europe. Grassy places, Sussex and elsewhere, very rare. Flo. June–Aug.*

Euphorbia uralensis Fisc., ex Link. Twiggy spurge. *E. virgata* auct., non Waldst. & Kit. and non Desf. Rhizome creeping; branches long; leaves 2–8 cm, narrowly oblong; glands with long horns. Introd. E. Europe. Grassy places, etc., mostly S. and E. England. Flo. May–July.*

Euphorbia esula L. Leafy spurge. Rhizome creeping; branches short; leaves 2–4.5 cm, oblanceolate, widest near apex; glands with short horns. Introd. Europe. Grassy places, etc., rare, and much confused with *E. uralensis*. Flo. May–July.*

Euphorbia cyparissias L. Cypress spurge. Rhizome creeping; leaves narrowly linear, numerous; bracts yellowish; glands with short horns. Perhaps native on downs on calcareous soil, S. E. England, elsewhere in grassy places as a garden escape. Flo. June–Sept.

Euphorbia paralias L. Sea spurge. Leaves oblong, blunt, thick and fleshy; glands with short horns; seeds smooth. Sandy shores, mostly S. and W. England, Wales and Ireland. Flo. June–Sept.

Euphorbia portlandica L. Portland spurge. Similar to *E. paralias*; leaves obovate-lanceolate, apiculate, glaucous; glands with long horns; seeds pitted. Sandy shores, S. and W. coasts of England and Wales, and N. and E. coasts of Ireland. Flo. June–Sept.

Euphorbia peplus L. Petty spurge. Stem 10–30 cm; leaves ovate, stalked; bracts ovate; umbel rays 3; glands with long horns. Cultivated ground, widespread and common. Flo. May–Oct.

Euphorbia exigua L. Dwarf spurge. Stem 5–30 cm; slender; leaves linear, tapering, acute; bracts lanceolate; glands with long horns. Cultivated ground, mostly S. and E. England, local or rare elsewhere and introd. in Ireland. Flo. June–Aug.

Euphorbia lathyrus L. Caper spurge. Stem 30–120 cm; leaves large, narrowly oblong; bracts ovate-acute; glands with horns; capsule large. Woods, local, mostly S. half of Britain. Flo. June–July.

Mercurialis annua L. Annual mercury. Annual; stem branched, subglabrous; female flo. subsessile in leaf axils. Introd. Europe. Cultivated ground, common in S. and E. England, local or rare elsewhere. Flo. July–Sept.*

Mercurialis perennis L. Dog's mercury. Rhizome perennial; stem unbranched, hairy; female flo. long-stalked. Woods, England, Wales, and S. Scotland, local in Ireland, rare in N. Scotland. Flo. March–April.

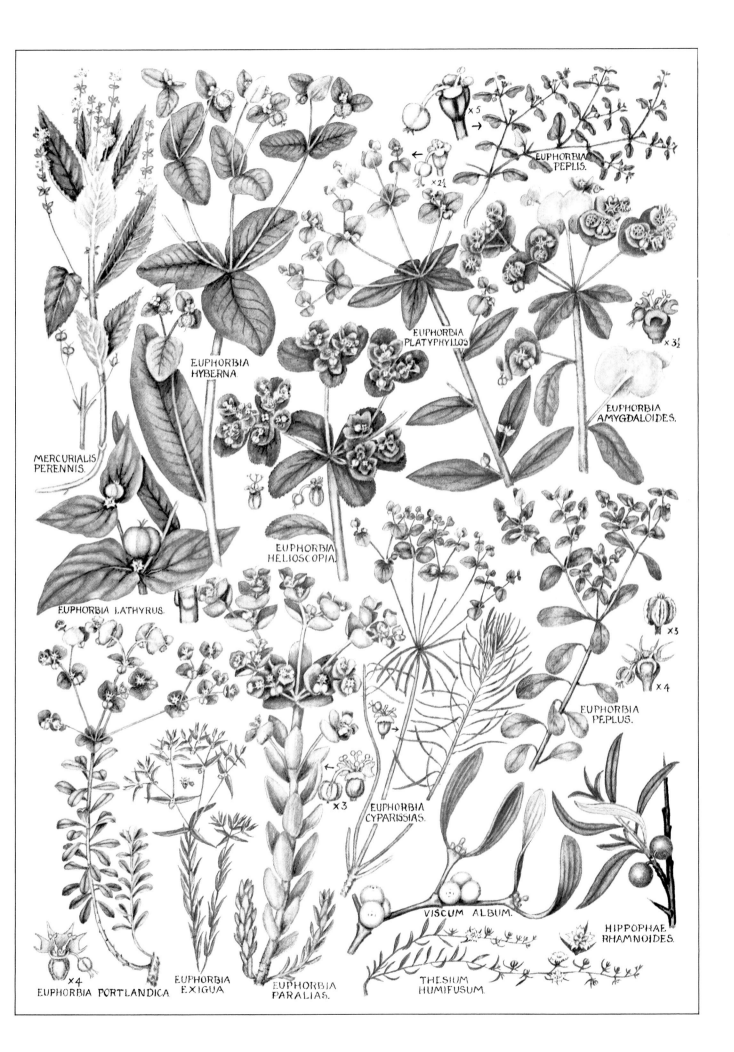

EUPHORBIA
PEPLIS.

×5

×2½

EUPHORBIA
PLATYPHYLLOS.

×3½

EUPHORBIA
AMYGDALOIDES.

EUPHORBIA
HYBERNA

MERCURIALIS
PERENNIS.

EUPHORBIA
HELIOSCOPIA.

EUPHORBIA LATHYRUS.

×3

×4

EUPHORBIA
PEPLUS.

EUPHORBIA
CYPARISSIAS.

×3

×4

EUPHORBIA PORTLANDICA.

EUPHORBIA
EXIGUA

EUPHORBIA
PARALIAS.

VISCUM ALBUM.

HIPPOPHAE
RHAMNOIDES.

THESIUM
HUMIFUSUM.

Plate 76

Aristolochiaceae

Asarum europaeum L. Asarabacca. Rhizome thick; stem very short, pubescent, bearing 2 leaves, 2 scales and 1 purplish flo. Woods, widespread, but rare, perhaps native. Flo. May–Aug.

Aristolochia clematitis L. Birthwort. Rhizome long; stem 20–80 cm; flo. tube dull yellow; fr. *c.* 2 cm, pear-shaped. Garden escape. Naturalized in grassy places, rare. Flo. June–Sept.

Thymelaeaceae

Daphne mezereum L. Mezereon. Erect shrub, up to 90 cm; leaves thin, not evergreen; flo. red-purple, fragrant; fr. scarlet. Woods, on calcareous and limestone soils, mostly England, introd. elsewhere, very rare. Flo. Feb.–March.

Daphne laureola L. Spurge-laurel. Erect shrub, 40–100 cm; leaves evergreen, thick and glossy; flo. green; fr. black. Woods, on calcareous and limestone soils, mostly S. and E. England, local elsewhere, and introd. in Scotland. Flo. Feb.–May.

Ulmaceae

Ulmus glabra Huds. Wych elm. *U. montana* Stokes. Leaves obovate, 6–16 cm, with long tapering point, base of longer side rounded, hiding petiole. Hedges, etc., formerly widespread and common. Flo. Feb.–March.

Ulmus procera Salisb. English elm. *U. campestris* auct. Tall spreading tree; leaves 4–9 cm, suborbicular or ovate-acute, unequal at base, teeth curved. Hedges, etc., formerly widespread, England, Wales and Ireland, rare in Scotland. Flo. Feb.–March.

Ulmus minor Mill. Small-leaved elm. *U. carpinifolia* G. Suckow. *U. glabra* Mill., non Huds. Leaves long, obovate-lanceolate, acuminate, shining, biserrate, base unequal, lower part of long side often straight. Hedges, mostly England, formerly common. Flo. Feb.–March.*
Var. **plotii** (Druce) Tutin. *U. plotii* Druce. Branches spreading; leaves elliptic, subglabrous, base nearly equal sided. Midlands and E. England.*

Cannabiaceae

Humulus lupulus L. Hop. Stems long, rough, hairy, climbing; male inflo. much branched; female with broad bracts. Frequent in hedges, etc., S. and E. England and the Midlands, local in N. England, Wales and Ireland, and rare in Scotland. Flo. July–Aug.

Urticaceae

Urtica dioica L. Common nettle. Stoloniferous; stem 30–100 cm; leaves up to 8 cm, cordate; flo. spikes up to 10 cm. Hedgebanks, woods, etc., widespread and common. Flo. June–Sept.

Urtica urens L. Small nettle. Annual; stem 10–50 cm; leaves up to 4 cm, ovate, all hairs stinging; flo. spike 1 cm. Cultivated ground, mostly on light soils, common in the E. half of Britain, local in the W. half of Britain, and in Ireland. Flo. June–Sept.

Parietaria judaica L. Pellitory-of-the-wall. *P. diffusa* Mert. & Koch., *P. officinalis* auct. Red stems and leaves softly hairy; female flo. terminal, male lateral; filaments elastic. Crevices of old walls, rocks, etc., common in S. and E. England, the Midlands and Ireland, mainly coastal in Wales, local in N. England, and rare in Scotland. Flo. June–Sept.

Soleirolia soleirolii (Req.). Dandy. Mind-your-own-business. *Helxine soleirolii* Req. Stem slender, creeping, rooting, matted; leaves small, round; flo. small. Garden escape. Hedge banks, walls, etc., widespread, but mostly England and Ireland. Flo. May–Sept.*

Myricaceae

Myrica gale L. Bog myrtle. Stem up to 120 cm; leaves grey-green, with fragrant yellow glands; inflo. catkins; bracts and anthers red. Wet heaths and fens, mostly in N.W. England, Scotland and W. Ireland. Flo. April–May.

Betulaceae

Betula pendula Roth. Silver birch. *B. verrucosa* Ehrh. Bark white; twigs long, pendulous; leaves doubly serrate, glabrous; catkin scales reflexed. Woods, heaths, etc., common and widespread. Flo. April–May.

Betula × **aurata** Borkh. *B. pendula* × *pubescens*. Intermediate between the parents and often occurring in their absence. Widespread.*

Betula pubescens Ehrh. Downy birch.
Ssp. **pubescens**. Stems bushy, dark brown; leaves singly serrate, downy; catkin scales straight. Damp heaths, mostly S. Britain. Flo. April–May.
Ssp. **odorata** (Bechst.) E. F. Warb. Young twigs and leaves with brown resinous warts, viscid buds and smaller leaves. Scottish Highlands. Flo. April–May.*

Betula nana L. Dwarf birch. Dwarf shrub to 1 m; leaves small, suborbicular, crenate; catkins short, oval. Locally common on mountains, mid and N. Scotland, but rare in Upper Teesdale, N. England. Flo. May.

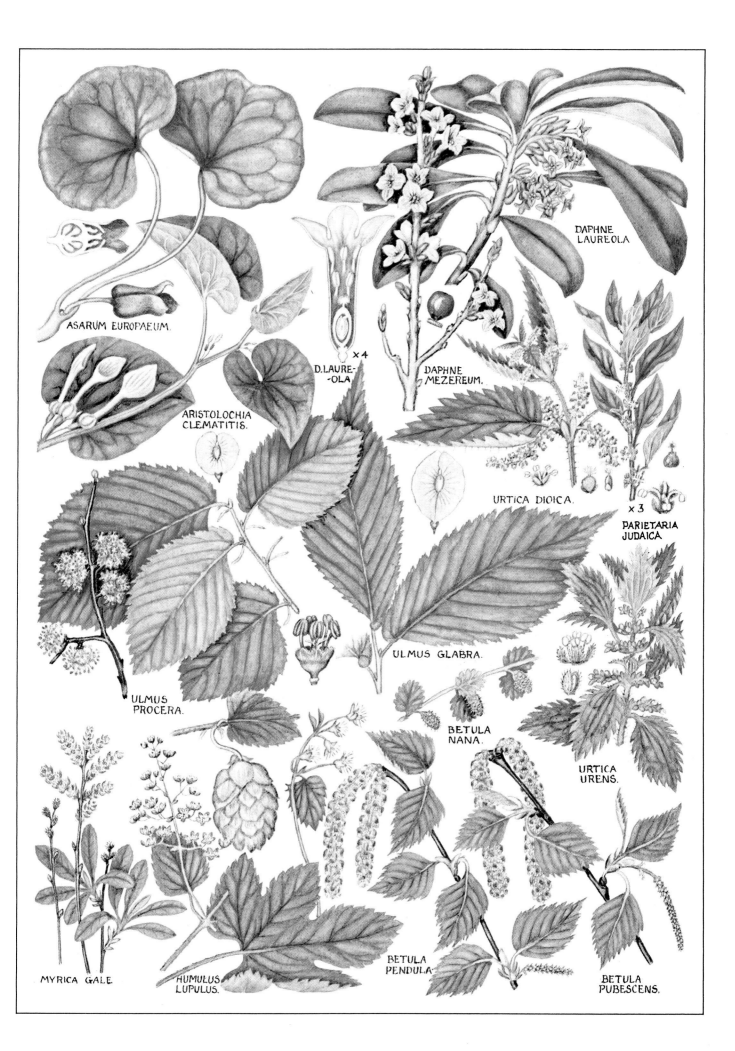

ASARUM EUROPAEUM.

ARISTOLOCHIA CLEMATITIS.

DAPHNE LAUREOLA

D. LAURE-
-OLA.   × 4

DAPHNE MEZEREUM.

URTICA DIOICA.

PARIETARIA JUDAICA.
× 3

ULMUS GLABRA.

ULMUS PROCERA.

BETULA NANA.

URTICA URENS.

MYRICA GALE.

HUMULUS LUPULUS.

BETULA PENDULA.

BETULA PUBESCENS.

Plate 77

Betulaceae *(continued)*

Alnus glutinosa (L.) Gaertn. Alder. *A. rotundifolia* Stokes. Bark dark brown; leaves blunt, green, veins few. Wet woods, by streamsides, etc., widespread and common. Flo. Feb.–March.

Alnus incana (L.) Moench. Grey alder. Similar to *A. glutinosa* but bark grey; leaves acute, grey-green above, veins many, pale and pubescent below. Introd. Europe. Planted by streams, etc., widespread but uncommon. Flo. Feb.–March.*

Corylaceae

Carpinus betulus L. Hornbeam. Leaves plaited, ovate, serrate; fr. subtended by a very large 3-lobed bract. Woods and hedges, common in England, local in Wales and rare in Scotland and Ireland. Flo. May.

Corylus avellana L. Hazel. Leaves rounded, cordate, stipulate, female flo. small, enclosed in green bracts. Woods and hedges, widespread and common. Flo. March–April.

Fagaceae

Quercus robur L. Pedunculate oak. Leaves subglabrous, mostly with a projecting auricle at base; flo. and fr. pedunculate. Woods, hedges, etc., common, especially on basic soils. Flo. April–May.

Quercus petraea (Mattuschka) Liebl. Sessile oak. *Q. sessiliflora* Salisb. Leaves with stellate hairs below, without auricle at base; flo. and fr. subsessile. Woods, hedges, etc., common, especially on acid soils. Flo. April–May.

Quercus × rosacea Bechst. *Quercus petraea × robur*. Intermediate between the parents, sometimes found where they grow together.*

Quercus ilex L. Evergreen oak. Leaves evergreen, dark green, glossy above, whitish-grey tomentose beneath; entire, or lightly toothed; fr. cup with small ovate scales. Introd. Mediterranean region. Planted in woods and hedges where it sometimes regenerates, mostly S. and E. England. Flo. April–May.*

Quercus cerris L. Turkey oak. Leaves with many acute lobes; fr. cup with spreading scales. Introd. Europe. Planted in woods and hedges, and regenerating freely, widespread. Flo. May.*

Quercus borealis Michx. f. var. **maxima** (Marsh.) Ashe. Red oak. *Q. rubra* L. sec. Duroi, *Q. maxima* Marsh. Leaves oblong, with 3–5 pairs of triangular-acute pointed lobes reaching half-way to midrib; glabrous except for reddish-brown tufts of hair on the primary veins beneath; fr. cup shallow, saucer-shaped, enclosing only base of fr. which is light brown and smooth. Introd. N. America. Planted in woods where it sometimes regenerates, uncommon. Flo. May.*

Castanea sativa Mill. Sweet chestnut. Tree to 30 m; leaves oblong-lanceolate, serrate; fr. 1–3 in a spinous involucre. Introd. S. Europe. Woods, hedges, etc., common. Flo. May.*

Fagus sylvatica L. Beech. Leaves ovate, silky; male catkins tassel-like; fr. triquetrous in woody spinous involucre. Woods, especially on calcareous soil, widespread and common, introd. in Ireland. Flo. March–April.

Salicaceae

Salix pentandra L. Bay willow. Shrub or small tree to 7 m; leaves lanceolate, glossy; catkin scales yellowish; stamens 5; capsule glabrous. Wet places, mostly N. England, Scotland and N. Ireland, introd. elsewhere. Flo. May–June.

Salix triandra L. Almond willow. Shrub or small tree to 7 m; leaves glabrous, paler below; catkin scales yellowish; stamens 3; capsule glabrous. Sides of streams, mostly S. and E. England, rare elsewhere. Flo. April.

Salix fragilis L. Crack willow. Tree to 25 m; twigs fragile at joints; leaves long; catkins long, pendulous; scales yellowish; stamens 2. By streams, ponds, etc., widespread and common. Flo. April.

Salix alba L. White willow. Tree to 25 m; leaves white and silky; catkin scales yellowish; stamens 2; stigma bifid. By streams, ponds, etc., widespread and common. Flo. April–May.

Salix purpurea L. Purple willow. Shrub to 3 m; leaves blue-green above, paler below; catkin scales dark at tip; stamens connate, purple. Fens and osier beds, widespread, but local. Flo. March–April.

Salix daphnoides Willd. Shrub or tree to 10 m; twigs bluish or purple; leaves oblong-lanceolate, dark green, glossy above, glaucous below; catkins cylindrical. Introd. Europe. Planted by ponds and rivers, widespread but uncommon. Flo. Feb.–March.*

Salix viminalis L. Common osier. Shrub to 5 m; twigs long and straight; leaves long, silky below; catkin scales dark at tip; anthers yellow. By streams and in osier beds, widespread and common. Flo. April–May.

Salix lapponum L. Downy willow. Shrub, 30–150 cm; leaves oblong, silky, especially below; scales dark at tip; anthers yellow and brown. Wet mountain rocks, Scotland and N. England. Flo. July.

Salix aurita L. Eared willow. Shrub 1–3 m, with raised striations under bark; leaves wrinkled, downy below, stipules large; scales dark at tip. Damp woods, heaths, by moorland streams, etc., widespread, but especially frequent in Scotland and N. Ireland. Flo. April–May.

ALNUS
GLUTINOSA.

× 5

CARPINUS
BETULUS

QUERCUS
PETRAEA.

CORYLUS
AVELLANA.

QUERCUS
ROBUR

FAGUS
SYLVATICA

SALIX
TRIANDRA

SALIX
ALBA.

SALIX
PENTANDRA.

SALIX
FRAGILIS.

SALIX
PURPUREA.

× 2

SALIX
VIMINALIS.

SALIX LAPPONUM.

SALIX AURITA.

— *Plate 78* —

Salicaceae *(continued)*

Salix caprea L. Goat willow. Shrub or small tree to 10 m; twigs without striations; leaves ovate, grey tomentose beneath; catkin scales dark at tip. Woods and hedgerows, widespread and common. Flo. March–April.

Salix cinerea L. Grey willow.
Ssp. **cinerea,** shrub to 10 m; twigs downy, with raised striations under bark; leaves obovate, grey beneath; anthers yellow. Fens, etc., E. England, local. Flo. March–April.*
Ssp. **oleifolia** Macreight. *S. atrocinerea* Brot., *S. cinerea* ssp. *atrocinerea* (Brot.) Silva & Sobrinho. Shrub to 10 m; twigs subglabrous, with raised striations under bark; leaves obovate, with rust-coloured hairs beneath; catkin scales dark at tip; anthers reddish. Woods, by streams and ponds, etc., widespread and common. Flo. March–April.

Salix repens L. Creeping willow. Stems mostly prostrate; leaves oblong-lanceolate with silky hairs; catkin scales brown at tip. Wet heaths, dunes, etc., widespread and common. Flo. April–May.

Salix nigricans Sm. Dark-leaved willow. Shrub to 4 m; spreading, striate under bark; leaves deep green, paler pubescent below, black when dry; scales dark at tip. Mountains, N. England, Scotland and N. Ireland. Flo. May.

Salix phylicifolia L. Tea-leaved willow. Shrub to 4 m; striate under bark; leaves glabrous, glaucous below, not black when dry; scales dark-tipped. Wet rocks, N. England and Scotland. Flo. April–May.

Salix hibernica Rech. f. Similar to *S. phylicifolia* but not striate under bark; leaves broadly lanceolate to elliptical, almost entire, broadly cuneate at base, apex shortly acuminate (not tapering as in *S. phylicifolia*). Rocks, etc., N.W. Ireland. Flo. April–May.*

Salix arbuscula L. Mountain willow. Low shrub; twigs striate; leaves glabrous above, glaucous beneath; scales brown-tipped, with white hairs; anthers reddish. Mountains, Scottish Highlands.

Salix lanata L. Woolly willow. Large shrub; buds large, woolly; leaves silky above, woolly beneath; scales with long yellow hairs. Mountain rocks, Scotland, rare. Flo. June.

Salix herbacea L. Dwarf willow. Plant small, from rhizome; leaves 10–20 mm, suborbicular, bright green; catkins terminal. Mountain tops, plentiful in Scotland, local in N. England, Wales and Ireland. Flo. June–July.

Salix myrsinites L. Whortle-leaved willow. Low shrub; twigs not striate; leaves green and shining; scales purple, dark-tipped, hairy; anthers purple. Wet mountain rocks, Scotland. Flo. May–June.

Salix reticulata L. Net-leaved willow. Stem creeping, rooting; leaves 10–30 mm, becoming subglabrous, oval, glaucous and reticulate beneath. Rocks, Scottish Highlands. Flo. June–July.

Hybrids are frequent in the genus *Salix* and are often intermediate between the parents. Although many are rare the following appear to have a wide distribution: *S. × ehrhartiana* Sm., *S. alba × pentandra*; *S. × meyerana* Rostk. ex Willd., *S. fragilis × pentandra*; *S. × rubens* Schrank., *S. alba × fragilis*; *S. × mollissima* Hoffm. ex Elwert., *S. triandra × viminalis*; *S. × rubra* Huds., *S. purpurea × viminalis*; *S. × sordida* A. Kern., *S. cinerea × purpurea*; *S. × sericans* Tausch. ex A. Kern., *S. caprea × viminalis*; *S. × calodendron* Wimm., *S. caprea × cinerea × viminalis*; *S. × stipularis* Sm., *S. aurita × viminalis × caprea*; *S. × smithiana* Willd, *S. × cinerea × viminalis*; *S. × fruticosa* Doell., *S. aurita × viminalis*; *S. × reichardtii* A. Kern., *S. caprea × cinerea*; *S. × capreola* A. Kern, ex Anderss., *S. aurita × caprea*; *S. × latifolia* Forbes, *S. caprea × nigricans*; *S. × multinervis* Doell., *S. aurita × cinerea*; *S. × laurina* Sm., *S. cinerea × phylicifolia*; *S. × subsericea* Doell., *S. cinerea × repens*; *S. × ambigua* Ehrh., *S. aurita × repens*; *S. × tetrapla* Walker, *S. nigricans × phylicifolia*.

Populus alba L. White poplar. Buds downy; leaves suborbicular, snowy-white beneath; catkin scales crenate; stigmas linear, cruciform. Introd. Europe. Planted in woods, by streams, etc., mostly S. England, uncommon. Flo. March–April.

Populus × canescens (Ait.) Sm. Grey poplar. *P. alba × tremula. P. × hybrida* Bieb. Buds downy, leaves grey beneath, broadly ovate, with 4–5 blunt teeth each side; scales laciniate. Damp woods, etc., mostly S. England. Flo. March (leaf only).

Populus tremula L. Aspen. Buds rather sticky; leaves glabrous, broader than long, petiole compressed; catkin scales deeply laciniate. Woods, heaths, etc., widespread and common. Flo. March.

Populus nigra L. Black poplar.
Ssp. **nigra.** Branches spreading; buds sticky; leaves glabrous, acuminate, with many small crenate teeth; catkin scales laciniate. Introd. Europe. Planted in woods, hedges, etc., uncommon. Flo. April.
Ssp. **betulifolia** (Pursh) W. Wettst. *P. betulifolia* Pursh. Similar to ssp. *nigra* but with smaller leaves, and a delicate pubescence on petioles, inflo. and young shoots. Perhaps native by streamsides, in wet woods, etc., S. and E. England, the Midlands and Wales, local. Flo. April.*
Both ssp. are frequently confused with *P. × canadensis* var. *serotina*.
Var. **italica** Duroi. Lombardy poplar. *P. italica* (Duroi) Moench. Branches and twigs all closely erect, fastigiate; leaf blades smaller. Often planted.*

Populus × canadensis Moench var. **serotina** (Hartig) Rehd. Italian poplar. *P. deltoidea × nigra. P. serotina* Hartig. Very similar to *P. nigra*; branches ascending; buds longer; leaves with teeth a little deeper, often with 2 glands at base of blade. Planted. Flo. April.*

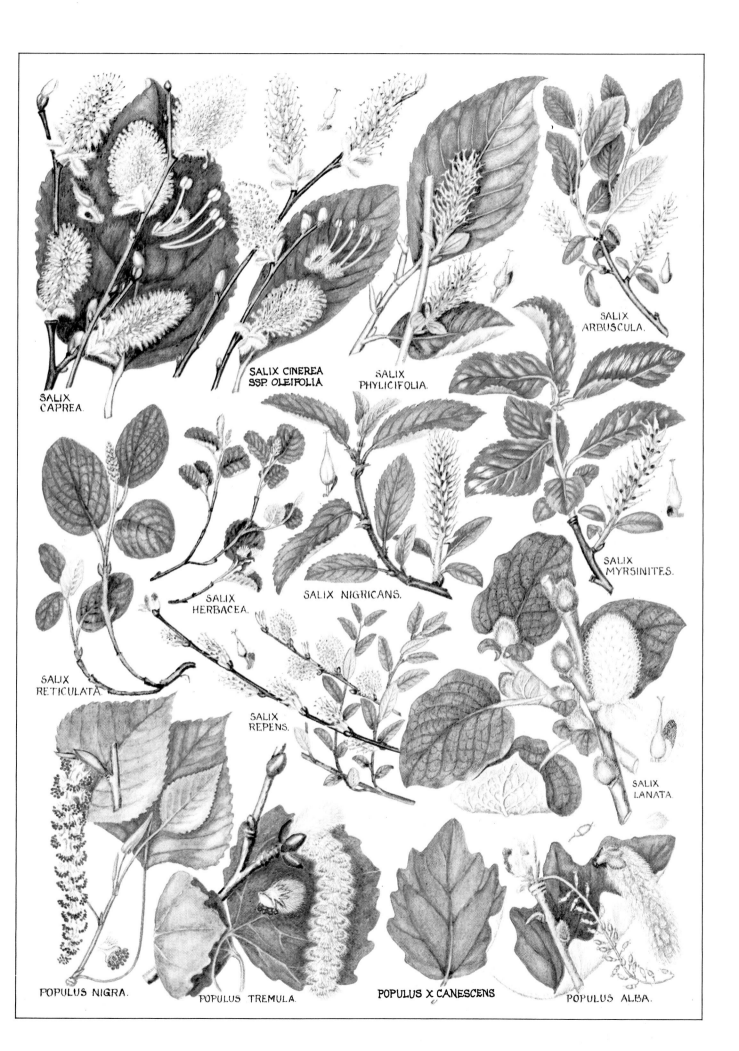

SALIX
CAPREA.

SALIX CINEREA
SSP. OLEIFOLIA

SALIX
PHYLICIFOLIA.

SALIX
ARBUSCULA.

SALIX
HERBACEA.

SALIX NIGRICANS.

SALIX
MYRSINITES.

SALIX
RETICULATA.

SALIX
REPENS.

SALIX
LANATA.

POPULUS NIGRA.

POPULUS TREMULA.

POPULUS X CANESCENS

POPULUS ALBA.

Plate 79

MONOCOTYLEDONES

Alismataceae

Baldellia ranunculoides (L.) Parl. Lesser water-plantain. *Alisma ranunculoides* L. Stems 6–40 cm; leaves narrow, lanceolate; flo. whorled, lilac; fr. head spherical. Beside streams and ponds, widespread but local. Flo. May–Aug.

Luronium natans (L.) Raf. Floating water-plantain. *Alisma natans* L. Stems long, floating; leaves long-petioled, small obtuse; flo. solitary, white. Lakes and canals, mostly Wales and Welsh border counties, rare. Flo. Aug.

Alisma plantago-aquatica L. Water-plantain. Leaves ovate, rounded at base; flo. pinkish; anthers twice as long as broad; style long, near base. Ponds and ditches, common, except in Scotland, where it is local. Flo. July–Aug.

Alisma lanceolatum With. Narrow-leaved water-plantain. Leaves lanceolate, narrowed below; anthers as long as broad; style short, near top of ovary. In similar habitats to *A. plantago-aquatica* but less common, mostly S. and E. England. Flo. July–Aug.

Alisma lanceolatum × plantago-aquatica. Intermediate between the parents, often occurs where they grow together.*

Alisma gramineum Lejeune. Ribbon-leaved water-plantain.*
Ssp. **gramineum**. Leaves submerged or aerial *c.* 45 mm wide, elliptic to oblong-elliptic; inflo. overtopping leaves; flo. petals white or purplish-white; stigma curled; fruitlets widest at top with lateral pericarp thick and opaque. Introd. N. Europe. Naturalized in rivers and streams, E. England and Worcestershire, rare. Flo. July–Sept.*
Ssp. **wahlenbergii** Holmb. Similar to ssp. *gramineum* but leaves usually submerged, 10.30 mm wide, narrowly linear; inflo. not overtopping leaves; flo. petals smaller, white; lateral pericarp of fruitlets thin and translucent. Introd. N. Europe. Naturalized in river in W. Norfolk, rare. Flo. July–Sept.*

Damasonium alisma Mill. Starfruit. *D. stellatum* Thuill. Leaves floating, oblong, 5-veined; flo. white; carpels with long beak, star-like. Ponds and ditches, with gravelly or sandy bottoms, formerly known from a number of localities in S. England, the Midlands and Yorkshire, now known only from a single locality in Surrey, very rare and almost extinct. Flo. June–July.

Sagittaria sagittifolia L. Arrowhead. Stoloniferous; aerial leaves arrow-shaped; scape longer than leaves; flo. white with purple centre. In mud by streams and ponds, common in S. and E. England and the Midlands, local in Ireland, rare in Wales, and introd. and very rare in S.W. England and Scotland. Flo. July–Aug.

Sagittaria rigida Pursh. Canadian arrowhead. *S. heterophylla* Pursh. non. Schreb. Similar to *S. sagittifolia* but aerial leaves ovate to elliptical; scape shorter than leaves; flo. white with pale yellow centre. Introd. N. America. Naturalized in Exeter Canal, S. Devon. Flo. July–Aug.*

Sagittaria latifolia Willd. Similar to *S. sagittifolia* but with larger flo. without purple centre. Garden escape. Naturalized in ponds in Surrey and Channel Islands, rare. Flo. July–Aug.*

Butomaceae

Butomus umbellatus L. Flowering-rush. Stem *c.* 1 m; leaves linear, triquetrous; flo. pink. By ponds and dikes, local, but widespread in most of England except the N. where it is rare, rather rare in Wales and Ireland, and introd. and very rare in Scotland. Flo. July–Sept.

Hydrocharitaceae

Hydrocharis morsus-ranae L. Frogbit. Stems floating; leaves in tufts; flo. dioecious, white, springing from pellucid sheaths. Canals, ponds, etc., locally common in S. and E. England and the Midlands, rare in Wales, N. England and Ireland and absent from Scotland. Flo. July–Aug.

Stratiotes aloides L. Water-soldier. Stem submerged, rising to surface for flo.; leaves spinous-serrate, aloe-like; flo. dioecious, white. Ponds and ditches, E. England, introd. elsewhere, rare. Flo. June–Aug.

Elodea canadensis Michx. Canadian pondweed. Stem robust, submerged; leaves up to 15 mm long, elliptic to ovate-lanceolate with rounded apex, dark green, 3 in whorl; flo. 5 mm diam., purplish, with long, slender, tube. Introd. N. America. Naturalized in still waters, formerly widespread but now decreasing. Flo. May–Sept.

Elodea nuttallii (Planch.) St. John. Nuttall's waterweed. *Hydrilla verticillata* auct., non (L.f.) Royle. Similar to *E. canadensis* but less robust; leaves up to 20 mm long, tapering to a pointed tip, flaccid, light green (but dark green and recurved in deep water), 2–6 in whorl; flo. 2 mm diam. Introd. N. America. Naturalized in still waters, widespread and increasing rapidly. Flo. May–Sept.*

Lagarosiphon major (Ridl.) Moss. Similar to *Elodea canadensis* but stems stout and rigid; leaves up to 25 mm long, spirally arranged, stiffly recurved, crowded, dark green; flo. dioecious, small, whitish, enclosed in long spathes, floating on water on reaching surface. Introd. S. Africa. Naturalized in ponds, slow streams, etc., mostly S. England. Flo. June–Sept.*

Hydrilla verticillata (L.f.) Royle. Similar to *E. nuttallii* but leaves translucent green, in whorls of up to 8; leaves 10–15 mm long, not reflexed, flaccid, with marginal teeth; flo. rarely seen in wild. Lake, W. Galway, Ireland, formerly in N. Lancashire but now lost.*

Vallisneria spiralis L. Submerged. Leaves ribbon-like, veined, long; flo. small, pinkish, male many together, female solitary; peduncle of latter becomes spirally twisted in fr. Introd. Tropics. Established in canals, etc., S. England, and probably elsewhere. Flo. July–Oct.*

Juncaginaceae

Triglochin palustris L. Marsh arrowgrass. Leaves filiform, semi-cylindrical to tip; fr. linear; carpels adhering at tip. In marshy places, local, but widespread. Flo. June–Aug.

Triglochin maritima L. Sea arrowgrass. Leaves fleshier, linear, flattened at tip; fr. ovoid, carpels separating. Seashores and salt marshes. Flo. July–Sept.

Scheuchzeriaceae

Scheuchzeria palustris L. Rannoch-rush. Stem 10–25 cm; leaves linear, semi-cylindrical, with a pore at top; flo. yellowish-green. Wet *Sphagnum* bogs, Perthshire, very rare, formerly in Shropshire, Cheshire, Yorkshire, Inverness-shire, Argyllshire and Offaly, but now lost. Flo. June–Aug.

LURONIUM NATANS.

BUTOMUS
UMBELLATUS

BALDELLIA
RANUNCULOIDES.

ALISMA
LANCEOLATUM.

SAGITTARIA
SAGITTIFOLIA.

ALISMA
PLANTAGO-
AQUATICA.

TRIGLOCHIN
MARITIMA.

DAMASONIUM
ALISMA.

TRIGLOCHIN
PALUSTRIS

SCHEUCHZERIA
PALUSTRIS.

HYDROCHARIS
MORSUS-RANAE.

STRATIOTES ALOIDES.

ELODEA
CANADENSIS

Plate 80

Orchidaceae

Hammarbya paludosa (L.) Kuntze. Bog orchid. *Malaxis paludosa* (L.) Sw. Stem 3–12 cm; leaves concave, bearing tiny bulbils; flo. green, with lip at back. *Sphagnum* bogs, mostly N. and W. Britain, very rare in S. England and Ireland. Flo. July–Sept.

Liparis loeselii (L.) Rich. Fen orchid. Stem 6–20 cm; flo. yellowish-green, lip oblong, mostly upwards; leaves lanceolate. Fens, E. England, very rare. Flo. June–July.
var. **ovata** Riddelsd. ex Godfery. Leaves broader, ovate-elliptical. Coastal dunes, Devon and S. Wales.*

Corallorhiza trifida Chatel. Coralroot orchid. Root fleshy with rounded lobes or branches; saprophyte with brown scales; stem 10–20 cm; flo. yellowish, lip white, purple-spotted, drooping. Boggy woods, N. England, and Scotland, rare. Flo. June–July.

Neottia nidus-avis (L.) Rich. Bird's-nest orchid. Roots many, thick, interlaced; saprophyte with brown scales; stem up to 50 cm; flo. brown. Shady woods, especially of beech, mostly S. half of Britain and in Ireland. Flo. June–July.

Listera ovata (L.) R. Br. Common twayblade. Stem up to 60 cm; leaves 2, large, 10–20 cm, ribbed; flo. spike long and green. Damp woods, shady pastures, etc., locally common except in N. Scotland. Flo. May–July.

Listera cordata (L.) R. Br. Lesser twayblade. Stem 3–20 cm; leaves small, 1–2 cm, opposite; flo. spike small, reddish. In *Sphagnum* under heather and in pinewoods, Scotland, N.W. England, rare in S.W. England, Wales and Ireland. Flo. May–June.

Spiranthes spiralis (L.) Chevall. Autumn lady's-tresses. *S. autumnalis* Rich. Tubers ovate; stem 5–15 cm; leaves radical, ovate; flo. white in 1 spiral row. Pastures, downs, etc., mostly on calcareous soils, England, W. Wales and S. Ireland, absent from Scotland. Flo. Aug.–Sept.

Spiranthes aestivalis (Poir) Rich. Summer lady's-tresses. Roots cylindrical; stem 10–35 cm, bearing lanceolate leaves; flo. white in 1 spiral row. Formerly in marshy ground, New Forest, Hampshire and in the Channel Islands, but probably now extinct. Flo. July–Aug.

Spiranthes romanzoffiana Cham. Irish lady's-tresses. Roots cylindrical; leaves cauline; flo. in 3 spiral rows. Flo. July–Aug.*

Originally thought to be distinct it is now known that the following two taxa are linked by intermediate forms and merge into each other:
Ssp. **gemmipara** (Sm.) Clapham. Cauline leaves fairly broad, not acuminate; flo. close together, white. Meadows, etc., S.W. Ireland and W. Devon, very rare.*
Ssp. **stricta** (Rydb.) Clapham. Leaves long, narrow, acuminate; flo. greenish-white; spike long and lax. Boggy pastures, lake verges, etc., N.E. Ireland, Hebrides and Argyll.*

Goodyera repens (L.) R. Br. Creeping lady's-tresses. Rhizome creeping; stem glandular; leaves net-veined; flo. white; lip pouched. Pine woods, N. England and Scotland, also in E. Anglia where it may have been introd. Flo. July–Aug.

Epipogium aphyllum Sw. Ghost orchid. Stem 5–25 cm; saprophyte with brown scales; flo. few; petals long, lanceolate, yellowish; lip upwards, cordate, pinkish with purple spots. Woods in deep shade, S. England, formerly in Herefordshire and Shropshire, very rare. Flo. June–Sept.*

Cephalanthera rubra (L.) Rich. Red helleborine. Stem 20–60 cm; leaves lanceolate-acute; flo. rose-red; lip white tipped with purple; ovary downy, shorter than bract. Beechwoods on limestone and calcareous soils, Gloucestershire and Buckinghamshire, very rare. Flo. June–July.

Cephalanthera longifolia (L.) Fritsch. Narrow-leaved helleborine. *C. ensifolia* (Schmidt) Rich. Stems 15–60 cm; leaves long and narrow; flo. white, petals acute; ovary glabrous, longer than bracts. Woods on calcareous soil, widespread, but local and rare. Flo. May–June.

Cephalanthera damasonium (Mill.) Druce. White helleborine. *C. grandiflora* Gray. Stem 15–60 cm; leaves ovate-oblong; petals white, oblong, blunt; lip with yellow spot. Woods, especially beech, on calcareous soil, mostly S. England. Flo. May–June.

The British taxa of *Epipactis* were revised by Young (1949 & 1952) and his treatment is followed below.

Epipactis phyllanthes G. E. Sm. Green-flowered helleborine. Stem 10–40 cm; flo. cernuous or hanging down, open or closed until fertilized, pale green; lip-like lateral petals, not fully differentiated. Woods on calcareous soil and dunes. Flo. July–Aug.*
Var. **phyllanthes**. Lip undifferentiated, ovate or lanceolate; flo. sometimes not opening. Woods, S. England.*
Var. **pendula** (C. Thomas) D. P. Young. *E. pendula* C. Thomas. Lip more differentiated, depression at base (hypochile) as long as reflexed tip (epichile). Woods, dunes, etc., N.W. England and N. Wales.*
Var. **vectensis** (T. & T. A. Stephenson) D. P. Young. Lip with small green hypochile and longer straight tip (epichile). Woods, S. and E. England, Midlands and S. Wales.*
Var. **degenera** D. P. Young. Lip with shallow, rudimentary depression at base. Woods, S. and E. England.*

Epipactis leptochila (Godfery) Godfery. Narrow-lipped helleborine. Stem 20–60 cm; flo. spreading and open, green; lip green with hypochile red-spotted within, tip long, spreading. Shady woods, mostly S. England, local, very rare in N. England. Flo. June–July.

Epipactis dunensis (T. & T. A. Stephenson) Godfery. Dune helleborine. Stem up to 80 cm; flo. incompletely open; epichile as broad as long. Coastal dunes, Anglesey, Lancashire and Northumberland, very local. Flo. June–July.*

Epipactis helleborine (L.) Crantz. Broad-leaved helleborine. *E. latifolia* (L.) All. Stem up to 90 cm; leaves broadly ovate; sepals green; lip purple, fully differentiated, tip recurved; ovary subglabrous. Woods, widespread and locally common, except in Scotland where it is rare. Flo. July–Sept.

Epipactis purpurata Sm. Violet helleborine. *E. sessilifolia* Peterm. Stem up to 90 cm; leaves narrower, ovate-lanceolate, purple beneath; bracts long; sepals greenish; lip whitish with recurved tip; ovary hairy. Woods on calcareous soil, mostly S. England and Midlands, local. Flo. Aug.–Sept.*

Epipactis atrorubens (Hoffm.) Schult. Dark-red helleborine. *E. atropurpurea* Raf. Stem 20–60 cm, pubescent; leaves small, elliptic; petals dark red-purple; lip broad with rugose swellings and reflexed tip. Limestone rocks, N. England, N. Wales, N. Scotland and W. Ireland, local and rare. Flo. June–July.

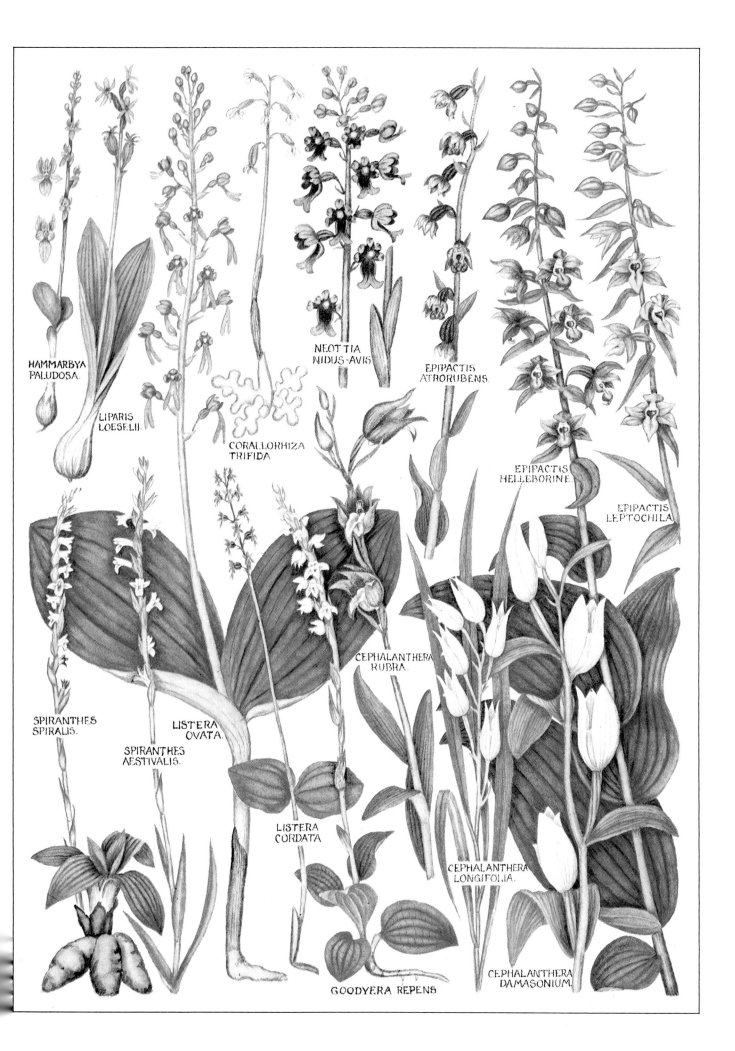

HAMMARBYA
PALUDOSA.

LIPARIS
LOESELII.

CORALLORHIZA
TRIFIDA

NEOTTIA
NIDUS-AVIS.

EPIPACTIS
ATRORUBENS.

EPIPACTIS
HELLEBORINE.

EPIPACTIS
LEPTOCHILA

SPIRANTHES
SPIRALIS.

SPIRANTHES
AESTIVALIS.

LISTERA
OVATA.

LISTERA
CORDATA

CEPHALANTHERA
RUBRA.

CEPHALANTHERA
LONGIFOLIA.

GOODYERA REPENS

CEPHALANTHERA
DAMASONIUM.

Plate 81

Orchidaceae *(continued)*

Epipactis palustris (L.) Crantz. Marsh helleborine. Rhizome creeping; Stem 20–60 cm; outer sepals greenish, inner white, flushed with pink; lip crenate, with red veins and yellow spots. Fens, marshes and dunes, widespread, but local. Flo. July–Aug.

Anacamptis pyramidalis (L.) Rich. Pyramidal orchid. *Orchis pyramidalis* L. Stem up to 60 cm, slender; spike pyramidal; flo. rose; lip with 3 oblong lobes and 2 tubercles; spur long and slender. Grassy places on calcareous and limestone soils, and dunes, widespread, but local in England and Ireland, rare in Wales and Scotland. Flo. June–Aug.

Himantoglossum hircinum (L.) Spreng. Lizard orchid. *Orchis hircina* (L.) Crantz. Stem 30–70 cm; flo. green and brown, smelling strongly of goats; lip with 3 linear lobes, central lobe very long and twisted. Wood margins and rough grassy places mostly on calcareous soil, mostly S. and E. England, very rare. Flo. June–July.

Aceras anthropophorum (L.) Ait. f. Man orchid. Tubers ovoid; stem 10–40 cm; sepals green, forming a hood; lip yellowish with 4 linear lobes; spur 0. Grassy slopes and scrub on calcareous soil, mostly S. and E. England, local. Flo. June–July. Illus. on pl. 82.

Orchis simia Lam. Monkey orchid. Tubers ovoid; stem 10–30 cm; flo. pale or crimson, hooded; lip with 4 narrow crimson lobes; spur cylindrical Bushy places on calcareous soil, mostly S. and E. England, very rare. Flo. May–June.

Orchis militaris L. Military orchid. Tubers ovoid; stem 20–60 cm; flo. pale purple with darker veins; lip 4-lobed with upturned ends. Woods and thickets on calcareous soil, S. and E. England, very rare. Flo. May–June.

Orchis purpurea Huds. Lady orchid. Tubers ovoid; stem 15–90 cm; sepals forming hood, veined dark purple; lip broad, whitish, spotted red. Woods and shady places on calcareous soils, mostly Kent, local. Flo. May–June.

Orchis ustulata L. Burnt orchid. Tubers ovoid; stem 5–15 cm; flo. small; hood dark purple, becoming white; lip white, spotted red. Downs and pastures on calcareous and limestone soils, mostly S. England, rare. Flo. June–July.

Orchis morio L. Green-winged orchid. Tubers ovoid; stem 6–20 cm; flo. hood with dark green veins; lip crimson-purple with pale centre. Moist meadows, etc., England, Wales and mid Ireland, widespread, formerly locally common but now rapidly decreasing. Flo. May–June.

Orchis mascula (L.) L. Early-purple orchid. Tubers ovoid; stem 20–60 cm; leaves blotched; flo. rich red-purple; lip nearly flat, spotted on pale centre. Woods, copses, etc., widespread and locally common. Flo. April–May.

Orchis laxiflora Lam. Loose-flowered orchid. Tubers ovoid; stem 20–60 cm; leaves ribbed, not blotched; sides of lip recurved, centre not spotted. Wet meadows, Channel Islands. Flo. May–June.

Dactylorhiza incarnata (L.) Soó. Early marsh-orchid.
Ssp. ***incarnata***. Stem up to 40 cm, hollow; leaves yellow-green, unspotted; flo. flesh colour; sides of lip reflexed. Wet meadows and marshes, widespread, but local. Flo. May–July.
Ssp. ***coccinea*** (Pugsley) Soó. Stem shorter, more robust; flo. smaller, bright red. Coastal dunes, E. Anglia, Wales, N.W. England, N. Scotland and N. Ireland, local.*
Ssp. ***pulchella*** (Druce) Soó. Flo. reddish-purple, lip nearly flat. Peat bogs, etc., mostly Wales.*
Ssp. ***cruenta*** (O. F. Muell.) P. D. Sell. Leaves often spotted on both surfaces; flo. lilac. Calcareous peat bogs, W. Ireland.*
Ssp. ***gemmana*** (Pugsley) P. D. Sell. Plant large with 6 leaves or more; lip more than 9 mm wide and spotted. Fens, E. Anglia and W. Ireland.*
Ssp. ***ochroleuca*** (Boll) P. F. Hunt & Summerhayes. Stem taller; flo. yellowish, lip unspotted and 3-lobed. Calcareous marshes, E. Anglia and S. Wales.*

Dactylorhiza majalis (Reichb.) P. F. Hunt & Summerhayes.
Ssp. ***occidentalis*** (Pugsley) P. D. Sell. Broad-leaved marsh-orchid. *D. kerryensis* (Wilmott) P. F. Hunt & Summerhayes. Stem up to 20 cm; leaves up to 10 cm, long with or without spots; flo. red-purple; lip 8–12 mm, mid lobe triangular; spur cylindrical. Marshy meadows, dunes, etc., N.W. Scotland and W. Ireland, local. Flo. May–June.*
Ssp. ***purpurella*** (T. & T. A. Stephenson) D. Moresby Moore & Soó. Northern marsh-orchid. *D. purpurella* (T. & T. A. Stephenson) Soó. Stem up to 30 cm; leaves up to 12 cm long, slightly spotted; flo. deep red-purple to magenta; lip 6–8 mm, entire; spur broad. Fens, damp pastures, etc., Staffordshire, Shropshire and mid Wales northwards, local; widespread in Ireland. Flo. June–July.
Ssp. ***praetermissa*** (Druce) D. Moresby Moore & Soó. Southern marsh-orchid. *D. praetermissa* (Druce) Soó. Stem up to 60 cm; leaves up to 24 cm long, mostly without spots; flo. reddish-purple; lip 9–14 mm, mid lobe short; spur broad. Marshes, damp pastures, etc., S. and W. England and Wales to Yorkshire, local. Flo. June–July.
Ssp. ***cambrensis*** (R. H. Roberts) R. H. Roberts. Similar to ssp. *purpurella* but leaves longer and narrower and more rigid, heavily marked with purple-brown spots or blotches; flo. light red-purple, marked with dark lines and dots. Marshes, W. and N. Wales and N.W. Scotland, very local. Flo. June–July.*

Dactylorhiza traunsteineri (Sauter) Soó. Narrow-leaved marsh-orchid. Stem 20–45 cm, slender; leaves up to 15 cm, long, narrow (up to 2 cm wide), spreading, without spots or marked with faint spots or blotches; flo. reddish-purple; lip 3-lobed. Calcareous fens, S. and E. England to Wales, S. Scotland and Ireland, local and rare. Flo. May–June.*

Dactylorhiza maculata (L.) Soó.
Ssp. ***elodes*** (Griseb.) Soó. Heath spotted-orchid. Ssp. *ericetorum* (E. F. Linton) P. F. Hunt & Summerhayes. Stem solid; lower leaves acute, spotted; flo. pale lilac or whitish, spotted; outer lobes of lip broad, rounded; spur slender. Moors, heaths, etc., widespread. Flo. May–July.

Dactylorhiza fuchsii (Druce) Soó.
Ssp. ***fuchsii***. Common spotted-orchid. Stem 10–45 cm, solid; lower leaves blunt, spotted; flo. lilac or whitish; lip with 3 deep triangular lobes. Woods, meadows, etc., on basic soils, widespread, but local. Flo. June–Aug.
Ssp. ***hebridensis*** (Wilmott) Soó. Stem 10–15 cm; flo. bright rose; lobes of lip rounded. Dunes, etc., N.W. Scotland and W. Ireland. Flo. June–Aug.
Ssp. ***okellyi*** (Druce) Soó. Leaves slender, unspotted; flo. white, without lines or dots, fragrant. Pastures, etc., on limestone soils, N.W. Scotland and W. Ireland. Flo. June–Aug.*

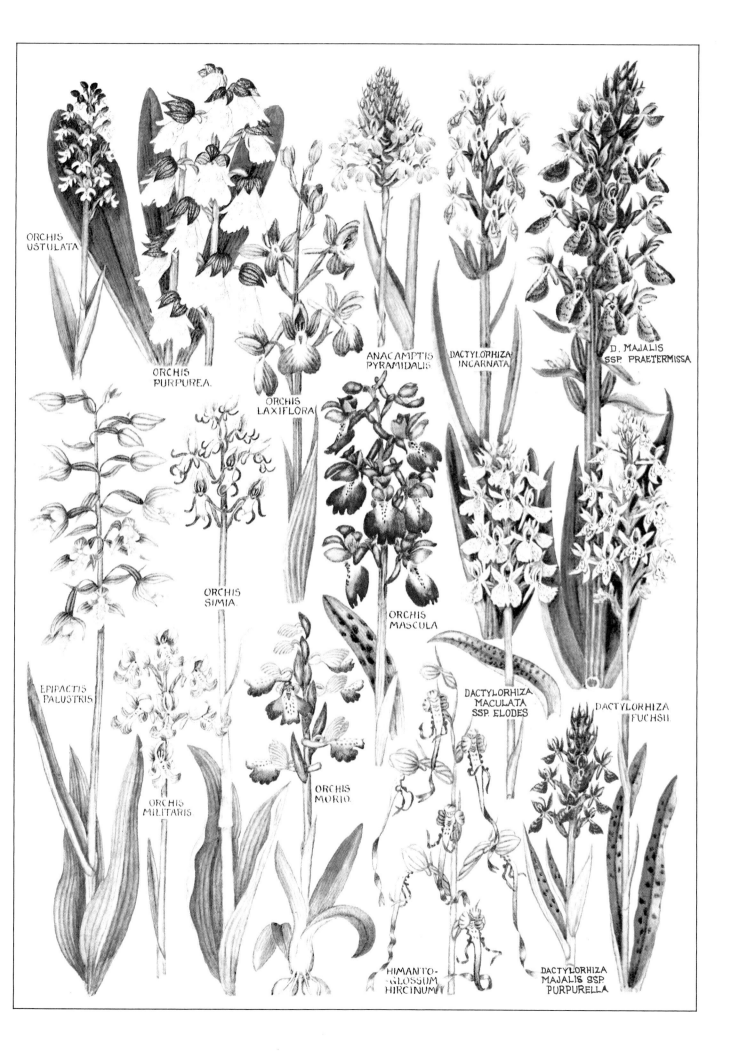

ORCHIS
USTULATA

ORCHIS
PURPUREA.

ORCHIS
LAXIFLORA

ANACAMPTIS
PYRAMIDALIS

DACTYLORHIZA
INCARNATA

D. MAJALIS
SSP. PRAETERMISSA

ORCHIS
SIMIA.

ORCHIS
MASCULA

EPIPACTIS
PALUSTRIS.

ORCHIS
MILITARIS

ORCHIS
MORIO.

DACTYLORHIZA
MACULATA
SSP. ELODES

DACTYLORHIZA
FUCHSII

HIMANTO-
-GLOSSUM
HIRCINUM

DACTYLORHIZA
MAJALIS SSP.
PURPURELLA

Plate 82

Orchidaceae *(continued)*

Ophrys apifera Huds. Bee orchid. Stems 15–45 cm; sepals pink or whitish, inner small; lip very convex with tip recurved and hidden; side lobes hairy. Grassy places on calcareous and basic soils, mostly S. and E. England and the Midlands, rare in N. England and Ireland, mostly coastal in Wales, and absent from S.W. England and Scotland. Flo. June–July. Var. **trollii** (Heg.) Druce. Lip more yellow, nearly flat, tip spreading. Gloucestershire.

Ophrys holosericea (Burm. f.) Greuter. Late spider-orchid. *O. fuciflora* (F. W. Schmidt) Moench. *O. arachnites* (L.) Reichard. Stem 15–50 cm; outer sepals pink; inner narrow, downy; lip broad, brown, velvety, becoming convex; tip upturned. Downs and grassy slopes on calcareous soil, E. Kent, very rare. Flo. June–July.

Ophrys sphegodes Mill. Early spider-orchid. *O. aranifera* Huds. Stem 10–20 cm; outer sepals green, inner green or brown; lip broad, brown, velvet with green edges, without a point. Downs and grassy places on calcareous soil, S. England, rare. Flo. April–May.

Ophrys insectifera L. Fly orchid. *O. muscifera* Huds. Stem up to 60 cm, slender; outer sepals pale green, inner filiform; lip narrow, oblong, rich brown with pale blue centre. Wood borders, shady places, etc., on calcareous and limestone soils, and bogs, mostly S. half of Britain and W. Ireland. Flo. May–June.

Herminium monorchis (L.) R. Br. Musk orchid. Stem 10–15 cm; flo. very small; sepals greenish; lip narrow, green, 3-lobed, pouched below. Short turf on downs and pastures on calcareous and limestone soils, mostly S. England, rare. Flo. June–July.

Gymnadenia conopsea (L.) R. Br. Fragrant orchid. *Habenaria conopsea* (L.) Benth. Stem 15–40 cm; flo. many, rose-pink to reddish-purple, rarely white, fragrant; lip with 3 equal lobes and long slender spur. Pastures, downs, etc., on basic or calcareous soil, heaths and bogs, widespread. Flo. June–Aug.

Neotinea maculata (Desf.) Stearn. Dense-flowered orchid. *N. intacta* (L.) Reichb. Stem 12–25 cm; leaves oblong, often slightly spotted; flo. greenish-white, streaked with pink; lip with lateral lobes narrow; spur short. Pastures on limestone, W. Ireland, and on calcareous sand and gravel soils in Ireland and the Isle of Man. Flo. May–June.*

Pseudorchis albida (L.) Á. & D. Löve. Small-white orchid. *Leucorchis albida* (L.) E. Mey. ex Schur. Root of fleshy fibres; stem 10–30 cm; flo. small, pendulous, greenish-white; lip 3-lobed; spur short. Hilly pastures, Derbyshire and N. Wales northwards, local, widespread but local in Ireland. Flo. May–July.

Coeloglossum viride (L.) Hartm. Frog orchid. Stem 6–25 cm; flo. green; lip linear, brownish-green, tubercled; spur short. Upland pastures, widespread, but local. Flo. June–Aug.

Platanthera chlorantha (Custer) Reichb. Greater butterfly-orchid. *Habenaria chlorantha* (Custer) Bab. Stem up to 45 cm; flo. white, tinged green, scented; pollinia diverging below; spur curved downwards. Moist woods on basic soils, widespread, but local. Flo. May–July.

Platanthera bifolia (L.) Rich. Lesser butterfly-orchid. *Habenaria bifolia* (L.) R. Br. Stem up to 40 cm; flo. white, scented; pollinia parallel; spur slender, horizontal. Open woods, pastures, heaths, etc., on basic soils, widespread but local. Flo. May–July.

Cypripedium calceolus L. Lady's-slipper. Stem up to 50 cm; flo. sepals maroon, lateral twisted, 2 lower often connate; lip large, inflated, yellow. Wood borders on limestone soil, Yorkshire, and formerly elsewhere, very rare. Flo. May–June.

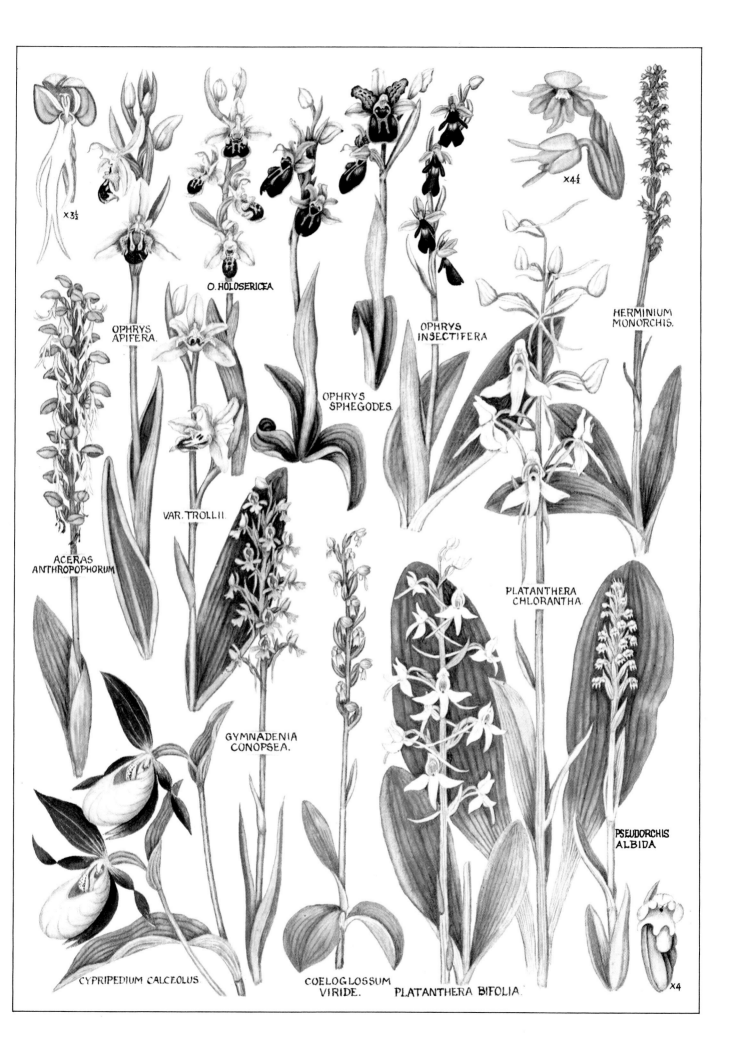

x3½

O. HOLOSERICEA

x4⅓

OPHRYS
APIFERA.

OPHRYS
INSECTIFERA

HERMINIUM
MONORCHIS.

OPHRYS
SPHEGODES.

ACERAS
ANTHROPOPHORUM

VAR. TROLLII.

PLATANTHERA
CHLORANTHA.

GYMNADENIA
CONOPSEA.

PSEUDORCHIS
ALBIDA

CYPRIPEDIUM CALCEOLUS

COELOGLOSSUM
VIRIDE.

PLATANTHERA BIFOLIA.

x4

Plate 83

Iridaceae

Iris pseudacorus L. Yellow iris. Stem up to 100 cm; leaves stiff, sword-like; flo. 2–3, large, bright yellow; seeds brown. Wet fields and marshes, common. Flo. May–July.

Iris foetidissima L. Stinking iris. Stem up to 80 cm; leaves weak; flo. 3–4, mauve with dark veins, rarely yellow; seeds scarlet. Woods and thickets on dry calcareous soil, S. half of Britain, introd. elsewhere. Flo. May–July.

Iris spuria L. Blue iris. Stem up to 60 cm; leaves linear; flo. violet and whitish; capsule with long point. Garden escape. Naturalized in ditches, Dorset and Lincolnshire, and probably elsewhere. Flo. June–July.

Iris versicolor L. Purple iris. Stem up to 100 cm; leaves broad, greyish; flo. pale pinkish-purple. Garden escape. Naturalized in wet places, mostly Lake District and Scotland, rare. Flo. June–July.*

Iris germanica L. Stem up to 100 cm; leaves broad, greyish; flo. bluish-violet with yellow beard. Garden escape. Naturalized in ditches, etc., mostly S. England and Midlands, uncommon. Flo. May–June.*

Hermodactylus tuberosus (L.) Mill. Snake's-head iris. *Iris tuberosa* L. Tubers finger-like; stem 30–40 cm; leaves linear, 4-angled; flo. sepals dark purple, inner thread-like. Garden escape. Naturalized in damp places, S.W. England and Channel Islands. Flo. April.*

Crocus nudiflorus Sm. Autumn crocus. Corm stoloniferous; leaves in spring; flo. in autumn, purple; stigma finely divided. Introd. Europe. Meadows, mostly the Midlands. Flo. Sept.–Oct.*

Crocus vernus (L.) Hill. Spring crocus. *C. purpureus* Weston. Corm not stoloniferous; leaves appearing with the purple or white flo.; stigmas blunt, orange. Garden escape. Naturalized in meadows, mostly S. and E. England, local. Flo. March–April.

Crocus tommasinianus Herbert. Similar to *C. vernus* but flo. lilac to purple with white tube. Garden escape. Naturalized in meadows, mostly S. and E. England, rare. Flo. March–May.*

Crocus flavus Weston. *C. aureus* Sibth. & Sm. Leaves appearing with 1–4 pale yellow to orange flo. Garden escape. Naturalized in meadows, S. and E. England, rare. Flo. March–April.*

Romulea columnae Seb. & Mauri. Sand crocus. *R. parviflora* Bub. Corm *c.* 8 mm; leaves very narrow, recurved; flo. pale lilac, midribs darker; fr. recurved. Sandy turf near the sea, S. Devon and Channel Islands. Flo. April.

Tritonia × crocosmiflora (Lemoine) Nicholson. Montbretia. *T. aurea × pottsii. Crocosmia × crocosmiflora* (Lemoine) N. E. Br. Corm *c.* 2 cm; stem up to 80 cm, slender; leaves sword-like; inflo. spike-like; flo. vivid orange, funnel-shaped, tube 2.5–3 cm long, with oblong wide spreading perianth segments. Garden escape. Naturalized in ditches, by streams, etc., widespread, but locally common in S.W. England. Flo. July–Aug.*

Sisyrinchium graminoides E. P. Bicknell. Blue-eyed-grass. *S. bermudiana* auct. *S. angustifolium* Mill. Leaves grass-like; spathe 2–3-flowered; flo. blue, paler outside; filaments united. Wet meadows and hills, W. Ireland, introd. elsewhere. Flo. July.

Sisyrinchium californicum (Ker-Gawl) Dryander. Yellow-eyed-grass. Similar to *S. graminoides* but more robust; flo. yellow turning orange. Introd. N. America. Naturalized in wet places, Cornwall, W. Wales and W. Ireland, local. Flo. June.*

Gladiolus illyricus Koch. Wild gladiolus. Stem 40–80 cm; leaves glaucous; flo. sepals crimson-purple or paler with dark centres; anthers shorter than filaments. Bushy heaths, New Forest, very rare, formerly in the Isle of Wight. Flo. July.

Amaryllidaceae

Narcissus pseudonarcissus L. Wild daffodil. Stem 15–35 cm; flo. petals pale; corona deep yellow, irregularly lobed. Damp woods and riversides, locally plentiful, though often introd. Flo. March–April.

Narcissus obvallaris Salisb. Tenby daffodil. Stem 20–30 cm; flo. petals deep yellow; corona distinctly 6-lobed, spreading. Formerly in pastures in Shropshire, and W. Wales, but not lost. Flo. April.

Narcissus poeticus L. *N. majalis* Curt. Flo. petals white; corona very short, yellow with red rim. Garden escape. Naturalized in grassy places, rare. Flo. May.*

Narcissus × medioluteus Mill. Primrose peerless. *N. poeticus × tazetta. N. × biflorus* Curt. Stem with 2 flo.; petals white; corona short, yellow. Garden escape. Naturalized in grassy places, widespread, but uncommon. Flo. April–May.

Galanthus nivalis L. Snowdrop. Leaves glaucous; flo. white, pendulous, with green spot on short inner petals. Perhaps native in damp woods, S.W. England, Wales and adjacent counties, introd. elsewhere. Flo. Jan.–March.

Leucojum aestivum L. Summer snowflake. Stem 30–50 cm; spathe green at apex, with 3–6 flo., white with green tips. Wet meadows and withy beds, mostly S. England and S. Ireland, introd. elsewhere. Flo. May.

Leucojum vernum L. Spring snowflake. Stem 15–20 cm; spathe green in middle, with 1 flo., white with green tip. Stream banks and damp places, Dorset and Somerset, introd. elsewhere, vary rare. Flo. Feb.–March.

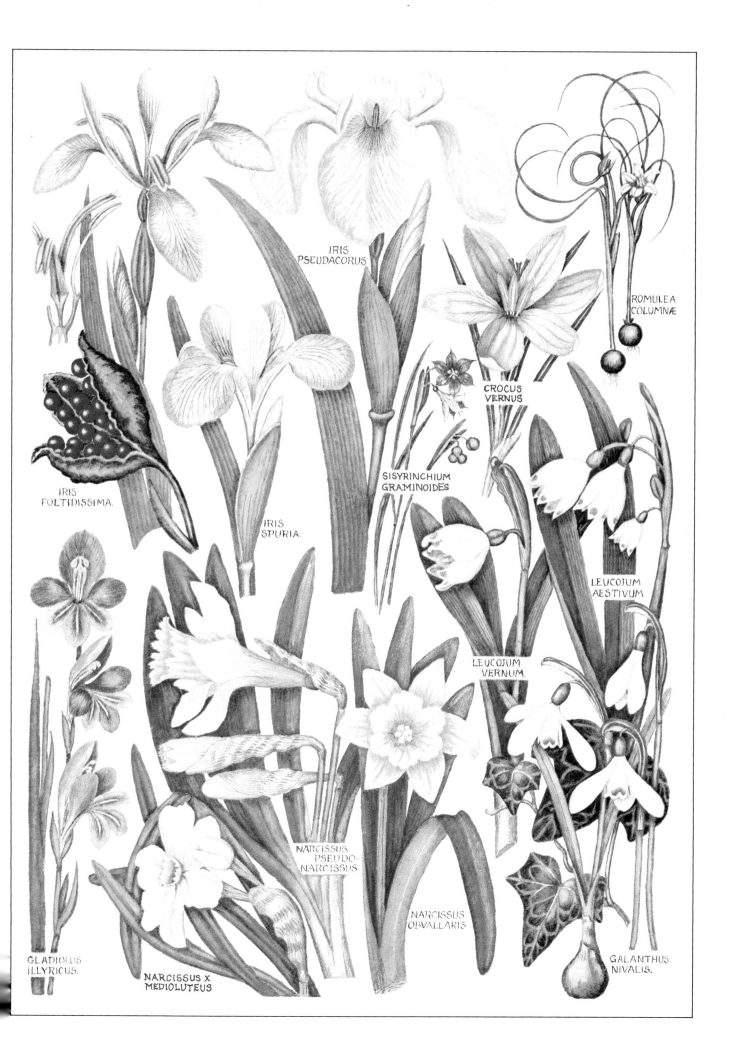

IRIS
PSEUDACORUS

ROMULEA
COLUMNÆ

CROCUS
VERNUS

SISYRINCHIUM
GRAMINOIDES

IRIS
FŒTIDISSIMA.

IRIS
SPURIA.

LEUCOJUM
AESTIVUM

LEUCOJUM
VERNUM.

NARCISSUS
PSEUDO-
NARCISSUS

NARCISSUS
ORVALLARIS

GLADIOLUS
ILLYRICUS.

NARCISSUS X
MEDIOLUTEUS

GALANTHUS
NIVALIS.

Plate 84

Dioscoreaceae

Tamus communis L. Black bryony. Root a tuber; stem very long, twining; flo. dioecious, yellow-green; fr. red. Woods and hedgerows, common in England and Wales, except in the N., introd. and very rare in Scotland, and absent from Ireland. Flo. May–July.

Liliaceae

Ruscus aculeatus L. Butcher's-broom. Stem up to 80 cm; flo. small, greenish, in centre of leaf-like branch or cladode; fr. red. Woods, thickets, cliffs, etc., mostly S. and E. England, and S. Wales, introd. elsewhere. Flo. Feb.–April.

Polygonatum verticillatum (L.) All. Whorled Solomon's-seal. Stem 30–70 cm; leaves whorled; flo. 1–4, constricted in the middle; filaments papillose; fr. red. Mountain woods, Perthshire, and formerly in Northumberland and Angus, very rare. Flo. June–July.

Polygonatum odoratum (Mill.) Druce. Angular Solomon's-seal. Stem 15–20 cm; flo. 1–2, cylindrical, often solitary; filaments glabrous; fr. bluish-black. Woods on calcareous and limestone soils, W. and N. England and Wales, introd. elsewhere, very local. Flo. June–July.

Polygonatum multiflorum (L.) All. Solomon's-seal. Stem 40–80 cm; flo. 2–5, constricted in the middle; filaments downy; fr. black. Woods, mostly S. England and Wales, introd. elsewhere, local. Flo. May–June.

Polygonatum × hybridum Brügg. *P. multiflorum × odoratum.* Intermediate between the parents. Garden escape. Thickets, etc., widespread, but uncommon. Flo. June.*

Asparagus officinalis L.
Ssp. ***prostratus*** (Dumort.) Corb. Wild asparagus. Stems prostrate; leaves minute, scarious; cladodes clustered, rigid; flo. yellow-green; fr. red. Sea cliffs and sand, S.W. England, Channel Islands, Wales and S.E. Ireland. Flo. June–Aug.
Ssp. ***officinalis.*** Stems erect, tall; cladodes slender and flexuous; flo. yellow-green; fr. red. Garden escape. Naturalized in grassy places, etc., common in S. and E. England, local or rare elsewhere. Flo. July–Oct.*

Maianthemum bifolium (L.) Schmidt. May lily. Stem 10–20 cm; leaves 2; flo. petals 4, whitish, fragrant; fr. red. Acid woods, mostly N. England, very local, introd. elsewhere. Flo. May–June.

Convallaria majalis L. Lily-of-the-valley. Stem 15–20 cm, angular; leaves large; bracts scarious; flo. white, scented; fr. red. Dry woods, mostly on calcareous soil, widespread, introd. in Ireland. Flo. May.

Simethis planifolia (L.) Gren. Kerry lily. *S. bicolor* (Desf.) Kunth. Stem 15–30 cm; leaves grass-like; flo. purple outside, whitish within. Heathy places near sea, Kerry, introd. in Dorset and Hampshire, rare. Flo. June.

Phormium tenax J. R. & G. Forst. New Zealand flax. Rhizome short, fleshy; leaves 1–3 m long, radical, sword-shaped, very tough; scape up to 5 m; flo. 3–6 cm, tubular, reddish, numerous. Introd. New Zealand. Naturalized on sea cliffs, etc., S.W. England, Isle of Man, Channel Islands, and S.W. Ireland. Flo. July–Aug.*

Allium ampeloprasum L. Wild leek. *A. babingtonii* Borrer. Stem 60–150 cm; leaves 12–35 mm wide; umbel compact; flo. many; usually without bulbils. Rocky coasts, Cornwall, Steep Holm, Pembrokeshire and Guernsey, introd. elsewhere. Flo. July–Aug.*

Allium scorodoprasum L. Sand leek. Stem 30–75 cm; leaves 10–20 mm wide; spathes 2; flo. rose with purple bulbils. Grassy places, scrub, etc., on dry soils, mostly N. England and Scotland, rare elsewhere. Flo. May–Aug.

Allium sphaerocephalon L. Round-headed leek. Leaves tubular; spathes 2; umbels without bulbils; flo. rose; stamens with lateral points shorter than anthers. Limestone rocks, St. Vincent rocks, Bristol and in Jersey. Flo. June–July.*

Allium vineale L. Wild onion. Stem 30–75 cm; leaves tubular; spathe 1; flo. rose with many bulbils; stamens with lateral points longer than anthers. Roadsides, etc., common in S. half of Britain, less frequent in N., becoming rare in Scotland, very local in Ireland. Flo. June–Aug.

CONVALLARIA
MAJALIS.

POLYGONATUM
MULTIFLORUM.

TAMUS
COMMUNIS.

POLYGONATUM
ODORATUM.

ALLIUM
SCORODOPRASUM.

SIMETHIS
PLANIFOLIA.

MAIANTHEMUM
BIFOLIUM.

POLYGONATUM
VERTICILLATUM.

ALLIUM VINEALE.

ASPARAGUS
OFFICINALIS
SSP. PROSTRATUS

RUSCUS
ACULEATUS.

Plate 85

Liliaceae *(continued)*

Allium oleraceum L. Field garlic. Leaves fleshy, solid; spathes 2, long; flo. few, pink or brownish, with bulbils; stamens not trifid, equalling petals. Field borders, etc., widely distributed but rare. Flo. July–Aug.

Allium carinatum L. Keeled garlic. Similar to *A. oleraceum*, but leaves flat, grooved; petals bright pink; stamens longer than petals. Introd. Europe. Established by roadsides, on banks, etc., widespread, but mostly N. England and Scotland. Flo. Aug.*

Allium schoenoprasum L. Chives. Leaves cylindrical; spathes 2; flo. umbel dense, globose; stamens half as long as spreading pink petals. Grassy places, mostly on limestone soil, W. and N. England, Wales, introd. elsewhere, rare. Flo. June–July.
A. sibiricum auct. of W. Cornwall and Pembrokeshire is now regarded as a form of *A. schoenoprasum*.

Allium roseum L. Leaves linear, flat; spathes 2–4, short; flo. pink, with bulbils. Introd. Mediterranean region. Naturalized in grassy places, mostly S. and W. England, uncommon. Flo. June.*

Allium triquetrum L. Three-cornered leek. Stem triquetrous; leaves radical, linear, keeled; spathes 2, short; flo. large, nodding, white, introd. Mediterranean region. Naturalized in woods, etc., in England, S. Wales, S.W. Ireland and Guernsey. Flo. April–June.

Allium paradoxum (Bieb.) G. Don. Few-flowered leek. Similar to *A. triquetrum*, but smaller, with brighter green stem and leaves; inflo. 1–4-flowered with numerous bulbils; flo. small white. Introd. Caucasus. Naturalized in woods, thickets, plantations, by roadsides, etc., widespread and increasing. Flo. April–May.*

Allium ursinum L. Ramsons. Stem triquetrous; leaves broad, elliptic; flo. white, petals acute. Moist woods, streamsides, etc., widespread and common. Flo. April–June.

Allium neopolitanum Cyr. Superficially like *Ornithogalum umbellatum* but stem up to 50 cm; triquetrous, slender, overtopping leaves; flo. many and larger. Garden escape. Established by roadsides, on walls, etc., mostly S. and S.W. England, uncommon. Flo. March–April.*

Nothoscordum inodorum (Ait.) Nicholson. *Allium fragrans* Vent. Stem 20–40 cm; spathes 2; inflo. many; flo. 10–15 mm, whitish above with pinkish midrib, greenish below, honey-scented. Introd. N. America. Established by paths, beneath walls and as a flower-bed weed, Isles of Scilly and Channel Islands, uncommon. Flo. April–May.*

Muscari neglectum Guss. exten. Grape hyacinth. *M. atlanticum* Boiss. & Reut. *M. racemosum* auct. Stem up to 20 cm; leaves narrow, flaccid; bracts minute; flo. dark blue, uppermost smaller, sterile. Sandy fields, E. England, introd. elsewhere. Flo. April–May.

Scilla autumnalis L. Autumn squill. Leaves autumnal; flo. pale purple, without bracts; anthers purple. Dry pastures, mostly near the sea, S. England, introd. elsewhere. Flo. July–Sept.

Scilla verna Huds. Spring squill. Leaves in spring; flo. pale blue, with bracts; anthers blue. Coastal pastures, widespread, locally plentiful. Flo. April–May.

Hyacinthoides non-scripta (L.) Chouard ex Rothm. Bluebell. *Endymion non-scriptus* (L.) Garcke. *Scilla nutans* Sm. Flo. nodding, cylindrical, petal tips recurved; anthers yellow. Woods, widespread and common, Britain, less frequent in Ireland. Flo. May.

Hyacinthoides hispanica (Mill.) Rothm. Spanish bluebell. *Endymion hispanicus* (Mill.) Chouard. Flo. erect, paler; petals more open, tips not recurved; anthers purple. Garden escape. Naturalized in grassy places, etc., widespread and common. Flo. May.*

Hyacinthoides hispanica × non-scripta. Intermediate between the parents, it is commonly grown in gardens, and occurs in scrub, fields, etc., as an outcast or escape. Flo. May.*

Ornithogalum umbellatum L. Star-of-Bethlehem. Stem up to 30 cm; leaves green with white midrib; flo. 6–15, subumbellate, erect, large, white. Perhaps native in grassy places, S. and E. England, introd. elsewhere. Flo. April–June.

Ornithogalum nutans L. Drooping star-of-Bethlehem. Leaves glaucous; flo. 2–10, nodding in a raceme, greenish-white, petals *c*. 3 cm long. Introd. Europe. Naturalized in grassy places, mostly S. and E. England, rare. Flo. April–May.

Ornithogalum pyrenaicum L. Spiked star-of-Bethlehem. Leaves in spring, fading early; flo. 20+, small, in erect spike, petals spreading. Woods and scrub, mostly S. and S.W. England, local. Flo. June–July.

Lilium pyrenaicum Gouan. Pyrenean lily. Stem 40–80 cm; leaves alternate, lanceolate; flo. nodding, yellow with black spots. Garden escape. Naturalized in woods and hedge banks, widespread, but locally frequent in S.W. England and Wales. Flo. June–July.

Lilium martagon L. Martagon lily. Stem 50–100 cm; leaves mostly whorled; flo. nodding, pale purple with dark warts. Garden escape. Woods, mostly S. England, local, introd. elsewhere. Flo. Aug.–Sept.*

Fritillaria meleagris L. Fritillary. Leaves few, linear; flo. nodding, red-purple, or white, chequered dark and light; fr. erect. Damp meadows, mostly S. and E. England, and the Midlands, very local. Flo. May.

Tulipa sylvestris L. Wild tulip. Leaves linear; flo. bright yellow; fr. oblong, trigonous. Introd. Europe. Naturalized in meadows, etc., mostly S. and E. England. Flo. April–May.

LILIUM
PYRENAICUM.

ALLIUM
SCHOENOPRASUM.

"ALLIUM
SIBIRICUM".

ALLIUM
OLERACEUM.

FRITILLARIA
MELEAGRIS.

ALLIUM
TRI-
QUETRUM.

ALLIUM
URSINUM.

TULIPA
SYLVESTRIS.

SCILLA
AUTUMNALIS.

MUSCARI
NEGLECTUM.

SCILLA
VERNA.

ORNITHOGALUM
PYRENAICUM.

HYACINTHOIDES
NON-SCRIPTA.

ORNITHOGALUM
NUTANS.

ORNITHOGALUM
UMBELLATUM.

Plate 86

Liliaceae *(continued)*

Gagea lutea (L.) Ker-Gawl. Yellow star-of-Bethlehem. Bulb solitary; stem 10–30 cm with 1-hooded radical leaf and 2 bracts; perianth segments 15–18 mm; flo. 1–7, greenish-yellow. Woods and grassy places in Britain, widespread, but very local. Flo. March–May.

Gagea bohemica (Zauschner) J. A. Schultes & J. H. Schultes. Similar to *G. lutea*, but bulbs 2 in a common tunic; stem up to 3 cm; perianth segments 6–8 (–18) mm, blunt; flo. 1 (rarely up to 3), yellow. Rocks, mid Wales, very rare. Flo. Jan.–March.*

Lloydia serotina (L.) Reichb. Snowdon lily. Bulb small; stem 5–15 cm; leaves slender, triquetrous; flo. white with red-purple veins. Rock ledges, Snowdonia, very rare. Flo. June–July.

Colchicum autumnale L. Meadow saffron. Leaves large, oblong, 12–30 cm in spring; flo. in autumn, pale purple, like crocus but with 6 stamens. Meadows, mainly S. half of Britain, very local, and very rare in Ireland. Flo. Sept.–Oct.

Narthecium ossifragum (L.) Huds. Bog asphodel. Leaves radical, rigid, linear; flo. bright yellow; anthers orange. Bogs, acid moors, etc., mostly W. and N. Britain, widespread in Ireland. Flo. July–Sept.

Tofieldia pusilla (Michx.) Pers Scottish asphodel. Leaves sword-shaped; spike dense; bracts small, 3-lobed; flo. greenish-white. By mountain streams, mostly Scotland, local. Flo. June–Aug.

Paris quadrifolia L. Herb-Paris. Leaves 4, whorled; flo. solitary; sepals 8, acute, green; fr. a black berry. Woods, on calcareous soil, widespread, but very local over most of England except the S.W., where it is rare; rare in Wales, very rare in Scotland, and absent from Ireland. Flo. May–July.

Juncaceae

Juncus foliosus Desf. Stem up to 35 cm; leaves more than 1.5 mm wide, bright green; flo. mostly 1–3; sepals usually with a dark line on either side of midrib; anthers usually 3–5 times as long as filaments. Pond and stream verges, wet fields, marshes, etc., mostly S. and W. England and Wales, widespread in Ireland. Flo. May–Sept.*

Juncus bufonius L. Toad rush. Similar to *J. foliosus* but leaves up to 1.5 mm wide, dark green; flo. mostly 1–5, often widely spaced; sepals without dark lines; anthers usually shorter than filaments. Muddy pond verges, marshes, etc., widespread and common. Flo. May–Sept.

Juncus ranarius Song. & Perr. *J. ambiguus* auct., non Guss. Similar to *J. bufonius* but stem up to 16 cm; leaves 0.5–1 mm wide; flo. mostly 2–4. Coastal mud-flats, dunes, etc., inland on mud and waste ground, widespread. Flo. May–Sept.*

Juncus trifidus L. Three-leaved rush. Rhizome creeping; stems crowded, with 1 leaf; flo. 1–3, between 2 long leafy bracts. Mountain tops, Scotland. Flo. June–Aug.

Juncus squarrosus L. Heath rush. Leaves rigid, pressed to ground; bracts broad; inflo. terminal; flo. brown. Acid heaths and moors, widespread and common. Flo. June–July.

Juncus compressus Jacq. Round-fruited rush. Stems tufted; inflo. terminal, shorter than bract; flo. *c.* 30; anthers equalling filaments; capsule subglobose. Marshes, damp meadows, etc., widespread, but local, in England; rare in Wales and Scotland and very rare in Ireland. Flo. June–July.

Juncus subulatus Forsk. Rhizomatous; stems leafy, up to 1 m; leaves glaucous, hollow; bract short; flo. many, green; stamens 6, short; styles twisted; capsule trigonous. Introd. Mediterranean region. Salt marsh, Somerset, very local. Flo. June–July.*

Juncus gerardii Lois. Salt marsh rush. Rhizome creeping; inflo. terminal, few-flowered, longer than bract; anthers 3 times length of filaments; capsule acute. Salt marshes, widespread. Flo. June–July.

Juncus tenuis Willd. Slender rush. *J. macer* S. F. Gray. leaves with long scarious auricles; inflo. terminal, overtopped by long bracts; flo. straw-coloured. Introd. N. America. Waysides, heaths and woodland tracts, widespread and common. Flo. July–Aug.

Juncus dudleyi Wieg. Similar to *J. tenuis* but stiffer and more erect; auricles shorter, not scarious. Introd. N. America. Naturalized in marshy ground, Perthshire and Isle of Rhum, rare. Flo. Aug.*

Juncus balticus Willd. Baltic rush. Rhizome widely creeping; leaf sheaths broad; inflo. lateral at $\frac{2}{3}$ height; flo. *c.* 12, brown; stamens 3. Dune slacks, Lancashire and Scotland, rare. Flo. June–Aug.

Juncus filiformis L. Thread rush. Rhizome creeping; stems slender; inflo. lateral at $\frac{1}{2}$ height; flo. 6–8, pale; stamens 6. Lakesides, etc., mostly N. England and S. Scotland, local. Flo. June–Sept.

Juncus inflexus L. Hard rush. *J. glaucus* Sibth. Stem 25–90 cm, glaucous, with 12–18 striae; pith interrupted; inflo. lateral, lax, with straight branches. Wet places, widespread and common. Flo. June–Aug.

Juncus effusus L. Soft rush. *J. communis* auct. Stem up to 100 cm, glossy green, with 40–80 striae; inflo. lateral; bract not expanded; flo. greenish; capsule yellowish, retuse, not apiculate. Wet places, widespread and common. Flo. June–Aug.

Juncus conglomeratus L. Compact rush. Stem up to 100 cm, greyish-green; inflo. dense, subglobose; base of bract expanded; flo. brown; capsule retuse, apiculate. Wet heaths, fields, etc., locally common. Flo. May–July.

GAGEA
LUTEA.

PARIS
QUADRIFOLIA.

JOFIELDIA
PUSILLA.

LLOYDIA
SEROTINA.

JUNCUS
CONGLOMER-
-ATUS.

NARTHECIUM
OSSIFRAGUM.

COLCHICUM
AUTUMNALE.

JUNCUS
BALTICUS.

JUNCUS
GERARDII.

JUNCUS
TRIFIDUS.

JUNCUS
INFLEXUS

JUNCUS
COMPRESSUS.

JUNCUS
FILIFORMIS

x2

x2

JUNCUS
TENUIS

JUNCUS
SQUARROSUS.

x2

JUNCUS
EFFUSUS

JUNCUS
BUFONIUS

Plate 87

Juncaceae *(continued)*

Juncus maritimus Lam. Sea rush. Stem up to 100 cm; leaves wiry, pointed; inflo. shorter than bract, erect; sepals lanceolate, outer acute, pale straw-coloured. Salt marshes, widespread and common. Flo. July–Aug.

Juncus acutus L. Sharp rush. Stem up to 150 cm, stout; leaves sharply pointed; sepals ovate, blunt, reddish-brown with scarious margins. Dunes, etc., S.W. and E. England, Wales and S. Ireland, rare. Flo. June–July.

Juncus subnodulosus Schrank. Blunt-flowered rush. *J. obtusiflorus* Ehrh. ex Hoffm. Stem 50–100 cm; leaves septate; secondary branches on inflo. at a wide angle; sepals obtuse; capsule ovoid. Marshes on basic soil, locally abundant in E. England, rare elsewhere. Flo. July–Sept.

Juncus acutiflorus Ehrh. ex Hoffm. Sharp-flowered rush. *J. sylvaticus* auct. Stem 30–100 cm; leaves septate; secondary branches of inflo. at acute angle; sepals very acute, shorter than acute tapering capsule. Marshes, especially on acid soils, widespread and common. Flo. July–Sept.

Juncus articulatus L. Jointed rush. *J. lampocarpus* Ehrh. ex Hoffm. Stem 30–60 cm; leaves curved, septate; inflo. branches few; sepals acute; capsule shining, blackish, ovoid-acuminate. Wet places, especially on acid soils. Flo. June–Aug.

Juncus alpinoarticulatus Chaix ex Vill. Alpine rush. *J. alpinus* Vill. Leaves septate; inflo. small; sepals obtuse, outer mucronate; capsule obtuse, mucronate. Wet places on mountains, N. England and Scotland, rare. Flo. July–Aug.*

Juncus nodulosus Wahlenb. Marshall's rush. Similar to *J. alpino-articulatus* with inflo. irregular, some flo. subsessile, others on long peduncles in small umbels. Stony shores of lochs, Aberdeenshire and E. Ross., rare. Flo. July–Sept.*

Juncus bulbosus L. Bulbous rush. *J. supinus* Moench. Stems and leaves slender, often prostrate or floating; inflo. irregular; stamens 3; anthers equalling filaments; flo. viviparous. Wet heaths, bogs, pond verges, etc., on acid soils, widespread and common. Flo. June–Sept.

Juncus kochii F. W. Schultz. Similar to *J. bulbosus*, but more upright; stamens 6; anthers shorter than filaments. Probably common, but confused with *J. bulbosus*. Flo. June–Sept.

Juncus castaneus Sm. Chestnut rush. Stem 8–30 cm; leaves and long bract tapering to blunt point; heads 1–3; flo. very large, rich brown; capsule *c*. 8 mm. Mountains, Scotland. Flo. June–July.

Juncus triglumis L. Three-flowered rush. Stem 5–10 cm, terete; leaves of 2 tubes; auricles large; flo. usually 3, level; capsule ovate. Wet places on high mountains, N. England and Scotland. Flo. June–July.

Juncus biglumis L. Two-flowered rush. Stem 5–12 cm, channelled; leaves of 1 tube; auricles small; flo. 2, 1 above; capsule retuse. High mountains, Scotland, very rare. Flo. June–July.

Juncus capitatus Weigel. Dwarf rush. Annual; stem 1–5 cm; leaves setaceous, without auricles; flo. clusters terminal, sessile, overtopped by a bract. Damp heaths, Cornwall and Channel Islands, rare, and formerly in Isles of Scilly and Anglesey. Flo. May–June.

Juncus mutabilis Lam. Pigmy rush. *J. pygmaeus* Rich. Annual; stem 2–8 cm, purplish; leaf sheath long, auricled; flo. cylindrical in purplish, sessile clusters. Damp hollows, Lizard Peninsula, Cornwall. Flo. May–June.

Juncus planifolius R. Br. Stem up to 45 cm, slender; leaves 3–7 mm wide, flat, all basal, shorter than stem; inflo. lax; flo. brown, usually 8–10 in compact head. Introd. S. America. Naturalized on lake shores and streamsides, W. Ireland, very local. Flo. June–July.*

Luzula forsteri (Sm.) DC. Southern wood-rush. Branches suberect in flo. and fr.; leaves narrow; flo. reddish; capsule short, acuminate; seed appendage short. Woods, etc., S. England and Wales. Flo. April–June.

Luzula pilosa (L.) Willd. Hairy wood-rush. Branches spreading, deflexed in fr.; flo. brown; leaves 4 mm wide; capsule obpyriform to cover long seed appendages. Woods, common throughout Britain, except E. Anglia, where it is rare, local in Ireland. Flo. April–June.

Luzula sylvatica (Huds.) Gaudin. Great wood-rush. *L. maxima* (Reichard) DC. Large tussocks; leaves 6–20 mm wide; inflo. broadly spreading; flo. brown. Woods, especially on acid soil, common over most of Britain, especially N., but rare in E. Anglia, local in Ireland. Flo. May–June.

Luzula luzuloides (Lam.) Dandy & Wilmott. White wood-rush. *L. albida* (Hoffm.) DC. Similar to *L. sylvatica* but smaller; leaves *c*. 6 mm wide; flo. dirty white or pinkish. Introd. Europe. Woods, mostly N. England and Scotland, rare. Flo. June–July.*

Luzula spicata (L.) DC. Spiked wood-rush. Stem 2–8 cm; leaves small; inflo. drooping, dense, spike-like; sepals finely pointed. Mountains, Scotland. Flo. June–July.

Luzula arcuata Sw. Curved wood-rush. Dwarf, 3–8 cm; leaves narrow; flo. clusters on few arcuate branches; sepals exceeding capsule. High mountains, N. Scotland. Flo. June–July.

Luzula campestris (L.) DC. Field wood-rush. Stem 10–20 cm; inflo. of 1 sessile and a few stalked clusters; anthers prominent, much longer than filaments; seeds subglobose. Grassy places, etc., widespread and common. Flo. April–May.

Luzula pallescens Sw. Fen wood-rush. Stem 10–30 cm; inflo. subumbellate of several clusters; flo. small, pale; capsule obovoid; seeds oblong. Fens, Huntingdonshire, introd. elsewhere, very rare. Flo. April–May.*

Luzula multiflora (Retz.) Lejeune. Heath wood-rush. *L. erecta* Desv. Stem 20–40 cm; inflo. dense, subspherical or of several short-stalked clusters; anthers equalling filaments; seeds oblong. Peaty moors, open woods on acid soils, etc., widespread and common. Flo. April–June.

JUNCUS
CAPITATUS.

JUNCUS
MUTABILIS

JUNCUS
ARTICULATUS.

JUNCUS
ACUTIFLORUS.

JUNCUS
MARITIMUS

JUNCUS
ACUTUS.

JUNCUS
BIGLUMIS.

JUNCUS
TRIGLUMIS.

LUZULA
PILOSA.

JUNCUS
SUBNODULOSUS.

LUZULA
MULTIFLORA

LUZULA
FORSTERI.

JUNCUS
CASTANEUS

LUZULA
SPICATA.

LUZULA
ARCUATA.

JUNCUS
KOCHII.

JUNCUS BULBOSUS.

LUZULA
SYLVATICA.

LUZULA
CAMPESTRIS.

Plate 88

Typhaceae

Typha latifolia L. Bulrush. Up to 2.5 m; leaves 10–20 mm wide; male and female inflo. contiguous, female without bracteoles. Beside streams and ponds, common throughout most of England, but local in Wales and Ireland, and rare in Scotland. Flo. June–July.

Typha angustifolia L. Lesser bulrush. Up to 3 m; leaves 4–8 mm wide; male and female inflo. separated, female with slender bracteoles. Beside streams and ponds, widespread, but local. Flo. June–July.

Sparganiaceae

Sparganium erectum L. Branched bur-reed. *S. ramosum* Huds.
Ssp. **erectum**. Stem 60–90 cm, branched, whitish below; leaves keeled; fr. *c.* 8 mm, angled, abruptly contracted to beak. Beside ponds and ditches, widespread and common. Flo. June–Aug.
Ssp. **neglectum** (Beeby) Schinz & Thell. *S. neglectum* Beeby. Stem red below; fr. *c.* 10 mm, terete, tapering to beak. In similar situations to ssp. *erectum* but less frequent.*

Sparganium emersum Rehm. Unbranched bur-reed. *S. simplex* Huds. Stem 30–80 cm, unbranched; leaves keeled; male heads with elongate anthers; lowest fr. head stalked. By ponds and ditches on basic soils, widespread and common but less frequent than *S. erectum*. Flo. June–July.

Sparganium angustifolium Michx. Floating bur-reed. *S. natans* auct. Stem 50–90 cm; leaves floating, base expanded; anthers small; fr. tapering above and below; lowest head stalked. Mountain lakes and streams, mostly Wales, N. England, Scotland and Ireland. Flo. July–Sept.

Sparganium minimum Wallr. Least bur-reed. Stem 10–35 cm; leaves thin, floating, base not expanded; male flo. head usually solitary; fr. oval. Lakes and pools, especially on acid soils, mostly Wales, N. England, Scotland and Ireland, local. Flo. June–July.

Araceae

Lysichiton americanus Hultén & St. John. Robust rhizomatous perennial; leaves 40–100 cm long, ovate, truncate at base, following flo.; spathe up to 25 cm, yellow; spadix greenish; foetid. Garden escape. Naturalized in swamps, bogs, etc., widespread, but mostly S. England and S. Scotland. Flo. April–May.*

Arum maculatum L. Lords-and-ladies. Leaves in early spring, spotted or not; midrib dark green; spadix usually purple, ½ length of erect spathe. Hedge banks, common in England and Wales and local in Scotland and Ireland. Flo. April–May.

Arum italicum Mill. Italian lords-and-ladies.
Ssp. **italicum**. Leaves before winter, unspotted, dark green with prominent white midrib, apex pointed, almost acuminate; spadix orange, ⅓ length of greenish-white, drooping spathe. Garden escape. Shady places, etc., widespread, but mostly England, uncommon. Flo. April–May.*
Ssp. **neglectum** (Townsend) Prime. *A. neglectum* (Townsend) Ridley. Similar to ssp. *italicum* but leaves lighter green and white midrib absent or inconspicuous, apex rounded at side, acute. Shady places, mostly near coast, S. England and Channel Islands, very rare in Wales and introd. in Scotland. Flo. April–May.

Acorus calamus L. Sweet-flag. Stem up to 1 m; spathe stem-like; leaves with wavy edges, scented when crushed; flo. crowded. Introd. S. Asia, margins of pools, canals, etc., mostly England, rare in Wales, Scotland and Ireland. Flo. June–July.

Calla palustris L. Stem creeping; leaves broadly cordate or rounded; spathe oval, whitish; spadix green crowded with flo.; fr. red. Introd. Europe, etc. Swamps, pond sides, etc., mostly S. England, rare. Flo. June.*

Lemnaceae

Lemna trisulca L. Ivy-leaved duckweed. Frond thin, stalked, mostly submerged, branching at right angles, with single root. Ponds, etc., locally common in England and Ireland, rare in Wales and Scotland. Flo. June–July.

Lemna minor L. Common duckweed. Frond ovate, 3–5-veined, budding freely, with single root. Ponds, etc., common, except in N. Scotland. Flo. June–July.

Lemna miniuscula Herter. Similar to *L. minor* but smaller, both faces more convex; frond 1-veined. Introd. N. America. Naturalized in ponds, slow streams, etc., S. and E. England, uncommon but spreading. Flo. June–July.*

Lemna gibba L. Duckweed. Frond hemispherical, flattish above, rounded below, with single root. Ponds, etc., mainly S. and E. England and the Midlands, local, rare in Wales, Scotland and Ireland. Flo. rare, summer.

Spirodela polyrhiza (L.) Schleid. Greater duckweed. *Lemna polyrhiza* L. Frond 5–8 mm wide; roots many. Flo. very rare. Ponds, mostly S. and E. England and the Midlands, local, rare in Wales, Scotland and Ireland. Flo. July.

Wolffia arrhiza (L.) Hork. ex Wimm. Rootless duckweed. Frond 1 mm, ovoid, rootless. Ponds, etc., mostly S. England, very rare. The smallest British flowering plant, though flo. not recorded from Britain.*

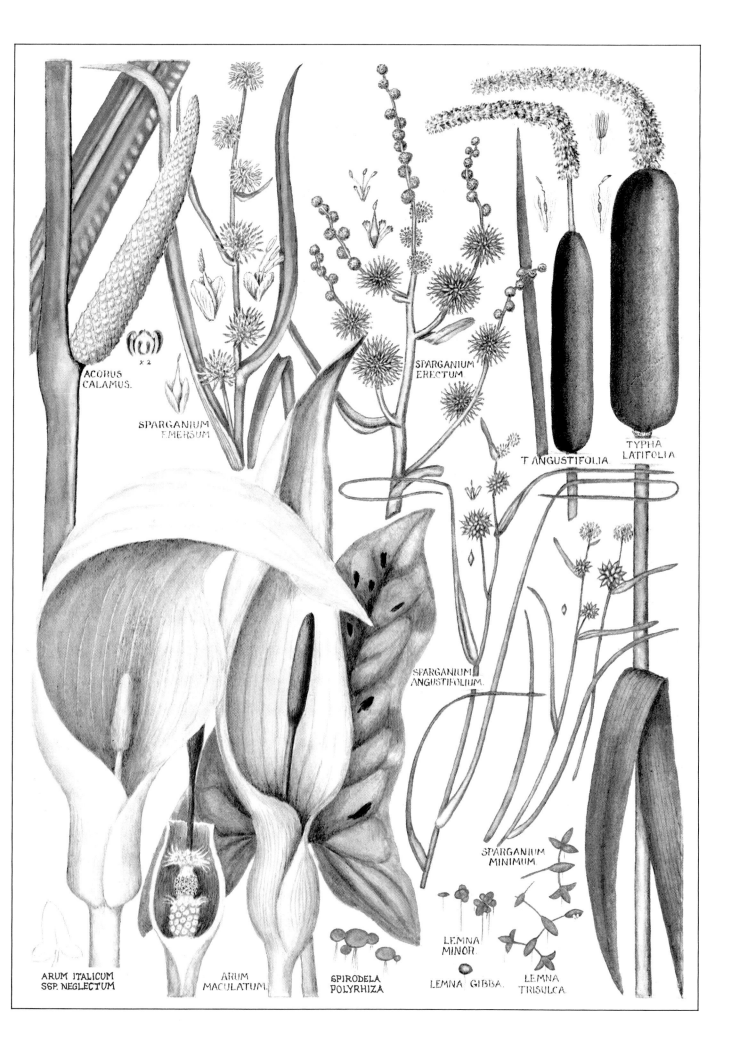

ACORUS
CALAMUS.

×2

SPARGANIUM
EMERSUM.

SPARGANIUM
ERECTUM.

T. ANGUSTIFOLIA.

TYPHA
LATIFOLIA.

SPARGANIUM
ANGUSTIFOLIUM.

SPARGANIUM
MINIMUM.

ARUM ITALICUM
SSP. NEGLECTUM

ARUM
MACULATUM.

SPIRODELA
POLYRHIZA.

LEMNA
MINOR.

LEMNA GIBBA.

LEMNA
TRISULCA.

Plate 89

Potamogetonaceae

Groenlandia densa (L.) Fourr. Opposite-leaved pondweed. *Potamogeton densus* L. Leaves opposite; stipules o except in involucre, where they adhere to the leaves; spike very short, recurved. Clear streams and ponds, mostly England, rare in Wales, Scotland and Ireland. Flo. May–Aug.

Potamogeton natans L. Broad-leaved pondweed. Submerged leaves without blades; blade of floating leaves elliptical, jointed at base. Lakes and ponds, widespread and common. Flo. May–Aug.

Potamogeton polygonifolius Pourr. Bog pondweed. *P. oblongus* Viv. Blade of submerged leaves lanceolate, of floating leaves elliptical, not jointed at base. Bogs and acid pools, common, except in mid and E. England, where it is local or rare. Flo. June–Sept.

Potamogeton coloratus Hornem. Fen pondweed. Leaves mostly elliptical, stalked, thin, beautifully net-veined; fr. very small, green; stalk slender. Calcareous fen pools, mainly E. England and Ireland, local, rare in Scotland and Wales. Flo. June–July.

Potamogeton lucens L. Shining pondweed. Leaves all submerged, large, oblong, short-stalked; stipules large; fr. spike *c.* 6 cm; stalk thickened above. Ponds, streams, etc., mostly S. and E. England and the Midlands, locally common, rare in Wales and Scotland, local in Ireland. Flo. June–Sept.

Potamogeton nodosus Poir. Loddon pondweed. Leaves long-stalked, elliptical, beautifully net-veined; fr. stalk long, stout, not thickened above. In Rivers Avon, Stour and Loddon, S. and W. England, local, formerly in Thames. Flo. Aug.–Sept.

Potamogeton alpinus Balb. Red pondweed. *P. rufescens* Schrad. Leaves narrowly oblong, reddish, short stalked; fr. spike *c.* 4 cm, stalk not thickened. Lakes and ditches, widespread, but local. Flo. June–Sept.

Potamogeton gramineus L. Various-leaved pondweed. *P. heterophyllus* Schreb. Densely branched at base; submerged leaves lanceolate, sessile; floating leaves oblong, long-stalked; fr. stalk thickened above. Mostly in acid waters, E. Anglia, N. England, Scotland and Ireland, very rare in S. England and Wales. Flo. June–Aug.

Potamogeton × zizii Koch ex Roth. *P. gramineus × lucens.* Like *P. lucens* but with some oblong, stalked floating leaves; submerged leaves sessile. Widespread, but local.*

Potamogeton × nitens Weber. *P. gramineus × perfoliatus.* Little branched at base; submerged leaves cordate below; floating leaves long stalked or o. Widespread but local.*

Potamogeton epihydrus Raf. American pondweed. Submerged leaves very long, linear, *c.* 8 mm, wide; with broad air tissue; floating leaves broad, elliptical, stalked; peduncle slender. Lochs, Outer Hebrides, introd. in W. Yorkshire. Flo. June–Aug.*

Potamogeton praelongus Wulf. Long-stalked pondweed. Leaves submerged, strap-shaped, narrowed to apex, rounded at sessile base; fr. stalk long. Lakes, etc., mostly Midland counties northwards, rare in S. England, Wales and Ireland. Flo. May–Aug.

Potamogeton perfoliatus L. Perfoliate pondweed. Leaves clasping the stem, cordate-ovate, but sometimes narrower; stipule small, soon falling; fr. stalk stout. Ponds, streams, etc., widespread, common. Flo. June–Aug.

POTAMOGETON
POLYGONIFOLIUS.

POTAMOGETON
GRAMINEUS.

POTAMOGETON
NATANS.

POTAMOGETON
COLORATUS.

POTAMOGETON
LUCENS.

POTAMOGETON
PERFOLIATUS.

POTAMOGETON
PRAELONGUS.

POTAMOGETON
ALPINUS.

POTAMOGETON   NODOSUS.

GROENLANDIA
DENSA.

Plate 90

Potamogetonaceae *(continued)*

Potamogeton crispus L. Curled pondweed. Leaves oblong, blunt, sessile, wavy, denticulate; fr. with a long beak. Ponds, streams, etc., widespread and common. Flo. May–Sept.

Potamogeton rutilus Wolfg. Shetland pondweed. Leaves very narrow, 1 mm wide or less, tapering to a fine point; stipules strongly veined, acuminate. Lochs, Inverness-shire, Ross-shire, Inner and Outer Hebrides, and Shetland. Flo. Aug.*

Potamogeton pusillus L. Lesser pondweed. *P. panormitanus* Biv. Leaves very narrow, 1 mm wide, blunt; lateral veins faint; stipules ⅔ tubular; beak of fr. nearly central. Ponds, streams, etc., mostly England, rare elsewhere. Flo. June–Sept.

Potamogeton berchtoldii Fieb. Small pondweed. Leaves long, narrow, 1–2 mm wide, acute; lateral veins meeting central at right angles near tip; stipules open. Ponds, streams, etc., widespread and common. Flo. June–Sept.

Potamogeton trichoides Cham. & Schlecht. Hairlike pondweed. Leaf width 1 mm or less, tapering to long point; stipules open; usually ripening only 1 fr. per flo. Ponds, streams, etc., mostly S. and E. England and Midlands, local, rare in N. England, Wales and Scotland, and absent from Ireland. Flo. June–Aug.

Potamogeton obtusifolius Mert. & Koch. Blunt-leaved pondweed. Leaf width 3–4 mm, rarely 2 mm; tip rounded apiculate; midrib with air cell, lateral veins rejoining at wide angle; stipules broad; peduncle short. Ponds, streams, etc., widespread, but local. Flo. June–Aug.

Potamogeton compressus L. Grass-wrack pondweed. *P. zosteraefolius* Schumach. Stem flattened; leaves very long, 2–4 mm wide; tip rounded; main veins 3–5, with others smaller. Ponds, streams, etc., mostly C. and E. England. Flo. June–Sept.

Potamogeton acutifolius Link. Sharp-leaved pondweed. Stem flattened; leaves with air tissue, long, linear, pointed; veins many; fr. stalk short. Lakes, ponds, etc., S. and E. England, local. Flo. June–July.

Potamogeton friesii Rupr. Flat-stalked pondweed. Stem flattened, with many short, leafy branches; leaves 2–3 mm wide, 5-veined; fr. whorls separated; stalk 2.5–5 cm. Ponds, streams, etc., mostly England, local, rare elsewhere. Flo. June–Aug.

Potamogeton filiformis Pers. Slender-leaved pondweed. Leaves slender, of 2 tubes; base sheathing; spike widely interrupted; stalk very long; fr. beak central. Lakes, etc., Scotland, Anglesey and Ireland, mostly near coast.

Potamogeton pectinatus L. Fennel pondweed. *P. flabellatus* Bab. Upper leaves slender, of 2 tubes; sheath long, open; ligule longer; fr. large; beak near inner margin. Lowland waters, common in England, except S.W., rare in Wales and Scotland, and local in Ireland. Flo. June–Sept.

Ruppiaceae

Ruppia cirrhosa (Petagna) Grande. Spiral tasselweed. *R. spiralis* L. ex Dumort. Leaves 1 mm wide, sheaths inflated; peduncle very long, often spirally twisted; fr. ovoid. Ditches near the sea, mostly S. and E. England and N.E. Ireland, rare. Flo. July–Aug.

Ruppia maritima L. Beaked tasselweed. *R. rostellata* Koch. Leaves narrower, filiform, sheaths small; peduncle short, equalling pedicels; fr. gibbous. Ditches near the sea, widespread but local. Flo. June–Aug.*

Zannichelliaceae

Zannichellia palustris L. Horned pondweed. Variable; leaves slender; stipules semi-tubular; flo. subsessile in minute spathe; carpels muricate. Ditches, streams, etc., mostly England, rare in Wales and Scotland, and local in Ireland. Flo. May–Aug.

Najadaceae

Najas flexilis (Willd.) Rostk. & Schmidt. Slender naiad. Submerged annual; stems slender, brittle, branching; leaves 10–20 mm long (usually in whorls of 3), subentire; sheaths ciliate; fr. 3 mm. Lochs, Scotland and W. Ireland, and formerly Lancashire. Flo. Aug.*

Najas marina L. Holly-leaved naiad. Leaves with many, larger, spinous pointed teeth; sheaths entire, not ciliate; fr. 4 mm, ovoid. Norfolk Broads, rare and decreasing. Flo. July–Aug.

Zosteraceae

Zostera marina L. Eelgrass. Leaves very long, 4–6 mm wide, rounded at apex; stigma twice as long as style; seeds ribbed. In the sea below tide-level, widespread, but local. Flo. June–Sept.

Zostera angustifolia (Hornem.) Reichb. Narrow-leaved eelgrass. Leaves *c*. 2 mm wide; margin of flo. sheath 2 mm, sheaths closed; flo. stems branched; stigma equalling style; seeds ribbed. Estuary mud, half tide to low tide, widespread, but local. Flo. June–Sept.*

Zostera noltii Hornem. Dwarf eelgrass. *Z. nana* auct. Leaves 7.5–15 cm × 1 mm; flo. stems simple; flo. few, male enclosed in bracts; sheaths inflated; seeds smooth. Estuary mud, widespread but local. Flo. June–Sept.*

Eriocaulaceae

Eriocaulon aquaticum (Hill) Druce. Pipewort. *E. septangulare* With. Roots and rhizomes white, septate; leaves septate; flo. stalk furrowed, twisted flo. in scaly head, lead-coloured. Shallow water in acid lochs, bogs, etc. Inverness-shire, Inner Hebrides and W. Ireland, locally abundant. Flo. July–Sept.

POTAMOGETON
ACUTIFOLIUS.

POTAMOGETON
FRIESII.

POTAMOGETON
CRISPUS.

POTAMOGETON
BERCHTOLDII.

POTAMOGETON
OBTUSIFOLIUS.

POTAMOGETON
PUSILLUS.

.×2

POTAMOGETON
TRICHOIDES.

ERIOCAULON
AQUATICUM

POTAMOGETON
COMPRESSUS.

×2½

ZOSTERA
MARINA.

RUPPIA
CIRRHOSA

×
2E

POTAMOGETON
FILIFORMIS.

POTAMOGETON
PECTINATUS.

NAJAS
MARINA.

ZANNICHELLIA
PALUSTRIS

Plate 91

Cyperaceae

Eriophorum angustifolium Honck. Common cottongrass. Leaves triquetrous, 3–6 mm wide; upper sheath loose; peduncle smooth; glumes 1-nerved, brown, margin broad, hyaline. Acid bogs, widespread but local. Flo. May–June.

Eriophorum gracile Koch ex Roth. Slender cottongrass. Leaves triquetrous, 1–2 mm wide, short, obtuse; peduncles hairy; glumes ovate, many-nerved, not hyaline. Acid bogs, S. England, Wales and W. Ireland, very local and rare. Flo. June–July.*

Eriophorum latifolium Hoppe. Broad-leaved cottongrass. Leaves flat with short triquetrous point; sheath close-fitting; peduncles rough; glumes blackish-green. Bogs on basic or calcareous soils, widespread, but mostly N. Britain and Ireland. Flo. May–June.

Eriophorum vaginatum L. Hare's-tail cottongrass. Leaves triquetrous, 1 mm wide; upper sheath much inflated, usually leafless; spike solitary. Bogs, mostly N. Britain and Ireland. Flo. May.

Eleocharis parvula (Roem. & Schult.) Link ex Bluff, Nees & Schau. Dwarf spike-rush. *Scirpus parvulus* Roem. & Schult. Small; runners whitish, capillary, tipped with tubers; stem 2–8 cm, with 1 leafless sheath; spikelet 2–3 mm. On estuary mud, S. England, N. Wales and Ireland, very local. Flo. July–Aug.*

Eleocharis acicularis (L.) Roem. & Schult. Needle spike-rush. Rhizome slender, brown; stem 4-angled, subulate; lowest glume $\frac{1}{3}$ length of spikelet; nut ribbed. Wet heathy places, mostly England and N.E. Ireland, local. Flo. July–Aug.

Eleocharis quinqueflora (F. X. Hartmann) O. Schwarz. Few-flowered spike-rush. *E. pauciflora* (Lightf.) Link. Rhizome creeping; stem with scales and 1 leafless sheath; obliquely truncate glume more than $\frac{1}{2}$ length of spikelet. Moors and fens, mostly N. Britain. Flo. June–July.

Eleocharis palustris (L.) Roem. & Schult. Common spike-rush. Rhizome creeping; stem reddish or brownish at base, up to 60 cm; sheath almost transversely truncate; stigmas 2; spikelet $\frac{1}{3}$ encircled by glume; variable. Marshes, etc., widespread and common. Flo. May–July.

Eleocharis austriaca Hayek. Northern spike-rush. Stem not reddish or brownish at base, vascular bundles widely open; spikes many, short and conical; fr. with narrow style base, and often with 5 bristles instead of 4. Moorland streamsides and marshes, N. England and S. Scotland, local. Flo. May–July.*

Eleocharis uniglumis (Link) Schult. Slender spike-rush. Similar to *E. palustris* but stigmas 2; lowest glume encircling spikelet; nut biconvex. Marshes, mostly near the coast, widespread. Flo. June–July.

Eleocharis multicaulis (Sm.) Desv. Many-stalked spike-rush. Stem up to 25 cm, tufted; sheath obliquely truncate, acute; stigmas 3; nut trigonous; spikelet often viviparous. Wet heaths, widespread but local. Flo. July–Aug.

Scirpus cespitosus L. Deergrass. *Trichophorum cespitosum* (L.) Hartm. Ssp. **cespitosus**. Upper sheath fitting tightly, opening 1 mm, with short blade; glumes brown with yellowish midrib. Moors, N. Britain and Ireland, uncommon. Flo. May–June.*
Ssp. **germanicus** (Palla) Broddesson. Upper sheath fitting loosely, opening larger; glumes brown with green midrib. Moors, widespread. Flo. May–June.

Scirpus setaceus L. Bristle club-rush. *Isolepis setacea* (L.) R. Br. Bract longer than inflo.; spikelets 1–3; glumes dark brown, margins white, keel green; nut trigonous, ribbed. Damp sandy places, etc. Flo. June–July.

Scirpus cernuus Vahl. Slender club-rush. *S. filiformis* Savi, non Burm. *S. pygmaeus* (Vahl) A. Gray. Bract not exceeding inflo.; longer, usually solitary spikelet; glumes green and brown; nut subglobose, nearly smooth. Damp sandy places, mostly near the sea, widespread but local. Flo. July.*

Scirpus lacustris L.
Ssp. **lacustris**. Common club-rush. Stem 1–3 m, often with long basal leaves; bracts stem-like; glumes smooth, shortly awned. Rivers, ponds, etc., widespread, but local in S.W. England and Wales. Flo. Aug.–Sept.
Ssp. **tabernaemontani** (C. C. Gmel.) Syme. Grey club-rush. *S. tabernaemontani* C. C. Gmel. Similar to ssp. *lacustris* but stem more slender and glaucous; glumes clothed with dark brown papillae. Streams, ditches, ponds, etc., mostly near the sea, widespread, but local. Flo. June–July.

Scirpus fluitans L. Floating club-rush. *Eleogiton fluitans* (L.) Link. Stem floating, leafy; spike small, solitary, greenish. Acid ponds, ditches, etc., widespread but local. Flo. June–Aug.

Scirpus triqueter L. Triangular club-rush. Stem up to 150 cm, triquetrous; bract exceeding inflo.; glumes brown with shallow rounded lobes. Muddy estuaries, S. W. England and S. Ireland, very local, and formerly elsewhere. Flo. Aug.–Sept.*

Scirpus pungens Vahl. Sharp club-rush. *S. americanus* auct. eur., non Vahl. Stem triquetrous; leaves 2–3; bract long; spikelets dense, sessile; glumes with acute lobes. Ponds near the sea, Jersey. Flo. June–July.*

Scirpus maritimus L. Sea club-rush. Stem 30–100 cm; leaves long and keeled; bracts several; spikelets large; glumes chocolate-brown, sharply 2-lobed, awned. Estuary mud, etc., widespread. Flo. July.

Scirpus sylvaticus L. Wood club-rush. Stem 30–100 cm; leaves broad; bracts many; inflo. compound; spikelets many, green; glumes entire. Wet shady places, widespread but local. Flo. July.

Scirpus holoschoenus L. Round-headed club-rush. *Holoschoenus vulgaris* Link. Stem terete, 50–100 cm; upper sheaths with short blades; spikes many in stalked globular clusters. Sea sand, Devon and Somerset, introd. elsewhere. Flo. Aug.*

Blysmus compressus (L.) Panz. ex Link. Flat-sedge. *Scirpus caricis* Retz. Leaves flat, keeled, rough; spikelets 10–12; lowest bract long, green; upper shorter than spikelets, many ribbed. Marshes, widespread but local. Flo. June–July.

Blysmus rufus (Huds.) Link. Saltmarsh flat-sedge. *Scirpus rufus* (Huds.) Schrad. Leaves involute, smooth; spikelets 4–8; bracts mostly equalling spikelets, 1–3-ribbed. Salt marshes, etc., Wales, N. Britain and Ireland, local. Flo. June–July.

Cyperus fuscus L. Brown galingale. Annual; stem up to 20 cm; inflo. subcapitate or small umbels; glumes reddish. On mud from ditches or dried pools, S. England, very rare. Flo. Aug.–Sept.

Cyperus longus L. Galingale. Rhizome aromatic; stem 50–100 cm; inflo. an irregular umbel; bracts very long. By ponds and ditches, mostly S. England, very local. Flo. Aug.–Sept.

Schoenus nigricans L. Black bog-rush. Stem wiry, 20–70 cm; sheaths black; leaves $\frac{3}{4}$ length of stem; spikelets 5–10, blackish, sessile. Bogs on calcareous or basic soils, widespread but local. Flo. July.

Schoenus ferrugineus L. Brown Bog-rush. Stem 10–40 cm; sheaths reddish-brown; leaves $\frac{1}{4}$ length of stem; spikelets 1–3, reddish. Peaty margins of Loch Tummel, Perthshire. Flo. July.*

Cladium mariscus (L.) Pohl. Great fen-sedge. Stem up to 2 m; leaves long, sharply serrate; inflo. of many branches, each with small reddish spikelets. Fens and marshes, widespread but local. Flo. Aug.

Rhynchospora alba (L.) Vahl. White beak-sedge. Stems tufted; lower sheaths leafless; bracts about equalling inflo.; spikelets white. Bogs on acid moors, widespread. Flo. July–Aug.

Rhynchospora fusca (L.) Ait. f. Brown beak-sedge. Rhizome creeping; lower sheaths mostly with blades; bracts exceeding inflo.; spikelets brown. Damp heaths and bogs, local and rare. Flo. July.

Kobresia simpliciuscula (Wahlenb.) Mackenzie. False sedge. *K. caricina* Willd. stem 5–20 cm; leaves slender; upper flo. (or spikelets) male, lower female, with 2 glumes. Moors, N. England and Perthshire, local. Flo. June–July.

SCHOENUS
NIGRICANS.

B. RUFUS.

SCIRPUS
SETACEUS

ERIOPHORUM
ANGUSTIFOLIUM.

SCIRPUS
LACUSTRIS.

SCIRPUS
MARITIMUS.

ERIOPHORUM
VAGINATUM.

ERIOPHORUM
LATIFOLIUM

BLYSMUS
COMPRESSUS.

CYPERUS
LONGUS.

S. LACUSTRIS
SSP.
TABERNAEMONTANI

CLADIUM
MARISCUS.

KOBRESIA
SIMPLICIUS-
-CULA.

E.PALUSTRIS.

E.MULTI-
-CAULIS.

SCIRPUS FLUITANS.

CYPERUS
FUSCUS.

SCIRPUS
CESPITOSUS.

RHYNCHOSPORA
ALBA.

RHYNCHOSPORA
FUSCA.

ELEOCHARIS
ACICULARIS.
ELEOCHARIS
QUINQUEFLORA

ELEOCHARIS
UNIGLUMIS.

SCIRPUS
SYLVATICUS.

Plate 92

Cyperaceae *(continued)*

The British species of *Carex* were monographed by Jermy and Tutin (1968) and the following account follows their treatment.

1. *Primocarex*. Spike solitary, of one or both sexes.

Carex microglochin Wahlenb. Bristle sedge. Stem 5–12 cm; leaves short; fr. 4–6 mm, yellow, with a bristle exserted at apex beside the stigma. By mountain flushes above 760 m, Breadalbanes, Perthshire, very rare. Flo. July.

Carex pauciflora Lightf. Few-flowered sedge. Stem 7–27 cm; leaves short; spike male at top; fr. 4.5–6 mm, yellow or reddish, without central bristle. Wet moors, N. England and Scotland, very rare in Wales and Ireland. Flo. June.

Carex pulicaris L. Flea sedge. Stem and leaves 10–30 cm; spike male at top; fr. 5–6 mm, shortly stalked, brown and shiny. Wet moors, etc., widespread and locally common. Flo. June.

Carex dioica L. Dioecious sedge. Stem 5–30 cm; leaves short; male and female spikes usually on separate plants; fr. 3.5 mm, sessile. Wet moors, etc., mostly N. England and Scotland, local. Flo. May.

Carex rupestris All. Rock sedge. Leaves 1–1.5 mm wide, equalling stem, point wavy; spike male at top; glumes ovate; fr. obovoid. Mountain rocks, Scotland, local. Flo. June–July.

2. *Arenariae*. Creeping plants; spikes clustered, mostly male at top.

Carex maritima Gunn. Curved sedge. *C. incurva* Lightf. Creeping; terete stems and leaves curved; spikes clustered in dense head, male at top; fr. smooth. Coastal dunes, N. England and Scotland. Flo. June.

Carex arenaria L. Sand sedge. Creeping stems triquetrous, 10–90 mm, spikes separated a little, upper male; fr. ribbed and winged. Coastal sand dunes, rare inland, widespread and common. Flo. June.

Carex disticha Huds. Brown sedge. Stem triquetrous, 20–100 cm; lowest and uppermost spikes female, central, narrower, male; fr. ribbed and serrate. Wet meadows and fens, widespread but local. Flo. June.

Carex divisa Huds. Divided sedge. Creeping; stem slender; bract often long and green; spikes oval, mostly contiguous, terminal male at top. Meadows near sea or estuaries, mostly S. and E. England, rare in N. England and Wales and very rare in Ireland. Flo. May–June.

Carex chordorrhiza L. f. String sedge. Stem stout, trigonous; leaves few, short; bract small; inflo. subcapitate, small. Bogs, W. Sutherland, very rare. Flo. June–July.*

3. *Paniculatae*. Spikes many, male at top, inflo. panicled or spike-like; stigmas 2.

Carex diandra Schrank. Lesser tussock sedge. *C. teretiuscula* Good. Stem slender; leaves grey-green; ligule very short; glumes 3 mm; fr. suborbicular, beaked, reddish. Damp meadows, widespread but local. Flo. May–June.

Carex paniculata L. Greater tussock sedge. Tufted; stem up to 150 cm; leaves 3–7 mm wide; inflo. branched; fr. gradually narrowed above. Marshes, pond verges, etc., widespread and common. Flo. June.

Carex appropinquata Schumach. Fibrous tussock sedge. *C. paradoxa* Willd., non J. F. Gmel. Tufted; stem up to 150 cm; leaves 1–2 mm wide; inflo. branched; fr. ribbed below, abruptly narrowed above. Calcareous meadows and fens, E. Anglia, Yorkshire, W. Wales, S. Scotland and S. Ireland, very local, formerly elsewhere. Flo. June.

Carex cuprina (Sandor ex Heuffel) Th. Nendtvich ex Kerner. *C. otrubae* Podp. *C. vulpina* auct., non L. Stem triquetrous, not winged; ligule long, 10–15 mm; 1 or 2 bracts very long; fr. greenish, ribbed. Damp, shady places, widespread and common. Flo. May–June.

Carex vulpina L. True fox sedge. Stem angles winged; ligule 2–5 mm; bracts all short; fr. reddish-brown. Damp, grassy places on clay soils, mostly S. England, local. Flo. May–June.

4. *Spicatae*. Spikes subsessile, male at top; stigmas 2.

Carex spicata Huds. Spiked sedge. *C. contigua* Hoppe. Leaves 3–4 mm wide; ligule 5 mm; spikes male at top; glumes long, purplish; fr. tapering at base. Hedge banks on basic and gravelly soils, mostly S. and E. England and Midlands, local. Flo. June.

Carex muricata L. Prickly sedge.
Ssp. **muricata**. Stem robust, strongly scabrid above; spikes globose; female glumes blackish or dark reddish-brown, much shorter than utricles; utricles 4–4.5 mm, rounded at base. Dry grassy places, mostly N. England, very rare. Flo. June.*
Ssp. **lamprocarpa** Celak. *C. pairaei* F. W. Schultz. Similar to ssp. *muricata* but stem slender, weakly scabrid; spikes ovoid; female glumes pale brown, almost as long as utricle; utricles 3–3.5 mm, truncate at base. Dry grassy places, widespread. Flo. June.

Carex divulsa Stokes.
Ssp. **divulsa**. Grey sedge. Stem rather weak; leaves 2–3 mm wide; ligule as wide as long; utricles 3.5–4 mm, pale to yellowish-brown. Dry hedge banks, etc., mostly England, Wales and S. Ireland, rare elsewhere. Flo. June–July.
Ssp. **leersii** (Kneucker) Walo Koch. Similar to ssp. *divulsa* but stems more robust; leaves 3–4 mm wide; ligule wider than long; utricles 4.5–5 mm, dark brown. Dry banks, etc., on calcareous soils, local. Flo. June–July.*

5. *Elongatae*. Spikes male at base; stigmas 2.

Carex echinata Murr. Star sedge. *C. stellulata* Good. Spikes *c.* 4, slightly separate, male at base; glumes reddish-brown; fr. spreading, star-like. Wet heaths, etc., widespread. Flo. May–June.

Carex elongata L. Elongated sedge. Stem 30–80 cm; spikes several, oblong, overlapping, male at base; glumes 2 mm, brown, edges pale; fr. 4 mm. Marshes, wet meadows, etc., mostly England, local and rare. Flo. June.

Carex ovalis Good. Oval sedge. Stem 10–90 cm, spikes oval, clustered, male at base; glumes brown, edges pale; fr. 4–5 mm. Wet meadows, etc., common. Flo. June.

6. *Canescentes*. Spikes male at base; stigmas 2; glumes short and pale.

Carex lachenalii Schkuhr. Hare's-foot sedge. *C. lagopina* Wahlenb. Stem up to 30 cm; spikes 3–4, contiguous, male at base; glumes short, reddish, edges pale; fr. yellow, beak short. Mountain bogs and wet rocks, Scotland. Flo. July.*

Carex curta Good. White sedge. *C. canescens* auct. Stem 10–50 cm; spikes 4–6, oblong, male at base; glumes 2 mm, white, midrib green; fr. yellowish, beak short. Bogs, widespread but local. Flo. July.

Carex remota L. Remote sedge. Bracts very long, leaf-like; spikes very distant, male at base; glumes white, midrib green; fr. green. Damp shady places, common. Flo. June.

CAREX MICROGLOCHIN.

CAREX DIOICA

CAREX PULICARIS.

CAREX PAUCIFLORA.

×2

CAREX MARITIMA.

CAREX DISTICHA

CAREX DIANDRA.

CAREX DIVISA.

CAREX PANICULATA

×2

CAREX RUPESTRIS.

CAREX ARENARIA.

CAREX ECHINATA

CAREX DIVULSA.

CAREX REMOTA.

CAREX SPICATA.

CAREX ELONGATA

CAREX CURTA.

CAREX MURICATA
SSP. LAMPROCARPA

CAREX VULPINA.

CAREX CUPRINA

CAREX APPROPINQUATA

CAREX OVALIS

Plate 93

Cyperaceae *(continued)*

7. *Altratae*. Terminal spike partly male; stigmas 3.

Carex norvegica Retz. Close-headed alpine-sedge. *C. alpina* Liljeb. Bract leaf-like; spikes small, erect, black, terminal male at base; fr. small, obovoid. Wet alpine rocks, Central Scotland. Flo. June–July.

Carex atrata L. Black alpine-sedge. Leaves broad, 5 mm; bract leaf-like; spikes oval, black, stalked, terminal male at base. Wet mountain rocks, N. England and Scotland, and formerly N. Wales. Flo. July.

Carex buxbaumii Wahlenb. Club sedge. *C. fusca* auct. Leaves narrow, glaucous; bract leaf-like; spikes subsessile, terminal male at base; glumes narrow, blackish; fr. broad, glaucous green. Fens, Inverness-shire. Flo. July.

Carex atrofusca Schkuhr. Scorched alpine-sedge. *C. ustulata* Wahlenb. Leaves short and broad; bracts brown, sheathing; spikes black, lower nodding, terminal male above or throughout. Mountain bogs, Perthshire, and Inverness-shire, rare.

8. *Acutae*. Spikes dense-flowered, terminal male; bracts leafy; stigmas 2; beak very short.

Carex recta Boott. Estuarine sedge. *C. kattegatensis* Fr. ex Krecz. Stem 30–100 cm; leaf ligule 2–3 mm; lower spikes long-stalked; female glumes long, 4–5 mm, midrib pale excurrent. Estuary sands, N. Scotland, local and rare. Flo. July–Aug.*

Carex elata All. Tufted-sedge. *C. hudsonii* A. Benn. Stem 25–100 cm; leaf ligule 5–10 mm, upper bracts small; spikes long, subsessile; fr. in straight rows. Riversides and fen ditches, mostly E. Anglia and C. Ireland, local. Flo. June.

Carex acuta L. Slender tufted-sedge. *C. gracilis* Curt. Stem 30–120 cm; leaf ligule 2–3 mm; lowest bract equalling inflo.; spikes long; glumes narrow, black, nerve often excurrent. Pond verges, marshes, etc., widespread, but rare in Scotland. Flo. May–June.

Carex aquatilis Wahlenb. Water sedge. Stem 20–110 cm; leaf ligule 10 mm; 2 or 3 bracts equalling inflo.; female spikes narrowed below; glumes dark. By mountain lakes and streams, N. Britain and Ireland. Flo. July.

Carex bigelowii Torr. ex Schwein. Ssp. **rigida** Schulte-Motel. Stiff sedge. *C. rigida* Good. Stem 4–30 cm, stoutly triquetrous; leaves keeled and recurved; spikes shorter, *c.* 15 mm; glumes short and black. Stony places on mountains, N. Britain and Ireland. Flo. June–July.

Carex nigra (L.) Reichard. Common sedge. *C. goodenowii* Gay. Stem 7–70 cm; lower bract leaf-like; spikes dense, cylindrical, obtuse; glumes black, narrower than green fr. Wet grassy places on acid soils, widespread and common. Flo. May–June.

9. *Limosae*. Peduncles slender; fr. elliptic; beak very short; stigmas 3.

Carex flacca Schreb. Glaucous sedge. *C. glauca* Scop *C. diversicolor* auct. 10–60 cm, stem and leaves glaucous; spikes cylindrical; stalks slender; glumes dark; fr. minutely papillose. Grassy places on calcareous and limestone soils, widespread and common. Flo. May–June.

Carex magellanica Lam. ssp. **irrigua** (Wahlenb.) Hiitonen. *C. paupercula* Michx. Tall bog-sedge. 10–40 cm, stem smooth; leaves broader, 3 mm; spikes nodding, 8–10-flo.; female glumes lanceolate, narrower than pale, ovate fr. Bogs, N. England, N. Wales and Scotland, rare. Flo. June.

Carex rariflora (Wahlenb.) Sm. Mountain bog-sedge. Up to 20 cm, stem and leaves smooth; spikes nodding, 8–10-flo.; male glumes ovate, female glumes obovate. High mountain bogs, Scotland, local. Flo. June.*

Carex limosa L. Bog-sedge. 10–40 cm, stem and narrow leaves rough; spikes nodding, 10–20 flo.; male glumes lanceolate, female glumes ovate; fr. elliptic, ribbed. Peaty pools, local. Flo. June.

10. *Digitatae*. Inflo. finger-like; flo. few; fr. pale, pubescent; beak short.

Carex digitata L. Fingered sedge. Stem up to 25 cm; leaves 3–4 mm; spikes lax, 6–8-flo.; glumes pale; fr. pubescent. Grassy places on limestone soil, N. Somerset to N. England, rare. Flo. April–May.

Carex ornithopoda Willd. Bird's-foot sedge. Stem 5–25 cm; leaves narrower; spikes small, lax, 4–5-flo.; glume shorter than pyriform fr. Banks on limestone soil, Derbyshire to Lake District, local. Flo. May.

Carex humilis Leyss. Dwarf sedge. Dwarf, 2–10 cm; leaves very narrow; bracts broad, enclosing 3–5-flo. female spike. Dry turf and crevices on limestone soil, Herefordshire to Hampshire. Flo. April.

11. *Montanae*. Spikes sessile subglobose or oblong; fr. pubescent; beak short.

Carex montana L. Soft-leaved sedge. Shortly creeping; stem 10–40 cm; leaves 2 mm wide; glume dark, shorter than pubescent fr. Pastures on limestone soil, England and Wales, very local. Flo. May.

Carex ericetorum Poll. Rare spring-sedge. Stems tufted, 2–30 cm; leaves wider, 3–4 mm, short; glumes dark, edges pale; fr. obovate, pubescent. Dry grassy places on calcareous soil, Suffolk to Lake District. Flo. April–May.

Carex pilulifera L. Pill sedge. Stem 10–30 cm; leaves narrow, 2 mm; glumes light brown; fr. globose, green; bract sometimes long. Damp heaths, etc., common. Flo. May–June.

Carex caryophyllea Latourr. Spring-sedge. *C. praecox* auct. Stem 2–30 cm; bracts sheathing; spikes oblong; glumes ovate, brown, midrib green; fr. elliptic, green. In short turf, common. Flo. April–May.

Carex tomentosa L. Downy-fruited sedge. *C. filiformis* auct., non L. Stem 20–50 cm; leaves narrow; bracts shortly leaf-like; spikes oblong; fr. small, obovoid, very downy. Wet meadows, woodland rides, etc., Wiltshire, Surrey, Oxfordshire and Gloucestershire, local and rare, formerly elsewhere. Flo. May–June.

12. *Paniceae*. Spikes stalked; fr. large, oval, glabrous, pale.

Carex pallescens L. Pale sedge. Stem 20–60 cm; bract leaf-like; female spikes dense, slender-stalked; glumes white with green midrib; fr. bright green. Damp meadows and woods, widespread. Flo. June.

Carex panicea L. Carnation sedge. Stem 10–60 cm; leaves very glaucous; bract sheath tight; spikes lax, few flo.; fr. curved. Damp pastures, common. Flo. May–June.

Carex vaginata Tausch. Sheathed sedge. Stem 10–60 cm; leaves bright green; bract sheath very loose; spikes lax, few flo.; fr. curved. High mountains, Scotland. Flo. July.

13. *Nutantes*. Lower bract sheath long; spikes nodding; fr. narrow-beaked.

Carex capillaris L. Hair sedge. Stem 10–40 cm, very slender; spikes lax, few flo., nodding; glumes and fr. small, brown, shiny. Mountain slopes, Teesdale to N. Scotland, local. Flo. June–July.

CAREX
HUMILIS.

CAREX
LIMOSA

CAREX
PILULIFERA.

CAREX
DIGITATA

CAREX
BUXBAUMII.

C.ORNITHO
PODA.

CAREX
MONTANA

CAREX
ERICETORUM

CAREX
ELATA.

CAREX
ATRATA

CAREX
NIGRA.

CAREX
ACUTA

C.MAGELLANICA
SSP. IRRIGUA

CAREX
ATROFUSCA.

CAREX
TOMENTOSA

CAREX
PALLESCENS.

CAREX
NORVEGICA

CAREX
CARYOPHYLLEA

CAREX
AQUATILIS.

CAREX
CAPILLARIS.

×3

CAREX
FLACCA

CAREX
BIGELOWII

CAREX
VAGINATA.

CAREX
PANICEA.

×2   ×2   ×2

×2   ×2   ×2

Plate 94

Cyperaceae *(continued)*

Carex strigosa Huds. Thin-spiked wood-sedge. Stem up to 70 cm; leaf width *c.* 8 mm; female spikes lax, flo. slender, 25–80 mm, long; fr. lanceolate, green. Damp shady places, local. Flo. May–June.

Carex pendula Huds. Pendulous sedge. Stem 60–180 cm; leaf width 15–20 mm; flo. spikes dense, very long, 10–15 cm, drooping; fr. lanceolate, green. Damp woods and shady places, common in S. and E. England, local in Wales and Ireland and rare in Scotland. Flo. May–June.

Carex sylvatica Huds. Wood-sedge. Stem 15–60 cm; female spikes 20–65 mm, lax, nodding; stalks slender; glumes pale; fr. green with long beak. Woods on stiff soils, common. Flo. May–June.

14. *Distantes.* Bracts long sheathing; spikes distant, oblong; beak long, bifid.

Carex depauperata Curt. ex With. Starved wood-sedge. Spikes with few flo., 3–4 only, lower distant, stalked; fr. very large, 8 mm, ribbed; beak long. Dry woods and hedge banks on limestone soil, Somerset and Cork, very rare; formerly in Surrey. Flo. May.*

Carex binervis Sm. Green-ribbed sedge. Spikes distant, lowest 20–45 mm, dense, long-stalked; glumes dark; fr. with strong green submarginal ribs. Acid heaths, moors, etc., widespread and common. Flo. June.

Carex distans L. Distant sedge. Spikes distant, 10–20 mm; stalks included in sheath; glumes greenish-brown; fr. many, ribbed. Marshes, etc., mostly near the sea, widespread. Flo. May–June.

Carex hostiana DC. Tawny sedge. *C. hornschuchiana* Hoppe, *C. fulva* auct. Spikes distant, 8–20 mm, lower long-stalked; glumes brown with white margin; fr. many, ribbed. Moors, marshes, etc., widespread but local. Flo. June.*

Carex flava L. Yellow-sedge. Stem stout, leaves 4–7 mm wide; terminal spike sessile, often partly female; fr. large, 6–7 mm, deflexed, golden. Fens on base-rich soils, N. Lancashire, very rare. Flo. June.

Carex lasiocarpa Ehrh. Slender sedge. *C. filiformis* auct. Leaves narrow, glabrous; female spikes distant, subsessile, 10–30 mm; glumes brown; fr. very downy. Peat bogs and reed swamps, widespread but local. Flo. June.

Carex hirta L. Hairy sedge. Wider leaves and sheaths hairy; spikes distant; glumes long, greenish, awned; fr. green, very pubescent. Damp meadows, shady places, etc., widespread and common. Flo. May–June.

15. *Extensae.* Bracts deflexed; female spikes short, dense; fr. spreading.

Carex extensa Good. Long-bracted sedge. Leaves narrow, involute; bracts very long; spikes subsessile; glumes light brown; fr. ribbed. Salt marshes, locally common. Flo. June.

Carex lepidocarpa Tausch. Long-stalked yellow-sedge.
Ssp. **lepidocarpa.** Stem slender, twice as long as leaves; leaves 2–3.5 mm wide; male spike stalked; female spikes rarely contiguous; glumes orange or red-brown. Base-rich fens, widespread. Flo. May–June.
Ssp. **scotica** E. W. Davies. Similar to ssp. *lepidocarpa* but stem three times as long as leaves; leaves 4.5 mm wide; glumes dark brown, not falling before utricle. Rocky shores, etc., on limestone soils, N. Wales, N. England and Scotland. Flo. May–June.*

Carex serotina Mérat. Small-fruited yellow-sedge.*
Ssp. **serotina.** Leaves 2–3 mm wide, channelled; male spike sessile; female glumes pale yellow-brown with green midrib; utricles 2–3.5 mm; fr. not curved, abruptly contracted to short beak. Marshes, bogs, etc., widespread, but local. Flo. July–Aug.
Ssp. **pulchella** (Lönnr.) Ooststr. *C. scandinavica* E. W. Davies. Similar to ssp. *serotina* but leaves grey-green; female glumes darker; utricles 1.75–2 mm. Salt marshes, etc., Scotland. Flo. July–Aug.*

Carex demissa Hornem. Common yellow-sedge. *C. tumidicarpa* Anderss. Stems spreading; male spike short-stalked; lowest female spike often distant and stalked; fr. swollen, green, lower deflexed. Wet places on acid soils, widespread. Flo. July.

Carex punctata Gaudin. Dotted sedge. Spikes distant; stalks included in bract sheath; glumes pale reddish; fr. pale green with pellucid dots. Sandy places by the sea, mostly S.W. England, Wales, S. Scotland and W. Ireland, local. Flo. June–July.*

16. *Vesicariae.* Stems leafy; lower spikes on slender stalks; fr. ovoid; beak long.

Carex pseudocyperus L. Cyperus sedge. Stem 40–90 cm; leaves wide; ligule 12 mm; female spikes nodding; fr. 5–6 mm, ribbed; beak long. By ponds and slow rivers, local, in England and Ireland, rare in Wales and very rare in Scotland. Flo. May–June.

Carex laevigata Sm. Smooth-stalked sedge. *C. helodes* Link. Stem 30–120 cm; leaf ligule 10 mm; male spike 1; lower female spike nodding; glumes 3 mm; fr. 5–6 mm, ovoid, inflated. Shady places on acid soil, widespread. Flo. June.

Carex rostrata Stokes. Bottle sedge. *C. ampullacea* Good. Stem 20–100 cm; leaf ligule 2–3 mm; male spikes 2–3; lower female spikes 3–7 cm, suberect; glumes 5 mm; fr. 5–6 mm, yellowish. Swamps, marshes, etc., widespread. Flo. June.

Carex vesicaria L. Bladder-sedge. Stem 30–120 cm; leaf ligule 5–8 mm; female spikes 2–4 cm; glumes 3 mm; fr. 4–5 mm, ovoid, yellow. Wet places, widespread but local. Flo. June.*

Carex saxatilis L. Russet sedge. *C. pulla* Good. Stem 15–40 cm; leaves concave; ligule 1 mm, rounded; male spike usually 1; female spikes oval; fr. 3 mm, smooth. Bogs on high mountains, Scotland, local. Flo. July.

Carex × grahami Boott. Mountain bladder-sedge. *C. saxatilis × vesicaria. C. stenolepis* auct., non Less. Stem 30–120 cm; leaf ligule 3–4 mm, acute; female spikes broadly oval; fr. 4–5 mm, inflated, ribbed. Mountain bogs, Argyll, Perthshire and Angus, rare. Flo. July.

17. *Paludosae.* Plants tall; leaves wide; spikes many, large, erect, dense.

Carex acutiformis Ehrh. Lesser pond-sedge. *C. paludosa* Good. Stem 60–150 cm; leaf width 7–10 mm; ligule 5–15 mm; male glumes 5–6 mm, obtuse; female spikes 2–5 cm; glumes 4–5 mm; fr. 4 mm. Ponds and canals, widespread, but rare in Scotland. Flo. May–June.

Carex riparia Curt. Greater pond-sedge. Stem 60–130 cm; leaf width 6–15 mm; ligule 5–10 mm; male glumes long, 8 mm; pointed female spikes 3–10 cm; female glumes 7 mm; fr. 8 mm. Rivers, ditches, etc., widespread and common, but rare in Scotland. Flo. May–June.

CAREX
PENDULA

CAREX
STRIGOSA.

CAREX
ROSTRATA.

CAREX
PSEUDO-
-CYPERUS.

CAREX
ACUTIFORMIS

CAREX
RIPARIA.

CAREX
DISTANS.

CAREX
SYLVATICA.

C. EXTENSA

CAREX
FLAVA.

CAREX X
GRAHAMI

CAREX
LASIOCARPA

CAREX
HIRTA.

CAREX
LEPIDOCARPA

CAREX
LAEVIGATA

CAREX
BINERVIS

CAREX
DEMISSA.

CAREX SAXATILIS

Plate 95

Gramineae

The British grasses were monographed by Hubbard (1968) and the lines of that work have been followed here as far as possible. We are also indebted to the late Dr. C. E. Hubbard for permission to use some of his 'points of difference' and for looking through the text of the original edition and making useful suggestions.

Digitaria ischaemum (Schreb.) Muhl. Smooth finger-grass. Annual; leaf ligule membranous; spikelets stalked on 1 side of axis; lower glume suppressed; lower lemma barren. Sandy fields, S. and E. England, rare. Flo. Aug.*

Cynodon dactylon (L.) Pers. Bermuda-grass. Perennial; leaf ligule a ring of hairs; spikelets sessile on 1 side of axis; glumes narrow, subequal. Coastal sand, S. W. England, introd. elsewhere. Illus. on pl. 96.

Setaria viridis (L.) Beauv. Green bristle-grass. Annual; inflo. spike-like; spikelet stalks bearing long rough bristles; upper glume equalling spikelet, lower very short. Introd. Europe. Cultivated and waste ground, uncommon. Flo. Aug.–Oct.*

Spartina maritima (Curt.) Fernald. Small cord-grass. *S. stricta* (Ait.) Roth. Stem up to 50 cm; leaf width 6 mm, spikelets 4–12 mm, hairy; upper glume 3-nerved; anthers 4–6 mm. Salt marshes, mostly S. England. Flo. July–Sept.*

Spartina × townsendii H. & J. Groves. Townsend's cord-grass. *S. alterniflora × maritima*. Stem 30–130 cm; leaf width 4–12 mm; spikelets 11–15 mm, hairy; anthers 5–8 mm. Spreading on coastal mud flats, mostly S. and E. England, local, planted. Flo. July–Nov.

Spartina anglica C. E. Hubbard. Common cord-grass. Similar to *S. × townsendii* but upper leaf-blades broader and more widely spreading; ligular hairs longer; spikelets longer, wider and more hairy; anthers 8–12 mm. Tidal mud flats, widespread. Flo. July–Nov.*

Spartina alterniflora Lois. Smooth cord-grass. Stem 40–100 cm; leaf width 5–12 mm; spikelets 10–18 mm, subglabrous; upper glumes 5–9-nerved; anthers 4–6 mm. Mud flats, Hampshire, now very rare. Flo. July–Nov.*

Danthonia decumbens (L.) DC. Heath-grass. *Sieglingia decumbens* (L.) Bernh. *Triodia decumbens* (L.) Beauv. Stem spreading; leaf ligule of short hairs; spikelets plump and shiny; flo. usually self-fertilizing. Heaths, moors, etc., widespread and common. Flo. July. Illus. on pl. 96.

Molinia caerulea (L.) Moench. Purple moor-grass. Stem tufted, 15–120 cm; leaves long, dying in winter; ligule of short hairs; inflo. up to 40 cm long, purple. Moors, heaths, fens, etc., common. Flo. July–Sept. Illus. on pl. 97.

Phragmites australis (Cav.) Trin. ex Steud. Common reed. *P. communis* Trin., *Arundo phragmites* L. Stem stout, 1.5–3 m; leaf width 10–30 mm; ligule of hairs; inflo. densely branched; spikelet 10–16 mm. Marshes, pools, etc., common. Flo. Aug.–Oct.*

Leersia oryzoides (L.) Sw. Cut-grass. Stem 30–120 cm; leaf sheaths hairy, often enclosing inflo.; glumes 0; lemma and palea hairy. Wet meadows, riversides, etc., Surrey to Somerset and Dorset, local and rare. Flo. Aug.–Oct.*

Nardus stricta L. Mat-grass. Stem and inrolled leaves wiry; spikes 1-sided, very slender; spikelets narrow, pointed. Heaths and moors, common. Flo. June–Aug. Illus. on pl. 99.

Parapholis strigosa (Dumort.) C. E. Hubbard. Hard-grass. *Lepturus filiformis* Trin. Stem up to 40 cm; leaves 1–6 cm; spikes long, narrow; spikelets alternate, embedded in the stem; anthers 2–4 mm. Salt marshes, widespread. Flo. June–Aug. Illus. on pl. 99.

Parapholis incurva (L.) C. E. Hubbard. Curved hard-grass. *Lepturus incurvatus* Trin. Smaller, up to 20 cm; stems and spikes curved; leaves 5–30 mm; anthers very small, 0.5–1 mm. Salt marshes, Somerset and Dorset to Yorkshire. Flo. June–July.*

Phalaris arundinacea L. Reed canary-grass. Stem 60–200 cm; leaf width 6–18 mm; ligules 2.5–16 mm; panicle with rough branches; small sterile lemmas, fertile one hairy. Wet places, common. Flo. June–Aug.

Phalaris canariensis L. Canary-grass. Stem 20–120 cm; inflo. spike-like, 1.5–6 cm; glumes large, pale yellow, with green winged keels. Introd., Mediterranean region. Waste ground, common. Flo. July–Sept.*

Polypogon monspeliensis (L.) Desf. Annual beard-grass. Stem up to 80 cm, leaves and ligules long; panicle spike-like; ripe spikelets falling; glumes

rough, long-awned. Coastal marshes, S. and S.E. England, rare, introd. elsewhere. Flo. July.

Milium effusum L. Wood millet. Stem 45–180 cm; leaf width 5–15 mm; ligule long; inflo. long and wide spreading; spikelets isolated, oval, green. Woods, shady places, etc., widespread. Flo. May–July.

Alopecurus alpinus Sm. Alpine foxtail. Stem 10–45 cm; spikes short and broad; glumes very hairy; lemma ovate, awn short or 0. Wet places on mountains, N. England and Scotland. Flo. June–Aug.

Alopecurus pratensis L. Meadow foxtail. Stem 30–120 cm; spikes soft, 2–13 cm long; spikelets 4–6 mm; glumes acute, united below; lemma awn long. Meadows, etc., common. Flo. April–July.

Alopecurus geniculatus L. Marsh foxtail. Stem prostrate below; leaf sheaths pale, inflated; spikelets 3 mm; glumes blunt, nearly free; anthers violet. Wet margins of pools and ditches, common. Flo. June–Aug.

Alopecurus bulbosus Gouan. Bulbous foxtail. Stem 15–20 cm; bulbous at base; upper sheaths inflated; glumes sharply pointed; lemma awn long. Salt marshes, S. England and Wales, local, rare elsewhere. Flo. May–Aug.

Alopecurus aequalis Sobol. Orange foxtail. *A. fulvus* Sm. Prostrate at base; sheaths inflated; glumes blunt; lemma awn short; anthers orange. Margins of pools, mostly England, local. Flo. June–Sept.

Alopecurus myosuroides Huds. Black-grass. *A. agrestis* L. Stem 20–80 cm; spikes 2–12 cm, narrow; glumes pointed, half united; lemma awn long. Arable land, common. Flo. May–Aug.

Phleum alpinum L. Alpine cat's-tail. *P. commutatum* Gaudin. stem 10–50 cm; leaf ligule short; spikes short and broad; glumes truncate; keel ciliate; awns 2–3 mm. High mountains, N.W. England and Scotland, rare. Flo. July–Aug.

Phleum pratense L. Timothy-grass. Stem 40–150 cm; leaves rough; ligule 4–6 mm; spike 6–15 cm; glumes truncate; keel ciliate; awn 1–2 mm. Meadows, common. Flo. June–Aug.

Phleum bertolonii DC. Cat's-tail. *P. nodosum* auct. Stem swollen at base; leaf ligules 2–4 mm; spikes 1–6 cm, dense; glumes truncate, ciliate; awn short. Pastures, common. Flo. June–Aug.

Phleum phleoides (L.) Karst. Purple-stem cat's-tail. Leaves narrower, ligules 1–2 mm; spikes 2–10 cm; glumes bluntly narrowed; keel hairs very short. Dry grassy places on sandy and calcareous soils, local, E. England. Flo. June–Aug.

Phleum arenarium L. Sand cat's-tail. Stem 3–20 cm; leaves short, ligules long; spikes dense, narrowed below; glumes gradually narrowed above. Coastal sands, locally common. Flo. May–July.

Lagurus ovatus L. Hare's-tail. Stem 5–60 cm, hairy; leaves short, softly hairy; spikes ovoid, hairy, bristly; glumes narrow, subulate, hairy. Sandy places, Channel Islands, naturalized in S. England, rare. Flo. July.*

Mibora minima (L.) Desv. Early sand grass. Stem slender, tufted, 2–15 cm; leaves small; spike slender, 1-sided; spikelets 1-flo.; glumes blunt. Damp sandy places near the sea, Channel Islands and Wales, introd. elsewhere. Flo. Feb.–May. Illus. on pl. 96.

Agrostis stolonifera L. Creeping bent. Stolons leafy; stem up to 40 cm; panicle contracted, branches short, palea ⅔ length of lemma. Grassy places, etc. Flo. July–Aug.

Agrostis capillaris L. Common bent. *A. tenuis* Sibth. *A. vulgaris* With. Rhizome short; stem 10–70 cm; ligule short; panicle spreading, brown; lemma awnless; palea ½ length of lemma. Heaths, fields, etc., common. Flo. June–Aug.

Agrostis gigantea Roth. Black bent. *A. nigra* With. Rhizomatous; stem 40–120 cm; leaves large; ligule long; panicle open; lemma awnless; palea 1–1.3 mm. Waste ground, etc., common. Flo. June–Aug.*

Agrostis canina L. Brown bent. Stolons creeping, bearing tufts of slender leaves; panicle branches bare below; lemma awned; palea minute. Moors and meadows, common. Flo. June–Aug.

Agrostis vinealis Schreb. *A. canina* ssp. *montana* (Hartm.) Hartm. Similar to *A. canina* but smaller with scaly rhizome, dense tufts of stiffer leaves and contracted panicle. Heaths, etc., common. Flo. June–Aug.

Agrostis curtisii Kerguelen. Bristle bent. *A. setacea* Curt. Many shoots of very fine leaves; panicle narrow; lemma awned; palea very small. Heaths and moors, S. and S.W. England and S. Wales, local. Flo. June–July.

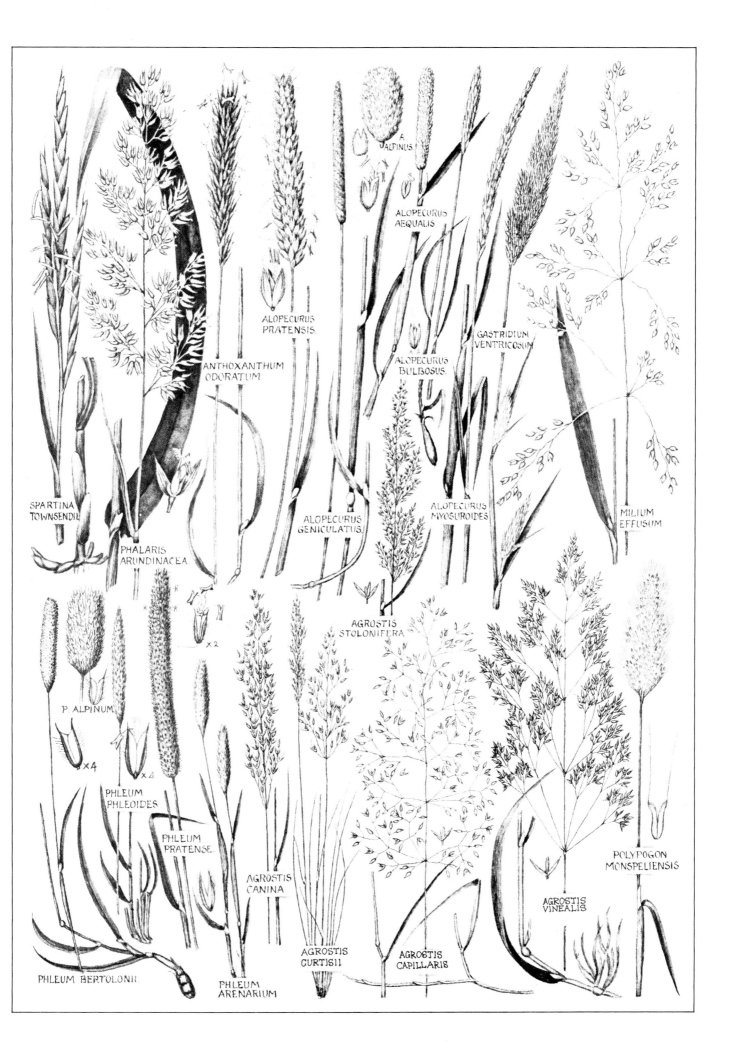

SPARTINA
TOWNSENDII

PHALARIS
ARUNDINACEA

ANTHOXANTHUM
ODORATUM

ALOPECURUS
PRATENSIS.

A.
ALPINUS

ALOPECURUS
AEQUALIS

GASTRIDIUM
VENTRICOSUM

ALOPECURUS
BULBOSUS.

ALOPECURUS
GENICULATUS.

ALOPECURUS
MYOSUROIDES

MILIUM
EFFUSUM

AGROSTIS
STOLONIFERA

P. ALPINUM.

×4

PHLEUM
PHLEOIDES

×4

PHLEUM
PRATENSE.

PHLEUM
ARENARIUM

PHLEUM BERTOLONII.

AGROSTIS
CANINA

AGROSTIS
CURTISII

AGROSTIS
CAPILLARIS

×2

AGROSTIS
VINEALIS

POLYPOGON
MONSPELIENSIS

Plate 96

Gramineae *(continued)*

Apera spica-venti (L.) Beauv. Loose silky-bent. Stem 20–100 cm; leaves and ligules long; panicle branches long, spreading; lemma awn long; anthers 2 mm. Cultivated and waste ground on light soils, mostly S. England. Flo. June–Aug.*

Apera interrupta (L.) Beauv. Dense silky-bent. Stem and leaves short; panicle branches short, erect, dense; anthers minute. Cultivated and waste ground on sandy soil. E. Anglia, very rare elsewhere. Flo. June–July.*

Gastridium ventricosum (Gouan) Schinz & Thell. Nit-grass. *G. lendigerum* (L.) Desv. Stem 10–60 cm; leaves short; panicle spike-like, pale green; spikelets swollen at base, shiny. Dry grassy places on sandy and calcareous soils, mostly near the sea, S. and S.W. England and S. Wales, local. Flo. June–Aug. Illus. on pl. 95.

Calamagrostis epigejos (L.) Roth. Wood small-reed. Stem 60–200 cm; leaves wide, glabrous; ligule long; panicle dense; glumes narrow; hairs much exceeding lemma. Damp woods and fens, local. Flo. June–July.

Calamagrostis canescens (Weber) Roth. Purple small-reed. *C. lanceolata* Roth. Stem 60–120 cm; leaves hairy above; panicle loose; glumes rather narrow; hairs slightly exceeding lemma. Marshes and fens, widespread but rather rare. Flo. June–July.

Calamagrostis stricta (Timm) Koel. Narrow small-reed. *C. neglecta* auct. Stem 30–100 cm; leaves hairy above; ligule short; panicle narrow, dense; glumes 3–4 mm, broadly lanceolate; hairs shorter than lemma. Bogs, widespread but rare. Flo. July.*

Calamagrostis scotica (Druce) Druce. Scottish small-reed. Stem up to 90 cm; leaves hairy above; panicle rather narrow, dense; glumes 4–6 mm, lanceolate; hairs shorter than lemma. Marshes and bogs, Roxburghshire and Caithness, very rare. Flo. July–Aug.*

Ammophila arenaria (L.) Link. Marram. *A. arundinacea* Host. Rhizomes long; stem 50–120 cm, leaves inrolled, sharp-pointed; ligule very long; panicle large, spike-like; glumes 8–12 mm. Coastal sands, widespread and common. Flo. July.

Ammocalamagrostis baltica (Flügge ex Schrader) P. Fourn. *Ammophila arenaria × Calamagrostis epigejos*. Leaves flatter; inflo. purplish; lemma hairs longer; anthers small. Dunes, etc., mostly E. England.*

Anthoxanthum odoratum L. Scented vernal-grass. Perennial; stem unbranched; spike 1–12 cm; glumes hairy, unequal; awns of sterile lemmas not conspicuous. Meadows, etc., common. Flo. April–June. Illus. on pl. 95.

Anthoxanthum aristatum Boiss. Annual vernal-grass. *A. puelii* Lecoq & Lamotte. Annual; stem branched; spike 1–4 cm; glumes glabrous; awns of sterile lemmas conspicuous. Sandy fields, S. and E. England, rare. Flo. June–Aug.*

Hierochloe odorata (L.) Beauv. Holy-grass. Creeping; stem 20–50 cm; upper leaves short, pointed; panicle spreading; spikelets rounded; glumes broad. Wet places, Scotland, rare, and Lough Neagh, N. Ireland, very rare. Flo. March–May.*

Holcus mollis L. Creeping soft-grass. Rhizomes creeping; stems hairy at nodes; glumes ovate, acute, hairy; upper lemma long-awned. Dry woods, heaths, etc., common. Flo. June–Aug.

Holcus lanatus L. Yorkshire-fog. Tufted; stems downy; glumes ovate, blunt, hairy, upper aristate; upper lemma short-awned. Meadows, waste land, etc., common. Flo. May–Aug.

Aira caryophyllea L. Silver hair-grass. Stem 3–40 cm, slender; leaf sheaths rough; panicle spreading; glumes silvery; lemmas awned. Dry soils, banks and wall tops, common. Flo. May–July.

Aira praecox L. Early hair-grass. Tufted; stem 2–20 cm, slender; leaves very small; sheaths smooth; panicle spike-like; glumes shiny; lemmas awned. Heaths, dry fields, etc., on sandy and acid soils, common. Flo. April–June.

Corynephorus canescens (L.) Beauv. Grey hair-grass. *Aira canescens* L. Tufted; leaves many, very slender, rough; panicle narrow; lemma awn with apex club-like. Coastal dunes, Norfolk, Suffolk and Channel Islands. Flo. June–July.

Deschampsia setacea (Huds.) Hack. Bog hair-grass. Leaves very narrow, bristle-like; sheaths smooth; ligules long, pointed; lemma broad, unequally 4-pointed. Boggy heaths, mostly Scotland, local, rare elsewhere. Flo. July–Aug.

Deschampsia flexuosa (L.) Trin. Wavy hair-grass. Leaves narrow, bristle-like; sheaths slightly rough; ligules blunt; lemma ovate, apical teeth microscopic. Heaths, dry woods, etc., widespread and common. Flo. June–July.

Deschampsia cespitosa (L.) Beauv.
Ssp. **cespitosa**. Tufted hair-grass. Large tussocks; stem 20–200 cm; leaves flat, coarse, ribs rough; ligule long; lemma tip toothed. Wet fields, moors, etc., widespread and common. Flo. June–Aug.
Ssp. **alpina** (L). Tzvelev. Alpine hair-grass. *D. alpina* (L.) Roem. & Schult. Stem 10–40 cm, tufted; leaves short, channelled; sheath smooth; ligule long; flo. often proliferous; lemma toothed. Wet rocks and grassy slopes above 930 m, N. Wales, Scotland and S. Ireland, rare. Flo. July–Aug.*

Trisetum flavescens (L.) Beauv. Yellow oat-grass. Stem 20–80 cm; leaves flat, pointed; ligule short; panicle yellow; spikelets *c.* 3-flo.; lemma 2-toothed, awned. Pastures, roadsides, etc., widespread but rare in Scotland. Flo. June–July.

Koeleria macrantha (Ledeb.) Schultes. Crested hair-grass. *K. gracilis* Pers. *K. cristata* (L.) Pers. p.p. Tufted, stem up to 40 cm; leaves mostly inrolled; sheaths hairy; panicle dense, spike-like, pale. Grassy places on basic soils, common. Flo. June–July. Illus. on pl. 97. Var. *albescens* DC., appears to be a sand-dune form with white panicles. Illus. on pl. 97.

Koeleria vallesiana (Honck.) Gaudin. Somerset hair-grass. Similar to *K. macrantha* but with the basal leaf sheaths persisting, split and fibrous, forming a dense thickened base to stems. Rocky limestone slopes, Somerset. Flo. June–July.*

Avena ludoviciana Durieu. Winter wild-oat. Spikelet jointed and breaking only above the glumes; lemmas awned, hairy; apex 2-toothed, without bristles. Introd. weed. Flo. July–Aug.*

Avena fatua L. Wild-oat. Spikelet jointed and breaking between the lemmas; lemmas hairy, awned; apex 2-toothed, without bristles. Cultivated and waste ground, common in England, local or rare elsewhere. Flo. June–Aug.

Arrhenatherum elatius (L.) J. & C. Presl. False oat-grass. *A. avenaceum* Beauv. Stem 50–150 cm, often bulbous at base; spikelets 2-flo.; lower lemma long-awned, 7-nerved. Waste ground, hedgerows, etc., common. Flo. June–Sept.

Seslaria albicans Kit. ex Schultes. Blue moor-grass. *S. caerulea*.
Ssp. *calcarea* (Čelak.) Hegl. Stem 10–45 cm; leaves flat, blunt, hooded; spike bluish with scales at base; spikelets 2–3-flo. Grassy and rocky places on limestone soil, N. England, Scotland, W. Ireland, local. Flo. April–June.

Avenula pratensis (L.) Dumort. Meadow oat-grass. *Avena pratensis* L. *Helictotrichon pratense* (L.) Pilg. Stem 30–80 cm; leaf sheaths glabrous; spikelets large, 3–6-flo.; axis short-haired; lemmas long-awned. Grassy places, mostly on calcareous and limestone soils, widespread. Flo. June–July.

Avenula pubescens (Huds.) Dumort. Downy oat-grass. *Avena pubescens* Huds. *Heliototrichon pubescens* (Huds.) Pilg. Stem 30–100 cm; leaves and lower sheaths hairy; spikelets 2–3-flo.; axis with long hairs; lemmas long-awned. Damp calcareous soils, widespread. Flo. May–July.

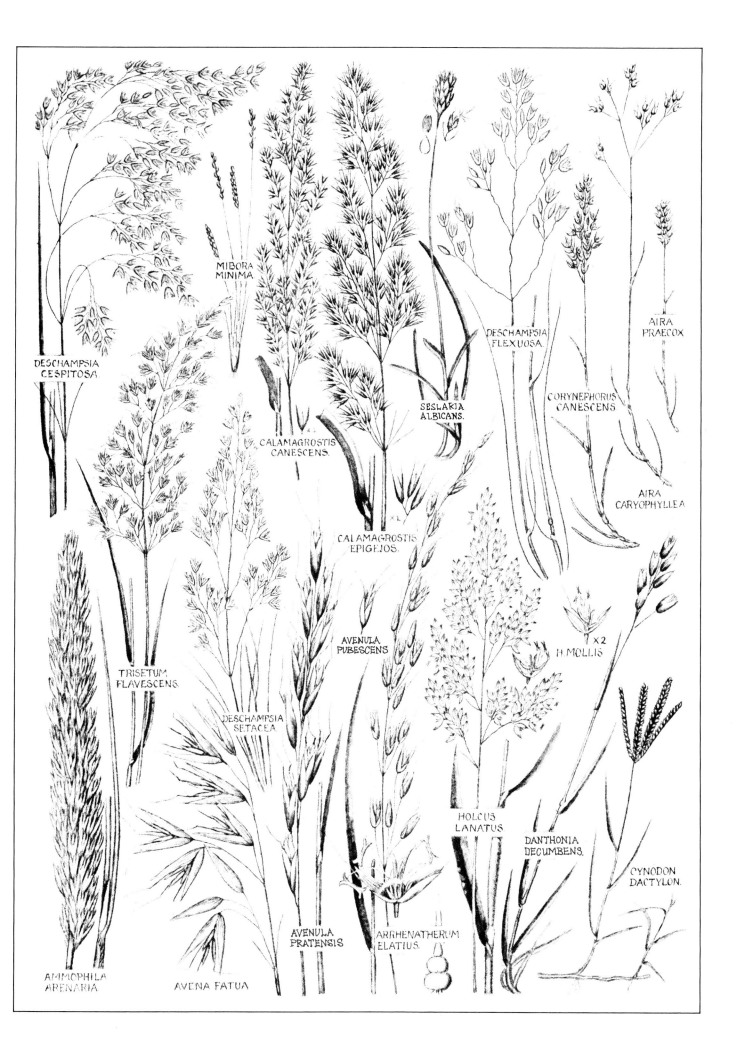

DESCHAMPSIA
CESPITOSA.

MIBORA
MINIMA

CALAMAGROSTIS
CANESCENS.

CALAMAGROSTIS
EPIGEJOS.

SESLARIA
ALBICANS.

DESCHAMPSIA
FLEXUOSA.

AIRA
PRAECOX

CORYNEPHORUS
CANESCENS

AIRA
CARYOPHYLLEA

TRISETUM
FLAVESCENS.

AVENULA
PUBESCENS

×2
H. MOLLIS

DESCHAMPSIA
SETACEA

HOLCUS
LANATUS.

DANTHONIA
DECUMBENS.

CYNODON
DACTYLON.

AMMOPHILA
ARENARIA.

AVENA FATUA

AVENULA
PRATENSIS

ARRHENATHERUM
ELATIUS.

— *Plate 97* —

Gramineae *(continued)*

Melica uniflora Retz. Wood melick. Slender; leaf sheath with small pointed extension; panicle branched; 1-flo. fertile and sterile lemmas in each spikelet. Woods and shady banks, widespread and common but local or rare in Scotland. Flo. May–June.

Melica nutans L. Mountain melick. *M. montana* Huds. Leaf sheaths without pointed extension; panicle usually unbranched; 2–3-flo. in spikelet; peduncle bent. Woods, shady banks, etc., on calcareous and limestone soils, Gloucestershire and Herefordshire northwards, local. Flo. May–July.

Glyceria maxima (Hartm.) Holmberg. Reed sweet-grass. *G. aquatica* (L.) Wahlb., non J. & C. Presl. Stems 90–250 cm; leaves 30–60 cm; panicle much branched; spikelets many, 4–10-flo.; lemmas oval, 3–4 mm. Ponds, fens and slow rivers, widespread. Flo. June–Aug.

Glyceria fluitans (L.) R. Br. Floating sweet-grass. Stem up to 1 m; leaves 5–25 cm; panicle branches few, appressed; spikelets long, 8–16-flo.; lemmas long, 6–7 mm, bluntly pointed. Ponds and streams, common. Flo. May–Aug.

Glyceria × pedicellata Townsend. *G. fluitans × plicata*. Intermediate between the parents, with minutely scabrid sheaths; sterile. Widespread.*

Glyceria plicata (Fr.) Fr. Plicate sweet-grass. Stem 30–75 cm; leaf sheaths rough; branches spreading; lemmas rounded, 3–5 mm, palea teeth included. Ponds, ditches, etc., widespread, but less frequent than *G. fluitans*. Flo. June–Aug.

Glyceria declinata Bréb. Small sweet-grass. Stem 10–45 cm; leaves grey-green; branches few, appressed; lemmas 3-lobed, 4–5 mm; palea teeth projecting. Marshes and moors, widespread. Flo. June–Sept.

Catabrosa aquatica (L.) Beauv. Whorl-grass. Stoloniferous; stem 5–75 cm; leaves blunt; spikelets mostly 2-flo.; lemmas much exceeding glumes. Sides of ponds and streams, widespread but local. Flo. May–July.

Cynosurus cristatus L. Crested dog's-tail. Stem 5–75 cm; leaves pointed; inflo. spiked; sterile spikelets of empty glumes concealing fertile spikelets of 3–4 flo. Meadows, etc., common. Flo. June–Aug.

Cynosurus echinatus L. Rough dog's-tail. Leaves wide; inflo. dense, oval; lemmas with long rough awns; sterile glumes short-awned. Introd. Mediterranean region. Waste ground, etc., mostly S. England, uncommon. Flo. June–July.*

Dactylis glomerata L. Cocks-foot. Stem stout, 15–140 cm; leaves valuable grazing; inflo. in dense clusters; keels of glumes and lemmas rough or hairy. Meadows, etc., common. Flo. June–Sept.

Briza media L. Quaking-grass. Perennial, leaf width *c.* 2–4 mm; ligules short; lemmas as broad as long; anthers long. Dry pastures, particularly on calcareous soils, common. Flo. June–Aug.

Briza minor L. Lesser quaking-grass. Annual; leaves soft, 3–4 mm wide; ligules longer; lemmas small, broader than long; anthers small. Roadsides, arable land, etc., S.W. England, uncommon. Flo. June–Sept.

Briza maxima L. Great quaking-grass. Spikelets very large, 7–20-flo. Introd. Mediterranean region. Naturalized in Isles of Scilly and Channel Islands. Flo. May–July.*

Poa infirma Kunth. Early meadow-grass. Annual, 1–25 cm; inflo. lax; spikelets small, 2–4-flo.; glumes small; lemmas short and hairy; anthers small. Bare ground, etc., W. Cornwall, Isles of Scilly and Channel Islands. Flo. March–May.*

Poa annua L. Annual meadow-grass. Stem 3–30 cm; leaves crinkled, broad and blunt; spikelets *c.* 6-flo.; lemmas longer, overlapping; anthers medium. Abundant everywhere. Flo. Feb.–Nov.

Poa bulbosa L. Bulbous meadow-grass. Shoots bulbous at base; stem 5–40 cm; leaves very narrow; inflo. dense; spikelets 3–6-flo.; short hairs on nerves of lemmas. Sandy coasts, mostly S. and E. England, local, introd. inland, rare. Flo. March–April.

Poa alpina L. Alpine meadow-grass. Stem 5–40 cm; leaves broad, blunt; spikelets large, 2–5-flo.; glumes and lemmas large, ovate, margins broad and white; anthers long, 2 mm. Often proliferous. Stony places on mountains, N. Wales to N. Scotland, S. Ireland, rare. Flo. July–Aug.

Poa flexuosa Sm. Wavy meadow-grass. *Poa laxa* auct. Similar to *P. alpina*, but leaves narrow, tapering; inflo. narrower; spikelets fewer, smaller, not proliferous; anthers 1 mm. Mountain screes and ledges, 800–1100 m, Scotland. Flo. July–Aug.*

Poa nemoralis L. Wood meadow-grass. Stem 15–90 cm; leaves narrow, pointed; ligules short; inflo. long, slender; spikelets small, few-flo. Woods and shady places, common, except N. Scotland and Ireland where it is local or rare. Flo. June–July.

Poa glauca Vahl. Glaucous meadow-grass. *P. balfourii* Parnell. Stiff stems and leaves glaucous, whitish; inflo. branches short, erect; glumes broader ovate. Rocky slopes and ledges, 300–900 m, N. England, N. Wales and Scotland, rare. Flo. July–Aug.*

Poa palustris L. Swamp meadow-grass. Stem 30–150 cm; leaves pointed; sheaths smooth; ligules long, blunt; inflo. large; lemma tips yellowish. Introd. Europe. Damp waste ground, widespread but rare. Flo. June–July.*

Poa chaixii Vill. Broad-leaved meadow-grass. Large, tufted; stem 60–120 cm; leaves long and broad; ligules short; spikelets 5–6 mm; lemma nerves glabrous. Introd. Europe. Naturalized in woods, etc., widespread but rare. Flo. May–July.*

Poa trivialis L. Rough meadow-grass. Stoloniferous; leaves glossy below; sheaths keeled, rough, drooping, often purple; ligule long, pointed; lemma base long-haired. Meadows, roadsides, etc., common. Flo. June–July.

Poa pratensis L. Smooth meadow-grass. Rhizomes slender; stems tufted; sheaths smooth; ligules short; spikelets up to 6 mm; glumes abruptly pointed. Old pastures, roadsides, etc., very common. Flo. May–July.

Poa subcaerulea Sm. Spreading meadow-grass. *P. irrigata* Lindm. Rhizomes long; stems scattered, solitary; lower inflo. branches in pairs; spikelets 4–7 mm; glumes finely pointed. Damp meadows, marshes, etc., common. Flo. June–July.

Poa angustifolia L. Narrow-leaved meadow-grass. Rhizomes slender; stems tufted; leaves stiff and narrow; ligules short; spikelets smaller, up to 5 mm. Dry places, common in England, rare elsewhere. Flo. May–June.*

Poa compressa L. Flattened meadow-grass. Rhizomes long; stems scattered, flattened, wiry; inflo. branches short; spikelets 3–8 mm. Dry banks, old walls, etc., widespread but local. Flo. June–Aug.

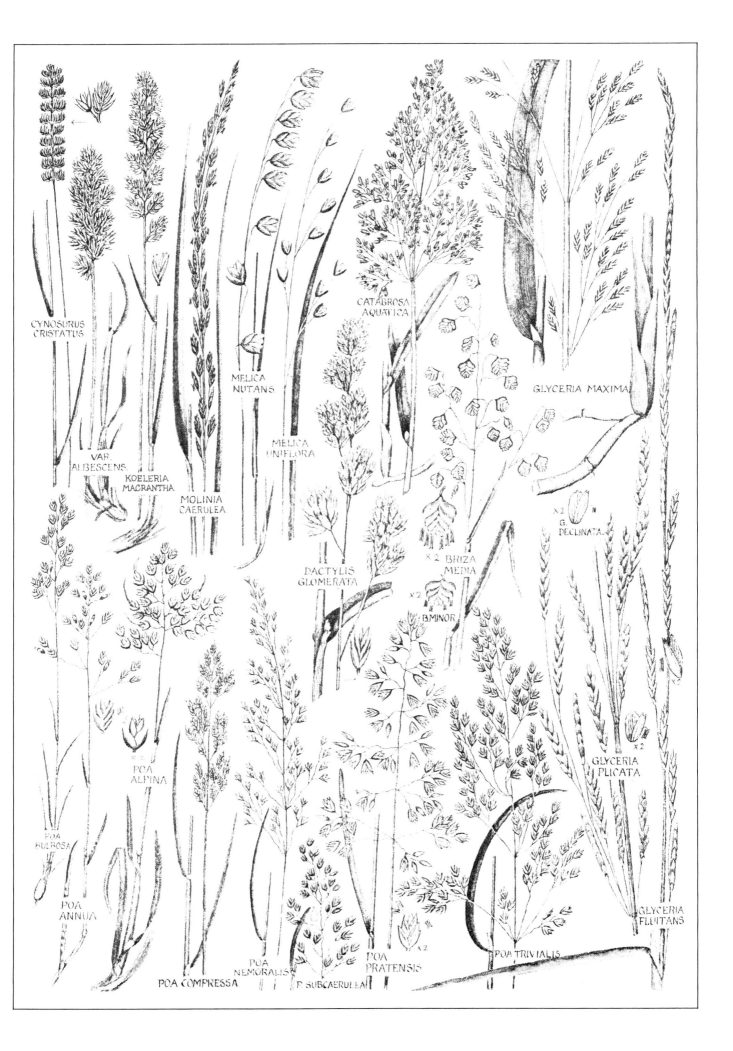

CYNOSURUS
CRISTATUS

VAR.
ALBESCENS.

KOELERIA
MACRANTHA

MOLINIA
CAERULEA.

MELICA
NUTANS

MELICA
UNIFLORA

DACTYLIS
GLOMERATA

CATABROSA
AQUATICA

GLYCERIA MAXIMA

×2
G.
DECLINATA.

×2 BRIZA
MEDIA

×2
B.MINOR.

POA
ALPINA

×2

POA
BULBOSA

POA
ANNUA

POA COMPRESSA

POA
NEMORALIS

P. SUBCAERULEA

POA
PRATENSIS

×2

POA TRIVIALIS

GLYCERIA
PLICATA

×2

GLYCERIA
FLUITANS

— *Plate 98* —

Gramineae *(continued)*

Puccinellia fasciculata (Torr.) Bicknell. Borrer's saltmarsh-grass. *Glyceria borrei* (Bab.) Bab. Perennial; tufted; inflo. rather dense; branches short; spikelets up to 6 mm; lemmas small, 2 mm; anthers short. Salt marshes, S. and E. England and S. Wales, local, and S. Ireland, very rare. Flo. June–Sept.

Puccinellia distans (L.) Parl.
Ssp. **distans**. Reflexed saltmarsh-grass. Perennial; stem 10–60 cm; leaves 1–4 mm wide; panicles very loose; spikelets 3–7 mm; lemmas 2–5 mm. Salt marshes, waste ground, etc., both near the sea and spreading inland along sides of main roads, widespread. Flo. June–July.
Ssp. **borealis** (Holmb.) W. E. Hughes. Northern saltmarsh-grass. *P. capillaris* (Liljeblad) Jansen. Similar to ssp. *distans* but smaller, stem 6–40 cm; leaves 1–2 mm wide; panicles contracted and dense; spikelets 3.5–5 mm; leaves 2–3 mm. Sea cliffs, rocks, etc., Scotland, local. Flo. June–Aug.*

Puccinellia maritima (Huds.) Parl. Common saltmarsh-grass. *Glyceria maritima* (Huds.) Wahlb. Stoloniferous; stems spreading; spikelets up to 13 mm; lemmas large, 4 mm; anthers long. Salt marshes and brackish areas, common. Flo. June–July.

Puccinellia rupestris (With.) Fernald & Weatherby. Stiff saltmarsh-grass. *Glyceria procumbens* (Curt.) Dumort. Stems spreading or prostrate; leaves flat; spikelets up to 9 mm; lemmas large; anthers short. Salt marshes and shingle banks, England, local. Flo. May–Aug.

Desmazeria rigida (L.) Tutin. *Poa rigida* L. *Catapodium rigidum* (L.) C. E. Hubbard. Fern-grass. Stem rigid, 2–30 cm; inflo. branches stiff, spreading on 1 side of axis; often purplish. Dry banks, walls, etc., widespread, but rare in Scotland. Flo. May–July.

Desmazeria marina (L.) Druce. Sea fern-grass. *Catapodium marinum* (L.) C. E. Hubbard. *Festuca rottboellioides* Kunth. Stem short and stout; inflo. narrow, spike-like; branches short, appressed. Rocks and shingle by the sea, local. Flo. May–July.

Vulpia fasciculata (Forsk.) Samp. Dune fescue. *V. membranacea* auct., non (L.) Dumort. *V. uniglumis* (Ait.) Dumort. *Festuca uniglumis* Ait. Upper sheath inflated; spikelets large, 12–16 mm; lower glume minute or 0, upper 3-nerved. Coastal dunes, S. and E. England, Wales and E. Ireland. Flo. June.

Vulpia ciliata Dumort. Ssp. **ambigua** (Le Gall) Stace & Auquier. Bearded fescue. *V. ambigua* (Le Gall) More. *Festuca ambigua* Le Gall. Sheath nearly reaching straight inflo.; spikelets 5–7 mm; lower glume very small, upper 1-nerved. Coastal dunes, S. and E. England. Flo. May–June.

Vulpia myuros (L.) C. C. Gmel. Rat's-tail fescue. *Festuca myuros* L. Stem sheathed to top; inflo. long, curved; spikelets 7–10 mm; lower glume about ¼ length of upper. Cultivated and waste ground, sandy land and railway tracks, locally plentiful. Flo. June–July.

Vulpia bromoides (L.) S. F. Gray. Squirreltail fescue. *Festuca sciuroides* Roth. Stems and sheaths slender; spikelets few, 7–14 mm; lower glume ½–¾ length of upper. Dry banks, sandy heaths, etc., common. Flo. May–July.

Festuca ovina L. Sheep's-fescue. Without rhizomes; leaves narrow, inrolled, up to 25 cm; sheaths open; spikelets 5–10 mm; lemma awn short, *c.* 1 mm. Heaths, moors, etc., common. Flo. May–July.

Festuca filiformis Pourr. Fine-leaved sheep's-fescue. *F. tenuifolia* Sibth. *F. capillata* Lam. *nom, illeg.* Slender, tufted; leaves inrolled, hair-like; ligules short; sheaths open; spikelets up to 7 mm; lemma awnless. Heaths, moors, etc., common. Flo. May–June.

Festuca altissima All. Wood fescue. *F. silvatica* Vill., non Huds. Stem 50–120 cm; leaves wide and flat; ligules long; inflo. large; spikelets 5–8 mm; lemma awnless. Woods and shady places, mostly N. and W. England and Scotland. Flo. May–July.

Festuca vivipara (L.) Sm. Similar to *F. filiformis* but spikelets always producing young plants. Mountain rocks, etc., N. Wales to Scotland and Ireland.*

Festuca trachyphylla (Hack.) Krajina. Hard fescue. *F. duriuscula* auct. *F. longifolia* auct., non Thuill. Similar to *F. ovina* but stouter; leaves up to 30 cm; inflo. often pyramidal; lemmas a little longer; awn up to 4 mm. Introd. Europe. Sown, and naturalized in grassy places, mostly S. England. Flo. June.*

Festuca longifolia Thuill. Blue fescue. *F. caesia* Sm. *F. glauca* Lam., non Vill. Similar to *F. trachyphylla* but with leaves very bluish-white. Native on E. Anglian heaths, rare. Flo. May–June.*

Festuca heterophylla Lam. Various-leaved fescue. Stem 60–120 cm, without rhizomes; basal leaves hair-like, 30–60 cm long, 3-angled; stem leaves short, flat, 2–4 mm wide. Introd. Europe. Woods, mostly S. England and Scotland, rare. Flo. June–July.*

Festuca rubra L. Red fescue. Rhizomes long; leaves narrow, basal, inrolled; sheaths tubular; spikelets 5–14 mm; lemma 5–6 mm, awned. Dunes, heaths, woods, etc., common. Flo. May–June.

Festuca nigrescens Lam. Chewing's fescue. *F. rubra* ssp. *commutata* Gaudin. Similar to *F. rubra* with sheaths tubular, but without rhizomes. Introd. Established on dry soils, downs and roadsides.*

Festuca juncifolia St-Amans. rush-leaved fescue. Rhizomes long; stem 20–90 cm; leaves stiff, inrolled, sharply pointed; spikelets 10–18 mm; lemmas 7–10 mm, hairy, short-awned. Coastal dunes, mostly S. and E. England and Wales. Flo. June–July.

Festuca pratensis Huds. Meadow fescue. Tufted, 30–120 cm; leaves flat; sheath auricles glabrous; shorter branch of each pair with 1–2 spikelets; lemma awnless. Meadows, etc., widespread and common. Flo. June–Aug.

Festuca arundinacea Schreb. Tall fescue (Huds.) P. Fourn. Tufted; stem 45–200 cm; leaves long, flat, coarse; sheath auricles hairy; shorter branch of each pair with 3–6 spikelets; lemmas 6–9 mm, often short-awned. Damp grassy places, meadows, etc., widespread and common. Flo. June–July.

Festuca gigantea (L.) Vill. Giant fescue. *Bromus giganteus* L. Tufted; stem 45–150 cm; leaves flat, 30–60 cm, up to 18 mm wide; sheath auricles glabrous, shorter branch with several spikelets; lemma awn 10–18 mm. Woods, shady places, etc., widespread and common but local in N. Scotland. Flo. July.

× **Festulolium loliaceum** (Huds.) P. Fourn. *Festuca pratensis* × *Lolium perenne*. Intermediate between the parents. Common where the two grow together.*

PUCCINELLIA
RUPESTRIS

×2

DESMAZERIA
MARINA

VULPIA
BROMOIDES

PUCCINELLIA
DISTANS

DESMAZERIA
RIGIDA

VULPIA
FASCICULATA

P. FASCIC-
-ULATA.

VULPIA
CILIATA

PUCCINELLIA
MARITIMA

VULPIA
MYUROS

×1

FESTUCA
OVINA.

×2

FESTUCA
FILIFORMIS

FESTUCA
RUBRA

FESTUCA
ARUNDINACEA

×2

FESTUCA
PRATENSIS.

FESTUCA
JUNCIFOLIA

FESTUCA
ALTISSIMA.

FESTUCA
GIGANTEA.

Plate 99

Gramineae *(continued)*

Lolium perenne L. Perennial rye-grass. Perennial; tufted; stem 10–90 cm; leaf width up to 6 mm; glumes shorter than spikelets; lemma awnless. Pastures, etc., common. Flo. May–Aug.

Lolium multiflorum Lam. Italian rye-grass. *L. italicum* A. Braun. Annual; stem 30–100 cm, soft; leaf width up to 10 mm; glumes shorter than spikelets; lemma long-awned. Introd. Europe. Roadsides, field borders, etc., common. Flo. June–Aug.*

Lolium temulentum L. Darnel. Leaves wide; glumes equalling spikelets; lemma broad, oval, awned or awnless. Introd. Europe. Waste ground, etc., rare.*

Bromus sterilis L. Barren brome. *Anisantha sterilis* (L.) Nevski. Annual; leaves hairy; inflo. branches long, mostly with single wedge-shaped spikelet; lemma long-awned. Roadsides, waste ground, etc., common. Flo. May–July.

Bromus madritensis L. Compact brome. *Anisantha madritensis* (L.) Nevski. Annual; stem 10–60 cm, lower sheaths hairy; inflo. branches erect, shorter than wedge-shaped spikelets; lemma long-awned. Dry grassy places on limestone soils, Somerset, Gloucestershire, Pembrokeshire and Channel Islands, introd. elsewhere on waste ground, old walls, etc. Flo. June.

Bromus carinatus Hook. & Arn. California brome. Perennial; stem 30–80 cm, erect, glabrous; panicle with long nodding branches; spikelets 25–30 mm, linear-lanceolate; lemmas 7–8-nerved, awn 5–10 mm long. Introd. N. America. Naturalized by rivers on waste ground, etc., widespread but uncommon, except W. London and Oxford. Flo. June–Oct.*

Bromus ramosus Huds. Hairy-brome. *Zerna ramosa* (Huds.) Lindm. Perennial; stem 45–190 cm, leaves wide; sheaths with reflexed hairs, auricled; inflo. branches in pairs; spikelets oblong, 2–4 cm. Woods and hedgerows, widespread. Flo. July–Aug.

Bromus benekenii (Lange) Trimen. Lesser hairy-brome. Similar to *B. ramosus* but with glabrous or minutely hairy upper leaf-sheaths; shorter ligules; shorter and narrower leaf blades; contracted panicles and smaller, fewer-flo. spikelets. Woods and shady places, S. and W. England, local. Flo. June–Aug.*

Bromus erectus Huds. Upright brome. *Zerna erecta* (Huds.) S. F. Gray. Perennial; stem 40–120 cm; leaves narrow; sheaths subglabrous; branches clustered, erect; spikelets oblong. Downs, grassy places, etc., on calcareous and limestone soils, common in S. England, rare in Scotland and local elsewhere. Flo. June–July.

Bromus lepidus Holmberg. Slender soft-brome. Similar to *B. hordeaceus* ssp. *hordeaceus*; leaves and lower sheaths hairy, but inflo. dense; spikelets short-stalked, usually glabrous, 7–15 mm; lemma 5.5–6.5 mm; the grain projecting at the top. Roadsides, waste ground, etc., widespread. Flo. May–June.*

Bromus interruptus (Hack.) Druce. Interrupted brome. Leaves and sheaths hairy; spikelets short, 10–15 mm, hairy, subsessile in clusters; palea split to base. Arable land, Cambridgeshire, very rare. Flo. June–July.

Bromus hordeaceus L.
Ssp. **hordeaceus**. Soft-brome. *B. mollis* L. Annual; stem 10–100 cm; leaves and sheaths softly hairy; spikelets 12–22 mm, 6–12 flo., hairy; lemma 8–11 mm, palea entire. Roadsides, waste ground, etc., common. Flo. May–July.
Ssp. **thominii** (Hardouin) Maire & Weiller. Lesser soft-brome. *B. thominii* Hardouin. Differs from ssp. *hordeaceus* in its glabrous spikelets with lemmas 6.5–8 mm. Hayfields, roadsides, etc., widespread. Flo. May–July.*
Ssp. **ferronii** (Mabille) P. M. Sm. Least soft-brome. *B. ferronii* Mabille. Differs from ssp. *hordeaceus* in its stiffly erect panicles and densely hairy

spikelets with lemmas 6.5–7.5 mm. Short turf on sea cliffs, mostly S. and S.W. England and Wales, local. Flo. May–July.*

Bromus racemosus L. Smooth brome. Stem 25–100 cm; leaves and sheaths hairy; inflo. erect; spikelets 12–16 mm, glabrous, oblong; lemma 6.5–8 mm. Riverside meadows, mostly S. England, local. Flo. June–July.*

Bromus commutatus Schrad. Meadow brome. *B. pratensis* Ehrh. ex Haffm., non Lam. Stem 40–120 cm; sheaths hairy; inflo. branches longer; spikelets 18–28 mm, mostly glabrous; lemma 8–11 mm. Riverside meadows, arable land, etc., widespread. Flo. June.

Brachypodium sylvaticum (Huds.) Beauv. False-brome. Stem 30–90 cm; leaves broad, soft and flat; spikelets hairy; awn as long as lemma. Hedge banks and shady places, common. Flo. July–Aug.

Brachypodium pinnatum (L.) Beauv. Tor-grass. Stem 30–120 cm; leaves narrow; stiff and glabrous; spikelets glabrous; awn shorter than lemma. Grassy places on calcareous and limestone soils, common in S. England, local or rare elsewhere. Flo. June–Aug.

Elymus donianus (F. B. White) Á. & D. Löve. Don's couch. *Agropyron donianum* F. B. White. Without rhizomes; leaves flat with slender ribs; spike rigid; lemma with short awn. Limestone rocks, Perthshire and N. Scotland, rare. Flo. Aug.–Sept.*

Elymus caninus (L.) L. Bearded couch. *Agropyron caninum* (L.) Beauv. Without rhizomes; leaves flat with slender ribs; spike slender, curved; lemma narrowed to long awn. Hedgerows and shady places, widespread but rare in N. Scotland and Ireland. Flo. June–Aug.

Elymus repens (L.) Gould. Common couch. *Agropyron repens*. Rhizomes long; leaves flat with slender ribs; lemma usually awnless; ripe spikelets falling entire. Weed of arable and waste ground, common. Flo. June–Aug.

Elymus pycnanthus (Gordon) Melderis. Sea couch. *Agropyron pungens* auct., non (Pers.) Roem. & Schult. Rhizomes long; leaves with thick ribs, inrolled and pointed; sheath auricled; lemmas usually awnless. Salt marshes, seaside sand and gravel, widespread, but mostly England. Flo. June–Aug.

Elymus farctus (Viv.) Runemark ex Melderis ssp. **boreali-atlanticus** (Simonet & Guinochet) Melderis. Sand couch. *Agropyron junceiforme* (Á. & D. Löve) Á. & D. Löve. *A. junceum* auct. Rhizomes long; leaf ribs pubescent; sheath without auricles; spike brittle; glumes and lemmas blunt, awnless. Coastal dunes, widespread. Flo. June–Aug.

Leymus arenarius (L.) Hochst. Lyme-grass. *Elymus arenarius* L. Rhizomes stout; stem 60–200 cm; leaves glaucous, pointed; spikes 15–35 cm; spikelets in pairs, 3–6 flo. Coastal dunes, widespread. Flo. June–Aug.

Hordelymus europaeus (L.) Harz. Wood barley. *Hordeum europaeum* (L.) All. Without rhizomes; stem 40–120 cm; sheaths mostly hairy; spikelets usually in threes and 1-flo.; glumes and lemmas awned. Woods on calcareous and limestone soils, mostly England. Flo. June–July.*

Hordeum murinum L. Wall barley. Annual; stem 6–60 cm; sheaths inflated; spikelets in threes, middle 1 fertile; glumes and lemmas long-awned. Waste ground, common. Flo. May–Aug.

Hordeum marinum Huds. Sea barley. Annual; stem 10–40 cm; sheath inflated; spike short with long spreading awns; glume of lateral spikelet widened at base. Verges of salt marshes, sea walls, etc., mostly England. Flo. June–July.

Hordeum secalinum Schreb. Meadow barley. Perennial; stem 20–80 cm; sheath not inflated; spike with shorter awns; all glumes bristle-like. Meadows on heavy soils, mostly S. England, local or rare elsewhere. Flo. June–July.

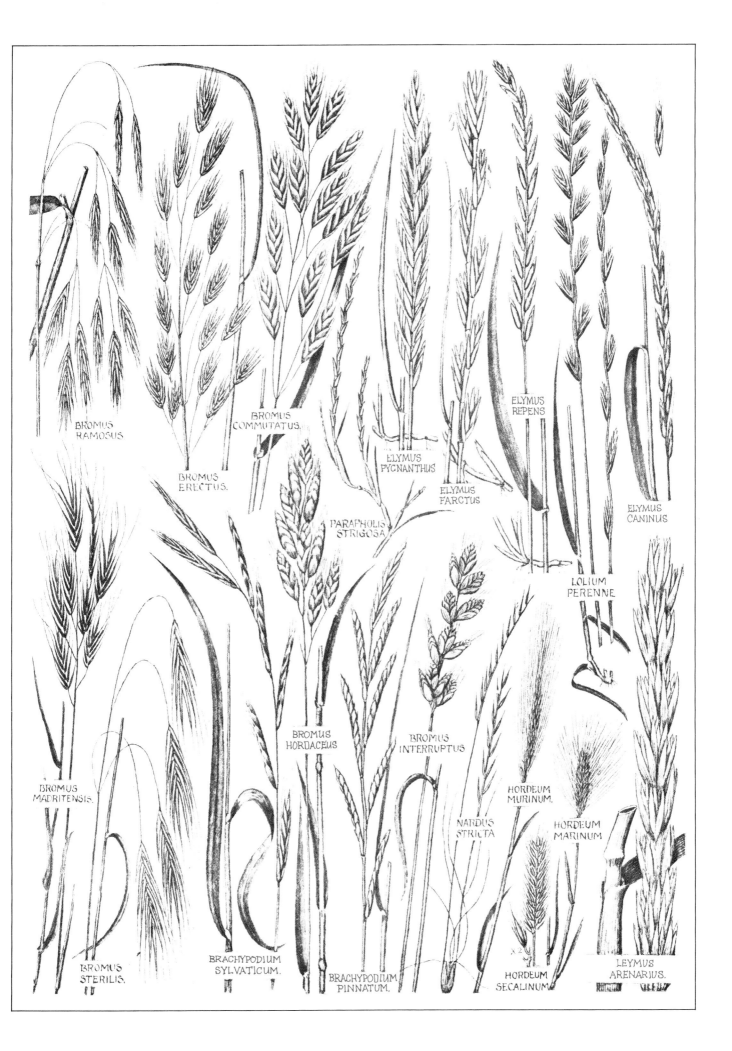

BROMUS
RAMOSUS

BROMUS
COMMUTATUS.

BROMUS
ERECTUS.

PARAPHOLIS
STRIGOSA

ELYMUS
PYCNANTHUS

ELYMUS
FARCTUS

ELYMUS
REPENS

ELYMUS
CANINUS

LOLIUM
PERENNE

BROMUS
MADRITENSIS.

BROMUS
HORDACEUS

BROMUS
INTERRUPTUS

HORDEUM
MURINUM.

NARDUS
STRICTA

HORDEUM
MARINUM

BROMUS
STERILIS.

BRACHYPODIUM
SYLVATICUM.

BRACHYPODIUM
PINNATUM.

HORDEUM
SECALINUM

LEYMUS
ARENARIUS.

Plate 100

GYMNOSPERMAE

Pinaceae

Picea abies (L.) Karst. Norway spruce. Twigs pendulous; leaves 10–20 mm, many on each leaf cushion. Much planted.*

Larix decidua Mill. European larch. Leaves deciduous, 12–30 mm, bright green, many on each shoot. Much planted.*

Pinus sylvestris L. Scots pine. Bark reddish-brown, in scales; old trees flat-topped; leaves 2 on each short shoot; cones 3–7 cm. Native in Scottish Highlands, planted elsewhere.

Pinus nigra Arnold. Tree pyramidal; bark greyish; buds sticky; scales flat; cones 5–8 cm. Planted.*

Pinus pinaster Ait. Maritime pine. Bark reddish; leaves 2; buds not sticky; scales reflexed; cones large. Planted, naturalized in S.E. England.*

Taxaceae

Taxus baccata L. Yew. Small male and female cones usually on separate plants; ovule 1, surrounded by a red fleshy cup or aril. Wood borders, rocky places, etc., on limestone and calcareous soils, widespread but often planted. Flo. March–April.

Cupressaceae

Juniperus communis L. Juniper.
Ssp. **communis**. Shrub suberect and prickly; leaves spreading, narrow, tapering to a point. Scrub, mostly on chalk and limestone soils, widespread but local. Flo. May–June.*
Ssp. **nana** Syme. *J. sibirica* Burgsd. More procumbent; leaves wider and ascending, bluntly pointed. Mountains, etc., on acid soils, N. Wales, Lake District, Scotland and Ireland. Flo. May–June.

PINUS SYLVESTRIS

JUNIPERUS
COMMUNIS.

TAXUS
BACCATA.

JUNIPERUS COMMUNIS SSP NANA

References

Cook, C. D. K., 1966. A monographic study of *Ranunculus* subgenus *Batrachium. Mitt. bot. St. Samml. Munchen* **6**: 47–237.

Dony, J. G., *et al.*, 1980 (reprint with corrections). *English Names of Wild Flowers. A Recommended List of the Botanical Society of the British Isles.* London.

Hubbard, C. E., 1968. *Grasses.* Revised edition. Penguin Books, Harmondsworth.

Jermy, A. C. and Tutin, T. G., 1968. *British Sedges.* Botanical Society of the British Isles. London.

Lousley, J. E. and Kent, D. H., 1981. *Docks and Knotweeds of the British Isles.* BSBI Handbook no. 3. London.

Perring, F. H. and Farrell, L., 1977. *British Red Data Books: 1. Vascular Plants.* The Society for the Promotion of Nature Conservation with the financial support of The World Wildlife Fund. SPNC. Lincoln.

Pritchard, N. M., 1959–1960. *Gentianella* in Britain. *Watsonia* 4: 169–193 and 218–237.

Pugsley, H. W., 1948. A Prodromus of the British *Hieracia. Journ. Linn. Soc. London (bot.)* 54.

Richards, A. J., 1972. The *Taraxacum* flora of the British Isles. *Watsonia* 9. Suppl.

Rostański, K. and Ellis, G., 1979. Evening Primroses (*Oenothera* L.) in Wales. *Nature in Wales* 16:238–249.

Stace, C. A. (Editor), 1975. *Hybridization and the Flora of the British Isles.* Published in collaboration with the Botanical Society of the British Isles by Academic Press. London.

Tutin, T. G., 1980. *Umbellifers of the British Isles.* BSBI Handbook no. 2. London.

Tutin, T. G., *et al.*, 1964–1980. *Flora Europaea* vols. 1–5. Cambridge University Press.

Walters, S. M., 1949. *Alchemilla vulgaris* in Britain. *Watsonia* 1: 6–18.

Walters, S. M., 1953. *Montia fontana* L. *Watsonia* 3: 1–6.

Watson, W., 1958. *Handbook of the Rubi of Great Britain and Ireland. Watsonia. Journal and Proceedings of the Botanical Society of the British Isles.* 1949→

Yeo, P. F., 1978. A taxonomic revision of *Euphrasia* in Europe. *Bot. Journ. Linn. Soc. London* 77: 233–334.

Young, D. P., 1949 & 1952. Studies in the British *Epipactis*, 1. *Watsonia* 1: 102–113; 2. *loc. cit.* 2: 253–276.

Young, D. P., 1958. *Oxalis* in the British Isles. *Watsonia* 4: 51–69.

Index of Botanical Names

Species only are indexed. Synonyms are shown in *italics*. *indicates a plant that is not illustrated.

Index of Common Names

*indicates plant is not illustrated

Notes